# Accepting Assistance in the Aftermath of Disasters

## Standards for States under International Law

SCHOOL OF HUMAN RIGHTS RESEARCH SERIES, Volume

The titles published in this series are listed at the end of this volume.

# Accepting Assistance in the Aftermath of Disasters

## Standards for States under International Law

Stefanie Jansen-Wilhelm

intersentia
Cambridge – Antwerp – Portland

Intersentia Ltd
Sheraton House | Castle Park
Cambridge | CB3 0AX | United Kingdom
Tel.: +44 1223 370 170 | mail@intersentia.co.uk

This publication is based on a doctoral dissertation defended at Tilburg University in June 2015.

Stefanie Jansen-Wilhelm
Accepting Assistance in the Aftermath of Disasters. Standards for States under International Law



ISBN 978-1-78068-329-4
D/2015/7849/70
NUR 828

Cover image: Leonardo da Vinci – 'Natural Disaster'
(c. 1517, Royal Library, Windsor Castle, London)
Royal Collection Trust/© Her Majesty Queen Elizabeth II 2015

British Library Cataloguing in Publication Data. A catalogue record for this book is available from the British Library.

*To Jeroen, Karen and Nico*

# ACKNOWLEDGEMENTS

There is more to life than working on a dissertation. There is a danger of getting sucked into the topic, to focus on everything that is remotely of relevance for the research, to wake up and go to bed with all kinds of novel ideas for finding that answer to the main question and to be too close to the research to see the bigger picture. I have been aware of that danger from the beginning and successfully avoided walking into that trap. Perhaps too succesfully, being at times too distracted and occupied with other very important things, as such lengthening the process of the research. Yet I am very thankful for the opportunity Tilburg University has given me to write this dissertation – on a topic of my own choosing and which has with every disaster occurring over the last six years proved its importance (at the time of writing these acknowledgements I hear the sad news that the death toll of the earthquake in Nepal (and other Himalayan countries) passed 2500) – and for allowing me to teach, to organize a conference on international humanitarian assistance, to visit conferences abroad and to do many other activities (not always directly related to the research). I would love to thank a whole list of people who enabled me to do this research and who distracted me at the same time, but there is too little room to write down the full list. A couple of names are mentioned here nonetheless.

First and foremost I would like to thank my supervisors, Willem van Genugten and Conny Rijken. You have patiently read all those draft chapters and given me feedback, comments and useful insights. During our 'tissues & issues' meetings (luckily the tissues were not always necessary) you helped me brainstorm on all those questions that still needed to be answered and also on the structure of the book (the question of which came first, the chicken or the egg, now has a new meaning). Although you both are extremely busy with your own work, you have always made time to read my drafts and give feedback. At the moments that I thought I was heading nowhere, you were both very encouraging. Willem, you put me on the PhD-track during the Master's programme at Tilburg University and you have always expressed your faith in me. I am happy that joking around did not lessen that faith (although to be fair, you were the one who once threw a breadroll at me during a staff meeting). Conny, you were my mentor during the Research Master and have kept the mentor-role throughout the PhD-track. The detailed feedback you give – although very welcome – can be daunting at times, yet it is amazing how you always see the tiniest of gaps in the reasoning, even when reading my draft chapters in a plane off to some major conference after only a few hours of sleep.

I would also like to express my gratitude towards the members of the reading committee, Professors Cees Flinterman, Jenny Goldschmidt, Nicola Jägers, Nico Schrijver and Eduardo Valencia-Ospina. Thank you for taking the time to read the manuscript and for your comments. Your feedback has been very valuable in finalizing the dissertation. A special word of thanks to Mr Valencia-Ospina for allowing me to assist with the preparation of his Fourth Report for the ILC. Also thanks to Pleased2ReadYou for proofreading my dissertation on such short notice (any remaining mistakes are my own).

To all my collegues at the Department of International and European Public Law (past and present): thank you so much for the wonderful time. It has been great working with you (and drinking coffee, and having lunch, and drinks, and dinner…). While the group as a whole creates such a great atmosphere, I would like to single out a few people. Bas, you were my partner-in-crime during the Master's, the Research Master and while we were roommates during our PhD. You always managed to stop me from worrying about the PhD ('its just a couple of theses put together'). Thanks for sharing in your endeavours for the rights of indigenous peoples and for agreeing that the window should always be open. Drazan, thank you for being an excellent new roommate (albeit with a closed window) and for putting up with two girls questioning everything you say. Perhaps one day I will learn to pronounce your name correctly. Laura and Zahra, thank you for introducing me to the phenomenon of statelessness and to the difficulties it poses in the lives of those without nationality and for giving me the opportunity to contribute to combating it, small as the contribution may be. Good luck with your Institute on Statelessness and Inclusion. Hopefully you will one day manage to eradicate statelessness and still have time inbetween all the research to visit a theme park again (with Eefje and me of course). To Simone, Byung Sook, Niels and others who joined in our daily lunches: thanks for the non-academic discussions and for agreeing that talking about unimportant topics is important too. I am grateful that the senior staff (Anna, Cees, Conny, Floor, Helen, Jonathan, Nicola, Willem, and all others) acknowledged this as well and made plenty of time available for drinks and outings. Finally, Femke, Inge and the other ladies at the secretariat, thank you for your support and for the many chats over coffee and cookies.

Throughout the years the research took place I have met wonderful fellow-PhD-students who made the PhD a social endeavour through drinks, lunches or other activities and who were available for 'complaining' about our 'hard' lives as PhD-students at times of getting stuck. Annemarie, Esther, Iris, Lorena, Pinar, Shamiso and all others: thank you for sharing in the experience. A special thanks to co-PhD-student Emilie, with whom I was also able to share in the frustration about the scarcity of conferences on the legal aspects of international humanitarian assistance (so we organized a conference ourselves). Good luck with finalizing your dissertation. Another word of gratitute goes to Chenny, who adjusted so easily to life in the Netherlands but found an amazing job back in China. I hope I can soon enjoy your cooking skills again (in China or in Tilburg).

I am also very lucky with all my non-academic friends who very patiently listened to my (probably) rather boring stories about doing research and writing a book. Thanks for all the great distractions, Joyce, Esther (no, a PhD does not make me scary, please keep texting), Richard, Floortje, Laura, Jeff, Jolanda, Sander, Claire, Laura and Teun. Also thanks to Chantal, Paul, Geerie and Bob for understanding that I was not always available for dinner-plans.

Coming to the end of what has become a very long list (and I guess that many are now just scanning for their name or have stopped reading entirely), I realise that I have trouble categorizing one person. Eefje, I have met you in the Research Master but you have become more than a fellow student, fellow PhD-student or colleague. Not only are you my business partner (yay!) and roommate, you have become one of my dearest friends also outside of the university. Thank you for all the fun years and for your support, and of course for being one of my paranimfs (I have made sure that the book is not too heavy to hold during the defense). Good luck with finishing your own dissertation and after that we will find some fun jobs together.

Last but not least (a cliché but so true) I would love to express my gratitude to my family, Karen, Nico, Rutger, Sofie, Thijs. Thank you for all your love and support during all those years and for putting up with me whenever I was moody because I got stuck or had to delete a chapter, again. You have always believed in me even when I did not. And, not to forget, thanks for babysitting Fabienne. Jeroen, thank you for distracting me by marrying me. The honeymoon to Hawaii certainly put the dissertation to the far, far back of my mind. You have been a tremendous support through all the years even while you are always so busy yourself. You took most of the punches in times I got stuck and you never complained. I could not wish for a better, sweeter, greater husband.

Lieve Fabienne, misschien zie je op een dag een boek in de kast staan met je mama's naam erop. Wellicht raak je nieuwsgierig en kijk je erin, en zie je tot je grote verbazing dat het boek is opgedragen aan papa, oma en opa en niet aan jou. Toch was je al één toen het boek klaar was?! Dat komt, lieverd, omdat papa, oma en opa een grote steun zijn geweest gedurende de hele studie en het promotieonderzoek en dat wil ik graag benadrukken door het boek aan hen op te dragen. Natuurlijk was jij tijdens het laatste jaar ook een hele grote afleiding (en dat bedoel ik vooral heel positief) en ben ik heel erg blij dat je er bent. Dankzij jou heb ik tijdens het laatste jaar heel veel gespeeld, gewandeld en gefietst en niet alleen maar gewerkt. Daarom is dit boek toch ook een beetje voor jou.

*Stefanie Jansen-Wilhelm*
*Tilburg, April 2015*

# CONTENTS

# List of Abbreviations

| | |
|---|---|
| AP | Additional Protocols to the Geneva Conventions |
| ASEAN | Association of Southeast Asian Nations |
| AU | African Union |
| CAT | Convention against Torture |
| CDERA | Caribbean Disaster Emergency Response Agency |
| CEDAW | Convention on Elimination of Discrimination against Women |
| CESCR | Committee on Economic, Social and Cultural Rights |
| CO | Concluding Observation |
| CRC | Convention on the Rights of the Child |
| CRED | Centre for Research on the Epidemiology of Disasters |
| CRPD | Convention on the Rights of Persons with Disabilities |
| DHA | UN Department of Humanitarian Affairs |
| ECOSOC | Economic and Social Council |
| ECtHR | European Court of Human Rights |
| ESC | European Social Charter |
| ESC-rights | Economic, social and cultural rights |
| FAO | Food and Agriculture Organisation |
| GA | General Assembly (UN) |
| GC | General Comments |
| GCI-IV | Geneva Conventions (I-IV) |
| GNP | Gross National Product |
| HRC | Human Rights Council |
| IASC | Inter-Agency Standing Committee |
| ICCPR | International Covenant on Civil and Political Rights |
| ICESCR | International Covenant on Economic, Social and Cultural Rights |
| ICISS | International Commission on Intervention and State Sovereignty |
| ICJ | International Court of Justice |
| ICRC | International Committee of the Red Cross and Red Crescent |
| IDP | Internally Displaced Persons |
| IDRL | International Disaster Response Laws |
| IFRC | International Federation of the Red Cross and Red Crescent Societies |
| IHL | International Humanitarian Law |
| ILC | International Law Commission |
| ILO | International Labour Organisation |
| IMF | International Monetary Fund |

| | |
|---|---|
| IRU | International Relief Union |
| ISDR | International Strategy for Disaster Reduction |
| $M_w$ | Moment Magnitude Scale |
| NATO | North-Atlantic Treaty Organisation |
| NGO | Non-governmental organisation |
| OCHA | Office for the Coordination of Humanitarian Affairs |
| OHCHR | Office of the High Commissioner for Human Rights |
| OP | Optional Protocol |
| RtoP | Responsibility to Protect |
| SC | Security Council |
| UDHR | Universal Declaration of Human Rights |
| UN | United Nations |
| UNDP | UN Development Programme |
| UNDRO | UN Disaster Response Organisation |
| UNESCO | UN Educational, Scientific and Cultural Organisation |
| UNHCR | UN Office of the High Commissioner for Refugees |
| UNRRA | UN Relief and Rehabilitation Administration |
| VCLT | Vienna Convention on the Law of Treaties |
| WHO | World Health Organisation |

# PART I

# CHAPTER I
# GENERAL INTRODUCTION

## 1 INTRODUCTION

### 1.1 Disaster strikes

Disasters will always have certain consequences in terms of casualties, injuries, and material damage, although the degree varies from one disaster to another.[1] It is up to the state on which territory the disaster takes place (that state will henceforth be referred to as the 'affected state') to address these consequences. In some cases, the damage as a result of the disaster is so severe that a state needs assistance from others – like states, international organisations, NGOs or a combination of these – to respond to a disaster and to work on reconstruction. The earthquake that struck Haiti in 2010 provides a clear example of a disaster where international assistance was needed and requested by the state.

In the late afternoon of 12 January 2010, an earthquake with a magnitude of 7.0 $M_w$ struck Haiti, its epicentre lying about 25 kilometres from Port-au-Prince.[2] Not only due to the enormous scale of the disaster but also because it is one of the poorest countries in the Americas, Haiti found itself struggling to cope with the consequences of the earthquake.[3] The damage was indeed of massive proportions. Over 200.000 people were killed and many homes were destroyed along with the capital's main infrastructure.[4] Survivors tried to find refuge with relatives in the countryside or – in most cases – found shelter in refugee camps. For the distribution of tents, water and food the refugees were largely depending on international humanitarian aid, delivered with the permission of Haiti's government.

---

[1] When referring to a 'disaster', an event with natural causes is meant rather than a man-made disaster, like an industrial or technical accident or armed conflict. In section 3 it will be explained in more detail what is understood with 'disaster' in this research.

[2] The references to the magnitude of an earthquake are according to the Moment Magnitudes Scale ($M_w$) and based on the information of the US Geological Survey <http://www.usgs.gov/>.

[3] According to the United Nations Development Programme's (UNDP) human development index of 2009, Haiti ranks 149 out of 182 of the most developed States. The Human Development Report of 2009, including the index, can be found at: <http://hdr.undp.org/en/statistics/> accessed 22 April 2010.

[4] Office for the Coordination of Humanitarian Affairs (OCHA) Haiti Earthquake Situation Report #34 of 16 April 2010, 1 <http://www.reliefweb.int/> accessed 22 April 2010.

Not in all disasters is the affected state willing to make use of aid offered by international actors. When the Italian city of L'Aquila was hit by an earthquake in 2009, the Italian government made clear that international assistance for reconstruction was not required. The L'Aquila earthquake, which struck on 6 April at 3:32 am local time with a magnitude of 6.3 $M_w$,[5] killed over 300 people and made around 55,000 people homeless.[6] Many buildings in the historic centre of the city were damaged. The total cost of the earthquake was estimated at 2.5 billion US dollars[7] and yet – at the time – Prime Minister Silvio Berlusconi stated that 'Italians were "proud people" and had sufficient resources to deal with the crisis'.[8] Italy did therefore not make use of offers of aid made by international actors.[9] This response by the Italian government was initially received with some scepticism and more critical voices could be heard around the earthquake's first anniversary when it was reported that approximately 4,000 people were still living in Red Cross accommodation and around 17,000 people were still living in hotels.[10] Moreover, at that time there did not seem to be a clear plan for the reconstruction of the non-historical parts of L'Aquila.[11] It was then questioned whether Italy should not have accepted aid since its own response did not yield satisfying results. This discussion was preceded and therefore probably influenced by a disaster of larger scale, namely cyclone Nargis that hit Myanmar, where the affected state's refusal of international assistance prompted much criticism on Myanmar's government from the international community.

When cyclone Nargis swept over the Irrawaddy Delta in southern Myanmar on 2 May 2008, approximately 140,000 people lost their lives and around 2.4 million people were affected as they lost their homes and livelihoods.[12] During the first days after the disaster the government of Myanmar did not accept international assistance. Other states and international organisations disapproved of this decision of the government, pressuring Myanmar to allow humanitarian relief into the country. After some time, the government indeed accepted assistance but insisted

---

[5] US Geological Survey <http://earthquake.usgs.gov/earthquakes/eqinthenews/2009/us2009fcaf/ #details > accessed 28 April 2010.

[6] According to the database used by the Centre for Research on the Epidemiology of Disasters (CRED) of the University of Louvain called 'EM-DAT'. When this database is used, reference is made to 'EM-DAT' (<http://www.cred.be/> and <http://www.emdat.be/>).

[7] EM-DAT.

[8] —— 'Death Toll Rises in Italy Quake' *BBC News* (7 April 2009) <http://news.bbc.co.uk/go/pr/fr/-/2/hi/europe/7987698.stm> accessed 28 April 2010.

[9] This does not mean that no international resources reached Italy. For example through the Red Cross system funding can easily be transferred. This system will be discussed in more detail in section 2.3 of Chapter II.

[10] —— 'L'Aquila Earthquake Survivors Plan Protest March' *The Guardian* (5 April 2010) <http://www.guardian.co.uk/world/2010/apr/05/laquila-earthquake-survivors-plan-protest-march> accessed 28 April 2010.

[11] Ibid.

[12] EM-DAT.

on distributing the relief goods itself. Later also aid workers were allowed to enter the country. Ten days after Nargis struck, only a quarter of the required aid was being allowed into the country.[13] Around three weeks after the disaster only an estimated 500,000 out of 2.4 million affected people had received some form of international assistance.[14] The decision of Myanmar's government to refuse assistance incited much international discussion. Not only were strong reactions found in the international media[15] but also an academic debate arose on the limits of international law in such situations.[16]

There is absolutely no guarantee that disaster recovery is better, faster, more effective, or of overall higher quality when the affected state accepts international assistance. From updates appearing in the media and being published by humanitarian organisations around the anniversaries of the Haitian earthquake, it becomes clear that many people are still struggling to get back on their feet year after year, despite the massive international response and the many international organisations and NGOs working in Haiti. Yet there is a feeling of common sense that when disaster survivors do not have access to food, water, health care or shelter because their state is unable or unwilling to provide it, these survivors do not need to suffer or even perish when offers of assistance are made by foreign actors. Problems therefore arise when the affected state is unable or unwilling to respond adequately to a disaster and refuses to accept offers of international assistance.

Cyclone Nargis and the earthquake in L'Aquila are only two examples where a state does not accept international humanitarian assistance. The scale of the problem exceeds these two examples. Three factors determine how many people are affected by the decision of affected states to refuse assistance: (i) the frequency with which disasters occur; (ii) the number of times states refuse international assistance; and (iii) the capacity of the affected state. The first factor, the frequency with which disasters happen, lies between 500 and 650 a year. In the years 2009 to 2013, a total of 598, 646, 592, 553 and 529 disasters occurred. In 2010, 304,472 people were killed (for a large part as a result of the earthquake in Haiti), in the other years the

[13] Alex J. Bellamy, 'Disasters and 'Responsibility to Protect': Should Nations Force Aid on Others? A Cyclone is Not Enough' (2010) 34 Natural Hazards Observer [3] 1, 9.

[14] United Kingdom Department for International Development (23 May 2008) <http://www.reliefweb.int> accessed 28 April 2010.

[15] See for example A. Buncombe, 'Burma under pressure to let outside world help after cyclone kills hundreds' *The Independent* (5 May 2008); B. Pisik, 'Cyclone toll feared above 100,000; Burma blocks aid; workers await visas' *The Washington Times* (8 May 2008); S. Sengupta, 'International Pressure on Myanmar Junta is Building' *The New York Times* (18 May 2008); M. Lillis, 'Debate Storms over Burma Aid' *Washington Independent* (20 May 2008).

[16] See for example John Arendshorst, 'The Dilemma of Non-Interference: Myanmar, Human Rights, and the ASEAN Charter' (2009) 8 Northwestern University Journal of International Human Rights 102; Morton Abramowitz & Thomas Pickering, 'Making Intervention Work. Improving the UN's Ability to Act' (2008) 87 Foreign Affairs 100; Rebecca J. Barber, 'The Responsibility to Protect the Survivors of Natural Disaster: Cyclone Nargis, A Case Study' (2009) 14 Journal of Conflict and Security Law 3.

numbers vary between 15,585 (2012) and 37,907 (2011). The numbers of people affected in these years vary from 99,837,000 in 2013 to 340,671,000 in 2010. The average amount of damage in these five years is 178,226 million US dollars per year.[17] Although 2013 shows a dip in the number of affected people, there is general concern for the ever growing impact disasters have. The number of disasters occurring each year is quite stable, but the number of affected people is likely to grow.[18]

An empirical study published in 2010 sheds light on the second factor, i.e. how often humanitarian assistance is refused. Of the disaster situations between 1989 and 2004 included in the research, aid was being refused to some extent in approximately 25% of the cases.[19] This number does not even include states which have a default policy to refuse international offers of assistance, like the US, China, India and Japan.[20] Reasons for refusing international offers of assistance are manifold, and since decades studies have looked into the arguments given by refusing states.[21] Some states declare that they are capable of responding to a disaster themselves so that international assistance is not needed, arriving at the third factor. If a state is indeed equipped to adequately respond to a disaster, victims can obtain sufficient assistance. In the cases where a state is not capable to respond adequately or is unwilling to use the resources at its disposal for responding to a disaster, the refusal of international humanitarian assistance poses a problem.

---

[17] These numbers are provided by the International Federation of the Red Cross (IFRC) in the World Disaster Report of 2014 (annexes, tables 1 to 4) and are based on data provided by EM-DAT. 'Disaster' according to these statistics are those events with a natural and or technological trigger, excluding wars, conflict-related famines, diseases or epidemics. IFRC, 'World Disaster Report 2014: Focus on Culture and Risk' (IFRC, Geneva 2014) 220-223 <http://www.ifrc.org/Global/Documents/Secretariat/201410/WDR%202014.pdf> accessed 27 October 2014.

[18] A number of factors cause this trend, like climate change, poverty and overcrowding in cities.

[19] Sometimes an affected state refused aid from one particular state, sometimes from a particular group of states, and more rarely from all states as a whole. Travis Nelson, 'Rejecting the Gift Horse: International Politics of Disaster Aid Refusal' (2010) 10 Conflict, Security and Development 379.

[20] Ibid.

[21] See for example an analysis from 1979 by Ellen Freudenheim, 'Politics in International Disasters: Fact, Not Fiction' in Lynn H. Stephens & Stephen J. Green (eds) *Disaster Assistance: Appraisal, Reform and New Approaches* (1979) 228. Freudenheim identifies four major political problems: domestic politics (the domestic politics obstruct formal acknowledgement of the disaster or the acceptance and coordination of relief); domestic corruption (e.g. misallocation of relief goods); rejection of aid (blatant rejection of offers of foreign governments); international politics (relief operations do not come off the ground due to international politics). A more recent study is done by Dorothea Hilhorst & Bram J. Jansen, 'Humanitarian Space as an Arena: A Perspective on the Everyday Politics of Aid' (2010) 41 Development and Change 1117, where for example distrust is used as an argument (at 1179).

## 1.2 Legal regulation of disaster response

Given the facts that people have been dealing with disasters for centuries, that disasters happen frequently worldwide, and that disasters can have strong international impacts like population displacement and the outbreak of diseases, it would be expected that a vast body of specialized international law regulates international disaster response and dictates whether or not a state should accept or is allowed to refuse international humanitarian assistance. The contrary is however true. According to the International Federation of the Red Cross (IFRC), '(d)isaster response is a "long-neglected facet of international law" and "it is unlikely that any other challenge looming so large in world affairs has received so little attention in the legal realm".'[22] Indeed, at first glance, public international law does not seem to offer many specific instruments dictating states' action in disaster situations, although at closer scrutiny a small number of legal instruments can be found that focus on aspects of international disaster response.[23]

Despite the absence of an explicit legal framework on disaster response, scattered sources of international law can nonetheless be found from which rights, rules and principles can be derived to be applied after the occurrence of a disaster. The principles of state sovereignty, non-intervention, non-interference and territorial integrity grant the freedom to an affected state to determine which aid is needed after a disaster and to decide which international actors are allowed to cross the borders of its territory to provide assistance.[24] Other rules of international law dictate states to take care of the persons living on a state's territory or who are under a state's jurisdiction. Human rights law, as the main example, has grown into a system of many international and regional instruments aimed at the protection of (groups of) persons. International humanitarian law, applicable in situations of armed conflict, explicitly deals with humanitarian assistance going for example into situations where a civilian population is in need of assistance and where this assistance would be delivered by international actors.

Nevertheless, even though some fields of public international law can be used, in situations where an affected state refuses international humanitarian assistance, the legal implications are not clear-cut:

> There is no definitive, broadly accepted source of international law which spells out the legal standards, procedures, rights and duties pertaining to disaster response and

---

[22] IFRC, 'World Disaster Report 2000' (IFRC, Geneva 2000) 157 cited by David P. Fidler, 'Disaster Relief and Governance after the Indian Ocean Tsunami: What Role for International Law?' (2005) 6 Melbourne Journal of International Law 458, 459.

[23] In the next Chapter an overview will be provided of the legal framework of international disaster response and the development of this framework. In that Chapter the instruments aimed specifically at disaster response will also be discussed.

[24] These principles are laid down in, *inter alia,* article 2 under paragraph (1), (4) and (7) of the Charter of the United Nations. Their role will be discussed in more detail in Chapter II.

> assistance. No systematic attempt has been made to pull together the disparate threads of existing law, to formalize customary law or to expand and develop the law in new ways. (...) At the dawn of the 21st century, a cohesive approach to international disaster response law is not much farther along than it was at the start of the 20th.[25]

Consequently, at first-face public international law does not provide a clear overview of the duties of affected states in responding to a disaster. It is therefore difficult to define how much freedom a state has to accept or refuse (offers of) international humanitarian assistance.

### 1.3 Research goal and main research question

Considering the problems that too often arise in the aftermath of a disaster with respect to acceptance and refusal of international humanitarian assistance and taking into account that the largely scattered legal framework is not helpful here, this research will look into the amount of freedom affected states have to refuse offers of international humanitarian assistance. While the body of specialized law on disaster response and international humanitarian assistance is not very extended, it is possible that standards can be found in the wider field of public international law. Formulated as a question, this research aims to seek an answer to the following:

*To what extent does public international law contain standards for affected states determining whether the affected state must accept international humanitarian assistance after the occurrence of a disaster?*

To come to an answer of this question, certain choices must be made with regard to the scope and content of the research. In the following, the scope will be demarcated. In section 3 of this Chapter it will be explained what is understood with 'disaster' and 'humanitarian assistance' and in the fourth section the structure and research methodology will be explained.

## 2 The Scope of the Research

### 2.1 Focus on affected states' obligations to accept

The focus of this research will lie on the obligation(s) for affected states with regard to accepting international humanitarian assistance. The nature of this research is legal and departs from public international law. Traditionally, public international law mainly evolved around states. Being created and ratified by states, treaties focused on regulating the relations between states in numerous aspects. Over time

[25] IFRC, 'International Disaster Response Laws, Principles and Practice: Reflections, Prospects, and Challenges' (Geneva 2003) 9 cited by Fidler (n 22) 465.

this body of state-centric law became increasingly concerned with rights and obligations of other actors in the international sphere.[26] Still, when looking at disaster response, it immediately becomes clear that a fundamental concept like state sovereignty lies at the centre of the issue. In Chapter II, sovereignty will be discussed in more detail, but in anticipation of that Chapter an implication of the concept is mentioned here. A traditional reading of state sovereignty includes territorial integrity and non-interference. In disaster-context this means that international actors cannot enter an affected state to deliver humanitarian assistance without the affected state's permission. During and right after a disaster the first and foremost responder and distributor of humanitarian relief is therefore the affected state itself. The obligations of this first responder are under scrutiny here to see what these rules of general international law mean in disaster-context, not the obligations of other actors. Consequently, it will not be considered whether non-state actors have any obligations in this respect.[27]

Accepting and offering humanitarian assistance are two sides of the same coin. Usually, a wide variety of actors offer assistance after a disaster. Here, only obligations to accept international humanitarian assistance will be researched. Whether or not there is an obligation for offering assistance is a different question than the research question posed here. The offering-side is only included insofar they are relevant for answering the main research question. Offers are in that case not limited to offers made by other states, but also offers made by international organisations and NGOs are included. If a state refuses an offer made by another state that happens to the state's political nemesis, there is less controversy than when a state refuses an offer made by a neutral humanitarian organisation.[28]

As a corollary to the obligations of the affected states, the thesis pays much interest to the position of disaster victims. The interests of disaster victims are a common theme throughout this research. Within the analysis of the legal framework fields like human rights law and refugee law will be included, fields that provide standards seeking to protect individuals while directing obligations to states.[29] When looking at the obligations of states to accept international humanitarian assistance, the protection of disaster victims (especially through human rights law) will continuously be under consideration.

---

[26] Take for example the developments taking place in trying to regulate the conduct of private corporations under international law.

[27] Non-state actors relevant in disaster situations are international organisations like the UN or UN-affiliated organisations, NGOs, individuals, and to increasing extent also private corporations.

[28] Joana Abrisketa, 'The Right to Humanitarian Aid: Basis and Limitations' in Humanitarian Studies Unit (ed.), *Reflections on Humanitarian Action: Principles, Ethics and Contradictions* (Pluto Press, London/Sterling 2001) 60.

[29] In this line many examples can be found of state-centric law which aim to protect individuals, like the parts of international humanitarian law which focus at protecting civilians in armed conflict, the developing doctrine of the Responsibility to Protect and the norms seeking to protect indigenous peoples.

## 2.2 Legal scope

To find an answer to the research question, it will be analysed what rules and principles on accepting humanitarian assistance can be found in public international law. Public international law is a very broad and extensive category of law, encompassing many fields that are not relevant for the present research. Only those fields of public international law that could potentially be relevant for answering the research question will be included. On the one hand, these are fields of law that are not developed for the purpose of disaster response, but which are nonetheless to a certain extent or with regard to a certain topic explanatory on what states should do after a disaster struck. Examples are international humanitarian law and refugee law. On the other hand, (soft law) instruments are included that deal specifically with elements of international disaster response. Taking all these sources together, it is possible to identify the rules and principles that currently dictate affected states' behaviour in the aftermath of a disaster, reflecting *lex lata*.

A remark must be made on the inclusion of international humanitarian law and the understanding of 'disaster' in this research. In the next section, it will be explained that situations of armed conflict are excluded from the definition of 'disaster' to be used. Nonetheless, international humanitarian law contains much information on international humanitarian assistance and is generally considered to be a well-developed and clear framework on delivering and accepting humanitarian assistance:

> Although far from constituting a comprehensive legal regime (...) the legal framework for humanitarian assistance in armed conflict constitutes a rather detailed one, in particular if compared with the regime for situations outside armed conflicts.[30]

Even though armed conflicts are excluded from the definition of 'disaster' and are outside the scope of this research, much can be learned from the rules of international humanitarian law because of the rather detailed legal framework on humanitarian assistance. Therefore, this field of law will be included in the legal analysis of Chapter II so that the rules and principles found within international humanitarian law can be used to explain and clarify the further findings of the legal analysis. At the same time, the existing rules and principles during peace-time disasters can be compared to the framework provided for situations of armed conflict to find out if the discrepancy is indeed as large as is commonly believed.

---

[30] Heike Spieker, 'The Right to Give and Receive Humanitarian Assistance' in Hans-Joachim Heintze & Andrej Zwitter (eds.), *International Law and Humanitarian Assistance: A Crosscut Through Legal Issues Pertaining to Humanitarianism* (Springer, Heidelberg/Dordrecht/London/ New York 2011) 28.

## 2.3 The phases of disasters and their correlative legal issues

Disaster studies focus on roughly three phases surrounding the occurrence of a disaster. First, there is the phase in which no disaster has taken place but where the state prepares for the possible future occurrence of a disaster. Some states are more disaster-prone than others and being aware of disaster risks can lead to a level of preparedness that limits the number of victims when disasters do in fact occur. Studies must identify disaster risks, and states are encouraged to invest in disaster preparedness. Legal questions in this respect relate to the actual duties that states have to prepare for a disaster, for instance when it comes to questions of liability after a disaster occurred. To what extent a state must prepare for a future event of which it is not sure that it will actually happen is an interesting but difficult question. This first phase, the disaster preparedness-phase, will not be included in this research because only affected states' obligations in the aftermath of a disaster will be considered.

The subsequent phase is the actual occurrence of a disaster and the immediate response to it (the disaster-proper phase). The type of disaster is determining how long the actual occurrence of a disaster lasts. Earthquakes are usually very short, but are often followed by aftershocks which can be as severe as the initial earthquake. Floods may also occur quickly, but not always does the water disappear again easily. A drought can be ongoing for years. No matter how long a disaster lasts, it is essential that there is immediate response to rescue people and to coordinate the assistance for survivors. If the immediate response is in any way flawed, it can result in further loss of life. Therefore, the main focus of this research lies on the immediate response-phase.

After the disaster and the first response, the phase of reconstruction starts. It is not always easy to pinpoint where the initial response ends and where reconstruction begins, and often these phases overlap. One way to distinguish between disaster response and recovery is by looking at the nature of assistance offered. In the disaster-proper phase or in immediate response, the assistance offered is humanitarian assistance. At a later stage, the humanitarian assistance can (in full or partly) turn into development assistance. The difference lies in the nature of the assistance: development assistance is usually the result of a policy and of agreements with the receiving state, and is long-term in nature. Humanitarian assistance is usually *ad hoc* and cannot have any conditions set for the affected state to comply with in return. The reconstruction-phase turns again into the disaster-preparedness phase, since reconstruction-planning should take into account the occurrence of another disaster and development assistance can be used for preparing for such an event. Development assistance is not included in this research. Although the disaster-proper and disaster recovery phases overlap, the line is drawn at the transition from humanitarian assistance to development assistance.

## 3 Definitions

### 3.1 The definition of 'disaster'

Disasters form the basis of this research. The legal obligations that are sought here apply in the event of a disaster, or – in other words – the occurrence of a disaster triggers a certain set of legal rules. Therefore, it is necessary to define what is understood with 'disaster'. In addition, throughout this research examples of disasters are used to illustrate points that are made.[31] The definition of 'disaster' also has the function of selecting these examples.

Generally, the word 'disaster' is associated with a certain event with a severe and dramatic impact on the society in which it occurs.[32] According to the Oxford English Dictionary a disaster is 'an unexpected event, such as a very bad accident, a flood or a fire, that kills a lot of people or causes a lot of damage'.[33] Nonetheless, it is difficult to pinpoint which events can be considered 'disasters' and which events are merely 'unfortunate incidents' and why. When looking closely at definitions used by various organisations, a number of elements can be identified that determine what a disaster is. These elements are generally related to the causes and the effects of an event that could potentially be a disaster. Of further influence is the goal with which a definition of disaster is made, like the collection of certain data for research.

Disasters can either be caused by a natural event, by human action, or both. Amongst natural disasters are earthquakes, floods, hurricanes, droughts, landslides, cyclones and volcanic eruptions. Man-made disasters are for example nuclear disasters (like the Chernobyl disaster which occurred in Ukraine in 1986 due to an explosion in the nuclear power plant), industrial disasters (of which the Bhopal disaster of 1984 where a gas-leak killed thousands of people in India is the main example), and technical disasters (which generally concern accidents in industrial transportation, like the Shell oil leaks in Nigeria, causing environmental damage and illnesses due to ground contamination). A disaster can also be caused by a natural trigger but have a clear man-made element at the same time (like the Fukushima disaster in Japan of 2011 which was the result of a tsunami hitting the nuclear power plant resulting in a nuclear disaster). Armed conflicts are sometimes considered to be man-made disasters.[34] However, there are also those who explicitly

[31] What exactly the function is of these cases and how they are used in this research will be explained in section 4 below on Structure and Methodology.

[32] Quite commonly there is an understanding of disasters as incredibly chaotic situations where people panic and turn on each other, resulting in situations of lawlessness and disarray. Such images are not helped by popular disaster films and are in most cases far from the truth.

[33] Oxford Advanced Learner's Dictionary (7th edition 2007) 432. The word 'disaster' comes from *disastro* or 'unfavourable (positioned) star'. The occurrence of a disaster was (and sometimes still is) usually subscribed to bad fortunes or a punishment by a deity.

[34] EM-DAT provides in its glossary a definition of 'disaster' which explicitly includes armed conflict: '(t)hough often caused by nature, disasters can have human origins. Wars (...) are

exclude armed conflict from the definition of disaster[35] and use the term 'complex disaster' to indicate a situation in which a disaster takes place within a context of violence and armed conflict.[36]

The causes of a disaster can be further divided in slow- and sudden-onset. A slow-onset disaster takes a longer time to develop and to reach its peak than a sudden-onset disaster. A very clear example of a slow-onset disaster is a drought for which it is necessary that rain stays out for a number of subsequent rainy seasons. Such a disaster is relatively easy to predict, yet not all states have the capacity to respond effectively. Even though sudden-onset disasters like earthquakes and tsunamis are more difficult to predict, early warning systems do help in decreasing the effects of such disasters.

Categorizing disasters according to cause is useful when looking at questions on liability and preparedness. Yet it is in many cases very difficult to determine whether a disaster had natural or man-made causes, as it is often a combination of both. An earthquake is a natural disaster, but when construction regulations for earthquake-prone areas are ignored, man-made elements are included.[37] Also a hurricane is a natural disaster, but when the affected state is slow in its response and the situation for survivors deteriorates as a result, the disaster becomes partly man-made. Moreover, many disasters are somehow related to climate change which arguably has a certain man-made element. To avoid the difficulty of determining if a disaster is truly natural or whether there are man-made elements, it is more convenient to define what a disaster is by looking at the consequences and not at the cause.[38]

Defining a disaster based on consequences can include a variety of elements, like the number of casualties, the number of people affected, the total costs of the damage, or the broader impact of the event on a particular society.[39] However, a certain line must be drawn to determine how many casualties or how much damage is required before an event can be called a disaster. If such a line is not drawn in absolute terms (e.g. ten casualties constitutes disaster), the definition would necessarily be relative because in that case impact is determined by the

---

included among the causes of disasters.' The database itself does not, however, include situations of armed conflict.

[35] See also the definition used in the Caribbean Disaster Emergency Response Agency (CDERA) Agreement article 1(d).

[36] IFRC <www.ifrc.org/what/disasters/about/types/manmade/conflict.asp> accessed 3 May 2010.

[37] In the case of L'Aquila, for example, a number of builders were found guilty for the deaths of eight students because their dormitory collapsed during the disaster. Faulty construction work weakened the dormitory. ——, 'Builders Found Guilty in L'Aquila Quake Deaths' *The Australian* (17 February 2013) <http://www.theaustralian.com.au/news/ world/builders-found-guilty-in-laquila-quake-deaths/story-e6frg6so-1226579660625> accessed 25 February 2013.

[38] It is possible to do this in this research because questions of blame and liability are not relevant. The only man-made element that is excluded is armed conflict.

[39] EM-DAT includes an event as a disaster when a minimum of ten persons have died or when the lives of at least one hundred persons are affected.

vulnerability of a society before a disaster strikes, the severity of the disaster and the capacity that the society has to rebuild. A group of disadvantaged victims is often less prepared than a more privileged group and a richer society is usually more capable to address the aftermath of a disaster, so that it depends on the circumstances whether an event is a 'disaster'. A hurricane can be considered a 'disaster' in one state based on the damage caused but not in the next if that other state was better prepared or has more capacity to respond. The IFRC uses the following formula to illustrate this relativity: $\frac{vulnerability+hazard}{capacity} = disaster$.[40] When looking at the definitions of 'disaster' which are created for different purposes, the options of departing from cause or from consequence can be recognized. A number of definitions will be discussed here that form the basis for the definition of 'disaster' that will be used in this research.

The definition used in the Tampere Convention on Telecommunication is often cited in legal contexts, possibly because it is a definition created for legal purposes. It is therefore also a good starting point here. The Tampere Convention's definition of disaster is the following:[41]

> Disaster means a serious disruption of the functioning of society, posing a significant, widespread threat to human life, health, property or the environment, whether caused by accident, nature or human activity, and whether developing suddenly or as the result of complex long-term processes.[42]

According to this definition there must in the first place be a 'serious disruption of the functioning of society', meaning that the effect of an event must influence the everyday life of people in a severe way. Consequences are formulated in a relative way. It is not determined in absolute numbers what a disaster is; it is the serious disruption that counts. Minor disruptions are not included, but when is a disruption serious enough to be considered a disaster? The description of consequences provides more insight in the level of 'seriousness' that is required to make a certain disruption a disaster. The disruption must be so severe to be a threat to 'human life, health, property or the environment'.[43] For the Tampere Convention's definition, it

---

[40] IFRC <http://www.ifrc.org/what/disasters/about/index.asp> accessed 3 May 2010.

[41] Officially called the Tampere Convention on the Provision of Telecommunication Resources for Disaster Mitigation and Relief Operations 1998, entered into force in January 2005. This Convention regulates the use of telecommunication in times of disaster, setting aside national regulations on telecommunication in order to make communication more efficient.

[42] Article 1 of the Tampere Convention. This definition is also considered by the ILC 'Second Report on the Protection of Persons in the Event of Disasters by Eduardo Valencia-Ospina, Special Rapporteur' (UN Doc A/CN.4/615 of 7 May 2009) para 33 and by the IFRC in its 'Guidelines': IFRC, 'Introduction to the Guidelines for the Domestic Facilitation and Regulation of International Disaster Relief and Initial Recovery Assistance' (IFRC, Geneva 2008).

[43] Some definitions are not specific on the type of consequences that must be included in their understanding of 'disaster', but speak generally of 'consequences'. See for example the UN Inter-Agency Standing Committee (IASC) in the 'Operational Guidelines': 'Natural disasters, i.e. the

is enough that a certain event could *potentially* have these effects: the definition does not require the *actual* loss of life or damage to property. The only requirement of the definition is that there is a disruption. Apart from looking at the consequences, this definition also names possible causes, including natural as well as man-made causes ('caused by accident, nature or human activity') and both slow- and sudden-onset disasters ('developing suddenly or as the result of complex long-term processes'). Even armed conflicts are not excluded.

Many other definitions are not satisfied with a 'threat' that certain effects will follow the disaster but require that a certain event or disruption must have caused actual negative effects like loss of life or damage. In its work on the 'Protection of Persons in the Event of Disasters', the UN International Law Commission (ILC) reflects this in its definition: '"Disaster" means a calamitous event or series of events resulting in widespread loss of life, great human suffering and distress, or large-scale material or environmental damage, thereby seriously disrupting the functioning of society'.[44] Noticeable in this definition is the absence of any reference to the cause of the 'calamitous event or series of events'. Apparently, it does not matter what caused it, but an event can be considered a disaster when there is 'widespread loss of life, great human suffering and distress, or large-scale material or environmental damage'. Again, it is required that this damage is severe enough to 'seriously' disrupt the everyday life of a society. The amount of suffering or damage that must be present before the ILC speaks of a disaster is determined by the degree in which the functioning of society is disrupted, where the word 'seriously' provides a minimum standard and indicators of what can be considered as 'seriously' are given through 'widespread', 'great', and 'large-scale'. The ILC excludes armed conflicts from its work because the ILC is of the opinion that 'a well-developed body of law exists to cover such situations'.[45]

An important organisation in disaster response is the Office for the Coordination of Humanitarian Affairs (OCHA) which is the successor of the UN Department of Humanitarian Affairs (DHA). When looking at the definition used by the DHA, it immediately becomes clear that the ILC used this as a source of inspiration:

> A serious disruption of the functioning of society, causing widespread human, material or environmental losses which exceed the ability of affected society to cope

---

consequence of events (...) that overwhelm local response capacity (...)', IASC, 'Protecting Persons Affected by Natural Disasters: IASC Operational Guidelines on Human Rights and Natural Disasters' (Brookings-Bern Project on Internal Displacement, Washington DC 2006) 8.

[44] ILC Drafting Committee, 'Protection of persons in the event of disasters: Texts of draft articles 1, 2, 3, 4 and 5 as provisionally adopted by the Drafting Committee' (UN Doc. A/CN.4/L.758 of 24 July 2009), draft article 3.

[45] The exclusion of armed conflicts does not follow from the definition, but is explained in the reports.

> using only its own resources. Disasters are often classified according to their cause (natural or manmade).[46]

In this definition the causes are only mentioned as a means of classification, but are not determining which situations can be considered as disasters. Again, there must be a 'serious' disruption, to be determined by the extent to which losses exist. Consequently, this definition refers to actual losses and damage, not merely to the threat that this might occur. Besides these elements that were also present in the ILC-definition, there is one very important element that was also taken into account in the formula of the IFRC. The DHA-definition states that a situation that disrupts societies by causing losses can only be considered a disaster when the losses 'exceed the ability' of the affected society 'to cope using only its own resources'. As a result, no matter how big or severe the event causing a disruption is, it is not considered to be a disaster as long as the affected state has the ability to deal with the consequences. This line is also followed by the Centre for Research on the Epidemiology of Disasters (CRED): 'a situation or event, which overwhelms local capacity, necessitating a request to national or international level for external assistance'.[47]

The definitions of disasters described in the foregoing may include choices which appear striking at first glance, yet it must be called to mind that definitions may serve to identify a certain dataset. Excluding armed conflicts means excluding a certain field of law and only taking into consideration those events that exceed the affected state's ability results in including cases in which international assistance becomes a major issue. In this line a definition of 'disaster' will be created here for the purpose of this particular research.

In the first place, the situations this research will focus on are events taking place in peace-time. The reason for excluding situations of armed conflict is the general presumption that international humanitarian law has a (relatively) clear-cut and comprehensive framework on international humanitarian assistance. It is more interesting to consider obligations of states to accept humanitarian assistance outside the scope of this relative legal clarity. Still, in the analysis of the legal framework in the next Chapter, international humanitarian law will be included to see what this field has to offer and to compare these findings with the findings of the rest of the legal framework. In addition, the rules found in international humanitarian law may be helpful to explain or interpret rules and concepts found in

---

[46] UNDHA, 'Internationally Agreed Glossary of Basic Terms Related to Disaster Management' (UN Doc. DHA/93/36 of December 1992) 27. The original uses 'manmade' rather than 'man-made'. The – more or less – same definition is used by the UN International Strategy for Disaster Reduction (ISDR): 'A serious disruption of the functioning of a community or a society causing widespread human, material, economic or environmental losses which exceed the ability of the affected community or society to cope using its own resources'. UN ISDR (2006), cited by George Kent, 'Disasters and 'Responsibility to Protect': Should Nations Force Aid on Others? Rights and Obligations' (2010) 34 Natural Hazards Observer [3], 18.

[47] See EM-DAT <http://www.emdat.be/glossary/9> accessed 7 October 2014.

other fields of law. In order not to enter into the difficult debate on what constitutes 'armed conflict', 'peace-time' is considered to be a state where international humanitarian law is not applicable.[48]

It is not necessary for answering the main research question to make any claims on the cause of a disaster. The goal is to find state obligations in the aftermath of a disaster, no matter what caused it. At the basis of this decision also lies a more practical consideration: it is often very difficult to determine whether a disaster is caused by nature or by human action or inaction (either in the disaster preparedness phase or in the response to a disaster). Therefore, to determine whether a certain event can be considered as a disaster the emphasis will lie on the consequences of the event.[49]

For the purposes of this research, situations in which a certain event took place but where the affected state could easily cope with the consequences using its own resources are not interesting to include. The definition of 'disaster' in this research must therefore include reference to the capacity of the affected state (as in the formula of the IFRC or in the definition of the DHA: 'which exceed the ability of (the) affected society to cope using only its own resources').[50] In addition, there are situations in which the affected state would be able to adequately respond to a disaster using solely its own resources, but where the state is unable to allocate its resources effectively (for example due to a weak government or corruption) or unwilling to help (parts of) its population. Here, the question whether the state has obligations to accept assistance is relevant as well. The definition of 'disaster' must therefore include cases where the capacity of the affected state is exceeded, where states are unwilling to deal with the consequences of a disaster, and situations that are a combination of the two.[51]

A rather pressing problem is announcing itself here. If the capacity of a state or the willingness of a state to respond to an event are determining whether or not that event can be considered to be a disaster, the question arises how it must be decided if the affected state's capacity is overwhelmed or if the state is indeed unwilling to respond adequately. To overcome this problem, the determination whether an event was beyond a state's capacity to address or whether a state was unwilling to respond adequately is based on a variety of sources and comments (resulting in a

[48] Complex disasters are therefore excluded from the definition as well.

[49] Following the approach taken by the organisations described above.

[50] UNDHA (n 46). That capacity is overwhelmed could mean that a disaster is of such a massive scale that it exceeds a state's ability to cope, but also the situation where in some small states, like island-states, the economy is too small to generally address the consequences of disasters. See e.g. Victoria Bannon, 'International Disaster Response Law and the Commonwealth: Answering the Call to Action' (2008) 34 Commonwealth Law Bulletin 843, 844.

[51] These are for example the cases in which a state appears to be willing to accept assistance but at the same time blocks it by strict customs regulations or other barriers; the cases in which assistance is only refused from a particular state or small group of states; or examples in which the affected state claims that it responded well enough but where the contrary can also be argued, placing the case in the scope of this research.

hint of subjectivity). Ultimately, the inclusion of human rights law will prove useful in determining whether the affected state has sufficient capacity to address the consequences of a disaster.

Taking all these considerations together, in this research a 'disaster' is: *an event occurring in peace-time with natural causes, man-made causes, or a combination of both, which causes harm to the affected population to an extent that it is beyond the affected state's capacity to address. This includes situations in which the affected state is not willing to address the consequences and refuses to accept international assistance.*

### 3.2 Humanitarian assistance

The term (international) 'humanitarian assistance' is part of the main research question. There is no universal definition of 'humanitarian assistance', so to define the concept a number of sources is used here.[52] 'Humanitarian assistance' includes the support that is offered to reduce human suffering after the occurrence of a disaster. It has already been explained that short-term humanitarian assistance must be distinguished from longer-term development assistance as it is 'an activity within 'humanitarian action', which is short term relief to rehabilitation and reconstruction, even leading to development cooperation'.[53] Development assistance is not directly connected to the occurrence of a disaster and constitutes long-term plans and agreements between donors and receiving parties.[54]

Alternative terms for 'humanitarian assistance' exist and will also be used throughout this study. 'Humanitarian aid' basically means the same as assistance, yet a certain prejudice nonetheless exists towards 'aid' in the sense that it appears to indicate that the receiving party is somehow weak. In this study 'humanitarian assistance' and 'humanitarian aid' are used as synonyms without having any prejudice towards the affected state's capacity. Other varieties are 'humanitarian relief', 'relief assistance' and 'relief action'.

Assistance can comprise many types of goods and services. Depending on what is required in a particular situation, assistance can consist of financial assistance, of goods, and of personnel delivering these goods or providing services (for example medical personnel or search and rescue teams). The International Court of Justice determined that humanitarian assistance includes 'food, clothing, medicine and other humanitarian assistance, and it does not include the provision of weapons, weapons systems, ammunition, other equipment, vehicles, or material which can be

[52] Rohan Hardcastle & Adrian Chua, 'Victims of Natural Disasters: The Right to Receive Humanitarian Assistance' (1997) 4 The International Journal of Human Rights 35, 36.

[53] Spieker (n 30) 7.

[54] Development cooperation is also sometimes indicated as 'foreign aid': 'Humanitarian assistance is to be distinguished from foreign aid by its emergency character and use for relieving victims of natural disasters'. Hardcastle & Chua (n 52) 36.

used to inflict serious bodily harm or death'.[55] Assistance is in the first place provided by the affected state and organisations working on the affected state's territory and when speaking of *international* humanitarian assistance foreign actors, like the UN or UN-affiliated organisations, other states sending goods and personnel, NGOs and private parties like individuals and corporations are the ones delivering (either through the affected state or directly to disaster victims).[56]

The word 'humanitarian' is often believed to relate to the humanitarian principles, which are the principles of humanity, impartiality, neutrality, and independence.[57] Varieties exist on the humanitarian principles. Some mention only the first three, others have more, like the seven principles of the IFRC.[58] The humanitarian principles must make sure that the assistance offered is meeting certain quality standards, so that aid is not conditional or tied in any way. In practice assistance that is called 'humanitarian' does not always meet these criteria. It is nonetheless a presupposition here that humanitarian assistance must always aspire to adhere to the humanitarian principles.[59] The implications of not bringing an offer of assistance in line with these principles will return throughout this research.

Finally, perhaps needless to say, the word 'humanitarian' in humanitarian assistance is not equal to the word 'humanitarian' in international humanitarian law. Truly, the field of international humanitarian law also contains rules on the delivery and acceptance of humanitarian assistance, but humanitarian assistance is not limited to conflict situations. Moreover, the research focuses on disasters occurring in peacetime. Although 'humanitarian' can cause confusion with regard to the legal implication that armed conflict is included, it is certainly not part of its meaning in the present research.

---

[55] ICJ, Military and Paramilitary Activities in and Against Nicaragua (Nicaragua v United States of America) (Merits) [1986] ICJ Rep 14, 47.

[56] The role of civil society in disaster response is ever increasing. When the Indian Ocean tsunami struck in 2004, private donations to NGOs and the UN exceeded governmental donations for the first time. David Fisher, 'Fast Food: Regulating Emergency Food Aid in Sudden-Impact Disasters' (2007) 40 Vanderbilt Journal of Transnational Law 1127, 1133.

[57] OCHA, 'What are Humanitarian Principles?' (2012) <https://docs.unocha.org/sites/dms/Documents/OOM-humanitarianprinciples_eng_June12.pdf> accessed 22 January 2015.

[58] Spieker (n 30) 7; the IFRC adds 'voluntary service', 'unity' and 'universality'. IFRC, 'The Seven Fundamental Principles' <http://www.ifrc.org/who-we-are/vision-and-mission/the-seven-fundamental-principles/> accessed 22 January 2015.

[59] Considering the possible obligation to accept international humanitarian assistance, it is of importance that an offer of assistance is purely humanitarian. If an offer is for example conditional or earmarked for members of a certain religious group, there is a strong argument for an affected state to refuse that offer. Naturally, what exactly the effect of the humanitarian nature of the offer is on the obligation to accept will be assessed in this research.

## 4 STRUCTURE AND RESEARCH METHODOLOGY

As said, there is no clearly demarcated field of public international law on disaster response, but in various areas of international law rules and principles can be found contributing to the total set of rules applicable in disaster settings. Instruments have been identified that contain the elements of a legal framework on accepting international humanitarian assistance, which will be analysed in Chapter II. This legal framework will contain the obligations for states on accepting (and refusing) assistance. To gain more insight into the origins of these rules, Chapter II will also consider developments within the main organisations working on disaster response and which are those stimulating legal developments most strongly. The outcome of this Chapter (an overview of the status of the law) will not only explain the rules but will at the same time make it possible to identify where the gaps in the framework lie. Chapter III will subsequently take these findings and place them in the reality of disaster response.

In this third Chapter examples of disasters are included based on which it is analysed to what extent the legal rules found in Chapter II direct states in accepting assistance. Based on this analysis, it is possible to identify the difficulties that application of the legal framework of Chapter II causes in practice. The examples that are included are disasters that occurred roughly since 2004.[60] In the selection of examples the definition of 'disaster' as used in this research forms the basis, meaning that the disasters are considered beyond the state's capacity to address. As already explained, determining whether this is the case is rather subjective and difficult: a state can deem its response adequate while others may disagree. There is, therefore, room for discussion on the cases selected, although that discussion is not held here; it is assumed that in the examples included throughout the research the disaster's consequences were beyond the state's capacity (or willingness) to address. This is determined based on a variety of sources, like statements or reports on the status of recovery after some time has passed since the actual occurrence of a disaster. Consequently, disasters on which hardly any reliable information is available are not included.[61] In addition, situations of armed conflict are excluded

---

[60] In 2004, the Boxing Day Tsunami (or Indian Ocean Tsunami) killed an enormous number of people and posed many difficulties in humanitarian efforts. Consequently, this tsunami renewed the (legal) attention to disaster response and sources on disasters since that time are more readily available than sources on disasters prior to 2004.

[61] There have for example been many cases of famine in North Korea in the last decades due to mismanagement of natural factors like drought. It is, however, difficult to find reliable information on these cases so the North Korean famines are not included. Even for disasters that are extensively documented information is not always reliable, as was seen after hurricane Katrina when it hit New Orleans in 2005. Many newspapers that are usually considered to be reliable, published stories of horrible crimes that were committed at the refuge Super Dome, like murder and rape. Also, people were supposedly looting and pillaging on a large scale, making New Orleans too dangerous a place for relief workers. Later, it became clear that many of these stories were not true, even though the post-Katrina situation did contain a few remarkable

from the definition of 'disaster' to be used here. Therefore, cases concerning armed conflict (even when a natural disaster occurs in the context of an armed conflict) are not included. Two exceptions are made: the cases of Syria (humanitarian emergency during an armed conflict while no natural disaster takes place) and Somalia (humanitarian emergency as the result of a natural disaster taking place in the context of an armed conflict). Both cases make a particular legal point (explained in Chapters II and III) which is important for the understanding of the legal framework as a whole. Finally, it must be stressed that the included cases do not have the purpose of an empirical study into disaster response. Only the elements of each example that illustrate a certain point are included in the research. No general conclusions can be made based on the examples alone.

What becomes clear from Chapters II and III is that a set of rules and principles exist which dictates what states must do in terms of seeking and accepting international humanitarian assistance, but when these rules are applied in practice, they are not concrete enough to set standards for state behaviour. It is therefore necessary to seek another way of concretizing the rules that are identified in Chapters II and III. There are multiple possibilities through which this can be attempted and it would be interesting to compare different options and outcomes.[62] In this research the approach is however taken to look at one possibility in-depth rather than exploring a variety of alternatives superficially. Underlying this decision is the promising potential of the option taken and the desire to be thorough in the analysis.

When considering the entire framework of laws, resolutions, guidelines and other instruments on humanitarian assistance and disaster response, the field of human rights law stands out for its standard-setting potential in disaster response. Human rights standards can be used to concretize and therefore define obligations to accept international humanitarian assistance. One human rights instrument in particular is of special relevance because of the rights it contains. The International Covenant on Economic, Social and Cultural Rights (ICESCR) provides the rights to housing, food, water and health, rights which are commonly affected by the occurrence of a disaster. In addition, under the general obligations stemming from this treaty states appear to be directed in their international disaster response through stating that parties must make use of 'international assistance and cooperation' and 'the maximum of its available resources' for the full realization of the rights.[63] In the second part of this research the ICESCR will therefore be closely

---

examples of unusual violence. See for example Lisa Grow Sun, 'Disaster Mythology and the Law' (2011) 96 Cornell Law Review 1131 and Lisa Grow Sun & RonNell Andersen Jones, 'Disaggregating Disasters' (2013) 60 UCLA Law Review 884, 931.

[62] These options do not only lie in the legal realm but can also be sought in the field of political science, philosophy and/or economics or at the cross-sections of public international law and politics or other disciplines.

[63] Article 2(1) ICESCR.

examined to establish to what extent the ICESCR can provide more concrete obligations for state parties on accepting international humanitarian assistance.[64]

Through treaty interpretation according to the rules of the Vienna Convention on the Law of Treaties (VCLT) it will be analysed in Chapter IV what exactly is meant with article 2(1) ICESCR in terms of concrete obligations. The findings will be placed in the light of disaster response in Chapter V. This Chapter will go in more detail into state parties' human rights obligations after a disaster. Here, the general obligations as found in Chapter IV will be specified further by including four substantive rights of the ICESCR: the rights to housing, food, water and health.[65] In the final conclusion it will be considered to what extent public international law is able to dictate states whether they should accept international humanitarian assistance and what concrete standards follow from the ICESCR.

[64] That the ICESCR may be useful to identify obligations for states in disaster contexts is recognized by others as well. For example, when considering the case in which Pakistan did not participate in international cooperation with the goal to help the victims of cyclones and floods in Southern Pakistan in 2007, Barber argues that Pakistan could as such violate its obligations under the ICESCR if it was a party to that Covenant. Rebecca J. Barber, 'Protecting the Right to Housing in the Aftermath of Natural Disaster: Standards in International Human Rights Law' (2008) 20 International Journal of Refugee Law 432, 459.

[65] The rights to housing and food are laid down in article 11 and the right to health in article 12. The right to water is an implied element of both articles. These rights have been selected for their relevance in most disaster situations, not implying that other rights are not relevant in disaster response. The right to education, for example, is probably not the first right springing to mind in relation to disasters, yet providing education is a valuable tool in protecting children against forced labour and other forms of exploitation and also to reduce child marriage. It would however go beyond the scope of this research to include all rights of the ICESCR. Committee on Economic, Social and Cultural Rights, General Comment 11 on 'Plans of Action for Primary Education' (UN Doc. E/C.12/1999/4 of 10 May 1999) para 4.

# CHAPTER II
# DISASTER RESPONSE AND INTERNATIONAL HUMANITARIAN ASSISTANCE: BACKGROUND AND LEGAL FRAMEWORK

## 1 INTRODUCTION

Various attempts have been made to create more clarity in the rules and principles that apply in disaster situations. However, the international legal developments of the last century

> Are all at the periphery of the issue. At the core is a yawning gap. There is no definitive, broadly accepted source of international law which spells out the legal standards, procedures, rights and duties pertaining to disaster response and assistance. No systematic attempt has been made to pull together the disparate threads of existing law, to formalize customary law or to expand and develop the law in new ways.[1]

Although there is no coherent system, this Chapter will look into the rules and principles that can be derived from legal sources. These sources consist of general international law that is relevant for the topic of humanitarian assistance as disaster response, and of sources that were developed especially for this topic.

Before going into the legal framework, a number of developments will be discussed that proved determining factors for the way international humanitarian assistance is perceived today. Over the centuries, different views have existed on what the role of international humanitarian assistance should be when a natural disaster struck. A number of these views were put into practice in setting up special organisations or attempts at codifying principles of disaster response. These developments will illustrate what have been successful or – in most cases – less successful approaches to international disaster response and humanitarian assistance. Moreover, keeping the past attempts in mind, it is possible to explain where certain rules and principles come from and to understand why certain developments and attempts at codification will (potentially) be successful or likely to fail.

---

[1] IFRC, 'World Disaster Report 2000' (IFRC, Geneva 2000) 157.

# 2 THE FIELD OF INTERNATIONAL DISASTER RESPONSE: BACKGROUND AND MAIN ACTORS

## 2.1 Introduction

Until roughly the end of the nineteenth Century and the beginning of the twentieth Century, the ideas on international disaster response, and more specifically the delivery of international humanitarian relief, developed along a more or less singular line of thought. A new way of looking at humanitarian assistance was proposed by diplomat Emer De Vattel during the 18th Century. After De Vattel's new insights, further developments led to major changes in the course of the nineteenth Century. Initiatives arose to bundle disaster relief efforts in a specialized organisation. A positive result is the establishment and the development of the Red Cross and Red Crescent Movement. Parallel, the less fruitful International Relief Union was created under auspices of the League of Nations, followed by further initiatives taken in UN context. After discussing the developments prior to the twentieth Century, this section will successively discuss the initiatives of the Red Cross and Red Crescent, the establishment and quiet ending of the International Relief Union and finally the activities within the UN-framework.

## 2.2 International disaster relief prior to the 20th Century

Going back to the Middle Ages, it becomes apparent that the attention for providing humanitarian assistance was wider than merely the provision of humanitarian assistance in response to a disaster. In a legal sense this can be recognized in the rules that started to develop early on the conduct of war trying to make battles more 'humane'. Humanitarian relief work was mainly organised in the form of 'Samaritan work'. This system of voluntary work responded to local needs for many centuries and can still be seen in a modern version today.[2] With the rise of Christianity, providing humanitarian assistance was placed within a more religious context and structure. Orders were established on a non-governmental basis to bring relief for those in need, like the Order of the Knights of St. John of Jerusalem of the 12th Century.[3] Being a non-military order of knights, the Order of St. John cared for those who were wounded and sick, both in war and in peacetime.[4] This way of

[2] Many examples exist today where private initiatives make altruistic efforts to provide relief when need requires so, like the many calls to fold paper-cranes for Japan after the tsunami hit in 2011 or marathon runners providing food to the victims of hurricane Sandy after the New York marathon was cancelled in October 2012.

[3] Peter Macalister-Smith, *International Humanitarian Assistance: Disaster Relief Actions in International Law and Organization* (Martinus Nijhoff Publishers, Dordrecht 1985) 9.

[4] David Fisher, 'Law and Legal Issues in International Disaster Response: A Desk Study' (IFRC, Geneva 2007) 25.

organizing the provision of relief can still be recognized today in the form of organisations like the Red Cross and Red Crescent.

Private initiatives formed the main body of humanitarian responders. Not much state activity could be found in this field, though bilateral agreements on the provision of humanitarian assistance between states as they exist today have been around for a very long time.[5] Nonetheless, the role of states in international disaster response and in the provision of humanitarian assistance was rather underexposed, although one author, inspired by a major disaster halfway the eighteenth Century, started to think about what the duties of states should be. This author is Emer de Vattel.

When an earthquake with an estimated magnitude of 8.7 $M_w$ destroyed major parts of Lisbon in 1755,[6] King George II of England appealed to parliament to send relief.[7] The Lisbon earthquake drew international attention due to the size of the disaster and the importance and fame of the city at the time of the earthquake. The initial shock of the earthquake was followed by heavy aftershocks, after which

> There appeared, at some small distance, a large body of water, rising as it were like a mountain. It came on foaming and roaring, and rushed towards the shore with such impetuosity, that we all immediately ran for our lives as fast as possible; many were actually swept away, and the rest above their waist in water at a good distance from the banks.[8]

The earthquake and tsunami were followed by fires: 'the whole city appeared in a blaze (…). It may be said without exaggeration, it was on fire at least in a hundred different places at once, and thus continued burning for six days together, without intermission, or the least attempt being made to stop its progress'.[9] As a result, about a quarter of the population of Lisbon died.[10] The appeal of King George II was not based on any sense of legal obligation but on religious and humanitarian considerations. Emer de Vattel, author of '*Les Droits des Gens*', [11] referred to the Lisbon earthquake as an example of natural international solidarity.[12] In addition,

---

[5] Macalister-Smith, *International Humanitarian Assistance* (n 3) 17.
[6] USGS <http://earthquake.usgs.gov/earthquakes/world/events/1755_11_01.php> accessed 12 November 2012.
[7] Macalister-Smith, *International Humanitarian Assistance* (n 3) 17.
[8] Eva March Tappan (ed), *The World's Story: A History of the World in Story, Song and Art* (14 Vols. Eyewitness report, Boston: Houghton Mifflin, Vol. V: *Italy, France, Spain, and Portugal,* 1914) 618-628, Internet Modern History Sourcebook: <http://www.fordham.edu/halsall/mod/1755 lisbonquake.asp> accessed 12 November 2012.
[9] Ibid.
[10] USGS <http://earthquake.usgs.gov/earthquakes/world/events/1755_11_01.php> accessed 12 November 2012. The eyewitness report states that at least 60,000 people lost their lives, which seems an accurate estimate based on a population at the time (250,000 people).
[11] Emerich de Vattel, *Les Droits des Gens. Ou Principes de la Loi Naturelle Appliques à la Conduite & Aux Affairs des Nations & des Souverains* (Book II, London 1758).
[12] De Vattel (n 11) 5, cited by Macalister-Smith, *International Humanitarian Assistance* (n 3) 17.

De Vattel introduced the possibility of looking at 'natural' solidarity from an angle of international legal obligations. In his work De Vattel describes the 'offices of humanities between nations'.[13] With this phrase he refers to altruistic 'obligations' of a state to do 'every thing in [its] power for the preservation and happiness of others, as far as such conduct is reconcilable with [its] duties towards [itself]'.[14] This means for example that states should help others in case of famine:[15]

> If a nation is visited with famine, all those who have provisions enough and to spare should come to its assistance, though not to the extent of self-impoverishment (...). Help in such an extremity is so much in accord with the dictates of humanity that no civilized nation could altogether fail to respond (...). Whatever the nature of the disaster that overtakes a nation, the same help is due to it.[16]

With the words 'should' and 'due', De Vattel refers to an obligation for states to assist or help other states that are 'visited with famine'. The basis for this obligation lies within humanity and is therefore not an obligation coming forth from any law. De Vattel also gives the limits of this obligation. In the first place, states should not give more than can reasonably be expected of them, which is indicated by stating that offering assistance must be reconcilable with the duties towards 'itself' and that assistance must not lead to self-impoverishment. Another limit to the obligation lies with the receiving state. 'Offices of humanities' cannot be forced upon other states as the receiving state is an independent and sovereign state.[17]

The novelty of De Vattel's work lies in his moving away from the system of private initiatives and bilateral agreements between states by creating a basis for an obligation for states to provide humanitarian assistance when another state needs this. The limits that he described are formed by the obligations towards a state's own population and by the willingness to accept the help of the receiving state. These limits found in the eighteenth Century can be still recognized in contemporary legal debates surrounding the provision of humanitarian assistance, as will be seen in this Chapter.

During the remainder of the eighteenth and later during the nineteenth Century, private relief schemes remained the most important mechanism of generating and providing humanitarian assistance. Even in the twentieth and twenty-first Centuries, private relief continued to be one of the most important sources of humanitarian aid. When Tokyo was hit by an earthquake in 1923, it was the British Mansion House funds – a private organisation with the purpose to collect money for disaster relief –

---

[13] De Vattel (n 11).

[14] De Vattel (n 11) 258, cited by Stéphane Beaulac, 'Emer de Vattel and the Externalization of Sovereignty' (2003) 5 Journal of the History of International Law 237, 263.

[15] De Vattel (n 11) 260-1, cited by Beaulac (n 14) 263.

[16] De Vattel (n 11) 5, cited by Peter Macalister-Smith, 'The International Relief Union: Reflections on the Convention Establishing an International Relief Union of July 12, 1927 (1986) 54 Legal History Review 363, 363.

[17] De Vattel (n 11) 262-3, cited by Beaulac (n 14) 264.

that managed to raise 6,600,000 gold francs to send to Japan.[18] In response to the Indian Ocean tsunami of 2004 the contribution of private donors to NGOs and international organisations exceeded that of states. Only when organisations were set up with the purpose of responding to disasters and providing humanitarian relief the role and duties of states returned to the centre of the legal stage. Ironically, this started with the establishment of a private organisation during the second half of the nineteenth Century when the Red Cross and Red Crescent Movement was created.

## 2.3 The Red Cross and Red Crescent Movement

The Red Cross and Red Crescent Movement has its roots in (humanitarian) response to armed conflicts. Founder Henry Dunant witnessed the battle of Solferino in 1859 and was horrified by the treatment of wounded soldiers. He started advocating rules for the protection of victims of international armed conflict and for the establishment of a relief organization caring for those victims.[19] As a result, the International Committee of the Red Cross (ICRC) was founded in Geneva in 1863 and in 1864 the first Geneva Convention was adopted.[20] In this Convention, humanitarian ideas were incorporated in an international legal document. Next to the establishment of the ICRC, national Red Cross (or in the case of some countries starting with Turkey: Red Crescent) Societies were founded aimed specifically to work within the borders of a state. Apart from looking at ways to make armed conflict more humane, Dunant also paid attention to peacetime relief activities.[21] To a large extent, the National Red Cross and Red Crescent Societies took this role upon themselves. Early efforts of National Societies consisted of forwarding supplies and contributions to the National Society of the affected country.[22] In 1919, after the First World War, the League of Red Cross Societies was established to promote the cooperation between the Societies and to respond to situations of natural disaster.[23] The League was renamed in 1991 into the International Federation of the Red Cross and Red Crescent Societies (IFRC).[24]

The ICRC (focusing on situations of armed conflict) and IFRC (focusing on humanitarian needs in peacetime) enjoy a special status as international actors. The Red Cross is a private organisation, and works closely together with governments.

[18] John F. Hutchinson, 'Disasters and the International Order – II: The International Relief Union' (2001) 23 International History Review 253, 255.

[19] Macalister-Smith, *International Humanitarian Assistance* (n 3) 9, see also Henry Dunant, *Memory of Solferino* (International Committee of the Red Cross, 1986, first published 1862).

[20] The Geneva Convention for the Amelioration of the Conditions of the Wounded in Armies in the Field. The Convention was revised (in 1906 and 1929) and formed the basis of the First Geneva Convention of 1949.

[21] Dunant (n 19).

[22] Macalister-Smith, *International Humanitarian Assistance* (n 3) 17.

[23] Macalister-Smith, 'The International Relief Union' (n 16) 365.

[24] In 1983, the name was first changed into the 'League of the Red Cross and Red Crescent Societies'.

After the Geneva Convention of 1864, the ICRC was the driving force behind a number of other Geneva Conventions, eventually leading to the Geneva Conventions of 1949 and their Additional Protocols of 1977. While the Red Cross and Red Crescent Movement is in itself a private initiative, states became parties to the Geneva Conventions, binding themselves to these rules. Consequently, the role of states in humanitarian assistance received a legal basis. Apart from binding states, the Conventions also emphasize the special status of the Red Cross and Red Crescent, for example where it is provided that the ICRC should be granted humanitarian access where others, like states, would not be accepted. The Red Cross is also helped in this by the fact that in most states, in 186 to be precise, National Societies are present. The ICRC and IFRC work closely together with these National Societies whenever a humanitarian emergency occurs and therefore often have access to states (or particular areas within states) even if other actors are not granted access.

Where the ICRC has a strong foundation in instruments like the Geneva Conventions and its Additional Protocols, the IFRC does not. Even so, the IFRC has produced or was involved in the creation of numerous instruments focusing on the provision of humanitarian assistance and otherwise responding to disasters. Some of these instruments will be discussed in section 3 below, like the Code of Conduct for the International Red Cross and Red Crescent Movement and NGOs in Disaster Relief, the Guidelines for the Domestic Facilitation and Regulation of International Disaster Relief and Initial Recovery Assistance, and the Humanitarian Charter and Minimum Standards for Disaster Response of the Sphere Handbook. The IFRC is also working on an ongoing project to prepare national legal systems for the possible future reception of international humanitarian assistance. This project, International Disaster Response Laws (IDRL) will also be discussed below.

## 2.4 The International Relief Union

Whereas the Red Cross and Red Crescent Movement is a private initiative closely involving states by promoting rules to bind them, the International Relief Union was an international organization. On 28 December 1908, the Sicilian city Messina was struck by an earthquake of a magnitude of 7.2 $M_w$.[25] This earthquake was followed by a tsunami and fires, killing an estimated 72,000 to 110,000 people in Messina and in Reggio di Calabria.[26] Among the approximately 40% of the population of Messina who died were many friends and family members of

[25] USGS <http://earthquake.usgs.gov/earthquakes/world/events/1908_12_28.php> accessed 13 November 2012.

[26] Ibid. The Italian government did not know how to relocate all the survivors, since many houses collapsed. While also relocating people within Italy, some survivors were sent to the US to 'start a new life' in New York. See the newspaper clipping describing how the survivors of the Messina earthquake almost perished at sea during the crossing: <http://www.pbs.org/wgbh/amex/rescue/peopleevents/pandeAMEX99.html> accessed 13 November 2012.

Giovanni Ciraolo, Italian senator and president of the Italian Red Cross Society. For the purpose of addressing the aftermath of disasters more effectively, Ciraolo made a plan to organise disaster relief. His idea was basically an insurance model that each state would establish for its citizens, together with the founding of an organization for mutual assistance based on the international Red Cross and Red Crescent Movement.[27]

After proposing his plan to the international Red Cross conference in 1921 and to governments at the Genoa economic conference, Ciraolo was allowed to present his plan to the League of Nations in 1922.[28] Within the framework of the League, the plan was further developed and negotiated. At an international conference held in Geneva in 1927, the Convention Establishing an International Relief Union (IRU Convention) was adopted along with the IRU's Statutes.[29] The IRU Convention entered into force in 1932 when the requirements of having sufficient ratifications contributing to the minimum amount of shares were fulfilled.[30]

The IRU was the first international organisation exclusively set up for providing disaster relief in non-armed conflict situations. Nonetheless, and although the IRU has existed for many decades, its story is not one of great success. Already in the years leading up to the adoption of the IRU Convention, it was clear that the ideas behind the IRU were rather controversial. Especially in the US and Great Britain, the idea of an insurance-scheme was not very well received.[31] The UK argued that according to the insurance-scheme it would have to contribute to the common fund of the IRU, but since hardly any major disasters occur in the UK, it would never get anything in return.[32] The US and the UK rather believed in national (individual) responses to disasters, either through public funds or private donations, as such following the line that was until then the trend throughout the previous centuries.

---

[27] Hutchinson (n 18) 253.

[28] Ibid. The League of Red Cross and Red Crescent Societies was involved in the development and presentation at the forum of the League of Nations: David P. Fidler, 'Disaster Relief and Governance After the Indian Ocean Tsunami: What Role for International Law?' (2005) 6 Melbourne Journal of International Law 458, 463.

[29] Macalister-Smith, 'The International Relief Union' (n 16) 363.

[30] According to article 18 of the IRU Convention a total of twelve ratifications was required before the Convention could enter into force and moreover that the contributions of these states must amount to 600 shares of the initial fund. From a discussion in the British parliament in 1928 it follows that by that time only five states ratified and that the UK, despite its critical attitude, also decided to ratify. Nonetheless, in 1928 thirty states already signed the Convention. See the House of Commons debate of 28 November 1928 at: <http://hansard.millbanksystems.com/commons/1928/nov/28/international-relief-union> accessed 13 November 2012.

[31] Although the US never joined the League of Nations, it was involved in the League's efforts on several issues. However '(c)onstant suspicion in Congress (…) that steady U.S. cooperation with the League would lead to de facto membership prevented a close relationship between Washington and Geneva.' US Department of State, Office of the Historian, 'Milestones: 1914-1920 – The League of Nations, 1920' <https://history.state.gov/milestones/1914-1920/league> accessed 4 November 2014.

[32] Hutchinson (n 18) 254.

An affected state would respond to the disaster occurring on its territory, where necessary assisted by private initiatives, either national or foreign. That more states besides the US and UK were not too enthusiastic about the plans is also illustrated by the lapse of time between the adoption of the IRU Convention and the moment on which sufficient ratifications were deposited for the Convention to enter into force on 27 December 1932: five and a half years.[33]

During the negotiations on the content of the Conventions, the original scheme of Ciraolo was altered almost beyond recognition. One of the major changes concerned the funding of the IRU. The idea of an annual donation to the IRU's fund by all member states was changed into the requirement that states must make a small payment for an initial fund, which would then be further filled with voluntary public or private donations.[34] This entailed a departure from the insurance model foreseen by Ciraolo, which generally prompted much criticism for its lack in feasibility and practical difficulties. Another important point was the focus on the persons who are in need of assistance. Ciraolo believed that affected people should have a right to receive international humanitarian assistance. The Preparatory Commission did not go so far, even though a legal foundation for an obligation to give and receive humanitarian assistance was established: 'it is not a question of introducing into international relations a positive obligation that would entail sanctions, but rather of accepting the notion that assistance should neither be given nor received as charity but as a matter of justice'.[35] By saying that giving and receiving assistance is a matter of 'justice', a first stone was laid in the foundation of perceiving humanitarian assistance as a right and/or obligation. This stone was, however, immediately hewed and chiselled by state representatives when negotiating the final texts. States were not ready to acknowledge anything that resembled the beginning of a right or obligation and in the final versions indeed no reference to such language can be found.

Another element that was limited compared to the plans of Ciraolo was the scope of the IRU's work. In the draft-statutes it was laid down that to be eligible for response by the IRU a disaster should meet four criteria: the disaster must be caused due to *force majeur*;[36] it must affect an entire population; the consequences must

---

[33] The states that ratified the Convention prior to the entry into force and who were accordingly responsible for a minimum of 600 shares of the initial fund are (the thirteen states that withdrew their ratification later on are in italics): Albania, Belgium, the *UK* (including *Myanmar*), *New Zealand*, *India*, Bulgaria, *Czechoslovakia*, Ecuador, *Egypt*, Finland, *France*, Germany, *Greece*, *Hungary*, Iran, Italy, *Luxembourg*, Monaco, Poland, *Romania*, San Marino, Sudan, Switzerland, Turkey, Venezuela and Yugoslavia. China, *Cuba* and *Iraq* acceded after the entry into force in the 1930s, and nine other states signed the Convention but never ratified. UN Treaty Database at: <http://treaties.un.org/Pages/LONViewDetails.aspx?src=IND&id=564&lang=en> accessed 13 November 2012.

[34] Hutchinson (n 18) 259.

[35] Notes du Sénateur Ciraolo, LN 12/34734/20947, box R659, 3, cited by Hutchinson (n 18) 262.

[36] The requirement of *force majeur* excludes armed conflicts from the IRU's mandate. This does not follow from the explicit text of the IRU Convention, but is interpreted as such. See

exceed normal provisions of even a provident government; and the disaster must be of an exceptional character in the affected state.[37] That these requirements are unworkably strict was illustrated by a disaster that took place while negotiations on the IRU were underway. In 1923, Japan was hit by an earthquake with a magnitude of 7.9 $M_{w.}$[38] Followed by tsunamis and fires, the earthquake killed about 142,800 people, mainly in the Kanto area (the region around Tokyo and Yokohama).[39] Even though this earthquake can be considered one of the worst in history, applying the strict criteria of the IRU would make it doubtful whether this disaster would have been eligible for response by the IRU. Although an earthquake would be *force majeur,* this particular earthquake did not affect the entire population directly but hit Tokyo and Yokohama hardest. And while probably the normal provisions of Japan were exceeded by the earthquake, the occurrence of such a severe earthquake in itself is not exceptional in Japan.[40] Consequently, only two of the four criteria would be met.

Of all the plans and humanitarian intentions of Ciraolo not much remained. In the IRU Convention no reference is made to humanitarian motives, human misery, moral obligations to assist one another, mutual insurance, and the disastrous consequences of wars and revolutions.[41] Neither does it contain a right of an affected population to receive international assistance. What did remain was the objective of the IRU to provide first aid (and to assemble funds and other resources to this end) in the event of a disaster meeting the requirements as given above.[42] The IRU Convention further mentions other objectives of the IRU, like the coordination of efforts of organisations in case of a disaster, conducting research on prevention of disasters, and stimulating all peoples to render mutual international assistance.[43] All these activities were further limited by another requirement: the IRU could only operate in a state that has granted permission for these operations, thus safeguarding state sovereignty.[44] As a result, ever since its beginning, the IRU was rather handicapped. The operational scope was limited beyond recognition

---

Macalister-Smith, *International Humanitarian Assistance* (n 3) 19. It must be noted, though, that the IRU was requested to come to the assistance of victims of the Spanish Civil War in 1936. The IRU decided not to do this because the ICRC already had an aid scheme in place and the members of the League of Nations did not want to take sides in the civil war. See Hutchinson (n 18) 292-5.

[37] In the IRU Convention the elements of *force majeur*, exceptional gravity, and exceeding the limits of the powers and resources of the stricken people are maintained in article 2(1), where the element of 'affecting the entire population is arguably implied in 'stricken people'.

[38] USGS <http://earthquake.usgs.gov/earthquakes/world/events/1923_09_01.php> accessed 20 July 2010.

[39] Ibid.

[40] Hutchinson (n 18) 264.

[41] Ibid, 286.

[42] Article 2(1) IRU Convention.

[43] Article 2(2) IRU Convention.

[44] See articles 3 and 4 IRU Convention. The requirement of consent and the lack of financial obligations made the IRU a very safe organisation in terms of state sovereignty. Fidler (n 28) 463-4.

when compared to the initial ideas of Ciraolo, and the funding scheme of the IRU as established in the Convention was inadequate from the start. Due to these problems, the IRU was doomed to be a failure:

> Unless showered with contributions from philanthropists and the public, the IRU would have almost no money to put towards disaster relief, which was probably just as well, since it was restricted to acting only in the wake of disasters due to force majeure occurring in the territory of member states, where the affected state admitted that it was unable to cope with the consequences, and agreed to the intervention of the IRU.[45]

During the first few years that the IRU was operational, there had been severe natural disasters in Poland, China, the US, Greece, Italy, and India, but in all cases states claimed that no international aid was required since the national capacity sufficed.[46] The IRU did however act on two occasions. First, in 1934 it wanted to provide funding in the aftermath of an earthquake in India.[47] The Indian government refused the aid offered by the IRU, after which the IRU nonetheless assisted by channelling its aid through the Red Cross.[48] In 1935, the IRU responded to an earthquake in Balochistan (Pakistan).[49] Actually responding to disasters was not the main activity of the IRU. Most of its work consisted of conducting research on disasters.[50]

After the Second World War, when the League of Nations did no longer exist and the United Nations was created, the IRU decided that becoming a part of the UN would be the most sensible thing to do. It also acknowledged that it should be confined to its scientific tasks. The Red Cross, which supported the IRU since its establishment by fulfilling administrative tasks, withdrew in 1948. It did, however, recommend that the need for an IRU remained and that the Convention should be revised. In 1950, the UN's Economic and Social Council (ECOSOC) suggested to the IRU members states (those who were also a member of the UN) to disband the IRU. By 1957, only three states declared themselves in favour of maintaining the IRU, although the other remaining members did not yet withdraw from the organisation. Only in 1965 did the IRU Executive Committee recommend the transfer of the IRU's assets and responsibilities to the UN.[51] This transfer was fully

---

45 Hutchinson (n 18) 286.

46 Ibid, 291.

47 This earthquake in the Bihar area in India (also affecting Nepal) was of a magnitude of 8.1 $M_w$ and killed around 10,700 people. USGS <http://earthquake.usgs.gov/earthquakes/world/events/1934_01_15.php> accessed 15 November 2012.

48 Of which the Red Cross made no mention in its publication on the relief undertakings. Hutchinson (n 18) 291.

49 The Balochistan earthquake is also referred to as the Quetta earthquake. It had a magnitude of 7.5 $M_w$ and killed approximately 30,000 people. USGS <http://earthquake.usgs.gov/earthquakes/world/ historical_country.php> accessed 15 November 2012.

50 Macalister-Smith, 'The International Relief Union' (n 16) 370.

51 Ibid, 372.

completed in 1967 after which only the scientific activities of the IRU remained, which were now placed at the UN's Educational, Scientific and Cultural Organisation (UNESCO). This put an end to the only international organisation set up for the sole purpose of providing peace-time humanitarian assistance.

Clearly, the IRU is not an example of great success in the history of international disaster response. Even so, the fact that the IRU has existed provides some interesting insights. One is that there were states that did believe that the task of bringing relief to the victims of disasters should be placed in the hands of an international organisation. Also, the response to disasters was taken up by states rather than private parties, basing this on a more or less legal foundation and not merely departing from the idea of charity.[52] Still, it was clear that states were careful at the same time to grant too much power to an international organisation so that the IRU received a mandate that was too cautious, making it unworkable. Nonetheless, the ideas behind the IRU keep coming back in the discussion on disaster response today.

## 2.5 The United Nations' activities within the field of disaster response

Apart from imbedding the IRU in the UN framework, the UN has its own story of international disaster response and the provision of humanitarian assistance. At the beginning of this story, humanitarian response is closely interlaced with armed conflict. Although that is not the focus here, it is necessary to include to provide the full picture.

Already before the UN Charter was signed, the UN Relief and Rehabilitation Administration (UNRRA) was created. The agreement establishing UNRRA of 9 November 1943 was signed by forty-two states.[53] Established during the Second World War, UNRRA's active operations aimed at providing relief (food, fuel, clothing, shelter, etc.) to the survivors of this war and specifically in the areas under the control of UN member states.[54] During the period in which UNRRA was active, which lasted less than five years, the organisation was working with a total budget of approximately 3,7 billion US dollars.[55] This budget exceeded that of the IRU, making it more successful financially. Also when looking at the operations, it can be argued that UNRRA was doing better than the IRU. UNRRA operated in sixteen states even though it could only operate with the consent of the recipient nation, just

---

[52] Macalister-Smith, *International Humanitarian Assistance* (n 3) 21.

[53] Agreement for United Nations Relief and Rehabilitation Administration, 1943, Australian Treaty Series, 2 cited by Andrej Zwitter, 'United Nations' Legal Framework of Humanitarian Assistance' in Hans Joachim Heintze & Andrej Zwitter (eds), *International Law and Humanitarian Assistance: A Crosscut Through Legal Issues Pertaining to Humanitarianism* (Springer, Heidelberg/Dordrecht/ London/ New York 2011) 52.

[54] Grace Fox, 'The Origins of UNRRA' (1950) 65 Political Science Quarterly 561, 570.

[55] Wilbur A. Sawyer, 'Achievements of UNRRA as an International Health Organization' (1947) 37 American Journal of Public Health 41, 41.

like IRU.[56] The clear difference in operational success between UNRRA and IRU can be explained by looking at the support that the organisations received from states. While the IRU was focusing on an uncertain event to happen in the future (i.e. natural disasters), UNRRA was responding to a suffering as the result of a war, at that time clearly visible. For IRU, states were supposed to give a contribution to a general fund not knowing how it would be used, while the funds for UNRRA had a concrete destination. Because of the specific mandate of UNRRA, i.e. aiding the victims of the Second World War, this organisation was set up as a temporary organisation, making it easier for state contributors to oversee the extent of the costs and efforts.[57] What is illustrated by the success of UNRRA is that a collective response to humanitarian emergencies (albeit in this case as a result of armed conflict) could indeed be successful and receive the support of states. Also working with the consent of the recipient state is not problematic per se.[58]

Despite its relative success, UNRRA was not immediately succeeded by a new organisation focusing on the delivery of humanitarian assistance, yet was followed up by the International Refugee Organisation which later turned into the Office of the High Commissioner for Refugees (UNHCR).[59] After the Second World War, many organisations were assisting survivors of the war and when this assistance was no longer required, attention shifted towards the process of decolonization and the provision of development aid.[60] Attention turned back to delivering humanitarian assistance at the end of the 1960's due to a humanitarian disaster as the result of – again – armed conflict.

In 1967, civil war broke out in Nigeria when Colonel Ojukwu unilaterally declared the independent republic of Biafra, which would be the country of the Ibo, an ethnic group. The armed forces of Biafra, fighting against Nigeria, were losing ground during almost the entire period of the war (1967-1970), and the people living in Biafra barely had access to food, water and health care. During most of the war, Biafrans were cut off by Nigerian forces from any incoming humanitarian aid. As a result, the people living in Biafra did not have access to basic needs, but they were at the same time unable to obtain these needs in Nigeria. Many people died of malnourishment, starvation, lack of water and related diseases. Photographs of this humanitarian disaster were published all over the world and also the upcoming

---

[56] Agreement on the UNRRA, article 1 under 2(a); Fox (n 54) 582-3.

[57] Fox (n 54) 570.

[58] It is questionable whether the failure of the IRU can be completely attributed to 'design flaws' (e.g. no obligation to contribute financially and the requirement of state consent) or whether perhaps the interbellum was not the right time for success. Fidler (n 28) 464.

[59] Zwitter (n 53) 53.

[60] Ed Tsui and Thant Myint-U, 'The Institutional Response: Creating a Framework in Response to New Challenges' in OCHA, *The Humanitarian Decade: Challenges for Humanitarian Assistance in the Last Decade and into the Future* (Volume II: General Assembly Resolution 46/182: The Development of Practice, Principles and the Humanitarian Framework) United Nations, Geneva/ New York 2004, 2. One UN agency was, however, working on humanitarian assistance; the UN Relief and Works Agency for Palestine Refugees in the Near East (UNRWA); Zwitter (n 53) 53.

medium of television made the effects on the Biafrans visible, leading to international reactions of outrage and shock. Organisations started to work on humanitarian assistance next to development assistance. Moreover, the working method of the main organisation already specialized in humanitarian assistance, the Red Cross and Red Crescent Movement, was critically reviewed. The International Committee of the Red Cross (ICRC, working in armed conflict) and International Federation of the Red Cross and Red Crescent Societies (IFRC, working in peace-time disasters) strongly promote the humanitarian principles of humanity, impartiality, neutrality, independence (and characteristic for the IFRC the additional principles of voluntary service, unity, and universality). Consequently, the ICRC and IFRC are often not vocal on what is experienced in the field. In the case of Biafra, however, many were of the opinion that Nigeria, supported by the UK and US, was clearly causing the deaths and suffering of thousands of civilians by blockading aid. New organisations like *Médecins Sans Frontières* refused to understand principles like 'neutrality' and 'impartiality' as having to stay silent even when witnessing great misconduct.[61]

Also the UN started to direct its attention to humanitarian crises, not only those as a result of armed conflict (e.g. the third Indo-Pakistani war in 1971), but also those following natural disaster (like the earthquake in Peru in 1970).[62] Here, the activities started to take different roads: humanitarian response to natural disasters was separated from armed conflict. The Secretariat of the UN advised the organisation to leave humanitarian relief actions to specialized organisations such as the IFRC. Setting this advice aside, the UN General Assembly established the Disaster Relief Organisation (UNDRO)[63] in 1971 in order to organise and coordinate the UN's emergency response capacity, ensuring that 'relief was mobilized more rapidly and was better co-ordinated'.[64] Up till the establishment of UNDRO, the UN relief initiatives were mainly on an *ad hoc* basis. UNDRO was supposed to organise and coordinate all UN's relief activities, yet it is questionable whether it succeeded in doing this. *Ad hoc* operations kept taking place and seemed at times the most convenient solution to an emergency.[65]

In 1976 and 1982, UNDRO – in cooperation with the Red Cross – conducted studies aimed at identifying the main problems in peacetime disaster relief which were subsequently addressed in the Draft Convention on Expediting the Delivery of

---

[61] When discussing the extent to which states have a freedom to refuse humanitarian assistance, the fact that those offering the assistance hold a state accountable for its actions could be of importance. For more information on their way of working, see the website of MSF: <http://www.msf.org> accessed 15 November 2012.
[62] Tsui and Myint-U (n 60) 2.
[63] Established by Resolution 2816 (XXVI) of 14 December 1971.
[64] R. Wolfrum, 'Art. 55' in Bruno Simma (ed) *The Charter of the United Nations: A Commentary* (Vol. I, 2nd edition, Oxford University Press, Oxford 2002) 916 cited by Zwitter (n 53) 55; Tsui and Myint-U (n 60) 2-3. The UN was already involved in disaster *preparedness* through the United Nations Development Programme (UNDP): Zwitter (n 53) 54.
[65] Tsui and Myint-U (n 60) 3.

Emergency Assistance.[66] As a consequence, the Draft Convention contains provisions on a wide range of practical issues, like the basic conditions for the delivery of assistance, the exchange of information and communication, protection of and facilities for personnel, quality of assistance and matters relating to transportation (including import, export, and liability). The Draft Convention was presented to ECOSOC in 1984, after which ECOSOC referred the instrument to UN's Second Committee, but no further action was taken.[67] The Draft Convention did not receive broad support, but the most notable opponents were the IFRC and the ICRC, which feared that the Draft Convention over-emphasized sovereignty and the primary (controlling) role of the receiving states.[68]

Besides the not very successful Draft Convention, the General Assembly adopted a number of resolutions relating to humanitarian assistance and natural disasters dating back to 1965.[69] In the next section where the legal framework will be discussed, more detail will be provided on the content of these resolutions. For now, it will suffice to mention the Resolution that forms the basis for the majority of today's peacetime humanitarian relief operations.[70] This is UN General Assembly Resolution 46/182 of 19 December 1991. It is striking to see that according to Resolution 46/182 there apparently is a need for a central funding mechanism complementary to individual states' responses, which reminds of the ideas behind the International Relief Union.[71] Regardless of the lack of success in the IRU's context, the idea apparently survived the decades between the creation of the IRU and the adoption of Resolution 46/182. Besides the new central emergency fund, the Resolution also appointed the new Emergency Relief Coordinator.[72] The responsibility for the coordination of UN's humanitarian response was in this way placed in the hands of one individual. The office of the Emergency Relief

---

[66] UNGA and ECOSOC, 'Draft Convention on Expediting the Delivery of Emergency Assistance' (UN Doc. A/39/267/Add.2, E/1984/96/Add.2 of 18 June 1984). Victoria L. Bannon, 'Strengthening International Disaster Response Laws, Rules, and Principles' in C. Raj Kumar & D.K. Srivastava (eds.), *Tsunami and Disaster Management: Law and Governance* (Thomson Sweet & Maxwell Asia, Hong Kong 2006) 12.

[67] Fisher, 'Desk Study' (n 4) 27-8; Macalister-Smith, *International Humanitarian Assistance* (n 3) 222-30, Fidler (n 28) 464-5.

[68] The third article on 'principles' refers to respect for the sovereignty of the receiving state and non-interference in its internal affairs; cooperation with national authorities and respect for national laws; abstention from any commercial or political activity; and the responsibility of the receiving state for facilitating the coordination of operations.

[69] In 1965, UNGA Resolution on 'Assistance in the Case of Natural Disaster' (UN Doc. A/RES/2034 [XX] [195] of 7 December 1965) was adopted.

[70] See Heike Spieker, 'The Right to Give and Receive Humanitarian Assistance' in Hans-Joachim Heintze & Andrej Zwitter (eds.), *International Law and Humanitarian Assistance: A Crosscut Through Legal Issues Pertaining to Humanitarianism* (Springer, Heidelberg/Dordrecht/London/ New York 2011) 21.

[71] UNGA Resolution on 'Strengthening of the coordination of humanitarian emergency assistance of the United Nations' (UN Doc. A/Res/46/182 of 19 December 1991) para 22.

[72] Ibid, paras 23 and 34.

Coordinator was based in UNDRO and UNDRO was renamed in the Department of Humanitarian Affairs (DHA). In 1998, the DHA changed into the Office for the Coordination of Humanitarian Affairs (OCHA). The Emergency Relief Coordinator is also the Under-Secretary General for Humanitarian Affairs and the head of OCHA. [73] Next to these UN agencies specifically focused on disasters and humanitarian assistance, other UN agencies fulfil a role in this field. Examples are the World Food Programme, the World Health Organisation, UNHCR, and UNICEF. Only where relevant, these other agencies will be discussed.

## 3 Overview of relevant fields and instruments of international law

### 3.1 Introduction

In Chapter I it has been explained that the legal framework on disaster response and the delivery of humanitarian assistance is quite scattered. To give some structure to the discussion of the legal framework, a distinction is made between sources that are of a general nature but are nonetheless relevant for the present research and those sources created for the specific purpose of disaster response and humanitarian assistance. In the first category, the legal fields that will be included are international humanitarian law, human rights law, refugee law and the law on internally displaced persons. Other general sources will be mentioned briefly, as they are of less relevance for this particular study. In the second category, sources will be discussed varying from the UN General Assembly resolutions to current developments that are undertaken by the International Law Commission and the IFRC. It must be noted that the title of this section may lead to some disappointment since especially the second category of sources consists mainly of instruments of a nature that is commonly referred to as 'soft law'. Many instruments are mere policy briefs or guidelines hardly constituting any obligations for states. They are nonetheless included as they illustrate the developments in the field of disaster response and humanitarian assistance and reflect the (legal) way of thinking about these topics.[74]

### 3.2 International humanitarian law

Even though situations of armed conflict are not the object of research, it is nonetheless useful to take a look at the field of international humanitarian law (IHL) because it contains a number of rules and principles on humanitarian assistance and is generally considered to be quite clear in this respect. What can be learned from

[73] Arjun Katoch, 'International Natural Disaster Response and the United Nations' in IFRC, *International Disaster Response Laws, Principles and Practice: Reflections, Prospects and Challenges* (IFRC, Geneva 2003) 47-56, 47.

[74] Only the instruments most relevant for this research will be discussed in this section. For a full overview of legal sources see Fisher, 'Desk Study' (n 4).

IHL can be used to explain the meaning of the rules and principles identified for peace-time disasters.

IHL consists of a number of instruments of which the most relevant here are the Geneva Conventions of 1949 and their Additional Protocols of 1977.[75] The Geneva Conventions are developed under auspices of the ICRC and are clearly connected to the original intentions and goals of Henry Dunant. The first two Geneva Conventions deal with the treatment of wounded and sick combatants, and shipwrecked, wounded and sick combatants at sea. The Third and Fourth Convention seek to protect prisoners of war and civilians respectively. The Fourth Geneva Convention (GCIV) contains provisions on the delivery of humanitarian assistance to the civilian population in situations of armed conflict. Also the First and Second Additional Protocols of 1977 (API and APII) – which deal with the protection of victims of international and non-international armed conflicts – contain rules and principles on humanitarian assistance.[76]

The Fourth Geneva Convention on the Protection of Civilian Persons in Time of War contains a number of provisions on humanitarian assistance, starting with article 10 (which is part of the Convention's General Provisions). This article states that

> The provisions of the present Convention constitute no obstacle to the humanitarian activities which the (ICRC) or any other impartial humanitarian organization may, subject to the consent of the Parties to the conflict concerned, undertake for the protection of civilian persons and for their relief.

In part II of GCIV ('General Protection of Populations Against Certain Consequences of War') it is stated that the parties to the Convention 'shall allow the free passage of all consignments of medical and hospital stores and objects necessary for religious worship intended only for civilians of another (...) Party'.[77] The same has also been determined for 'consignments of essential foodstuffs, clothing and tonics intended for children under fifteen, expectant mothers and maternity cases'.[78] Part III on the 'Status and Treatment of Protected Persons' contains in its section II on 'Aliens in the Territory of a Party to the Conflict' the rule that aliens 'shall be enabled to receive the individual or collective relief that

---

[75] The Conventions of 1949 are generally considered to have customary law status. For the Additional Protocols of 1977 this status is not widely assumed: only a couple of provisions of the Protocols would constitute customary law. The International Committee of the Red Cross has conducted an extensive study on the customary law status of the GCs and APs, concluding that some provisions of the APs can be considered customary law. Jean-Marie Henckaerts & Louise Doswald-Beck (eds), *Customary International Humanitarian Law: Volume I: Rules* (Cambridge University Press, Cambridge 2005).

[76] In 2005, a third Additional Protocol has been adopted introducing a third symbol next to the Red Cross and the Red Crescent (the Red Crystal).

[77] Article 23 GCIV.

[78] Ibid.

may be sent to them'.[79] The section on occupied territories (section III of Part III) goes further than these provisions on humanitarian assistance: '(i)f the whole or part of the population of an occupied territory is inadequately supplied, the Occupying Power shall agree to relief schemes on behalf of the said population'.[80] According to the same article, such relief can be given by states or impartial humanitarian organizations (like the ICRC) and shall consist of consignments of foodstuffs, medical supplies and clothing. Although free passage of these goods must be guaranteed by state parties, they can be searched and checked upon passage.[81] In addition to humanitarian aid delivered by third parties, it is emphasized in GCIV that the occupying power has the main responsibility to care for the civilian population.[82] Finally, an occupying power is not allowed to terminate the activities of the ICRC or other humanitarian agencies except for urgent reasons of security.[83]

Also the Additional Protocols contain references to humanitarian assistance. In the API on the Protection of Victims of International Armed Conflicts a rather extensive article is included containing a number of important rules and principles on humanitarian assistance. In this article it is determined that

> If the civilian population of any territory under the control of a Party to the conflict, other than occupied territory, is not adequately provided (...) relief actions which are humanitarian and impartial in character and conducted without any adverse distinction shall be undertaken, subject to the agreement of the Parties concerned in such relief actions.[84]

Moreover, offers of relief 'shall not be regarded as interference in the armed conflict or as unfriendly acts'.[85] All parties to a conflict must make sure that relief moves rapidly and unimpeded, no matter the nationality of the population for whom the relief is meant, although parties have a right to prescribe the arrangements under which passage of relief is permitted, may make its permission conditional on distribution under local supervision, and shall not 'divert relief consignments from the purpose for which they are intended (...) except (...) in the interest of the civilian population concerned'.[86] In the same line, the Second Additional Protocol provides that 'if the civilian population is suffering undue hardship owing to a lack of supplies essential for its survival, relief actions shall be undertaken subject to the consent of the High Contracting Party concerned'[87]

---

[79] Article 38 GCIV. This could also include allowances from relief societies (article 39 GCIV).
[80] Article 59 GCIV.
[81] Ibid.
[82] According to articles 55, 56 and 59 as emphasized in article 60 GCIV.
[83] Article 63 GCIV.
[84] Article 70(1) API under section II on 'Relief in the Favour of the Civilian Population' (part of Chapter VI on Civil Defence).
[85] Article 70(1) API.
[86] Article 70(2) and (3) API.
[87] Article 18(2) APII.

When looking at all these provisions, two conclusions can be drawn. In the first place, there is a strong indication that states – whether occupying powers or parties to an armed conflict – are under an obligation to accept relief when the civilian population is in need of humanitarian assistance.[88] The second conclusion departs from this 'obligation to accept': before humanitarian relief can be delivered, consent must be obtained from the state ('subject to the consent'). Consequently, there are situations in which states must give their consent to humanitarian assistance. This can be explained by looking at the development of the Additional Protocols in the 1970s. When a duty to accept relief was discussed, there were some concerns for state sovereignty. To protect sovereignty, the requirement of consent was included with the remark that this requirement 'did not imply that the Parties concerned had absolute and unlimited freedom to refuse their agreement to relief actions. A Party refusing its agreement must do so for valid reasons, not for arbitrary or capricious ones'.[89] As a consequence, there is a clear rule that consent is required before aid can be delivered but this rule is not granting states unlimited discretionary freedom: consent may not be withheld arbitrarily.[90] What exactly falls under 'arbitrarily withholding consent' is however not entirely clear.[91]

Possibly, the requirement of consent and the rule not to withhold consent arbitrarily are rules of customary international law.[92] Under auspices of the International Committee of the Red Cross and Red Crescent, an extended study has been conducted into the status of various IHL provisions, resulting in an overview

---

[88] There is some discussion on whether such a 'duty' exists for a state's own nationals or only those of another party to the conflict, especially when considering the specific provision for occupying powers. See also Ruth A. Stoffels, 'Legal Regulation of Humanitarian Assistance in Armed Conflict: Achievements and Gaps' (2004) 86 International Review of the Red Cross 515, 519.

[89] ICRC, *Commentary on the Additional Protocols of 8 June 1977 to the Geneva Conventions of 12 August 1949* (1987) para 2805. See also UN ILC Special Rapporteur Eduardo Valencia-Ospina, 'Fourth Report on the Protection of Persons in the Event of Disasters' (UN Doc. A/CN.4/643 of 11 May 2011) para 66.

[90] See, amongst others, Stoffels (n 88) 534. During the negotiations it was stated that giving consent could not be refused on arbitrary grounds OR/II/SR.87, para 27.

[91] Arguably this has something to do with the humanitarian principles. If humanitarian aid meets these principles (impartiality, neutrality, humanity, independence) there is less freedom for a state to withhold its consent. See Valencia-Ospina, 'Fourth Report' (n 89) para 66 where this is indicated with reference to ICRC, *Draft Additional Protocols to the Geneva Conventions of August 12, 1949* (1973) 78-9.

[92] David Fisher, 'Domestic Regulation of International Humanitarian Relief in Disasters and Armed Conflict: A Comparative Analysis' (2007) 89 International Review of the Red Cross 350; Henckaerts & Doswald-Beck (n 75). For the argument that the duty to give consent in certain circumstances enjoys customary law status see the reasoning made by M. Bothe, 'Relief Actions: The Position of Recipient State' in Frits Kalshoven, *Assisting the Victims of Armed Conflict and Other Disasters: Papers Delivered at the International Conference on Humanitarian Assistance in Armed Conflict, The Hague, 22-24 June 1988* (Martinus Nijhoff Publishers, Dordrecht/Boston/London 1989) 92-3.

of rules of customary international law.[93] One of these rules dictates that 'parties to the conflict must allow and facilitate rapid and unimpeded passage of humanitarian relief for civilians in need, which is impartial in character and conducted without any adverse distinction, subject to their right of control'.[94] Even though consent is not mentioned in this rule, the study includes that it is 'self-evident that a humanitarian organisation cannot operate without the consent of the party concerned' and that 'such consent must not be refused on arbitrary grounds'.[95] When a civilian population is threatened with starvation, and the relief offered can remedy the situation while being impartial and non-discriminatory, there would even be an obligation to give consent.[96] The ICRC's customary rules are however not uncontroversial.[97] One question raised is whether 'state practice and *opinio iuris* have abandoned the precondition of consent in case the receiving State refuses such agreement arbitrarily'. [98] This question is closely linked to issues around intervention, such as humanitarian intervention and action within the framework of the Responsibility to Protect, which will be addressed below.[99] It is, however, a valid point to make when considering the words used in the Geneva Conventions and Additional Protocols compared to the 'customary rule' as identified by the ICRC: despite the far-reaching idea in the customary law study, practice shows that states refusing to give consent can block the delivery of aid, even when it refuses to give its consent on arbitrary grounds. In this line, it can be asked whether there is 'a right to impose humanitarian assistance – under certain circumstances – regardless of considerations of national sovereignty' or whether a right to access exists.[100]

One final issue, following from article 70(1) APɪ, must be addressed here because it will come back time and again throughout this research. As article 70(1) APɪ explicitly states, the offers of aid which meet the requirements of that paragraph (i.e. humanitarian and impartial in character and conducted without

[93] Henckaerts & Doswald-Beck (n 75).
[94] Rule 55, Henckaerts & Doswald-Beck (n 75) 193.
[95] Henckaerts & Doswald-Beck (n 75) 196-7.
[96] Henckaerts & Doswald-Beck (n 75) 196-7. This is also argued by Joakim Dungel who is of the opinion that offers that meet the criteria of humanity, impartiality, and neutrality cannot be refused without being arbitrary. Joakim Dungel, 'A Right to Humanitarian Assistance in Internal Armed Conflicts Respecting Sovereignty, Neutrality and Legitimacy: Practical Proposals to Practical Problems' (2004) Journal of Humanitarian Assistance, para 2.2, available at: <http://www.jha.ac/articles/a133.htm> accessed 14 October 2010.
[97] See for example the commentary written by Yoram Dinstein, 'The ICRC Customary International Humanitarian Law Study (2006) 36 Israel Yearbook on Human Rights 1-15.
[98] Spieker (n 70) 17.
[99] Spieker goes into this question from an IHL perspective and argues that 'an apparent inadequacy of supply of the civilian population, a lack of success of alternative means including mechanisms of the United Nations, provision of the civilian population as a last resort and the proportionality of assistance' are elements to be included when discussing intervention. Spieker (n 70) 17.
[100] Ibid. A right to access would in this case be based on the articles of GCɪᴠ, APɪ and APɪɪ cited above.

adverse distinction) should not be regarded as interference in an armed conflict or as unfriendly acts.[101] In other words, if (offers of) humanitarian assistance meets the humanitarian principles of neutrality, impartiality and humanity, it cannot be understood as unfriendly or as interference. This is in line with the case law of the International Court of Justice (ICJ) in the Nicaragua-case. In this case, the Court stated that 'there can be no doubt that the provision of strictly humanitarian aid to persons or forces in another country (...) cannot be regarded as unlawful intervention, or as in any other way contrary to international law'.[102] The Court did put some conditions to this statement by saying that

> If the provision of humanitarian assistance is to escape condemnation as an intervention in the internal affairs of Nicaragua, not only must it be limited to the purposes hallowed in the practice of the Red Cross, namely "to prevent and alleviate human suffering", and "to protect life and health and to ensure respect for the human being"; it must also, and above all, be given without discrimination to all in need in Nicaragua, not merely to the *contras* and their dependents.[103]

Taking this argument one step further, it can also be argued that there is less ground to refuse (offers of) assistance if it adheres to the humanitarian principles of neutrality, impartiality and humanity. Whether or not this is true and what the implications are must become clear below.

### 3.3 Human rights law

Disasters have great impact on the enjoyment of human rights, most notably the rights to life, housing, food, water and health. Including human rights standards in discussions on disaster response it therefore self-evident: 'the scale and impact of the economic and human damage done by natural disasters also helps experts connect disaster policy with international human rights law'.[104] Human rights law is even included to rekindle the discussion on rights and obligations: 'linkages between disaster policy and human rights emerged more strongly as international human rights law developed after World War II, and these linkages emphasized the duty of states to facilitate, and the right of individuals to have access to, disaster relief'.[105] In the light of the present research this sounds very promising, but

---

[101] Spieker argues that even though this provision is addressed to states, 'customary law has broadened this "right to offer" to all humanitarian actors'. This 'right' is argued to be part of the 'humanitarian mandate' of relief organisations. Spieker (n 70) 17.

[102] ICJ, Military and Paramilitary Activities in and Against Nicaragua (Nicaragua v United States of America) (Merits) [1986] ICJ Rep 14, para 242.

[103] Ibid, para 243.

[104] Fidler (n 28) 468. See also Ronan Hardcastle & Adrian Chua, 'Victims of Natural Disasters: The Right to Receive Humanitarian Assistance' (1997) 4 The International Journal of Human Rights 35.

[105] Fidler (n 28) 468 (footnotes omitted).

expectations must be tempered: using human rights in this way proves more complex than it appears and is in need of more careful consideration.

The rights-based approach to humanitarian assistance has received the necessary attention. The Office of the High Commissioner of Human Rights describes such an approach in relation to humanitarian assistance as follows: '(t)he rights-based approach to assistance uses the human rights framework to redefine the relationship between stakeholders in society as rights-holders with entitlements and duty bearers with correlative obligations'.[106] In disaster contexts, the right holders would be the survivors of a disaster and the duty-bearers would be the affected states.[107] Following this description of the rights-based approach, disaster survivors would have certain entitlements and affected states would have *correlative* obligations. If human rights indeed have this effect, it can be wondered whether a claim to a certain human right leads to a corresponding obligation for the affected state to provide, and if necessary, to accept humanitarian assistance. Turning the question around: if an obligation to accept assistance is found, can it result in human rights terms in a right for individuals to receive humanitarian assistance? These questions will be explored here.

The Universal Declaration of Human Rights (UDHR), the International Covenant on Civil and Political Rights (ICCPR), and the International Covenant on Economic, Social and Cultural Rights (ICESCR) contain a broad basis of fundamental human rights that are often affected in disaster situations.[108] Some of the rights in the UDHR have the status of customary law, yet this goes mainly for the civil and political rights of the UDHR.[109] The economic, social and cultural rights of the Declaration, like article 25 providing the rights to an adequate standard of living including food, housing and medical care, do not have this customary law status nor does the elaboration of these rights within the ICESCR. Still, arguably there is a certain core of (some of the) economic, social and cultural rights which are of such importance that they can achieve – if not already have achieved – the status of customary law.[110] For this core it would mean that states have a duty to

[106] OHCHR, 'Frequently Asked Questions on a Human Rights-Based Approach to Development Cooperation' (United Nations, New York/Geneva 2006) 15 (available at <http://www.ohchr.org/Documents/Publications/FAQen.pdf> accessed 7 June 2012. See also Brian Concannon Jr., & Beatrice Lindstrom. 'Cheaper, Better, Longer-Lasting: A Rights-Based Approach to Disaster Response in Haiti' (25) 2011 Emory International Law Review 1145, 1149. The Sphere Minimum Standards, a much used soft-law framework for providing assistance, subscribe using a rights-based approach; ibid, 1157.

[107] See also Concannon & Lindstrom (n 106) 1151.

[108] Article 6 of the ICCPR contains the right to life, which is closely connected to the rights to housing, food, water and health of articles 11 and 12 of the ICESCR.

[109] See *inter alia* Christian Tomuschat, *Human Rights: Between Idealism and Realism* (Oxford University Press, Oxford 2003) 34.

[110] The 'customary core approach'; Malcolm Langford, Fons Coomans & Felipe Gómez Isa, 'Extraterritorial Duties in International Law' in Malcolm Langford, Wouter Vandenhole, Martin Scheinin & Willem J.M. van Genugten (eds), *Global Justice, State Duties: The Extraterritorial*

'ensure that the rights are protected against interference and that a minimum essential level of the right is positively realised'.[111]

The rights that are of special importance in disaster settings (the rights to life, housing, food, water and health) are repeated in a number of other human rights instruments targeting special groups, like the Convention on the Rights of the Child (CRC, for example article 6 on the right to life), Convention on the Elimination of Discrimination Against Women (CEDAW, for example article 12 on access to health care), and the Convention on the Rights of Persons with Disabilities (CRPD, for example article 28 on the adequate standard of living). State parties to these human rights instruments are responsible for realizing the human rights for the people under their jurisdiction. It appears therefore that those people can claim their rights to life, housing, food, et cetera when these rights are affected by the occurrence of a disaster. However, it must first be considered to what extent the exceptional circumstance of a disaster influences human rights obligations of states.

One way in which a disaster potentially influences state party obligations is through the state of emergency, explicitly laid down in the ICCPR and a few other human rights instruments. In cases of emergency a state can, according to article 4 ICCPR, derogate from its obligations stemming from that instrument: in 'times of emergency the state parties may take measures derogating from some of the specific obligations contained therein'.[112] Derogation becomes possible when a state officially proclaims the 'state of emergency', which is often done in case of disaster. Apart from official proclamation, there are a number of other requirements to which a state must comply. Moreover, some rights are excluded from the option to derogate, as is for example provided in article 4(2) ICCPR. In this paragraph the right to life (amongst other rights) is excluded from derogation. Whether the rights of the ICESCR are open to derogation during a disaster is subject to debate. The Covenant does not contain a derogation clause like the one of the ICCPR, and common sense dictates that even if derogation is possible, this cannot be unlimited: it is unimaginable to allow people to starve to death because the right to food is

---

*Scope of Economic, Social and Cultural Rights in International Law* (Cambridge, Cambridge University Press 2013) 68. An example of the development of a certain core of ESC-rights into customary law can be found in the context of the ILO where the ILO Declaration on Fundamental Principles and Rights at Work of 1998 recognizes the special importance of the cores of four social rights (i.e. the freedom of association, elimination of forced labour, effective abolition of child labour and the elimination of discrimination in respect of employment and occupation). ILO 'Declaration on Fundamental Principles and Rights at Work' (adopted by the International Labour Conference at its 86$^{th}$ session, Geneva 1998) para 2.

[111] Langford, Coomans & Gomes Isa (n 110) 68.

[112] Rebecca J. Barber, 'Protecting the Right to Housing in the Aftermath of Natural Disaster: Standards in International Human Rights Law' (2008) 20 International Journal of Refugee Law 432, 434. The following instruments also contain such a 'derogation-clause': European Convention for the Protection of Human Rights and Fundamental Freedoms (ECHR) (article 15), European Social Charter (article 30), and the American Convention on Human Rights (article 27).

temporarily inoperative.[113] Generally speaking, it is safe to say that human rights cannot be set aside solely by the occurrence of a disaster. It is nonetheless clear that in some situations it is more difficult to respect, protect and fulfil human rights than in other situations. Especially fulfilling economic, social and cultural rights is often linked to the availability of resources.[114] At times of disaster, having sufficient resources available for the realisation of human rights may prove challenging, which is for example acknowledged in the case of Haiti:

> A successful disaster response must place human rights at the centre. Under international law, the Haitian government has the primary obligation to realize the human rights of its people, but natural disasters make it difficult for states, already lacking capacity due to resource constraints, to assert full control over policies that are central to their ability to fulfil their human rights obligations.[115]

Consequently, the state of emergency-clause does not have the effect of eliminating all human rights obligations during disasters and although human rights achievements are linked to the availability of resources, the obligations remain valid in principle. Claims to certain human rights during disasters therefore still require corresponding state obligations.

Another question posed above was whether corresponding obligations for affected states lead to an obligation to accept humanitarian assistance, for example when the affected state lacks the capacity to fulfil its obligations by itself. The ICESCR contains an interesting provision that appears to touch upon this question. In its general obligations, the ICESCR provides that state parties must 'undertake to take steps, individually and through international assistance and cooperation, to the maximum of its available resources, with a view to achieving progressively the full realization of the rights',[116] apparently telling state parties to make use of international assistance to realize the rights to housing, food, water, health and other rights of the Covenant. Comparable references can be found in articles 23 and 28 of the CRC (although in this context linked to particular rights and not formulated as a general obligation) and article 4(2) of the CRPD, but no clear understanding exist on whether or to what extent this entails an obligation to accept humanitarian assistance after a disaster.

Although various human rights bodies have made the link between human rights obligations and disasters, an answer to this question is not given. The Committee on the Rights of the Child for example provided that states should develop and make

---

[113] Philip Alston & Gerard Quinn, 'The Nature and Scope of State Parties' Obligations under the International Covenant on Economic, Social and Cultural Rights', (1987) 9 Human Rights Quarterly 156, 201 & 219.

[114] See for instance Jonathan Todres, 'Mainstreaming Children's Rights in Post-Disaster Settings' (2011) 25 Emory International Law Review 1233, 1243, stressing that although there might be resource constraints, this does not mean that a disaster sets human rights obligations aside.

[115] Concannon & Lindstrom (n 106) 1147.

[116] Article 2(1) ICESCR.

available 'strategic budgetary lines' in disaster situations for the protection of vulnerable children.[117] The Human Rights Council (HRC) 'expressed its concern over the effective denial of assistance to undocumented migrants in Thailand during the 2004 Indian Ocean Tsunami. The HRC held that humanitarian assistance should be provided effectively to all victims of the tsunami without discrimination, and thus regardless of their legal status'.[118] The CRPD refers in its article 11 explicitly to humanitarian emergencies and disasters and under this provision a special working group was set up on the protection of human rights in a number of specific disaster settings (i.e. China, Haiti and Chile).[119] Moreover, the CRPD's Committee urged those involved in disaster response after the 2010 Haiti earthquake to include 'a disability perspective in all humanitarian relief efforts' and to make sure that 'disabled, elderly and other vulnerable groups such as women and children in the community be given preferential access to food distribution, and proper sanitation facilities'.[120] It further urged that 'rescue efforts must include the provision of medical support, and related assistance to meet the basic needs of those in distress with food, water, clothing, temporary shelter and basic sanitation' in ensuring that victims of disaster would not become persons with disabilities.[121] Continuing the line of attention to disaster-specific duties, it would be interesting to see whether the general obligations of the ICESCR being considered in disaster-settings could constitute an obligation to accept international humanitarian assistance in any way.

The final question posed at the beginning of this section concerned the possible existence of a right to humanitarian assistance. Such a right would imply 'the right of the victims of armed conflicts and other disasters to receive assistance and protection with the purpose of satisfying their immediate needs'.[122] The right to receive humanitarian assistance gained attention during the 1990s, which was the 'International Decade for Natural Disaster Reduction' and during which it was acknowledged that the international legal framework did not have an answer to situations in which people are in urgent need of humanitarian assistance.[123] Some

---

[117] CRC, 'Concluding Observations Madagascar' UN Doc. CRC/C/MDG/CO/3-4 of 8 March 2012, para 18, cited by Marlies M.E. Hesselman, 'Establishing a Full 'Cycle of Protection' for Disaster Victims: Preparedness, Response and Recovery according to Regional and International Human Rights Supervisory Bodies' (2013) 18 Tilburg Law Review 106, 122.

[118] HRC, 'Concluding Observations Thailand' UN Doc. CCPR/CO/84/THA of 8 July 2005, para 23, cited by Hesselman (n 117) para 123.

[119] See the CPRD, 'Report of the Committee on the Rights of Persons with Disabilities to the General Assembly' UN Doc. A/66/55 of 2011 para 31; Hesselman (n 117) 123.

[120] CRPD, 'Statement of the CteeRPD on the Rights of Persons with Disabilities on the Situation in Haiti' (8 February 2010) cited by Hesselman (n 117) 124.

[121] CRPD, 'Statement of the CtRPD in Connection with the Earthquake in Qinghai China' of 23 April 2010, cited by Hesselman (n 117) 124.

[122] Joana Abrisketa, 'The Right to Humanitarian Aid: Basis and Limitations' in Humanitarian Studies Unit (ed), *Reflections on Humanitarian Action: Principles, Ethics and Contradictions* (Pluto Press, London/Sterling 2001) 55.

[123] The International Decade for Natural Disaster Reduction was proclaimed by the UN General Assembly: GA Resolution 44/236 of 22 December 1989. Hardcastle & Chua (n 104) 35.

argue that a right to receive humanitarian assistance is (emerging) customary law under IHL,[124] yet under human rights law such a customary rule does not exist.[125] Even though humanitarian assistance is quite commonly delivered in disaster situations, it is questionable whether there is an *opinio iuris* supporting this and it is especially doubtful whether such an *opinio* can be found for a right to receive assistance.[126] Consequently, a right to receive (or as some call it: demand) relief is deemed not to exist at this point.[127] This does not take away the fact that human rights law can provide a basis for a duty to accept international humanitarian assistance in order to fulfil human rights obligations, not being a right to receive assistance necessarily.[128]

The importance and relevance of human rights law in disaster settings is recognized, but it is not yet used to its full potential. Human rights standards could be helpful in disaster response and disaster policy, although what this would entail in terms of obligations for state parties cannot be said without more research. Standards under the rights to housing, food, water and health must give affected states indications of what is expected from them after a disaster. Read in conjunction with the ICESCR's general obligations to make use of international cooperation and assistance and to use the maximum of *available* resources, it is possible that the ICESCR can fill the gaps that remain in the legal framework on accepting humanitarian assistance after the occurrence of a disaster (as will become clear in Chapter III). For this reason, it will be considered in Chapters IV and V in detail what the ICESCR can contribute to concretizing norms and setting standards.

### 3.4 Refugees and internally displaced persons

The occurrence of a disaster often displaces the affected population. When fleeing the consequences of a disaster, people could stay within their state's borders (making them internally displaced persons or IDPs) or they could cross the border and seek refuge in another state. Although this latter group does not meet the definition of 'refugee' as provided by the Refugee Convention and can therefore strictly speaking not be called 'refugees', this group is nonetheless assisted by the

---

[124] Abrisketa (n 122); Dungel (n 96); Stoffels (n 88).
[125] Hardcastle & Chua (n 104) 35.
[126] Basing the existence of customary law on the requirements of ICJ North Sea Continental Shelf Case, where it has been determined that there must be a state practice supported by *opinio iuris sive necessitatis*. That the *opinio iuris* is missing with regard to providing humanitarian assistance and with regard to a right to receive humanitarian assistance is also concluded by Hardcastle & Chua (n 104) 39.
[127] Yoram Dinstein, 'The Right to Humanitarian Assistance' (2000) 53 Naval War College Review 77. Even so, among sceptics it is usually understood that such a right might sooner exist in situations of armed conflicts than in peace-time because of the basis in IHL.
[128] See for a more extended review of the right to humanitarian assistance: Emilie E. Kuijt, *Humanitarian Assistance and Sovereignty in International Law: Towards a Comprehensive Framework* (forthcoming, 2015).

UNHCR and are for purposes of protection standards considered as refugees in this research.[129] In either case, the people who became displaced are in need of assistance, putting a strain on resources available at the location of displacement. Through the creation of (legal) instruments on the treatment of refugees and IDPs it has been attempted to grant certain rights and safeguards to those who had to leave their lives and possessions behind.

Based on the Refugee Convention, refugees are granted a certain level of protection from the state on which territory the refugee finds himself through the recognition of certain rights and entitlements. These rights vary from the right of association (article 15) and access to courts (article 16) to those rights which are generally closer connected to humanitarian assistance, like equal treatment as nationals with regard to rationing, housing, and public relief (articles 20, 21 and 23).

No specific legally binding international instrument of law exists with regard to IDPs,[130] something which can easily be explained with reference to a variety of sources and principles of public international law, like sovereignty and human rights law, dictating states that they must protect the people living on their territory or the people that are under the state's jurisdiction. IDPs do not leave their own state and must therefore (in theory) be protected by their government. Nonetheless, IDPs find themselves in a vulnerable position and often require special protection. In 1998 the Guiding Principles on Internal Displacement were adopted containing specific guidelines on how to protect IDPs. Although not a 'hard' legal instrument, the Guiding Principles at least acknowledge that displacement can be caused by a natural disaster. In the introduction to the Principles, under (2), it is said that IDPs are persons (or groups of persons) who had been forced to flee as a result of, amongst other causes, natural or human-made disasters. It is further emphasized that IDPs should be treated the same as other persons in the country, but the Principles go further than that.

An explicit right to request and receive protection and humanitarian assistance from national authorities can be found in Principle 3(2). These national authorities have the primary responsibility and duty to provide assistance, which is in line with the human rights obligations that many states have.[131] Indeed, in Principle 18 a set of socio-economic rights can be found. In its first paragraph, it is established that IDPs have a right to an adequate standard of living. The minimum content of this right is described as supplying IDPs with and ensuring access to essential food and

---

[129] According to the Refugee Convention, a refugee is a person who 'owing to well-founded fear of being persecuted for reasons of race, religion, nationality, membership of a particular social group or political opinion, is outside the country of his nationality' (article 1 under A(2) Refugee Convention). Originally, the Refugee Convention only relates to those situations in which the refugee status is caused by events starting prior to 1 January 1951. With the adoption of the protocol of 1967 this scope has been broadened to those situations taking place after 1 January 1951.

[130] Since December 2012, a regional legal instrument on IDPs exists within the framework of the African Union. This Kampala Convention will be discussed further below in the present section.

[131] Guiding Principle 3(1).

potable water; basic shelter and housing; appropriate clothing; and essential medical services and sanitation, all regardless of the circumstances and without discrimination.[132] Section IV of the Principles deals specifically with humanitarian assistance, starting with Principle 24 which determines that humanitarian assistance must meet the (humanitarian) principles of humanity, impartiality and non-discrimination. The primary duty of national authorities is reiterated in Principle 25(1), where a right to offer services is granted to 'international humanitarian organisations and other appropriate actors'.[133] In line with the Nicaragua-Case, it is provided that such offers cannot be regarded as an unfriendly act or interference in a state's internal affairs. Moreover, it is determined that 'consent thereto shall not be arbitrarily withheld, particularly when authorities concerned are unable or unwilling to provide the required humanitarian assistance'.[134] As such, these Guiding Principles contain a quite clear structure for the provision of humanitarian assistance.

On a regional level, an instrument on IDPs in the form of a convention exists. In October 2009, the African Union adopted the Convention for the Protection and Assistance of Internally Displaced Persons in Africa (the Kampala Convention) which is the only international (although regional) legally binding instrument on IDPs.[135] With regard to preventing displacement, article 4(3) provides that states 'may seek the cooperation of international organizations or humanitarian agencies (...)', as such stimulating inclusion of international assistance. In the obligations relating to protection and assistance it is determined that states 'shall bear the primary duty and responsibility for providing protection of and humanitarian assistance to internally displaced persons within their territory or jurisdiction'.[136] Moreover, it is determined that states 'shall cooperate with each other upon the request of the concerned State Party' and that the states 'shall respect the mandates of the AU and the UN as well as the roles of international humanitarian organizations in providing protection and assistance to IDPs, in accordance with international law'.[137] The other paragraphs of article 5 contain rules and principles that are also found in international humanitarian law: state parties are required to 'take necessary steps' to organize humanitarian relief (humanitarian and impartial

[132] Guiding Principle 18(2).
[133] Guiding Principle 25(2).
[134] Ibid.
[135] The Kampala Convention entered into force on 6 December 2012 after the fifteenth instrument of ratification was deposited by Swaziland. The other fourteen states are Benin, Burkina Faso, Central African Republic, Chad, Gabon, Gambia, Guinea-Bissau, Lesotho, Niger, Nigeria, Sierra Leone, Togo, Uganda and Zambia. Over thirty states signed the Convention. ——, 'IDPs: African IDP Convention Comes into Force' IRIN (6 December 2012) <http://www.irinnews.org/Report/96984/IDPs-African-IDP-Convention-comes-into-force> accessed 7 December 2012.
[136] Article 5(1) Kampala Convention. Article 5 explicitly explains that measures shall be taken to protect those who became displaced due to natural or human made disasters, including climate change; article 5(4) Kampala Convention.
[137] Article 5(2) and (3) Kampala Convention.

in character; respect for the humanitarian principles of humanity, neutrality, impartiality and independence is provided in article 5(8)), including its unimpeded passage but with a right to 'prescribe the technical arrangements under which such passage is permitted'.[138] Also, the role of local and international organizations shall be enabled and facilitated by the state.[139] IDPs have, according to the Kampala Convention, a right to peacefully request or seek protection and assistance.[140] Article 5 further puts strong emphasis on international cooperation: (facilitation of) the assessment of needs is done in cooperation with international organizations or agencies; sufficient protection must be provided by the state and where available resources are inadequate, states shall cooperate in seeking assistance of international organisations and humanitarian agencies, who may offer their services to all those in need.[141] Finally, article 5(12) determines that 'nothing in this Article shall prejudice the principles of sovereignty and territorial integrity of states', as such stressing that although international cooperation is important, the sovereignty and territorial integrity of states trumps such cooperation.

### 3.5 Other fields of international law

Besides IHL, human rights law and the protection framework for refugees and IDPs, other fields exist that can be useful in disaster response and for the provision of humanitarian assistance. Delivering humanitarian assistance usually meets all kinds of practical barriers. Instruments have been created that can take away these barriers, although the instruments do not always aim at doing this but take away a barrier as a side-effect. Below, the main problems encountered when delivering relief and corresponding instruments are mentioned to illustrate difficulties that must be overcome in delivering humanitarian assistance.

In 1967, the first Food Aid Convention was adopted which has since then been replaced by updated versions.[142] This Convention 'sets out minimum commitments of annual food aid of certain types to be provided by each member' where emergency food aid is also included.[143] In the Conventions, standards are laid down for food aid, like – as a recurring theme in the legal framework – adhering to the humanitarian principles, taking into account dietary needs and habits of the recipient community, and long-term planning for rehabilitation and self-sustainability.

---

[138] Article 5(7) Kampala Convention.

[139] Ibid.

[140] Article 5(9) Kampala Convention. This provision adds 'in accordance with relevant national and international laws, a right for which they shall not be persecuted, prosecuted or punished'.

[141] Article 5(5) and (6) Kampala Convention.

[142] The latest version dating from 1999, but which is regularly updated. David Fisher, 'Fast Food: Regulating Emergency Food Aid in Sudden-Impact Disasters' (2007) 40 Vanderbilt Journal of Transnational Law 1127, 1142. See also the website of the Food Aid Convention: <http://www.foodaidconvention.org/en/Default.aspx> accessed 17 December 2012.

[143] Ibid, 1143.

Also instruments that arrange practical issues are relevant for the legal framework, like rules and regulations on customs through the 'Recommendation of the Customs Co-Operation Council to Expedite the Forwarding of Relief Consignments in the Event of Disasters',[144] on telecommunication through the Tampere Convention on the Provision of Telecommunication Resources for Disaster Mitigation and Relief Operations of 1998,[145] on the environment through instruments like the UN Convention to Combat Desertification in those Countries Experiencing Serious Drought and/or Desertification of 1994,[146] and on the prevention and mitigation of industrial and nuclear accidents through the Nuclear Accident Convention or the Oil Pollution Convention.[147] In the same line, instruments exist on granting visa and work permits to humanitarian personnel, transportation,[148] flight zones, privileges and immunities,[149] and even space law.[150] The topics that are covered by these instruments are usually of practical relevance in disaster response and determine the effectiveness of international humanitarian assistance. Having for example strict rules on custom clearance of relief goods or asking high import taxes could delay or prevent relief goods from entering a state. In the same line, limited use of airspace, territorial waters or overland infrastructure could also negatively affect the provision of humanitarian assistance. The examples of conventions mentioned here are created for functional coexistence of sovereign states, yet prove to create barriers when it comes to quickly responding to disasters. Having such national (legal) barriers proved to be problematic in disaster response in the USA and Pakistan, while the legal systems of Fiji and Guatemala are considered to be 'best practices'.[151] When considering the emphasis which is placed on the primary role of the affected state in responding to a disaster or a humanitarian emergency, it is quite important that the state's legal system is prepared. The IFRC project on International Disaster Response Laws (IDRL),

[144] Adopted in 1970 by the forerunner of the World Customs Organization. Fisher, 'Desk Study' (n 4) 40. See also OCHA, 'Customs Facilitation in Emergency Humanitarian Assistance', the Kyoto Customs Convention, the Convention on Temporary Admission, and the Customs Convention on the Temporary Importation of Professional Equipment.

[145] The Tampere Convention was also mentioned in Chapter I for its widely cited definition of disaster. It is not, however, widely ratified: as of January 2015 only 48 states are a party to the Convention. UN Treaty Collection, <https://treaties.un.org/pages/ViewDetails.aspx?src=TREATY&mtdsg_no=XXV-4&chapter=25&lang=en> accessed 6 January 2015.

[146] Here also instruments on climate change can be mentioned, along with instruments to prevent hazardous waste to spread. Fisher, 'Desk Study' (n 4) 48.

[147] Or the Industrial Accidents Convention. Fisher, 'Desk Study' (n 4).

[148] For example the Customs Convention on the Temporary Importation of Private Road Vehicles of 1954 or the Convention on Facilitation of International Maritime Traffic of 1965.

[149] For example the Convention on the Privileges and Immunities of the Specialized Agencies of 1947.

[150] UNGA Resolution on 'Principles Relating to Remote Sensing of the Earth from Outer Space' (UN Doc. A/41/65 of 3 December 1986) of which principle 11 states that 'remote sensing shall promote the protection of mankind from natural disasters'. Fisher, 'Desk Study' (n 4) 51.

[151] Fisher, 'Desk Study' (n 4) 83-4.

which will be discussed in section 3.8.1 below, aims to take these potential legal barriers away, at least at national levels.

## 3.6 Regional cooperation in disaster response

Moving now into the realm of instruments specifically designed for disaster response, the regional systems set up for this purpose will be discussed first. Many regional systems contain arrangements for disaster situations and many neighbouring states have created bilateral treaties for mutual assistance. Examples of regional arrangements are the 2005 'Agreement on Disaster Management and Emergency Response' by the Association of South-East Asian Nations (ASEAN)[152] and the Agreement Establishing the Caribbean Disaster Emergency Response Agency (CDERA) by the Caribbean Community (CARICOM), both aiming at facilitating disaster relief and assistance in (legal) preparation and coordination, and the European Commission Humanitarian Aid Office (ECHO), which provides humanitarian assistance and is responsible for 30% of the global total for humanitarian funding.[153] In African context, the Economic Community of West-African States (ECOWAS) is worth mentioning, which has established a 'Mechanism for Disaster Reduction' to coordinate disaster response. Next to ECOWAS, the African Union may also take decisions on common policies, which include humanitarian action and disaster response.[154] In the Americas, the Inter-American Convention to Facilitate Disaster Assistance adopted by the Organization of American States (OAS) could potentially arrange many issues of international disaster response, but it only has three parties. Finally, NATO has included disaster assistance in its activities since 1953. While originally only focussing on assistance between member states, the NATO policy changed to providing assistance to non-NATO states as well.

Bilateral agreements between states generally aim at setting procedures for initiation and termination of assistance, and more practically at exchanging information and sending relief goods across the border. While bilateral agreements have a limited scope, they could potentially help in lifting some of the national legal barriers in the provision of humanitarian assistance.

## 3.7 Resolutions, guidelines and other instruments on humanitarian assistance and disaster response

Currently, no legal instrument exists that is created solely for the purpose of delivering humanitarian assistance in response to disasters. There are, however, quite a number of instruments with a 'soft law' character (dictating behaviour but not in a legally binding and/or enforceable way). Here, only the most relevant

[152] ASEAN has played an important role in negotiating disaster relief after cyclone Nargis.
[153] Fisher, 'Desk Study' (n 4) 71.
[154] Article 13(1) under (e) AU Constitutive Act.

instruments for the purpose of identifying a set of rules and principles on accepting humanitarian assistance in response to a disaster will be discussed.

Due to their setting, formulations, and wide level of acceptance, the General Assembly (GA) Resolutions on disaster response and humanitarian assistance are perhaps resembling a legal instrument closest. In the Resolutions the starting point is that the affected state is first and foremost responsible for relief, which is expressed with the words 'primary role of each State in caring for the victims of disasters occurring in its territory'.[155] Acknowledging state sovereignty in such a way is a line followed since Resolution 36/225 of 1981. The attention for state sovereignty remained in Resolutions adopted throughout the 1980s and 1990s, and was further emphasized with references to 'territorial integrity' and 'national unity', and the requirement that assistance should be provided 'with the consent' of the affected country and based upon an 'appeal' by that country.[156]

The Resolution that currently forms the basis for most humanitarian assistance-operations in natural disaster contexts is GA Resolution 46/182. In this Resolution too, there is much emphasis on state sovereignty. It is stressed that the sovereignty, territorial integrity and the national unity of states must be fully respected, that assistance should only be provided with the consent of the affected country and on the basis of an appeal by the affected state.[157] Also, each state 'has the responsibility first and foremost to take care of the victims of natural disasters and other emergencies occurring on its territory' which also includes the initiation of humanitarian assistance.[158] The Resolution further recognizes that the 'magnitude and duration of many emergencies may be beyond the response capacity' of the affected state, emphasizing the role of international cooperation.[159] Resolution 46/182 also dictates that humanitarian assistance 'must be provided in accordance with the principles of humanity, neutrality and impartiality'.[160]

Another three Resolutions adopted by the General Assembly are worth mentioning here for their contributions to the general development of norms and principles. Resolution 43/131 of 1988 has been described as a 'monument to qualification and prudence'.[161] The reason for this is that while the Resolution is on the one hand created with the rationale to protect people from the effects of disasters, it strongly confirms, on the other hand, the principle of state

---

[155] UNGA Resolution on 'Strengthening the capacity of the United Nations system to respond to natural disasters and other disaster situations' (UN Doc. A/Res/36/225 of 17 December 1981), para 2.

[156] UNGA Resolution on 'Strengthening the effectiveness and coordination of international urban search and rescue assistance' (UN Doc. A/Res/57/150 of 27 February 2003).

[157] UNGA Resolution 46/182 (n 71) para 3.

[158] Ibid, under 4.

[159] Ibid, para 5.

[160] Ibid, para 2.

[161] O. Russbach, *ONU contre ONU. Le droit international confisqué* (La Découverte, Paris 1994) 44-7 and 52 cited by Abrisketa (n 122) 67.

sovereignty.[162] In Resolution 45/100 of 1990, the line of earlier Resolutions is maintained, although it 'strongly emphasizes the need to be able to gain access to affected zones.[163] Finally, another important Resolution adopted by the General Assembly is Resolution 57/150 of 2003, which 'called on States to facilitate the entry and operation of international urban search and rescue teams in disaster settings (...)'.[164] The trend that these Resolutions show is that the General Assembly seems to understand the problems around humanitarian access, but is still struggling to combine this with ideas of sovereignty.

Apart from the General Assembly Resolutions, other instruments on disaster response and humanitarian assistance has been created of which those most relevant for the current legal framework will be discussed. The 'Hyogo Framework for Action' was adopted at the UN World Disaster Reduction Conference in 2005.[165] The Hyogo Framework aims to reduce disaster losses in lives and in social, economic, and environmental assets of communities and countries substantially.[166] To this end, five priorities for action have been identified along with cross cutting issues that must diminish disaster vulnerability.[167] This framework constitutes a plan specifically for the years 2005 to 2015.[168] While this instrument focuses strongly on preparedness, one of the priorities clearly makes the link between preparedness and an effective response.

Another example of a soft law instrument on disaster response is the 1994 'Code of Conduct for the International Red Cross and Red Crescent Movement and NGOs in Disaster Relief' (Code of Conduct). This instrument provides ten principles that relief agencies and NGOs may – voluntarily – adhere to. With over 450 signatories, the Code of Conduct is a standard-setting document on how humanitarian response should be delivered, mentioning amongst others neutrality, non-discrimination,

---

[162] J. Oraá, 'Derecho international y posibilidades de intervención en situationes de emergencia' in *Convulsión y violencia en el mundo,* Seminario de investigación para la paz (Centro Pignatelli, Zaragoza 1995) 100-14 cited by Abrisketa (n 122) 67

[163] Abrisketa (n 122) 67.

[164] David Fisher, 'The Law of International Disaster Response: Overview and Ramifications for Military Actors' in M.D. Carsten (ed) *Command of the Commons, Strategic Communications and Natural Disasters* (International Law Studies, Naval War College, Newport, Rhode Island 2007) 300.

[165] The Hyogo Framework was adopted by 168 states: <http://www.unisdr.org/we/coordinate/hfa> accessed 4 December 2012.

[166] Hyogo Framework for Action, summary of the framework: <http://www.unisdr.org/files/8720_summaryHFP20052015.pdf> accessed 4 December 2012.

[167] The priorities are making disaster risk reduction a national and local priority; identifying, assessing and monitoring disaster risks and enhancing early warning; using knowledge and education to build a culture of safety and resilience; reducing underlying risk factors; and strengthening disaster preparedness for effective response.

[168] The Hyogo Framework for Action can be found at: <http://www.unisdr.org/eng/hfa/hfa.htm> accessed 13 October 2010.

independence, and respect for local custom and culture as values.[169] In the first Appendix to the Code of Conduct, governments are recommended to grant access to victims so that aid can be provided.[170] Here again, the problem of access that humanitarian organizations encounter is acknowledged. A different instrument developed by the IFRC helps national governments in preparing for the possibility that they may at a certain time need international assistance. These 'Guidelines for the Domestic Facilitation and Regulation of International Disaster Relief and Initial Recovery Assistance' explains how (legal) barriers can be removed for the provision of international aid.[171] One last example of a non-binding instrument is the 'Sphere Handbook' made in the context of the 'Sphere Project'. A group of NGOs and the Red Cross and Red Crescent started the Sphere Project in 1997 in order to improve aid delivery. In this project, humanitarian principles have been identified that govern humanitarian action. These principles have been established in the Humanitarian Charter, which forms the 'cornerstone' of the Sphere Handbook.[172] The Handbook contains very practical indicators for making humanitarian responses most efficient and effective as possible, going in depth into water supplies, food security, shelter, and health services. The Handbook is updated regularly to include (new) 'best practices'.[173]

## 3.8 Recent standard-setting initiatives

In Red Cross- as well as UN-context there are ongoing projects which attempt to establish general norms and rules for peacetime disaster response. These projects, the 'International Disaster Response Laws'-project of the IFRC and the 'Protection of Persons in the Event of Disasters' of the International Law Commission will be discussed in the following sections.

### *3.8.1 International Disaster Response Laws*

The IFRC started its International Disaster Response Laws, Rules and Principles (IDRL) programme in 2001 to explore the role of law in the response to disasters,

[169] See also Dorothea Hilhorst, 'Dead Letter or Living Document? Ten Years of the Code of Conduct for Disaster Relief' (2005) 29 Disasters 351, 354 *ff.*

[170] The Code of Conduct can be found at <http://www.ifrc.org/publicat/conduct/> 13 October 2010.

[171] IFRC, 'Introduction to the Guidelines for the Domestic Facilitation and Regulation of International Disaster Relief and Initial Recovery Assistance' (IFRC, Geneva 2008) 3-6. The 'IDRL Guidelines' are a part of the International Disaster Response Law project of the IFRC (see section 3.8.1 below).

[172] Sphere Project, 'Humanitarian Charter and Minimum Standards in Disaster Response' (Oxfam Publishing, Oxford 2004) 5.

[173] The first Handbook in trial edition was published in 1998, the first final edition in 2000. Updates have been published in 2004 and 2011.

particularly in international disaster relief.[174] It is considering a number of different approaches for strengthening and developing supportive laws and policies at all levels and is conducting consultations with governments and the humanitarian sector to identify the best ways forward.[175] IDRL describes the body of rules and principles for international humanitarian assistance in the wake of peacetime disasters.[176] In other words, IDRL applies when states and organisations offer, request, provide or accept cross-border disaster assistance.[177] Domestic legislation must be prepared for large scale disasters and the offerings of international aid, in order to ensure the speed and effectiveness of humanitarian assistance. Local Red Cross Societies conduct research on the status of the national laws and advice the government on the results. The idea is that states must be prepared before disaster strikes, instead of trying to solve difficulties in an emergency situation:

> Currently, most states figure that they will sort out their mechanisms for dealing with international assistance when the time comes. Unfortunately, this ad hoc approach is increasingly inadequate to deal with the very real complications of international assistance.[178]

The aforementioned 'Guidelines for the Domestic Facilitation and Regulation of International Disaster Relief and Initial Recovery Assistance' was adopted by the parties to the Geneva Conventions at the 30th International Conference of the Red Cross in 2007.[179] These Guidelines will help states in strengthening their laws and bilateral agreements. In its strategy until 2020, the Red Cross and Red Crescent movement will keep the IDRL programme on the agenda.

IDRL does not provide a solution to the problem of a state refusing international aid. The IDRL Guidelines depart from the idea that the process of international humanitarian assistance must be initiated by the affected state with a request (and not by unsolicited offers).[180] The initiative therefore lies with the affected state and IDRL therefore departs from the notion of a willing state, and aims at making the delivery of international aid run smoothly. IDRL does, however, help to diminish the problem of underhandedly refusing aid. When states say that they are willing to

---

174 See the IFRC <http://www.ifrc.org/what/disasters/idrl/programme/intro.asp> accessed 21 September 2010.

175 Bannon, 'Strengthening International Disaster Response Laws' (n 66) 29.

176 Michael H. Hoffman, 'What is the Scope of International Disaster Response Law?' in IFRC, *International Disaster Response Laws, Principles and Practice: Reflections, Prospects and Challenges* (IFRC, Geneva 2003) 13.

177 Hoffman (n 176) 15.

178 IFRC Secretary-General Bekele Geleta to the Overseas Development Association (Westminster, London, March 2009), cited by IFRC, 'IDRL Programme: Plan 2010-2011' (IFRC, Geneva 2010) 2.

179 Ibid.

180 Horst Fischer, 'International Disaster Response Law Treaties: Trends, Patterns and Lacunae' in IFRC, *International Disaster Response Laws, Principles and Practice: Reflections, Prospects and Challenges* (IFRC, Geneva 2003) 34.

accept foreign aid but delay the entry of goods or persons through requirements of national laws (customs, visa, etc.), IDRL could potentially take this option away. Rules derived from IDRL are that the affected state has the primary responsibility to ensure humanitarian assistance in its territory, that the affected state is required to 'seek international and/or regional assistance in case the affected State determines that a disaster situation exceeds national coping capabilities'.[181] Finally, IDRL also confirms that international relief and assistance can only be delivered with consent of the affected state.[182]

### *3.8.2 Protection of Persons in the Event of Disasters*

In 2006, the Planning Group of the UN's International Law Commission (ILC) recommended to include 'Protection of Persons in the Event of Disasters' in its long-term programme of work.[183] During the fifty-ninth session of the ILC, in 2007, a Special Rapporteur was appointed and the topic was included in the ILC's programme of work.[184] In a background study, the Codification Division of the ILC provided an extensive overview of issues, concepts, legal norms and other considerations somehow linked to the topic of 'Protection of Persons in the Event of Disasters'.[185] In addition, the Special Rapporteur traced the evolution of the protection of persons in the event of disasters in his preliminary report of 2008.[186] Using this background as a point of departure, the Special Rapporteur developed draft articles on this topic taking the whole spectrum of disaster response into account. In 2014 the Drafting Committee collected the draft articles adopted thus far with their full titles and texts in one document, providing an overview of what has been achieved up to that point.[187]

The draft articles are aimed at situations where 'a calamitous event or series of events (result) in widespread loss of life, great human suffering and distress, or large-scale material or environmental damage, thereby seriously disrupting the functioning of society' and which is not a situation in which international

[181] Spieker (n 70) 24, deriving this from IDRL Guidelines (n 171) Guideline 3.2.

[182] Spieker (n 70) 26; IDRL Guidelines (n 171) Guideline 10.1.

[183] ILC, Report of the International Law Commission, fifty-eight session (1 May-9 June and 3 July-11 August 2006) (UN Doc A/61/10 of 2006), para 256*ff.*

[184] ILC, Report of the International Law Commission, fifty-ninth session (7 May-5 June and 9 July-10 August 2007) (UN Doc. A/62/10 of 2007), para 375. Mr. Eduardo Valencia Ospina was appointed as Special Rapporteur.

[185] ILC, 'Protection of Persons in the Event of Disasters: Memorandum by the Secretariat' (UN Doc A/CN.4/590 of 11 December 2007).

[186] ILC 'Preliminary Report on the Protection of Persons in the Event of Disasters by Mr. Eduardo Valencia-Ospina, Special Rapporteur' (UN Doc. A/CN.4/598 of 5 May 2008).

[187] ILC Drafting Committee, 'Texts and titles of the draft articles adopted by the Drafting Committee on first reading' UN Doc. A/CN.4/L.831 of 15 May 2014. The numbering used in the Drafting Committee's overview is not entirely the same as the numbering of the Draft Articles in the reports by the Special Rapporteur. The references to Draft Articles in the present study refer to the original numbering of the Special Rapporteur's reports since the reports are taken into consideration for the background information.

humanitarian law is applicable.[188] In the situations thus described the draft articles must 'facilitate an adequate and effective response to disasters that meets the essential needs of the persons concerned, with full respect for their rights'.[189] This emphasis on the needs and rights of the people for whom these draft articles are most relevant returns in draft articles 6 to 8. In article 6 it is determined that disaster response must meet the humanitarian principles 'while taking into account the needs of the particularly vulnerable'. Articles 7 and 8 provide that actors bringing humanitarian assistance must respect and protect the 'inherent dignity of the human person' and that 'persons affected by disasters are entitled to respect for their human rights'.[190] Here again, the relevance of human rights law in disaster response is stressed, yet without specifying how human rights fulfil a role and what they mean for obligations of affected states. The challenge is, however, taken up in Part II of this research.

Besides the attention for the interests of disaster victims, the draft articles provide some clear rules for affected states. In the first place, the affected state has the 'duty to ensure the protection of persons and provision of disaster relief and assistance on its territory' and has the 'primary role in the direction, control, coordination and supervision of such relief and assistance'.[191] This primary role is granted to the affected state 'by virtue of its sovereignty', from which more rules are derived. Immediately linked to the primary role in response is the duty of the affected state to seek international assistance when a disaster exceeds the national response capacity, a formulation that was also seen in other sources.[192] Another rule laid down in the draft articles that has been discussed above is that external assistance can only be provided with the consent of the affected state, which may not be withheld arbitrarily.[193] Further, external actors like states, the UN and 'competent' international organizations have a right to offer assistance, and relevant NGOs 'may' also offer assistance.[194] The affected state may place conditions on the provision of external assistance (in accordance with international and national law

---

[188] ILC Drafting Committee, 'Protection of persons in the event of disasters: Texts of draft articles 1, 2, 3, 4 and 5 as provisionally adopted by the Drafting Committee' (UN Doc. A/CN.4/L.758 of 24 July 2009), draft articles 3 and 4.

[189] Ibid, draft article 2.

[190] ILC Drafting Committee 'Protection of Persons in the Event of Disasters: Text and titles of draft articles 6, 7, 8, and 9 provisionally adopted by the Drafting Committee' (UN Doc. A/CN.4/L.776 of 14 July 2010), draft articles 6, 7, and 8.

[191] Ibid, draft article 9.

[192] ILC Drafting Committee 'Protection of Persons in the Event of Disasters: Text and titles of draft articles 10 and 11 provisionally adopted by the Drafting Committee on 19 July 2011' (UN Doc. A/CN.4/L.794 of 20 July 2011), draft article 10. The formulation was also used in *inter alia* GA Res. 46/182 (n 71).

[193] Ibid, draft article 11 paras 1 and 2.

[194] ILC Drafting Committee 'Protection of Persons in the Event of Disasters: Text and titles of draft articles 5 *bis,* 12, 13, 14 and 15, provisionally adopted by the Drafting Committee from 5 to 11 July 2012' (UN Doc. A/CN.4/L.812 of 12 July 2012), draft article 12.

and while considering the needs of the affected persons), the affected states must take national measures to facilitate prompt and effective provision of external assistance, and this assistance shall be terminated based on consultations with the parties involved.[195] These rules are in line with the idea of a duty to international cooperation as provided in draft article 5 and 5bis. Draft article 5 tells states to cooperate among themselves and with the UN, IFRC, ICRC, other international organisations and NGOs.[196] This article has been specified at a later stage where international cooperation is understood as 'humanitarian assistance, coordination of international relief actions and communications, and making available relief personnel, relief equipment and supplies, and scientific, medical and technical resources'.[197]

The draft articles on the Protection of Persons in the Event of Disasters are not without controversy. There is a clear recognition of state sovereignty, yet at the same time it is emphasized that this sovereignty comes with duties towards disaster victims. States are granted the freedom to give or withhold consent, but with the condition that this consent may not be withheld for arbitrary reasons. Since states are not given a *carte blanche* to withhold consent, and considering the emphasis on the rights of disaster victims and the duty to international cooperation included in the draft articles, it is questionable how many states are willing to ratify the treaty – if the treaty will ever be opened for ratification.[198]

The ILC's work on the Protection of Persons in the Event of Disasters has again made clear that sovereignty is of great influence on the rules and principles of accepting humanitarian assistance after a disaster. Before arriving at the conclusion on what the rules and principles are, the concept of sovereignty and its effect on the legal framework will therefore be considered here.

## 4 Sovereignty and International Action

### 4.1 Traditional reading of state sovereignty

The way in which the concept of state sovereignty has influenced the legal framework of disaster response so far is an expression of a rather traditional reading

---

[195] Ibid, draft articles 13, 14, and 15.

[196] ILC Drafting Committee, 'Protection of persons in the event of disasters: Texts of draft articles 1, 2, 3, 4 and 5 as provisionally adopted by the Drafting Committee' (UN Doc. A/CN.4/L.758 of 24 July 2009), draft article 5.

[197] ILC Drafting Committee 'Protection of Persons in the Event of Disasters: Text and titles of draft articles 5 *bis,* 12, 13, 14 and 15, provisionally adopted by the Drafting Committee from 5 to 11 July 2012' (UN Doc. A/CN.4/L.812 of 12 July 2012), draft article 5*bis*.

[198] At the time of writing, the work of the Special Rapporteur is not yet completed. The Preliminary Report of the Special Rapporteur explains the form that the work must take and here it is acknowledged that the final decision must be taken by the General Assembly when the work is completed. Various options are open here ranging from a treaty to principles or guidelines. Preliminary Report (n 186) paras 59 and 60.

of the concept. A strong emphasis of the role of the affected state trumps the assistance offered by international humanitarian actors; only with consent are these actors allowed to conduct their activities. As such, sovereignty protects the interests of the affected state by allowing that state to decide which actor is permitted to enter its territory and under which conditions, being in line with the related concepts of territorial integrity and non-intervention. This function of sovereignty is a therefore a welcome practical tool preventing chaos in international aid delivery but the problem at the same time is that the affected state is not always willing to give its consent to international humanitarian assistance, even when the civilian population is in need of such relief. Questions therefore arise at this point on where the traditional reading of sovereignty comes from, what the developments are in this field and, accordingly, how to move forward in answering the research question while not disregarding the reality that sovereignty still fulfils a prominent role. To answer the first question it is necessary to look at the development of the concept of sovereignty. Over the years, the role and meaning of sovereignty has continuously been reinvented and adjusted. Only those parts of the story of sovereignty important for answering the questions posed above will be told.

The origins of sovereignty are regularly linked to the Treaty of Westphalia, which brought a temporary end to the wars raging over Europe in the seventeenth century. With the peace of Westphalia of 1648, the creation of the nation state as still known today is understood to be the basis of state sovereignty.[199] Through its meaning ('being the highest power') sovereignty indicates that all states are equal and that no higher power exists that can bind states. In other words:

> States are independent entities that can exercise supreme political authority over their territory. (...) Under the traditional view of sovereignty, States may shape and determine their own policies with respect to the treatment of their citizens and control over their domestic affairs without interference from other States.[200]

This reading of sovereignty has for a long time dominated – and often still dominates – international law and resulted in sometimes hidden situations of mistreatment of a domestic population.

Within the UN Charter, sovereignty can be recognized in, *inter alia*, article 2, which states that '(t)he Organization is based on the principle of the sovereign equality of all its Members';[201] '(a)ll Members shall refrain in their international relations from the threat or use of force against the territorial integrity or political independence of any state';[202] and '(n)othing contained in the present Charter shall

---

[199] See for example Lloyd Axworthy, 'RtoP and the Evolution of State Sovereignty' in Jared Genser & Irwin Cotler (eds), *The Responsibility to Protect: The Promise of Stopping Mass Atrocities in Our Time* (Oxford University Press, Oxford 2012).

[200] Tyra R. Saechao, 'Natural Disasters and the Responsibility to Protect: From Chaos to Clarity' (2006-7) 32 Brookings Journal of International Law 663, 668.

[201] Article 2(1) UN Charter.

[202] Article 2(4) UN Charter.

authorize the United Nations to intervene in matters which are essentially within the jurisdiction of any state or shall require the Members to submit such matters to settlement under the present Charter'.[203] The UN Charter also contains a very important mechanism to limit sovereignty. The Security Council received the power to take measures to maintain or restore international peace and security and these measures can be taken against (the will of) a state.[204] Since the establishment of the UN, situations have been seen in which a state's regime or non-state actors committed gross atrocities against its own population and where it proved difficult – if not impossible – to respond.

A gradual change occurred which became most visible after the end of the Cold War. It was recognized that

> Old notions of national security predicated on the defence of borders made little sense when the threat posed by violence and conflict, international networks of predators and criminals, global pandemics, and massive natural disasters required a new approach to the protection of peoples.[205]

While originally meant to maintain or restore international peace and security exclusively, it has been gradually accepted that the Security Council also uses its powers to react on gross and systematic human rights violations since also non-military causes of instability can form a threat against peace and security.[206] The new (non-legal) concept of 'Human Security' captured this and placed the protection of civilians and respect for human rights as priorities on the international agenda, arguing that gross human rights violations could also constitute a threat to international peace and security, and thus qualify for Security Council intervention.[207] With this focus on the protection of civilians a method of action in case of gross human rights violations was created. In addition, there have been situations in which the Security Council did not give its authorization and where a group of states nonetheless intervened to respond to situations of human suffering. Such an intervention for humanitarian purposes without prior Security Council authorization is referred to as 'humanitarian intervention'.

---

[203] Article 2(7) UN Charter.

[204] The non-military measures of chapter VI and the military measures of chapter VII UN Charter.

[205] Axworthy (n 199) 8.

[206] Willem J.M. van Genugten, Fred Grünfeld & Dick Leurdijk, 'Internationale Rechtshandhaving' in Nathalie Horbach, René Lefeber & Olivier Ribbelink (eds), *Handboek Internationaal Recht* (T.M.C. Asser Press, The Hague 2007) 393.

[207] Commission on Human Security, 'Human Security Now!' (New York, 2003). Independently from the development of the human security-construct, the Security Council also started to take the same approach to protection of peace.

### 4.2 Non-Authorised humanitarian intervention

Looking at the UN Charter, and especially aforementioned article 2(4), it is clear that the military intervention of states apart from the case of self-defence (not relevant in the present context) and on the territory of another state without prior Security Council authorization is in violation of international law and therefore illegal.[208] However, examples in which the concept of humanitarian intervention was used as a legal basis for an intervention show that in cases of extreme atrocities against a civilian population the intervention was considered to be a necessity and apparently the only option. An early case in which a civilian population was protected with the means of a humanitarian intervention was the assistance to the Kurds in Northern Iraq in 1991.[209] Over a hundred thousand Iraqi Kurds fled the repression by the Iraqi regime after the Gulf war. Many of the refugees attempted to reach the Turkish border but got stranded in the mountains where they were living in extreme conditions. The Security Council did not come to a decision to intervene with forceful means for the assistance of the Kurds, after which the US, UK and France unilaterally decided to create a safe zone, enforced by military means and supported by thirteen states.[210] Another example where a humanitarian emergency prompted the unauthorized intervention by states is that of Kosovo in 1999. The Security Council did not come to a resolution yet according to member states of NATO action was required to come to the aid of civilians.[211]

Returning to situations of disaster, it is possible that a civilian population is suffering undue hardship after a disaster as a consequence of their state's decision to not come to their aid and at the same time not accepting international humanitarian assistance. In extreme situations, this may prompt the international community to discuss the option of undertaking action to come to the assistance of the civilian population. Being such an extreme situation, in the case of cyclone Nargis in Myanmar it was debated whether a humanitarian intervention (if the other option under discussion, an intervention with Security Council authorization, would not be realized) should take place.[212] It was argued that a large-scale natural disaster and subsequent lack of response can be considered a factor that can cause instability and therefore a threat to peace and security, yet it has so far (not in the case of

---

[208] Malcolm N. Shaw, *International Law* (Cambridge University Press, New York 6th edition, 2008) 1155.

[209] In doctrine, this case is generally accepted to be the first case where a humanitarian intervention was used. Genugten, Grünfeld & Leurdijk (n 206) 429.

[210] Ibid, 430.

[211] UNSC Resolution 1244 (UN Doc. S/Res/1244 of 10 June 1999); there was no formal endorsement of the NATO action, but no condemnation. Shaw (n 208) 1157, Louis Henkin, 'Kosovo and the Law of "Humanitarian Intervention"' (1999) 93 AJIL 824, 826.

[212] For example Andrew O'Neill, 'Kosovo Aid: The Model for Burma' *The Australian* (14 May 2008) Features 26.

cyclone Nargis, nor in any disaster situation) never been an actual ground for a humanitarian intervention (or authorized intervention).[213]

Although used for humanitarian purposes, a humanitarian intervention is in violation of international law and this controversy in combination with a sometimes indecisive Security Council made former UN Secretary-General Kofi Annan wonder '(i)f humanitarian intervention is, indeed, an unacceptable assault on sovereignty, how *should* we respond to a Rwanda, to a Srebrenica – to gross and systematic violations of human rights that offend every precept of our common humanity?'.[214] This question is also relevant for disaster situations in which the affected state refuses to accept assistance and does not adequately respond itself. Kofi Annan's challenge was taken up by the Canadian government, which funded the International Commission for Intervention and State Sovereignty (ICISS). The ICISS issued a report in 2001 describing the concept of the Responsibility to Protect (RtoP).[215]

### 4.3 The Responsibility to Protect

The term RtoP is best known for its usage since the issuance of the ICISS-report, but is originally introduced by Frances Deng in his work on IDPs.[216] The ICISS was asked to respond to the question 'when, if ever, it is appropriate for states to take coercive – and in particular military – action, against another state for the purpose of protecting people at risk in that other state'.[217] In answering this question, the ICISS came with an understanding of sovereignty that is at times described as new or novel, but appears at closer scrutiny a logical interpretation of the traditional view of state sovereignty. Due to being the highest power, a state always has a duty to take care of its citizens as no other entity is capable to do this. The novelty lies in the recognition of a right to intervene.[218] Based on the concept of sovereignty, states have a responsibility to protect their own citizens. This means that the primary responsibility to protect a civilian population lies with the territorial state itself. If that state fails to protect its population against gross human rights violations and

---

[213] Linda A. Malone, 'The Responsibility to Protect Haiti' (2010) 14 ASIL Insights [7], 3. For more on humanitarian intervention and humanitarian aid see Danesh Sarooshi, 'Humanitarian Intervention and International Humanitarian Assistance: Law and Practice' Conference Report Based on Wilton Park Special Conference: 2-4 July 1993 (HMSO, London 1994) 84.

[214] The Millennium Assembly of the United Nations, 'We the Peoples: The Role of the United Nations in the 21st Century: Millennium Report of the Secretary General' (UN Doc. A/54/2000 of 27 March 2000) 48 <http://www.un.org/en/events/pastevents/pdfs/We_The_Peoples.pdf> accessed 25 January 2015.

[215] ICISS, 'The Responsibility to Protect: Report of the International Commission on Intervention and State Sovereignty (International Development Research Centre 2001).

[216] Roberta Cohen & Francis M. Deng, *Masses in Flight: The Global Crisis of Internal Displacement* (The Brookings Institution, Washington D.C. 1998).

[217] ICISS Report (n 215) cited by Axworthy (n 199) 11-2.

[218] Axworthy uses the term 'revolutionary' in this context. Axworthy (n 199) 13.

other security threats, 'the obligation to protect passes from the territorial state to the international community'.[219] According to the ICISS the first step is taking preventive measures against the occurrence of mass atrocities like genocide, war crimes, and crimes against humanity. This responsibility to prevent turns into a responsibility to react 'when preventive measures fail to resolve or contain the situation and when a state is unable or unwilling to redress the situation, then interventionary measures by other members of the broader community of states may be required'.[220] This may also include forceful (military) measures, but constitute all kinds of less intrusive measures first.

Recognizing the difficulties around Security Council authorization in case of forceful measures, the ICISS advises the Security Council's permanent members not to use their veto unless their vital interests are at stake, and when the Council reaches a deadlock, there must be recourse to the General Assembly.[221] Moreover, a number of criteria are established in the ICISS report to determine whether action is allowed. According to one of these criteria, there must be a 'just cause' and when describing which situations can fall under 'just cause' the Commission states that this would at least include 'overwhelming natural or environmental catastrophes, where the state concerned is either unwilling or unable to cope, or call for assistance, and significant loss of life is occurring or threatened'.[222] In theory, the concept of RtoP would in extreme cases provide a way to bypass the requirement of state consent in the view of the ICISS to deliver international humanitarian assistance. In practice, however, the concept of RtoP changed course.

It took a few years before the concept of RtoP was taken up on a global level.[223] At the World Summit of 2005, states endorsed the concept and it was laid down in the 2005 World Summit Outcome Document.[224] However, the two paragraphs dealing with RtoP in the Outcome Document cannot be compared with the extended report of the ICISS. Being a political compromise, this is not utterly surprising, yet for the purposes of this research the World Summit Outcome poses a problem: the ICISS's reference to application of RtoP in disaster situations has disappeared completely. According to paragraph 138 of the Outcome Document, RtoP can be invoked in situations of genocide, war crimes, ethnic cleansing, and crimes against humanity. The first two phases as designed by the ICISS (responsibility to prevent and react) are still distinguished: the primary obligation lies with the territorial state.

---

[219] Axworthy (n 199) 12; William W. Burke-White, 'Adoption of the Responsibility to Protect' in Jared Genser & Irwin Cotler (eds), *The Responsibility to Protect: The Promise of Stopping Mass Atrocities in Our Time* (Oxford University Press, Oxford 2012) 19.

[220] ICISS Report (n 215) para 29; Burke-White (n 219) 20.

[221] Axworthy (n 199) 12.

[222] ICISS Report (n 215) para. 4.20.

[223] Which still is a speedy development within the field of international law. See also Burke-White (n 219) 21.

[224] UNGA, '2005 World Summit Outcome' (UN Doc. A/Res/60/1 of 16 September 2005), paras 138-140. The concept was further endorsed by the Security Council: UNSC Resolution on 'Protection of Civilians in Armed Conflicts' (UN Doc. S/Res/1674 of 28 April 2006).

That state must prevent the occurrence of genocide, war crimes, ethnic cleansing, and crimes against humanity and is 'encouraged and helped' in this by the international community. The international community further has the responsibility to use 'appropriate diplomatic, humanitarian and other peaceful means in accordance with Chapter VI and VIII of the Charter' and is 'prepared' to use more forceful measures (of Chapter VII of the UN Charter) to protect populations from the aforementioned crimes.[225] The responsibility to rebuild is largely ignored in the Outcome Document.[226] Although adopted with broad support from states, the Outcome Document cannot be considered as a legally binding document (nor can the ICISS report, for that matter) leaving the legal status of RtoP rather ambiguous.[227] The way in which the Security Council has used the concept in recent years has not proved too helpful either.[228]

The question remains whether RtoP can still be invoked in disaster situations even though that option is not explicitly recognized in the Outcome Document. In the aftermath of cyclone Nargis, this question has been extensively debated.[229] Frustrated by the response of the government of Myanmar, French Minister of Foreign Affairs Bernard Kouchner argued that RtoP should be applied in this situation to impose aid upon the state.[230] However, before RtoP can be invoked, one of the four crimes mentioned in the Outcome Document should take place, leaving the debate circling around the question whether in a concrete case refusal of humanitarian assistance can be considered as genocide, a war crime, a crime against humanity, or ethnic cleansing, given the facts of that case.[231] This question will be discussed in detail in Chapter III in relation to Myanmar, but it can already be said that the application of RtoP in such situations is not helped by a statement by Ban Ki-moon, Secretary-General of the UN that RtoP should not be applied in situations of natural disasters until member states decide otherwise. He followed the stance of

[225] UNGA, '2005 World Summit Outcome' (n 224) para 138-9. Rebecca Barber, 'The Responsibility to Protect the Survivors of Natural Disaster: Cyclone Nargis, a Case Study' (2009) 14 Journal of Conflict & Security Law 3, 7.

[226] Burke-White (n 219) 27.

[227] Discussions are ongoing on the legal status varying from possibilities as soft-law to customary law. For a commentary on these options see Burke-White (n 219) 23.

[228] The SC has applied the concept in its response to the Libyan conflict in 2011, yet in many other situations only reminds states of their responsibilities. See for the full list of SC resolutions referring to RtoP the Global Centre for the Responsibility to Protect <http://www.globalr2p.org /resources/335> accessed 5 April 2015.

[229] The idea to use RtoP in situations of disaster response did already exist among scholars prior to Nargis, probably inspired by the ICISS Report (n 215). See for example Saechao (n 200).

[230] Kouchner was supported by others, for example Javier Solana, the EU's High Representative for the Common Foreign and Security Policy. Mely Caballero-Anthony & Belinda Chng, 'Cyclones and Humanitarian Crises: Pushing the Limits of R2P in Southeast Asia' (2009) 1 Global Responsibility to Protect 135, 140.

[231] See for example Barber, 'The Responsibility to Protect' (n 225) 17.

a number of scholars[232] in arguing that application in situations like Myanmar would 'undermine the 2005 consensus and stretch the concept beyond recognition or operational utility'.[233]

Leaving this debate for now, it must be emphasized what the adoption of RtoP has meant for the understanding of sovereignty. Instead of regarding sovereignty as a shield against interference in the internal affairs of a state – recall in this line of thought also the ICJ Nicaragua Case in which it was decided that the provision of humanitarian assistance cannot be considered as unlawful interference in the internal affairs of a state – there is now a notion of 'responsible sovereignty'.[234] As explained by Kofi Annan in relation to the ethnic cleansing taking place in Kosovo:

> Human life and basic security were being threatened, in an increasingly visible fashion, by conflicts that were internal to states, and this meant that we needed to reframe the relations between citizens and governments. We needed to convince the broader global community that sovereignty had to be understood as contingent and conditional on states' taking responsibility for the security of their own people's human rights – and for this to be taken as seriously as the states' expectations of non-interference in their internal affairs.[235]

It is clear however that a traditional reading of state sovereignty has left a mark on the legal framework of disaster response. Also, there is

> Little prospect for the development of rules of international law designed to limit state sovereignty with respect to disaster relief. Put another way, states typically craft international law where their interests converge on the need to regulate sovereignty. With natural disasters, the interests of both the victim and assisting states converge on maintaining as much sovereignty as possible – a convergence that does not stimulate the robust development of international law.[236]

While a change is becoming visible in the work of the ILC on the Protection of Persons in the Event of Disasters (where it is included that the affected state is under an 'obligation' due to state sovereignty to ensure 'protection and assistance in the event of a disaster', aiming at 'preserving the life and dignity of the victims of

---

232 See e.g. Alex J. Bellamy, 'Disasters and 'Responsibility to Protect': Should Nations Force Aid on Others? A Cyclone is Not Enough' (2010) 34 Natural Hazards Observer [3] 1, 10; Caballero-Anthony & Chng (n 230) 144.

233 UNGA, 'Implementing the Responsibility to Protect: Report of the Secretary-General' (UN Doc. A/63/677 of 12 January 2009), para 10(b).

234 Axworthy (n 199) 8*ff*; Bellamy (n 232) 11. Although sovereignty as responsibility is often linked to the concept of RtoP, its origins can be traced back to Cohen & Deng (n 216).

235 Kofi Annan (with Nader Mousavizadeh), *Interventions: A Life in War and Peace* (Allen Lane, London 2012) 84.

236 Fidler (n 28) 461. When looking at the development of General Assembly Resolutions between 1989 and 2002, even an increasing emphasis on sovereignty can be seen. Katoch (n 73) cited by Fidler (n 28) 472.

the disaster and guaranteeing the access of persons in need to humanitarian assistance')[237] there is no guarantee that the ILC's draft articles on this topic will become customary international law or turn into a treaty (and will be ratified widely).[238] To place these developments with regard to peace-time disasters into perspective, a short side-step is made here to the ongoing developments in situations of armed conflict. In this context, a way is found to bypass state sovereignty in extreme humanitarian emergencies. Although armed conflict is excluded from the definition of disaster and – therefore – from the scope of this research, it (again) provides an interesting angle.

After having adopted a number of resolutions on the duties of the parties in the Syrian conflict with regard to humanitarian access, the Security Council decided in 2014 that

> United Nations humanitarian agencies and their implementing partners are authorized to use routes across conflict lines and the border crossings of Bab al-Salam, Bab al-Hawa, Al Yarubiyah and Al-Ramtha, in addition to those already in use, in order to ensure that humanitarian assistance, including medical and surgical supplies, reaches people in need throughout Syria through the most direct routes, with notification to the Syrian authorities (...).[239]

Through this resolution, the Security Council is bypassing the requirement of consent from the affected state, yet it only comes to this decision after stressing the special circumstances of the case. These consist of references to earlier resolutions demanding humanitarian access, to the massive scale of suffering of civilians, to the duties of the parties to the conflict under IHL and to the impact of humanitarian operations so far.[240] In addition, the Security Council has built in an automatic ending of the mandate for humanitarian operations by providing that the mandate is valid for 180 days after which it will be reconsidered (which has been done in December 2014 for a period of twelve months).[241] Considering the special circumstances of the case this decision is exceptional even in armed conflict situations and it is questionable whether disasters occurring in peace-time could ever accumulate to such circumstances prompting the Security Council to make a comparable decision.

---

[237] Valencia-Ospina, 'Fourth Report' (n 89) para 57.

[238] Another possibility is that the draft articles will not be turned into a treaty but that they will be picked up by those working in the field of humanitarian assistance and disaster response and through this route gain importance.

[239] UNSC Resolution 2165 of 14 July 2014, para 2.

[240] See the rather extensive preamble of the resolution which sets out the special circumstances of this case. See also Willem J.M. van Genugten & Nico Schrijver, 'Kroniek Internationaal Publiekrecht' (2015) 90 Nederlands Juristenblad (De Staat van het Recht 15) 982, 984.

[241] Ibid, para 5. In UNSC Resolution 2191 of 17 December 2014, para 2 the decision of Resolution 2165 has been renewed until 10 January 2016.

In peace-time disasters, therefore, the legal situation of the 21st century does not differ much from Vattel's time due to the lack of clear rules of international law on the obligations of states to accept humanitarian assistance: 'both assisting and victim states retain virtually unfettered sovereignty in the context of natural disaster policy'.[242] Nevertheless, when looking at the developments around the concept of state sovereignty, a change is becoming visible. The outlook on sovereignty is gradually shifting from granting states freedom within national borders to do as they please, states are now increasingly considered to be accountable for their internal acts, even to such an extent that there is a responsibility to protect the population against gross human rights violations. Moreover, this responsibility to protect can under specific circumstances transfer to the international community so that others can take action in situations of gross human rights violations; 'the rights of sovereign states to non-interference in their internal affairs could not override the rights of individuals to freedom from gross and systematic abuses of their human rights'.[243] This idea, embedded *inter alia* in the Responsibility to Protect, is still relatively young, with the consequence that its exact scope and legal value is still subject to debate and its practical application proves complicated. It would therefore probably be too soon to speak of a paradigm shift, yet it cannot be denied that strong developments are taking place. In the words of the Special Rapporteur of the ILC: '(s)ince consent to assistance is sanctioned by international law, rather than disregarding it, a limitation on its exercise also grounded in international law may be justified.'[244] It is now time to see what the new chapter in the story of sovereignty means for rules and principles on accepting humanitarian assistance.

## 5 Conclusions: Rules and Principles on Accepting Humanitarian Assistance

### 5.1 Introduction

Based on the legal framework described here, it is possible to identify some common rules as generally applicable when delivering humanitarian assistance in response to a disaster. First, it is clear that the primary role to respond to a disaster lies with the affected state. If the state is in need of assistance, it can initiate the process of delivery of such assistance. Common rules exist on the way that this process is triggered. Finally, after considering the offers of assistance made to the affected state, that state is granted the right to give or withhold consent to international humanitarian assistance. The legal framework further gives indicators when the affected state must move from its primary response to initiating the process of international humanitarian assistance or when the state must accept humanitarian assistance. These topics will be summarized and discussed here.

---

[242] Fidler (n 28) 466.
[243] Annan (n 235) 89.
[244] Valencia-Ospina, 'Fourth Report' (n 89) para 54.

## 5.2 Primary role of the affected state

Quite a number of the instruments discussed in the foregoing depart from the assumption that the primary role in responding to a disaster lies with the affected state.[245] This primary role entails 'the direction, control, coordination and supervision of (...) relief and assistance'.[246] Moreover, the affected state must also 'ensure disaster risk reduction (...) in their territory' next to providing relief and recovery assistance. The concept of state sovereignty lies at the basis of the primary role of affected states, as for example expressed by the ILC with the words 'by virtue of its sovereignty'.[247] Also the IDRL Guidelines base the primary role of the affected state on the concept of state sovereignty when providing that '(a)ffected States have the sovereign right to coordinate, regulate and monitor disaster relief and recovery assistance (…)'.[248]

Connecting the primary role of the affected state to sovereignty means, as was seen above, that the affected state is responsible for protection of the persons living in that state. As a consequence, 'if an affected State determines that a disaster situation exceeds national coping capacities, it should seek international and/or regional assistance to address the needs of affected persons'.[249] In the ILC draft articles on the Protection of Persons in the Event of Disasters, this rule is even formulated as a duty: '(t)o the extent that a disaster exceeds its national response capacity, the affected State has the duty to seek assistance (...)'.[250] Resolution 46/182 refers to the importance of international cooperation in the context of insufficient capacity, being less direct on indicating a duty to accept assistance.[251]

The affected state must know what its capacity is and it must also know 'timely' what is needed from international actors: '(t)he affected State should decide in a timely manner whether or not to request disaster relief (...) and communicate its decision promptly. In order to make this decision, the affected State should promptly assess needs'.[252] It is not specifically determined what 'timely' and 'promptly' mean, but the first seventy-two hours in disaster response are considered

---

[245] UNGA Resolution on 'Humanitarian assistance to victims of natural disasters and similar emergency situations' (UN Doc. A/Res/43/131 of 8 December 1988), second paragraph of the preamble; UN ILC draft articles 9 and 11; IDRL Guidelines (n 171) Guideline 3 paras 1 and 3 on 'responsibilities of the affected states'.
[246] See ILC Memorandum (n 185), paras 67 and 69; IDRL Guidelines (n 171) Guidelines 3(3) and 4(1).
[247] UN ILC draft article 9(1).
[248] IDRL Guidelines (n 171) Guideline 3 para 1 and 3 on the 'responsibilities of the affected states'.
[249] IDRL Guidelines (n 171) Guideline 3(2).
[250] ILC Drafting Committee 'Protection of Persons in the Event of Disasters: Text and titles of draft articles 10 and 11 provisionally adopted by the Drafting Committee on 19 July 2011' (UN Doc. A/CN.4/L.794 of 20 July 2011), draft article 10.
[251] UNGA Resolution 46/182 (n 71) under 5.
[252] IDRL Guidelines (n 171) Guideline no 10(1).

most critical. It is during this phase that certain legal effects are set in motion: the affected state's primary role means making a needs-assessment, judging whether the affected state's response will be adequate, and, when necessary, triggering the process of international assistance.[253]

Another consequence of the primary role of the affected state and of state sovereignty is that consent is required before an international actor can deliver humanitarian assistance to or in the affected state. The initiation of international humanitarian assistance and the role of consent are therefore necessary nuances to the primary role of the affected state.

### 5.3 The triggering and initiation of international humanitarian assistance

With regard to offers made by humanitarian actors, many instruments require an appeal or request by the affected state before an offer can be made.[254] UNGA Resolution 46/182 determines that 'humanitarian assistance should be provided (...) in principle on the basis of an appeal by the affected country'.[255] Also the IDRL Guidelines provide that '(d)isaster relief or initial recovery assistance should be initiated (...) in principle, on the basis of an appeal'.[256] After such an appeal, international actors can make offers of assistance, which the affected state then accepts or declines (i.e. giving consent or not).[257]

While some legal instruments explicitly require a prior request by the affected state as initiation of international assistance, other instruments give room to start with an offer.[258] Consequently, an 'unsolicited' offer of assistance 'should not be construed as an unfriendly act or interference in the affected State's internal affairs', which used to be the way unsolicited offers were perceived.[259] Even so, the

---

[253] Saechao (n 200) 699, also referring to Report on Wilton Park Conference, 'The Immediate Response to Disasters: Improving National Aid and International Frameworks (13-16 September 2004).

[254] The question whether an offer of assistance or the delivery of assistance must be preceded by an appeal or request is not for all actors relevant. Some organisations (for example National Red Cross or Red Crescent Societies) already have operations on the affected state's territory and therefore encounter less difficulty in providing humanitarian assistance.

[255] UNGA Resolution 46/182 (n 71); Guiding Principle no 3.

[256] IDRL Guidelines (n 171) Guideline no 10(1).

[257] ILC Memorandum (n 185) para 51.

[258] Fisher, 'Desk Study' (n 4) 92. For example in the ASEAN Agreement it is provided that 'assistance can only be deployed at the request, and with the consent, of the Requesting Party, or when offered by another Party or Parties, with the consent of the Receiving Party'. Article 11(2) ASEAN Agreement on Disaster Management and Emergency Response (26 July 2005). Also the IDRL Guidelines provide that the initiation of international assistance is 'in principle' based on an appeal, so other forms of initiation are also possible. IDRL Guidelines (n 171) Guideline 10(1).

[259] ILC Memorandum (n 185) para 64. See also the Council of the International Institute of Humanitarian Law, 'Guiding Principles on the Right to Humanitarian Assistance' (1993) 33 International Review of the Red Cross [297] principle 5 and, stemming from much earlier ILA Resolution on International Medical and Humanitarian Law (1976) part I para 2: '(t)he offer of

existence of an actual right to offer or provide relief may be a bridge too far, although it can be found in some soft law instruments: '(w)here the government or other authority is unable or manifestly unwilling to provide life-sustaining aid, the international community has the right and obligation to protect and provide relief (...)'.[260]

## 5.4 The affected state's right to withhold consent and limitations of this right

Based on the primary role of the affected state (as a result of state sovereignty) there is a widespread understanding that consent of the affected state is required before aid can be delivered.[261] In the words of UN General Assembly Resolution 46/182:

> The sovereignty, territorial integrity and national unity of States must be fully respected in accordance with the Charter of the United Nations. In this context, humanitarian assistance should be provided with the consent of the affected country and in principle on the basis of an appeal by the affected country.[262]

The affected state can also choose to withhold its consent: '(a)s a matter of international law, the affected State has a right to refuse an offer. However, this right is not unlimited'.[263] When looking closely at what has been discussed at the foregoing, three rules can be identified in the legal framework that direct a state in its choice to give or withhold consent.

First, some sources within the legal framework argue that there is an 'obligation of the affected State to request international assistance where its domestic response capacity is overwhelmed'.[264] It cannot be said with full certainty to what extent this duty is actually considered to be a legal obligation in practice. In the words of some of the instruments, states should make use of international cooperation when their own resources are insufficient, although the link between capacity and an obligation to make use of international cooperation is not explained clearly in the legal instruments. Another difficulty here lies in the fact that it is up to the affected state to determine that its capacity is overwhelmed.

---

foreign emergency relief shall in no way whatsoever be considered an unlawful intervention in the domestic affairs of a State nor shall it be deemed under any circumstances to constitute an unfriendly action'.

[260] Mohonk Criteria for Humanitarian Assistance in Complex Emergencies (1995), section II.4. See also the Guiding Principles on the Right to Humanitarian Assistance (n 259) principle 5; '(n)ational authorities (...) have the right to offer such assistance (...)'. More on the implications of the right to offer assistance is said in section 3.3 of the next Chapter.

[261] ILC Drafting Committee 'Protection of Persons in the Event of Disasters: Text and titles of draft articles 10 and 11 provisionally adopted by the Drafting Committee on 19 July 2011' (UN Doc. A/CN.4/L.794 of 20 July 2011), draft Article 11(1).

[262] UNGA Resolution 46/182 (n 71) under 3.

[263] Valencia-Ospina, 'Fourth Report' (n 89) para 52.

[264] ILC Memorandum (n 185) para 65.

Second, 'consent should not be withheld arbitrarily', a formulation seen in, *inter alia*, international humanitarian law limits the freedom of a state to withhold consent.[265] What 'arbitrarily' means does not become immediately clear. In the context of international humanitarian law some indications on the meaning can be found when it was argued that the requirement of consent 'did not imply that the Parties concerned had absolute and unlimited freedom to refuse their agreement to relief actions. A Party refusing its agreement must do so for valid reasons, not for arbitrary or capricious ones'.[266] A further argument was found that there is less ground to refuse an offer that meets the humanitarian principles (humanity, neutrality, impartiality and independence) than an offer that is somehow tied or conditional.[267] This is further clarified by stating that 'if the survival of the population is threatened and a humanitarian organization fulfilling the required conditions of impartiality and non-discrimination is able to remedy this situation, relief actions must take place. (...) The authorities cannot refuse such relief without good grounds'.[268] In the work of the ILC, the same line on 'arbitrarily withholding consent' can be found. According to the ILC's Special Rapporteur, offers of aid must meet the humanitarian principles as laid down in draft article 6,[269] and 'if an offer does indeed meet those criteria, the affected State must possess very strong and valid reasons for choosing not to give its consent. If it withholds its consent without such reasons being present, a State may be considered to have done so "arbitrarily".'[270] In coming to this conclusion, the Special Rapporteur made an

---

[265] This phrase is also used in other instruments. See ILC Memorandum (n 185) para 65 ; Valencia-Ospina, 'Fourth Report' (n 89) paras 52 and 68; Guiding Principles on Internal Displacement Principle 25; Institute of International Law, 'Duty of Affected States not Arbitrarily to Reject a Bona Fide Offer of Humanitarian Assistance' (2003).

[266] ICRC *Commentary* (n 89) paras. 2795 and 2805. In the context of IHL the question what can be understood with 'arbitrary' was asked to Professor Yoram Dinstein (who has been closely involved in the development of IHL) at the Conference 'International Humanitarian Assistance and International Law: A Legal Approach to Practical Problems', held in Leiden on 24 and 25 January 2013 by the University of Leiden and Tilburg University. Prof. Dinstein replied by stressing that "arbitrary is arbitrary, it means that there is no good reason".

[267] ICRC, *Draft Additional Protocols to the Geneva Conventions of August 12, 1949* (1973) 78-9; Valencia-Ospina, 'Fourth Report' (n 89) para 66.

[268] ICRC *Commentary* (n 89) para 4885 cited by Federica Donati & Margret Vidar, 'International Legal Dimensions of the Right to Food' in George Kent (ed), *Global Obligations for the Right to Food* (Rowman & Littlefield Publishers Inc., Lanham 2008) 39.

[269] Relief must not only be provided in accordance with the humanitarian principles, the Guidelines also provide a list with further requirements, including the requirement that aid must be delivered without discrimination, responsive to the needs of vulnerable groups, sensitive to culture and religious customs, provided by competent personnel, minimizing the negative impact on the local community's economy, development and environment. IDRL Guidelines (n 171) Guideline 4(2) a through d and 4(3) a through j.

[270] Valencia-Ospina, 'Fourth Report' (n 89) paras 68 and 73. Also the Institute of International Law provides that '(a)ffected States are under the obligation not arbitrarily and unjustifiably to reject a bona fide offer exclusively intended to provide humanitarian assistance or to refuse access to the victims'. Institute of International Law (n 265).

analysis of existing legal norms and interpreting what elements can be used to determine 'arbitrariness'. In the first place, being 'unable or unwilling to protect and assist persons on its territory affected by a disaster, a provision to reasonably limit the general rule on consent may be justified'.[271] This will also be discussed further below as the third potential limitation. Second, if there is no clear need for humanitarian assistance, refusal of aid would not be arbitrary. In any case, the Special Rapporteur comes to the conclusion that

> The determination of when a State's conduct amounts to that State being unable or unwilling is to be arrived at in light of the specific circumstances of each case and cannot be exhaustively dealt with. The objective element of inability may be satisfied if the affected State clearly lacks the required goods or services. A State can be considered to be unwilling to provide assistance when it does possess the necessary resources and capacity for adequate relief, but has indicated that it does not wish to use those resources or capacity.[272]

Consequently, 'whether or not a decision not to accept assistance is arbitrary depends on the circumstances of the case and should be determined on a case-by-case basis'.[273] He further acknowledges that 'the operational aspects involved may benefit from more clarity and transparency to enhance the response system, requiring the affected State to explain its conduct, in particular in case of refusal of humanitarian assistance.'[274]

The third limitation is – as pointed out above – closely linked to the arbitrariness-rule. This limitation can be found in the obligations stemming from the more general part of the legal framework, like human rights law and refugee law.[275] Based on such more general instruments, it can be argued that consent may not be withheld when 'authorities concerned are unable or unwilling to provide the required humanitarian assistance';[276] 'if the whole or part of the population of an occupied territory is inadequately supplied';[277] 'if the civilian population of any territory under the control of a Party to the conflict, other than occupied territory, is not adequately provided with (...) supplies (...)';[278] or when 'the affected State is a party to the Covenant [on Economic, Social and Cultural Rights] and is not capable of addressing the consequences of a disaster to a sufficient extent'.[279] In other words, when there is a general risk that not giving consent to humanitarian

[271] Valencia-Ospina, 'Fourth Report' (n 89) para 70.
[272] Ibid, para 71.
[273] Ibid, para 72.
[274] Ibid, para 76.
[275] Ibid, para 58.
[276] ECOSOC, Commission on Human Rights, 'Guiding Principles on Internal Displacement' (Annex) (UN Doc. E/CN.4/1998/Add.2 of 11 February 1998) principle 25(2).
[277] Geneva Convention IV, article 59.
[278] Geneva Conventions Additional Protocol I, article 70(1).
[279] Valencia-Ospina, 'Fourth Report' (n 89) para 60. Here, the potential violation of the ICESCR as a result of refusing assistance is seen as an arbitrary reason for withholding consent.

assistance would result in a violation of international law – like human rights law – an affected state should not be free to withhold consent.[280]

Some argue that in this case, the refusal to give consent could possibly constitute an international wrongful act.[281] Article 12 of the Articles on the Responsibility of States for Internationally Wrongful Acts provides: 'There is a breach of an international obligation by a State when an act of that State is not in conformity with what is required of it by that obligation, regardless of its origin or character'. Before state responsibility can be invoked, however, it must first be determined which international obligation has been breached exactly, whether the breach is attributable to the state, and whether the breach can be justified.[282] Since there are no clear obligations on the acceptance of international humanitarian assistance, it is difficult to determine exactly which obligation a state violates by not giving consent to humanitarian assistance. When a legal obligation is found that is violated by not giving consent to assistance, the framework of state responsibility would make it possible to claim the immediate ending of the wrongful act. In addition, the state committing the wrongful act can be held liable for damages.[283] When withholding consent could result in violation of obligations under international law, it can be argued that the refusal is based on arbitrary reasons and that a strong justification is required to base the refusal on valid reasons. In the same line, it can also be argued that refusing to give consent when the national capacity is overwhelmed is arbitrary. The idea that states may not withhold their consent for arbitrary reasons can therefore be a limitation in itself, but it can also be considered to be the general rule of which the other two limitations are specific examples.

## 5.5 Conclusion

When considering the entire legal framework, common rules are identified that direct states' behaviour on accepting humanitarian assistance in response to a disaster. State sovereignty fulfils an important role in these rules, making the primary role of the affected state the point of departure. The primary role of the affected state is the basis for the steps the affected state must take in the aftermath

---

280 Donati & Vidar (n 268) 40.

281 This possibility was discussed within the ILC; ILC Report of the International Law Commission, sixty-second session (3 May-4 June and 5 July-6 August 2010) (UN Doc. A/65/10 of 2010) para 318, cited by Dabiru S. Patnaik, 'Issues of State Consent and International Humanitarian Assistance in Disasters: The Work of the International Law Commission' in Andrej Zwitter *et al* (eds), *Humanitarian Action: Global, Regional and Domestic Legal Responses* (Cambridge University Press, Cambridge 2014) 111.

282 Nathalie Horbach & René Lefeber, 'Staatsaansprakelijkheid' in Horbach, Lefeber & Ribbelink (n 206) 313 and 322-3.

283 Zwitter and Lamont base the occurrence of an international wrongful act on a violation of an *erga omnes* obligation that could exist within human rights law. Their reasoning can be found in Andrej Zwitter & Christopher K. Lamont, 'Enforcing Aid in Myanmar: State Responsibility & Aid' in Zwitter *et al* (eds) (n 281) 349ff.

of a disaster to obtain international humanitarian assistance. The affected state must make a needs-assessment and trigger or initiate international humanitarian assistance accordingly. The primary role further entails that consent is required before assistance can be delivered. The freedom of affected states to withhold consent is however limited in various ways, determining when the state must accept humanitarian assistance. Consent may not be withheld when the national capacity to respond is overwhelmed, when refusing consent would result in a violation of a rule of international (human rights) law or when the refusal is based on arbitrary reasons.

Although the rules identified here return in various instruments and documents, it cannot be said that these are rule of customary international law.[284] There are no indications that the requirements of article 38(1)(b) ICJ Statute of general practice accepted as law are met in practice, although this must be further confirmed (or refuted) in the next Chapter.[285] At the most, it seems that a 'dotted pattern of behaviour' can be identified, which may or may not be the beginnings of customary international law.[286]

The goal of the legal analysis was to identify possible rules and principles applicable in natural disasters, and not in armed conflict. International humanitarian law was nonetheless included because it is generally understood to contain rather developed rules on humanitarian assistance and this could help in identifying and understanding the rules derived from the rest of the legal framework. Nevertheless, the common rules found on humanitarian assistance in disaster response are not that different from the rules that were described in the section on international humanitarian law. In IHL the requirement of consent is also clearly established, and as a limitation mainly the argument that consent may not be withheld for arbitrary reasons can be found. Within IHL, no clear description of what 'arbitrary' is can be found, as is the case within the broader legal framework. The other two limitations found for disaster-contexts are not explicitly present within IHL, although it is possible to argue that the phrase 'when a civilian population is in need of assistance'

---

[284] See also Saechao (n 200) 698.

[285] In case law described as practice and conviction of legal necessity. Gerald J. Postema, 'Custom in International Law: A Normative Practice Account' in Amanda Perreau-Saussine & James B. Murphy, *The Nature of Customary Law: Legal Historical and Philosophical Perspectives* (Cambridge University Press, Cambridge 2007) 279. PCIJ *Lotus* (Turkey v. France), Series A, No. 10, 1927; North Sea Continental Shelf-case; ICJ Libya/Malta, ICJ Reports 1995, pp. 13, 29; 81 ILR, p. 239; 'the substance of customary law must be looked for primarily in the actual practice and *opinio iuris* of states'. See also the ICJ Nuclear Weapons case, ICJ Reports 1996, pp. 226, 253; 110 ILR, p. 163. *Opinio juris* is supposed to distinguish a practice out of legal conviction from a practice out of social or moral belief: Shaw (n 208) 75.

[286] The phrase 'dotted pattern of behaviour' is ascribed to Em. Prof. Bert van Roermund, who, as a Professor in Legal Philosophy at Tilburg University, explained through this phrase the very beginnings of the process that may or may not result in rules of customary international law. While a dotted pattern of behaviour is not the same as consistent state practice, there may be clues that certain developments are underway. This explanation was given during an informal lecture series from September 2011 to March 2012 at Tilburg University, the Netherlands.

refers to a situation in which providing these needs is beyond a state's capacity (or perhaps willingness) to address. Despite its reputation, IHL is not that much clearer or more developed than the rules for peacetime humanitarian assistance.[287] Nonetheless, looking at the developments in Syria, the Security Council has found a way to bypass the requirement of consent in extreme situations. It is unlikely that such a decision to grant access to humanitarian organisations in the stead of the affected state will ever be taken in the context of peace-time disasters since such an accumulation of special circumstances would hardly ever occur in peace-time settings.

At this point it can be concluded, as a preliminary answer to the main research question, that within international law rules can be found which determine whether an affected state should accept international humanitarian assistance after a disaster occurred. Still, immediately a number of questions arise on the practical application of these rules. For example, how can it be determined that the capacity of the affected state is overwhelmed? Which supposedly breached rules of international law are invoked when a state refuses to give consent? What are arbitrary reasons for refusing to give consent and what are valid reasons? And what if a state should give its consent but does not do so? The next Chapter will look at the way that the rules are used in practice and what the consequences thereof might be for the legal framework.

[287] This also follows from the question asked by the Minister of Foreign Affairs of the Netherlands to the Advisory Committee on Issues of Public International Law in 2014 on humanitarian access in times of armed conflict. In the advice the conclusion is reached that much uncertainty exist with regard to the requirement of consent in armed conflict situations. CAVV, 'Advisory Report on Humanitarian Assistance' (Advisory report no 25, The Hague, August 2014) <http://cms.webbeat.net/ContentSuite/upload/cav/doc/Report_nr._25_-_Humanitarian_assistance%281%29.pdf> accessed 5 April 2015.

# CHAPTER III
# PRACTICAL APPLICATION OF THE RULES ON INTERNATIONAL HUMANITARIAN ASSISTANCE IN RESPONSE TO DISASTERS

## 1 INTRODUCTION

The goal of this Chapter is to illustrate the practical application of the rules that determine when an affected state moves from responding individually towards initiating the process of international humanitarian assistance and to giving consent to such assistance. As established in the previous Chapter, the legal framework on accepting humanitarian assistance in response to a disaster consists of three steps or layers. Underlying these three steps is the primary role of the affected state in responding to a disaster as a consequence of the sovereignty of the state. Due to this role, the affected state must in the first place make a needs-assessment (1). Based on this needs-assessment, the affected state must decide whether international humanitarian assistance is required and if so, the process of obtaining such assistance must be triggered (2). After valuing the offers of assistance available, the affected state must accept or decline these offers (3). At this stage, consent to offers of international humanitarian assistance may not be withheld for arbitrary reasons, when it would result in the violation of rules of international (human rights) law, or when the national capacity is overwhelmed.

The legal framework is established based on an analysis of the main (legal) sources on humanitarian assistance and disaster response. It is based on a theoretical understanding of what is expected of states. By looking at the way the legal framework is applied in practice, it is possible to further identify any problems and gaps that may exist. This way, it can be established whether the set of rules found in the previous Chapter is specific enough to speak of clear obligations for states to accept international humanitarian assistance. If not, it can be determined where the difficulties lie.

First, the individual response by the affected state will be discussed. The affected state is responsible for reacting to the occurrence of a disaster and must decide whether international aid is needed. If an affected state decides to accept international assistance, such assistance can be initiated through a request by the affected state or through an offer by another actor. The processes of initiation will be discussed in section 3. Accepting international humanitarian assistance is the point where the requirement of consent becomes visible. The role of consent will be explained in the fourth section. Less relevant for answering the main research question but completing the picture is the provision of international humanitarian assistance and termination of operations. These aspects will be discussed in section 5 before ending this Chapter by looking at situations in which consent of the affected state cannot be obtained yet where international humanitarian assistance is necessary (or even essential) for the survival of the civilian population.

## 2 The first response by the affected state: making a needs-assessment

That the affected state has the primary responsibility to respond to a disaster occurring in its territory means that it has the primary role in directing, controlling, coordinating, distributing and supervising relief.[1] The primary role of the affected state originates in the principles of sovereignty, territorial integrity, non-interference and national unity.[2] The role of the affected state can even be seen as an obligation 'to ensure such protection and assistance in the event of a disaster' which 'aims at preserving the life and dignity of the victims of the disaster and guaranteeing the access of persons in need to humanitarian assistance'.[3] In practice, this means that the affected state will initiate the response to a disaster before any other party does. Moreover, due to the primary role any other party has to coordinate its response with the affected state. This is translated in the legal framework as the prerequisite that consent from the affected state is required before humanitarian assistance can be delivered.

In principle, the response by the affected state (including the activities of organisations that were already on the ground prior to the disaster, like national Red Cross or Red Crescent Societies) remains the only response until the affected state gives its consent to relief coming in from outside the territory. To prevent problems relating to capacity deficits, the legal framework indicates – in a number of instruments – that the affected state should give its consent in situations where the national response capacity is overwhelmed or where not giving consent would result in the violation of international law. Even so, external humanitarian assistance can only be brought in after consent is obtained and the only standards explaining when the state should give its consent are not very concrete. Looking at the standards set in various guidelines and handbooks, it becomes clear that the affected state should decide in a 'timely' manner whether or not to request relief and 'communicate its decision promptly'.[4] This means that when a disaster occurs, the affected state must make a needs-assessment and decide what it can deliver itself and what it would need from others, and it must do so as soon as possible. If

---

[1] See ILC, 'Protection of Persons in the Event of Disasters: Memorandum by the Secretariat' (UN Doc. A/CN.4/590 of 11 December 2007), paras 67 and 69; IFRC, 'Introduction to the Guidelines for the Domestic Facilitation and Regulation of International Disaster Relief and Initial Recovery Assistance' (IFRC, Geneva 2008) Guidelines no 3(3) and no 4(1).
[2] ILC Memorandum (n 1) para 51.
[3] ILC 'Fourth Report on the Protection of Persons in the Event of Disasters by Eduardo Valencia-Ospina, Special Rapporteur' (UN Doc. A/CN.4/643 of 11 May 2011) para 57.
[4] IDRL Guidelines (n 1) Guideline 10(1).

an affected state can, with or without the assistance of organisations already present on its territory, supply for example sufficient food to disaster victims but does not have tents and field hospitals, it can very accurately request those items it still needs. Indeed, '(w)eaknessess in domestic administrative clarity and capacity to undertake valid needs assessments can be a major cause for problems in both the request and the provision of international assistance'.[5] Delays in the needs-assessment (for example as a result of communication problems between central and regional authorities) can hamper the relief operations, and although some organisations are capable of assisting the affecting state in making a needs-assessment, not all affected states are willing to let go (parts of) their control.[6] Also, if multiple parties are involved in the needs-assessment, it is more difficult to coordinate the various findings.[7] To date, there is no universally applicable set of standards that must assist in making a needs-assessment. Yet, being prepared for a disaster is a major factor for being able to make concrete requests for assistance and to start relief operations swiftly, as is illustrated by the example of Japan.

Japan is a disaster-prone country due to its geographical position. Based on experience, Japan is well-prepared for disasters and is trained in disaster response. On 11 March 2011, the country was hit by an earthquake with a magnitude of 9.0 $M_w$, its epicentre lying close to the coast of Honsu.[8] As the infrastructure was constructed in such a fashion that it could withstand the severe earthquake, the main disaster was the tsunami caused by the earthquake. Approximately 16,000 people lost their lives when waves as high as 37 metres flooded parts of Japan.[9] In the response to the disaster, Japan started with a needs-assessment: '(t)he first thing the government did right was to recognize the coordination challenge in the first place. They were very clear on what was needed, what wasn't needed, what could be accepted'.[10] As a consequence, Japan was clear which part of the response it would do by itself and for which part its capacity was not sufficient. On the other hand, this preparedness did not extend to the response to the subsequent nuclear disaster. According to an independent investigation panel, Japan failed in its disaster

[5] David Fisher, 'Law and Legal Issues in International Disaster Response: A Desk Study' (IFRC, Geneva 2007) 94.
[6] Ibid.
[7] This was experienced in the aftermath of hurricanes George and Mitch and after opening Aceh to aid organisations. See Fisher, 'Desk Study' (n 5) 94.
[8] US Geological Survey <http://earthquake.usgs.gov/earthquakes/recenteqsww/Quakes/usc0001xgp.php> accessed 26 June 2012.
[9] Ibid.
[10] Oliver Lacey-Hall, Head of OCHA in the Asia Pacific, ——, 'Disasters: Learning from Japan's Tsunami' *IRIN* 9 March 2012. This does not mean that the entire Japanese response was without errors. Eventually, the Prime Minister stepped down taking his responsibility for the flaws in the response. See for example Justin McCurry, 'Naoto Kan resigns as Japan's Prime Minister' *The Guardian* 26 August 2011 <http://www.theguardian.com/world/2011/aug/26/naoto-kan-resigns-japan-pm> accessed 4 December 2013.

planning and crisis management for a possible nuclear disaster as the result of a tsunami, an event that should have been anticipated.[11]

Although the international community of states, international organisations, NGOs and civil society can have an opinion on whether there is a need for an affected state to give its consent, it is ultimately the affected state only that can give its consent. Sometimes, an affected state's response is deemed 'sufficient' or 'effective' so that no discussion exists on whether the state should have accepted international aid.[12] To a larger extent, cases are part of a grey area where there is discussion on the quality of the affected state's response (as is the case in Japan). In the following, two examples will be discussed in which the affected state's response is considered by some to be sufficient, but is criticized by others. The purpose of these examples is to highlight the difficulty in determining when a state 'should' accept international assistance or not. The examples described here are not strictly speaking 'disasters' in the understanding of this research because the definition of 'disaster' in Chapter I refers to of events that overwhelm the capacity of the affected state. Situations in which no external aid is apparently required do not fall under the scope of the definition. However, as will be explained here, whether an event was beyond the affected state's capacity to address is subject to debate which makes the dividing line vague. The cases described here are considered to be 'disasters' in the understanding of the present research.[13]

The first example is the earthquake in L'Aquila (Italy). On 6 April 2009, the region around the Italian city of L'Aquila was hit by a 6.3 $M_w$ earthquake, killing at least 287 people and leaving over 40,000 people homeless.[14] In response, no international assistance was deemed necessary. According to – at that time – Prime Minister Silvio Berlusconi, Italians are 'proud people' and had sufficient resources to deal with the crisis.[15] Only for the reconstruction of historical buildings, Berlusconi would consider accepting funds from Washington.[16]

The individual response by Italy was praised by some. In a report of a company assessing construction damage it was said that 'the civil emergency response presented little challenge to Italian authorities. International support was not

[11] See ——, 'Fukushima One Year On: Poor Planning Hampered Fukushima Response' *SAGE Publications,* February 2012. An analysis of the report is available here: <http://www.alphagalileo.org/ViewItem.aspx?ItemId=117974&CultureCode=en> accessed 29 July 2013.

[12] The German response to the floods in the first half of June 2013, which affected thousands, can be mentioned as an example. See the status update at Deutsche Welle: Martin Koch, 'After the Floods: Relief Work and Cleanup' *DW* 21 June 2013 <http://www.dw.de/after-the-floods-relief-work-and-cleanup/a-16897279> accessed 29 July 2013.

[13] Therefore implying that the consequences were beyond the state's capacity to address.

[14] US Geological Survey <http://earthquake.usgs.gov/earthquakes/eqinthenews/2009/us2009fcaf/#summary> accessed 27 June 2012.

[15] ——, 'Death Toll Rises in Italy Quake' *BBC News* 7 April 2009.

[16] Ibid.

necessary.'[17] The government constructed apartment buildings for the people who lost their homes, and succeeded in providing shelter before the winter. According to an inhabitant of L'Aquila who witnessed the earthquake and its aftermath, the first response by the Italian government was 'fast and feverish,' referring to the construction of temporary homes on the outskirts of L'Aquila.[18] However, around the earthquake's first anniversary, some criticism could be found on Italy's individual response. Indeed, the government was able to resettle 17,000 people from tents to more adequate housing before winter, but one year after the earthquake it was rumoured that 4,000 people still lived in Red Cross accommodations and that around 7,000 people still lived in hotels.[19] In addition, work had not started to clear the historic centre of L'Aquila of rubble and to rebuild, making it impossible for businesses to return. Instead, the 'Aquilani' decided to do the work themselves, coming to the city centre on Sundays to clear out rubble using shovels and wheelbarrows.[20] Criticism on the response is probably best depicted by Italian filmmaker and satirist Sabina Guzzanti who made the documentary 'Draquila', arguing that the response by the government of Berlusconi was flawed, showing cases of corruption and claiming that resources earmarked for relief disappeared.[21]

It is very difficult to determine whether the Italian response to the earthquake met the standard of 'having sufficient capacity' to deal with the consequences and whether Italy's claim that no international assistance was needed was justified. When looking at the instruments available, many explain in general terms what needs to be done during disasters, and the Sphere Standards are most explicit on this. There is not, however, a set of principles that clearly explain what is expected from the affected state and how it can be measured if its national response capacity is overwhelmed. The achievements of affected states are often debated some time after the disaster occurred. Even then, it is up to interpretation and opinion what constitutes a response by the affected state that is sufficiently adequate and effective and whether the capacity of the affected state was overwhelmed or not. The second example illustrates this difficulty further.

On 12 May 2008, the Chinese province Sichuan was hit by an earthquake with a magnitude of $7.9M_w$. At least 69,195 people were killed, but another 18,392 people

[17] Global Risk Miyamoto, 'L'Aquila Italy Earthquake Field Investigation Report' (2009) 26 <http://www.grmcat.com/images/Italy-EQ-Report.pdf> accessed 20 April 2015.
[18] Laura Benedetti, 'After a Quake, Reclaiming their City' *The Washington Post* 11 April 2010.
[19] John Hooper, 'L'Aquila Earthquake Survivors Seek Answers from Government' *The Guardian* 5 April 2010.
[20] Benedetti (n 18).
[21] 'Draquila' was selected for the 2010 Cannes Film Festival. The Italian Minister of Culture at the time, Sandro Bondi, refused to visit the festival out of protest against this documentary. See Fiona Winward, 'Italy Snubs Cannes after Row Over Berlusconi Documentary' *The Guardian* 10 May 2010, 22.

went missing and were presumed dead.[22] More than 45.5 million people were affected.[23] China is a country that has experience with natural disasters and does in most cases not seek international assistance. Moreover, China is known for not being easily accessible for foreigners and information flows are checked by the government. Due to these factors, it is challenging to find information on China's response to the Sichuan earthquake that is reliable and which gives a realistic understanding of the processes. What on first face is available, are operation reports of a few international organisations that happened to be on the ground, for example the DREF Operation Reports by the IFRC.[24] These organisations want to safeguard their access to China and can therefore not afford to be overtly critical. Other information can be found in international newspapers, which have extensively reported on the Chinese people's outrage on the easy collapse of school buildings in the affected region.[25] A large number of schools and dorms collapsed during the earthquake while China has building regulations to make structures withstand earthquakes. According to many articles, parents were very angry with the Chinese government because the construction of schools conceivably did not meet building prescriptions due to corruption. To silence the protests, parents were supposedly bought off or put in prison.[26] One person who posted criticism on the government's response to the earthquake on his website, along with notes on the children who died in the collapsed schools and the treatment of the parents, was allegedly sentenced to three years imprisonment.[27]

Apart from these stories, other sounds can be heard. One independent consultant who worked in the disaster zone after the earthquake explains that China invited international assistance, but that few organisations could easily deploy and had knowledge on China, and that many organisations were already focusing on Myanmar which had just been hit by cyclone Nargis.[28] According to this consultant the response to the earthquake was described as efficient and comprehensive,

[22]US Geological Survey <http://earthquake.usgs.gov/earthquakes/eqinthenews/2008/us2008ryan/# summary> accessed 26 July 2013.

[23] Ibid.

[24] These reports are available on ReliefWeb: <http://www.reliefweb.int>. See for example operation update 2: <http://reliefweb.int/report/china/china-sichuan-earthquake-dref-operation-n%C2%B0-mdrcn005-operation-update-n%C2%B02> accessed 26 July 2013.

[25] See for example ——, 'Sichuan Earthquake' *New York Times* update of 6 May 2009 <http://topics.nytimes.com/top/news/science/topics/earthquakes/sichuan_province_china/index.ht> accessed 26 July 2013.

[26] See for example David Eimer, 'Sichuan Earthquake Anniversary: Parents of Victims Told Not to Hold Memorials' *The Telegraph* 8 May 2009 <http://www.telegraph.co.uk/news/worldnews/asia/china/5294397/Sichuan-earthquake-anniversary-Parents-of-victims-told-not-to-hold-memorials.html> accessed 26 July 2013.

[27] ——, 'China Jails Earthquake Activist' *The Guardian* 23 November 2009 <http://www.guardian.co.uk/world/2009/nov/23/huang-qi-jailed-sichuan-quake> accessed 26 July 2013.

[28] Brian Hoyer, 'Lessons from the Sichuan Earthquake' (2009) Humanitarian Exchange [43] 14, 15.

mainly due to the prevention of disease outbreak and prevention of an increase in victims as a result of subsequent flooding and landslides, yet he acknowledges that it is difficult to value the response by the government as information is not readily available.[29]

Apart from the outrage at the government reported by Chinese and international press, people were positive about the government's aid and '(a)ffected populations worked to reconstruct markets and establish a home in their government-issued tents, while awaiting further instructions from the local authorities'.[30] The Chinese-led response was not conventional in terms of holding 'cluster meetings, and the Sphere Standards and other guidelines common in the humanitarian community were not in evidence'.[31] Moreover, while the government succeeded in preventing the outbreak of diseases, provided food and shelter and prevented further deaths due to subsequent flooding and landslides, the response was not perfect:

> In order to get food to everyone who needed it nutritionally deficient instant noodles were provided for days on end in some locations. Shelter could not be manufactured quickly enough (despite temporary state seizure of suitable textile factories), resulting in up to 12 individuals sharing one family-size tent. The absence of water borne diseases may actually be attributed to a culture of boiling water, rather than the government's pervasive disinfection campaign.[32]

What becomes clear from this example is that there are many variables based on which it can be argued that an affected state's response was effective or not. China was successful in preventing further victims resulting from common post-disaster problems and people had access to basic facilities. However, the food was not completely sufficient nutrition-wise, for which for example the Sphere Handbook contains quite detailed indicators.[33] The same goes for shelter: the Sphere Handbook calculates a required living space of 3.5m$^2$ floor space which is difficult to achieve when living with twelve persons in one tent.[34] Consequently, although the first step in the affected state's response to a disaster appears quite straightforward (determining through a needs-assessment what it can do by itself and whether international assistance is required), it is difficult to pinpoint if and when the affected state should start the process of international humanitarian assistance. It is left to de discretion of the affected state to determine whether it

[29] Ibid, 15.
[30] Ibid, 16.
[31] Ibid, 16. The Sphere Standards were discussed in Chapter II and are created in the context of the Sphere Project. The standards are laid down in the Sphere Handbook which is used by relief workers to determine what detailed standards should be adhered to during post-disaster phases.
[32] Ibid, 16-7.
[33] See Sphere Project, 'Humanitarian Charter and Minimum Standards in Disaster Response' (Oxfam Publishing, Oxford 2011) ('Sphere Handbook') on Food, section 3: Minimum Standards in Nutrition, 135.
[34] Ibid, on Shelter and settlement standard 3: covered living space, 219.

needs such external assistance. At the final stage, the affected state must give its consent to assistance in a number of situations and these three limitation to the freedom to withhold consent can potentially be used as indicators in the needs-assessment. If a state fears that it will reach one of these three points, it must at least seek international humanitarian assistance. Still, it is up to the affected state to determine whether its capacity is overwhelmed and in practice no clear standards on this are used, no reference is made in practice to violation of a rule of international (human rights) law by withholding consent, and there is no practical reference to 'arbitrary reasons' for withholding consent. Possibly, more will become clear when looking at the next step: the initiation of international humanitarian assistance.

## 3 Initiating International Humanitarian Assistance

### 3.1 Introduction

If the affected state decides that its response capacity is insufficient or that there is a risk that the response capacity may turn out to be insufficient or that it will possibly violate a norm of international law by not giving consent, it can initiate international humanitarian assistance. There are two ways in which the process of delivering international assistance can be started: the affected state can make a request for assistance (in general or for certain (specified) relief items), or international actors can make an offer to which an affected state can react. In this section these two ways of initiating international assistance will be discussed based on their use in practice and legal implications. As quite a number of instruments discussed in Chapter II provide that 'humanitarian assistance should be provided with the consent of the affected country and in principle on the basis of an appeal by the affected country', the initiation of international assistance based on request will be discussed first.[35]

### 3.2 Requesting assistance

The request for international humanitarian assistance is an initiation to 'enter into a specific legal relationship'.[36] Depending on the particular circumstances of the disaster, certain legal consequences are triggered with the request for assistance. A disaster taking place, for instance, in a situation of armed conflict means that IHL must be taken into account. Requests made in the case of nuclear accidents must take into account the specific instruments made for such disasters. Bilateral agreements between states may also influence the legal implications of a request.[37] In general, it can be argued that as a result of the request, an international actor will

---

[35] UNGA Resolution on 'Strengthening of the coordination of humanitarian emergency assistance of the United Nations' (UN Doc. A/Res/46/182 of 19 December 1991) para 3.
[36] ILC Memorandum (n 1) para 52.
[37] Ibid, para 52 and 56.

become allowed to deliver humanitarian assistance without – in principle – breaching the affected state's sovereignty and territorial integrity. The delivery of the assistance, as will be explained further below, will still be subject to the affected state's control.[38]

The request made by the affected state must be specific and targeted. First, the state must decide whether a request will be made and its decision must be 'communicated promptly'.[39] In order to do this, the needs-assessment as mentioned above forms the basis for the decision to request aid and, in case of a request, what the content would be. It is not defined what is understood with 'promptly', but the first seventy-two hours after a disaster are commonly identified as the most critical, meaning that a needs-assessment and a request for assistance must be made within this time.[40] In addition, to make the delivery of humanitarian assistance as efficient and speedy as possible, the request must contain the necessary detail on what is required from international actors: '(r)equests (...) for assistance should be as specific as possible as to the types and amounts of goods as well as the services and expertise available or required, respectively'.[41] This can also be in a reversed manner by indicating in the request what goods and services are not needed.[42] Quite often, states have national mechanisms and legal frameworks in place to organise the needs-assessment and to formulate the request if necessary. Such mechanisms and rules can for example indicate which government body is responsible for (or authorized to) making a request. Moreover, it is possible that specific requirements are in place for a valid request.[43]

While rather straightforward in theory, in practice requests are surrounded by potential problems that could hamper relief efforts.[44] Sometimes, states use the option to communicate a 'willingness to accept' offers of assistance, which can be understood as a very general, unspecified request.[45] This option does not help speeding up the provision of aid, as it results in having to go through offers of relief to see what can be used.[46] A second problem relates to the way in which a request is

[38] See inter alia IDRL Guidelines (n 1) Guideline 4(1): 'Assisting actors and their personnel should abide by the laws of the affected State (...), coordinate with domestic authorities (...)'.
[39] IDRL Guidelines (n 1) Guideline 10(1).
[40] Tyra R. Saechao, 'Natural Disasters and the Responsibility to Protect: From Chaos to Clarity' (2006-7) 32 Brookings Journal of International Law 663, 699.
[41] IDRL Guidelines (n 1) Guideline no 10(2).
[42] Ibid.
[43] Some states require the declaration of the state of emergency before a request for relief can be made. This could be problematic for the application of human rights, as will be explained in Chapter V below. See also Fisher, 'Desk Study' (n 5) 90-1.
[44] The question whether or not a request functions as giving consent to humanitarian assistance is addressed in section 4 where the role of consent is discussed in more detail.
[45] Victoria L. Bannon, 'International Disaster Response Law and the Commonwealth: Answering the Call to Action' (2008) 34 Commonwealth Law Bulletin 843, 850. This option was for example used in the US after mixed messages were send out first.
[46] Fisher, 'Desk Study' (n 5) 91. This practice of requesting assistance without being specific will be discussed below in section 4.3.1.

communicated. If a request is not communicated in a clear and unequivocal way, it could delay the response by potential donors. This problem can be illustrated with an example that at the same time shows that difficulties do not merely arise in countries with limited resources or weak government structures. The US was overwhelmed when hurricane Katrina made landfall in a number of states in the south. On 29 August 2005, Katrina caused the flooding of New Orleans, which is probably the best-known affected area in Katrina's path, yet before arriving in New Orleans it destroyed parts of Louisiana, Mississippi, Alabama, and Florida.[47] After Katrina demolished parts of New Orleans' levee system, around eighty percent of the city flooded during an eighteen hour period, where water depths varied between six and twenty feet (1.80 to 6 metres).[48] Even though Katrina was an exceptionally large disaster,[49] the response by the US Government was highly criticized, mainly because of the weak response, the lack of preparedness and the many days it took for relief and personnel to reach New Orleans and other hurricane-devastated areas.[50] Former President George W. Bush acknowledged the United States' inadequate response to the hurricane by saying "Katrina exposed serious problems in our response capability at all levels of government and to the extent the federal government didn't fully do its job right, I take full responsibility".[51] One of the problems related to the US' request for assistance. While President Bush was quoted saying "I'm not expecting much from foreign nations because we haven't asked for it (...) I do expect a lot of sympathy, and perhaps some will send cash dollars. But this country is going to rise up and take care of it",[52] US Secretary of State Condoleezza Rice stated: "no offers of assistance will be refused".[53] Such a mixed-message can potentially delay the delivery of much needed humanitarian assistance. Besides sending out an ambiguous message, other problems around communication occur for example illustrated after the Indian Ocean tsunami. On Boxing Day in 2004, a massive earthquake (9.1 $M_w$) in the Indian Ocean caused a tsunami which hit fourteen countries, killed around 228,000 people and affected 1.7

---

[47] The White House, 'The Federal Response to Hurricane Katrina: Lessons Learned' (February 2006) 1 <http://www.disastersrus.org/katrina/White%20House%20Katrina%20report.pdf> accessed 3 July 2012.

[48] Ibid, 1-2.

[49] Based on the damage caused by the hurricane, not necessarily by the number of casualties (1882 people died according to EM-DAT).

[50] Saechao (n 40) 691.

[51] John King & Suzanne Malveaux, 'Bush: 'I take responsibility' for Federal Failures after Katrina' *CNN.com* 13 September 2005, cited by Saechao (n 40) 691.

[52] ——, 'Why Does the US Need Our Money?' *BBC News Magazine,* 6 September 2013 <http://news.bbc.co.uk/2/hi/uk_news/magazine/4215336.stm> accessed 29 July 2013.

[53] Ibid. See also Anne Richard, 'Role Reversal: Offers of Help from Other Countries in Response to Hurricane Katrina' (Center for Transatlantic Relations 2006) cited by Fisher, 'Desk Study' (n 5) 89-90. A number of offers of aid were nonetheless declined or were left unused.

million others.[54] The areas mostly affected were Sumatra, Thailand's west coast, Myanmar, Sri Lanka, India's east coast, the Maldives and parts of Africa. After Indonesia decided to allow relief workers into Aceh to assist the victims of the Indian Ocean tsunami, it took two days before this decision was made widely known, during which time many lives could have been saved or suffering relieved.[55] Such problems can be prevented by creating clear policies and plans on post-disaster action and communication.

A third problem that can be encountered when a request is issued is determining whether the sender of the request is indeed an authorised representative of the government.[56] The danger can arise that a request – and possibly the implied consent – is not made by a rightful representative of the government and that the response to the request as a result poses a threat to the affected state's sovereignty and territorial integrity. Especially in contexts where no effective government is present, difficulties can arise. This problem is illustrated by the case of Somalia, which was affected by a drought during some years.[57] In 2011 various relief organisations along with the UN warned for the effects of the drought in the Horn of Africa. In two Somali regions where the existence of a famine was declared, it was not the Somali government that held effective control, but instead the group Al-Shabab was the *de facto* controlling power. Al-Shabab expelled a number of aid agencies from the regions under its control during the period in which relief operations were necessary, cutting thousands off from humanitarian aid.[58] In that situation it would prove extremely difficult for the official government to coordinate a needs-assessment and to request assistance. Even when the government of Somalia would request assistance, it is questionable whether this would be the right authority: *de jure* it probably would, but *de facto* it would lack effect.

Although requests generally have an important status in the legal framework, it would go too far to argue the existence of a duty to request assistance. However, an evolution is going on 'towards greater recognition of a positive duty on affected States to request assistance, at least where the domestic response capacity is

[54] US Geological Survey <http://earthquake.usgs.gov/earthquakes/eqinthenews/2004/us2004slav/#summary> accessed 27 June 2012.

[55] Fisher, 'Desk Study' (n 5) 89-90. Other examples mentioned in the Desk Study are various storms in Fiji and the 1999 earthquake in Turkey.

[56] ILC Memorandum (n 1) para 53. The Memorandum mentions a few exceptions to this rule. In Fiji it is for example determined in national law that a request can also be made by a 'recognized NGO'. Some frameworks have decided that for example an international organization can make a request. It can be questioned whether other states are willing to answer to such requests in fear of breaching the affected state's sovereignty.

[57] The problems underlying the famine and difficulties in delivering aid will be discussed in slightly more detail in section 4.2.

[58] ——, 'Somalia: Al-Shabab Ban on Agencies Threatens Aid' *IRIN* 28 November 2011.

overwhelmed by a disaster'.[59] Due to the potentially implied consent in a specific, targeted request, it forms an essential part in this research.

### 3.3 Offers of assistance

After the affected state has made its request for assistance, international actors can make corresponding offers, which the affected state in its turn can refuse or accept. It is also possible that the affected state did not make any requests and that an unsolicited offer of assistance is made by an international actor (or that the affected state did not direct its request to that particular offering party). In these latter cases, the debate used to arise whether such an offer can be considered as an unlawful interference in the affected state's internal affairs. In the following, this issue will be addressed first because the discussion gives insight into the meaning of 'arbitrariness', after which it will be considered in more detail what conditions offers must meet and what their practical function is.

One of the fundamental principles of international law and of the UN is non-intervention, which includes non-interference.[60] An interpretation of this rule can be found within the UN General Assembly's Declaration of Principles of International Law Concerning Friendly Relations and Cooperation between States. According to this interpretation,

> no State or group of States has the right to intervene directly or indirectly, for any reason whatsoever, in the internal or external affairs of another State. Consequently, armed intervention and all other forms of interference or attempted threats against the personality of the State or against its political, economic, and cultural elements, are in violation of international law.[61]

In the light of this interpretation, the unsolicited offer of humanitarian assistance was at times considered as interference in domestic affairs. The ICJ addressed the issue in the Nicaragua-case where it was determined that 'there can be no doubt that the provision of strictly humanitarian aid to persons or forces in another country, whatever their political affiliations or objectives, cannot be regarded as unlawful intervention, or as in any other way contrary to international law'.[62] The Court also specified what can be understood with 'humanitarian aid': 'the provision of food, clothing, medicine and other humanitarian assistance, and it does not include the provision of weapons, weapons systems, ammunition, or other equipment, vehicles,

---

[59] ILC Memorandum (n 1) para 57.

[60] See article 2(7) UN Charter.

[61] UNGA, 'Declaration of Principles of International Law Concerning Friendly Relations and Cooperation between States' (GA Res. 2625 (XXV) of 24 October 1970) under para 1 of the annex.

[62] ICJ, Nicaragua v. the United States of America, Military and Paramilitary activities in and Against Nicaragua, Merits, Judgement, ICJ Reports 1986, para 242.

or material which can be used to inflict serious bodily harm or death'.[63] If the actual provision of humanitarian assistance cannot be considered as unlawful (although prior consent is at all times required), the mere offer of assistance that is truly humanitarian can certainly not be considered as an unfriendly act. Especially when the offer is made exclusively on humanitarian grounds and in accordance with the humanitarian principles, it cannot be considered as unlawful intervention, giving an affected state less ground to refuse the offer.[64] Consequently, when international actors respect the principles of humanity, impartiality and non-discrimination, offers of relief cannot be considered as intervening in the receiving state's affairs.[65] This is further acknowledged in *inter alia* the work of the ILC,[66] the Framework Convention on Civil Defence Assistance, which provides that '(offers of) assistance should not be viewed as interference in the internal affairs of the Beneficiary State',[67] and in the ILA Resolution on international medical and humanitarian law, which reads 'the offer of foreign emergency relief shall in no way whatsoever be considered an unlawful intervention in the domestic affairs of a State nor shall it be deemed under any circumstances to constitute an unfriendly action'.[68]

Even so, some instruments depart from the idea that no unsolicited offers should be made, like UNGA Resolution 46/182 or the Tampere Convention on the Provision of Telecommunication Resources for Disaster Mitigation and Relief Operations. Despite these references it is quite common in today's practice that international actors make offers of assistance even without prior request.[69] Usually, such offers do not lead to accusations of interference, but other problems arise when an affected state receives many offers of assistance. If an offer is made without prior request, the offering party is not sure whether the affected state actually needs whatever is being offered. The consequence is that the affected state must consider each separate offer to see whether it can be used or not, which may take valuable capacity away from the needs-assessment and from the preparation of targeted requests.

Now that it is established that an unsolicited offer is not an unlawful interference in the domestic affairs of a state (a state still has the right to withhold consent, so to

---

[63] Ibid, para 97.

[64] This is also clearly established in UNGA Resolution 46/182 (n 35), which was discussed in the previous Chapter.

[65] Which can also be read into some provisions of the Geneva Conventions, like common Article 3, Article 10 GCIV, and Article 70(1) of API.

[66] Valencia-Ospina, 'Fourth Report' (n 3) paras 107-109.

[67] Framework Convention on Civil Defence Assistance (22 May 2000) Article 3 under b) <http://www.ifrc.org/Docs/idrl/I319EN.pdf> accessed 4 December 2013.

[68] ILA, 'Resolution on international medical and humanitarian law' adopted at the 54th ILA Convention (The Hague, 1970) Part I, para 2. See further ILC Memorandum (n 1) para 64, fn. 226.

[69] As explicitly acknowledged in a number of instruments, like the ASEAN Agreement on Disaster Management and Emergency Response of 2005, which states that 'external assistance or offers of assistance shall only be provided upon the request or with the consent of the affected Party' (Articles 3(1) and 11(2)). ILC Memorandum (n 1) para 64; Fisher, 'Desk Study' (n 5) 91.

refuse the offer), it can be wondered whether this means that there is a 'right to offer assistance', or even a 'duty to offer assistance'?[70] As explained in the General Introduction, the offering-side is in principle excluded from the research, yet some remarks on the right or duty to offer assistance are in place for understanding the discretionary space a state has for valuing and refusing offers. If there is a right to offer assistance, there must also be those who can claim it and there must be duty bearers. The legal framework on humanitarian assistance does not seem to go this far, although there are exceptions within the frameworks provided by specific treaties. The Tampere Convention, for example, requires states to respond to requests directed to it.[71] Also, some treaties oblige parties 'to take action', like the 1999 Food Aid Convention. Yet it is probably safer to argue that offering assistance is based on moral convictions and charity, especially when acting outside the framework of a particular treaty. In most cases the discussion is not of particular practical importance, yet where not enough international assistance is available, the discussion becomes more significant.

In the situation of the Pakistan earthquake of 2005, not enough aid was available. The northern mountainous part of Pakistan was struck by an earthquake with a magnitude of 7.6 $M_w$ on 8 October 2005.[72] At least 86,000 people died as a result, 69,000 people were injured and around 4 million people were left homeless.[73] The northern part of Pakistan is logistically a difficult area to reach, but with damaged infrastructure due to the earthquake and with winter setting in, it was very difficult to come to the aid of the victims. While it was clear that the individual response of Pakistan could not be sufficient, it proved difficult to obtain enough international resources to address the situation. At a certain point, Kofi Annan made an appeal on the international community to give more donations, but at no point were states reminded of an obligation to offer.[74] When only a few offers are available to the

---

[70] See the discussion on a right to offer in Valencia-Ospina, 'Fourth Report' (n 3) paras 78-109 and ILC Memorandum (n 1) para 64. In the context of the ILC it is argued that a right to offer would implicitly exist in the absence of a specific prohibition to offering assistance. See for a more detailed discussion Dabiru S. Patnaik, 'Issues of State Consent and International Humanitarian Assistance in Disasters: The Work of the International Law Commission' in Andrej Zwitter *et al* (eds), *Humanitarian Action: Global, Regional and Domestic Legal Responses* (Cambridge University Press, Cambridge 2014) 113. A duty to offer assistance would be of particular importance if a right to receive assistance is recognized. As said, however, such a right is deemed not to exist in the context of this research.

[71] Article 4(3) Tampere Convention; example derived from the ILC Memorandum (n 1) para 61.

[72] US Geological Survey <http://earthquake.usgs.gov/earthquakes/eqinthenews/2005/usdyae/> accessed 4 July 2012.

[73] US Geological Survey <http://earthquake.usgs.gov/earthquakes/eqinthenews/2005/usdyae/#summary> accessed 4 July 2012.

[74] ——, 'Urging Greater Generosity: Annan Arrives in Pakistan for Quake Donor Conference', *UN News Centre* <http://www.un.org/apps/news/story.asp?/NewsID=16592&CR=Pakistan&CR1=quake#> cited by Saechao (n 40) 696. The appeal by Kofi Annan did not lead to fully satisfactory results: see ——, 'Pakistan: Forgotten 2005 Quake Victims Still Need Help' *IRIN* 18 August 2011.

affected state, the state has less room to refuse offers if its own capacity is insufficient and this stresses the importance of quality standards for offers of assistance.

Offers of assistance must meet the humanitarian principles of humanity, impartiality, neutrality, and independence. In the Red Cross' Guidelines from the International Disaster Response Laws-programme, this has been articulated as follows in Guideline 4:

> 2. Assisting actors should ensure that their disaster relief and initial recovery assistance is provided in accordance with the principles of humanity, neutrality and impartiality, and in particular: (...)
> c. It is provided without seeking to further a particular political or religious standpoint, intervene in the internal affairs of the affected state, or obtain commercial gain from charitable assistance;
> d. It is not used as a means to gather sensitive information of a political, economic or military nature that is irrelevant to disaster relief or initial recovery assistance.[75]

Not meeting such standards gives the affected state ground to refuse an offer of assistance. Although in approximately 25% of disaster situations aid is being refused to a certain extent, in some of these situations there is a legitimate ground to refuse assistance; not only because it is not needed, but also when the offer is not 'purely humanitarian'.[76] This leads to a new problem of determination: when can an offer be considered as purely humanitarian and when are there 'valid' grounds for refusing an offer?

To illustrate this issue, the case of hurricane Katrina can again be used. The US received various offers of assistance, a number of which were turned down. A shipment of ready-to-eat meals sent by the UK was not allowed to enter the US due to the ban on British beef. Offers of assistance by Cuba and Venezuela were refused because of the political relation between the US and these countries.[77] Iran offered oil in exchange for lifting the sanctions imposed on Iran.[78] For each offer the US had different reasons to refuse, but it is clear that some of the reasons are less controversial than others. The offer by Iran does not meet the humanitarian principles (being conditional to lifting sanctions), and does therefore not meet the international standards that exist on offering aid. Whether or not the US was rightfully refusing the other offers is already a more difficult question. The answer is further determined by other circumstances. Were there for example other relief items or offers available? If there already is plenty of food present or if there are alternative offers of food, refusing beef from a certain country is more easily acceptable.

---

[75] IDRL Guidelines (n 1) Guideline 4(2).
[76] The percentage of 25% is based on the research by Travis Nelson, 'Rejecting the Gift Horse: International Politics of Disaster Aid Refusal' (2010) 10 Conflict, Security and Development 379.
[77] Saechao (n 40) 693.
[78] Ibid, 693-4.

Taking the context of the affected state into account helps to determine whether a state can rightfully refuse certain offers. After the Indian Ocean tsunami of 2004, canned pork was offered to the population of Aceh, which is predominantly Muslim.[79] Indonesian customs officials recorded expired foodstuffs by the truckload.[80] In Thailand there were 'claims that some Christian charities were conditioning aid on religious conversion or participation in religious activities'.[81] After the Pakistan earthquake of 2005, clothes sent to survivors were mainly summer clothes, and survivors could do nothing but burn these clothes to stay warm. Similarly, powdered food items should not be sent to situations in which water is sparsely available. Offers which are clearly unsuitable clog the distribution of suitable items and states are generally excused for refusing such offers.

What becomes clear from these examples is that the legal framework grants the right to states to withhold consent to offers of assistance, and that in some cases a state makes use of this right for reasons that can be considered legitimate. However, there are no clear standards that decide which offers can be rightfully refused or not, apart from the 'arbitrariness-rule'. One argument that does follow from the analysis so far is that offers which meet the humanitarian principles should be accepted sooner than offers that are somehow tied. Even so, assistance that is purely humanitarian can also be unsuitable, giving legitimate ground for refusal. Arbitrariness therefore contains two components: the context in which the offer is made (political or tied) and the content of the offer. This will be more closely analysed in the next section on accepting assistance.

## 4 Accepting International Assistance: The Role of Consent

### 4.1 Introduction

After determining at what point and how international humanitarian assistance is initiated, the third step is the acceptance of assistance by giving consent. As this is a key-element in the distribution of international humanitarian assistance, a number of issues surrounding consent will be highlighted here. Giving consent to (offers of) international humanitarian aid means accepting that aid. Questions that arise relate to the situations in which consent should be given, the way (method) in which consent must be given, by whom it must be given and how fast it must be communicated. Linked to these questions are issues encountered in the practice of aid delivery, like giving blanket consent, delaying consent or not having the right authority to give consent.

[79] David Fisher, 'Fast Food: Regulating Emergency Food Aid in Sudden-Impact Disasters' (2007) 40 Vanderbilt Journal of Transnational Law 1127, 1137.
[80] Ibid.
[81] Fisher, 'Fast Food' (n 79) 1139.

## 4.2 General features of consent

According to the Special Rapporteur of the ILC, consent is 'the expression of the will of the sovereign who, thereby, permits activities on its territory that may otherwise constitute violations of the principle of non-intervention.'[82] Even though consent is as such crucial in the process of the delivery of humanitarian assistance, few instruments or documents provide any detail or rules on consent. Given the nature of consent, it can be argued that it is 'by definition (...) discretionary and may be withdrawn or be subjected to conditions'.[83] Yet it is practically nowhere explained in detail what the rules on giving, withdrawing and conditioning consent are.

What was already seen in the previous Chapter is that the freedom to give or withhold consent of states is limited. 'Restrictions on the right to refuse humanitarian assistance can be found in various legal regimes aimed at the protection of persons, such as international human rights law, the law concerning internally displaced persons and international humanitarian law.'[84] The restrictions found in the legal framework were not withholding consent arbitrarily; not withholding consent when the national capacity is overwhelmed; and not withholding consent when this would result in violation of a norm of international law. What also became clear in Chapter II – and also in the present Chapter – is that these restrictions do not seem concrete enough to be of use in practice. In this section, it will be analysed what the role is of consent in practice and which features it therefore must contain in order to construct more clarity on consent.

Given the role of consent to make activities on a state's territory permissible instead of constituting a violation of sovereignty and territorial integrity, consent must cover a number of issues. It must be clear which party (and which representatives of that party) receives the consent. It must also explain to which area(s) access is granted, for example only to the affected area, to designated areas around the affected area (as is for example the case in Blue Nile State in Sudan), or to the entire territory. Consent must also make clear during what time the consent remains valid. Humanitarian assistance offered after a disaster is a reaction to an extraordinary event, and must be temporary.[85] The nature of consent when it comes to disaster response is by definition temporary and must either be changed into development assistance or activities must be ended.

It is further possible to set conditions and restrictions to consent. One very important condition which is also recognized as a general precondition in many instruments is that the national authorities retain control over operations.[86] This may

---

[82] Valencia-Ospina, 'Fourth Report' (n 3) para 52.
[83] ILC Memorandum (n 1) para 65.
[84] Valencia-Ospina, 'Fourth Report' (n 3) para 58.
[85] Fisher, 'Desk Study' (n 5) 89.
[86] ILC Memorandum (n 1) para 67ff.

lead to difficult situations, especially when the authority in control is controversial, as was the case during the drought in Southern Somalia.

Despite many warnings issued months before severe problems existed, the drought in the Horn of Africa caused a famine when it reached its peak in 2011.[87] As a result of the drought and subsequent famine, between 50,000 and 100,000 people in the Horn of Africa lost their lives.[88] The region that was hit hardest was Southern Somalia, also being the region where many other problems already existed. By July 2011, according to the UN, tens of thousands died as a consequence of the drought in South Somalia. The UN declared the existence of a famine in two South Somali regions.[89] As already explained, most parts of South Somalia were at the time under control of Al-Shabab, and not of the official government of Somalia. This group was very reluctant to allow international assistance into the affected regions, causing delays in the delivery of aid.[90] In response to the attitude of Al-Shabab, the UN tried to reach parts of the affected population through an airlift.[91] Towards the end of July 2011, Al-Shabab started to grant access to some aid agencies, supporting the few agencies already working in the hardest hit areas.[92] According to Al-Shabab, the situation was not as bad as was being reported.[93] Even so, the humanitarian emergency proved incredibly difficult to address. When Al-Shabab started to allow some aid into the affected regions, it prevented victims at the same time to flee towards regions where aid could be obtained.[94] On top of this, fighting between Al-Shabab and troops of the Somali government and the African Union Mission AMISOM continued throughout the drought.[95] By August 2011,

[87] According to a report by Oxfam and Save the Children ('A Dangerous Delay: The Cost of Late Response to Early Warnings in the 2011 Drought in the Horn of Africa' of 18 January 2012) it was clear that a crisis was going to occur months before the actual outbreak of famine. Despite these warnings, many organisations started their work when the rains stayed out for the second year. This was not only too late, the response was insufficient. ——, 'Oxfam: Voorbode Hongersnood Steevast Genegeerd' *De Volkskrant* 18 January 2012.

[88] Ibid.

[89] ——, 'VN: Tienduizenden Doden Zuid-Somalië' *NOS* 20 July 2011. The regions in which a famine was declared are Bakool and Lower Shabelle. ——, 'Somalia: Aid Agencies Gain Access to Al-Shabab Areas' *IRIN* 26 July 2011.

[90] Already two years before the peak of the drought Al-Shabab was prohibiting aid workers to enter the regions under control of Al-Shabab. ——, 'VN Komt met Luchtbrug naar Noodlijdend Somalië' *De Volkskrant* 26 July 2011.

[91] With the airlift, the UN was hoping to reach 175,000 out of the 2.2 million people still in need of assistance. Ibid.

[92] The organisations Kuwait Direct Aid and the Red Cross and Red Crescent were working in Lower Shabelle since May 2011. ——, 'Somalia: Aid Agencies Gain Access to Al-Shabab Areas' *IRIN* 26 July 2011.

[93] Ibid.

[94] ——, 'Al-Shabaab Houdt Somali's Op Weg Naar Voedsel Vast' *De Volkskrant* 2 August 2011.

[95] Although the problems of the drought to which Al-Shabab was unable to respond made the position of Al-Shabab weaker. ——, 'Somalia: Al-Shabab Pullout – The Beginning of the End?' *IRIN* 9 August 2011.

famine was declared for five Somali regions and although more aid agencies were by that time operating in these regions, the response remained insufficient due to the difficult circumstances.[96] This situation continued to exist during the following months. In October 2011, the conflict with Kenya flared up and Al-Shabab banned sixteen aid agencies, among which many UN agencies, by November 2011.[97] Further escalation took place until one of the final aid agencies which still had access to South Somalia, the ICRC, suspended its aid deliveries because of the blocks of aid by Al-Shabab.[98] Al-Shabab wished to control the aid operations, which was unacceptable to many organisations working on the ground. Humanitarian organisations aim to operate based on the humanitarian principles, and independence and neutrality do not seem to stroke with the condition of control over the operations by national 'authorities'. As a result, these organisations were denied access.

### 4.3 Practical issues relating to consent

Not only is consent of essential importance for starting international operations in an affected state, it also has the function to lay down the terms for such an operation. During operations, those working in the affected state must comply with national and international law.[99] This is acknowledged in many legal or soft-law documents and is often included separately in agreements. Additionally, many practical conditions can be included in the consent given by the affected state. Examples are quantitative restrictions (like the proportionality requirement of the IDRL Guidelines);[100] that aid is delivered without distinction or discrimination;[101] that aid is delivered by competent and adequately trained, experienced and equipped personnel;[102] that there is sufficient cooperation and coordination with local authorities; that assistance is not used for other purposes than relief; and to provide only necessary goods and not inappropriate goods. Apart from this, agreements may contain rules on immunities, liabilities and settlement of disputes.[103] In the following, a number of common practical issues will be addressed, including blanket consent, delayed consent, not having or knowing the right authority to give consent, and the situation in which consent is being withheld for valid reasons.

---

[96] ——, 'Somalia: Coordinate Aid and Build for Long Term, Agencies Urged' *IRIN* 16 August 2011.
[97] ——, 'Al-Shabaab Dreigt Kenia Met Invasie' *De Volkskrant* 17 October 2011; ——, 'Somalia: Al-Shabab Ban on Agencies Threatens Aid' *IRIN* 28 November 2011.
[98] ——, 'Somalia: ICRC Suspends Aid Deliveries' *IRIN* 12 January 2012.
[99] ILC Memorandum (n 1) para 69ff.
[100] Ibid, para 76; IDRL Guidelines (n 1) art. 4(2)(a).
[101] ILC Memorandum (n 1) para 76.
[102] Ibid.
[103] Ibid, para 77.

*4.3.1 Blanket consent*

In principle, consent is given in response to an offer of assistance (which did or did not follow a request). As seen, the consent is not merely a 'yes' but usually indicates the conditions and terms under which the consent is given. A request for assistance can therefore not be considered as giving consent: it does not contain the necessary details for the operation. Moreover, the affected state must receive the room to value the offers given in reaction to the request to determine whether the offer is acceptable. Giving consent is an additional subsequent act by the affected state. It can be imagined that it is quite a task to keep track of offers, to consent or not to these offers, and to set terms and conditions. If the affected state made a needs-assessment and requested assistance accordingly, it can more easily determine which assistance is needed and which can be refused. In some cases, the affected state is not able (or willing) to make specific requests based on a needs-assessment or does not have the capacity to respond to each individual offer of assistance. A state could then make a statement that it 'welcomes assistance' or 'welcomes offers of assistance'. It can be questioned whether such a remark can be considered as a form of 'blanket consent' or 'advance consent'.

Giving 'blanket consent' to unspecified offers of assistance can be considered as a 'practical device' in difficult situations and on this basis seems to gain support.[104] It remains however questionable whether such a general remark can be considered to contain the legal content of actually allowing foreign entities on a state's territory without that entity violating norms of state sovereignty and territorial integrity. According to the ILC,

> Such a practice reveals the fact that, while the offer and request dynamic is the traditional approach, as a matter of treaty law and the practice of humanitarian agencies, other considerations may intercede in particular cases allowing for the lawful circumvention of the established mode for determining consent.[105]

The ILC does not exclude the legal option of giving blanket consent instead of concrete or targeted consent. Nonetheless, in more practical terms, in such cases the affected state is not concrete about its needs and the lack of details may hamper relief operations.[106] It does not solve the problem that the affected state still needs to decide which items are needed and which items need to be refused.[107] If a state does not do this, an excess of relief goods can clog distribution channels and consequently hamper relief operations.

If a state is not able or willing to make a needs-assessment and to give consent accordingly, a solution would be to call in the assistance of specialized agencies like the IFRC or OCHA. When Haiti was struck by the earthquake in 2010, the

[104] Fisher, 'Desk Study' (n 5) 91.
[105] ILC Memorandum (n 1) para 58.
[106] Fisher, 'Desk Study' (n 5) 91.
[107] ILC Memorandum (n 1) para 58.

government was assisted by OCHA (and the US) in coordinating relief, although President Préval later claimed that he was bypassed.[108] Haiti's governmental structure was so weak that Haiti could possibly be considered a failed state.[109] Yet even failed states are sovereign states and consent of the national authorities is required. Making use of organisations like OCHA helps to make targeted requests and to give consent to assistance which is actually needed, but such organisations or other states cannot give consent in the affected state's stead.[110]

The related phenomenon of having obtained consent to start general operations prior to a disaster and using that consent to target operation in response of a disaster will be discussed here in short. Some NGOs or organisations already have activities within a certain state, like the national Red Cross or Red Crescent Societies in most states. When a disaster occurs, assistance can be given by the IFRC through these national societies, in principle without further consent of the state. This system is based on rules in Statutes of the Movement and Principles and Rules of Red Cross and Red Crescent Disaster Relief to which states have unanimously agreed. There can be other NGOs and humanitarian organisations already operating within a state and which can combine efforts with others to bring assistance into that state. Whether or not consent is required separately for these operations is not entirely certain; it is assumed that the state should have the opportunity to consent to these additional operations (which indirectly also occurs through custom regulations).[111]

#### *4.3.2 Underhandedly refusing assistance and delayed consent*

It has already been explained in the foregoing that the speed with which humanitarian assistance is delivered after a disaster is essential. Affected states should therefore not delay their decision on giving consent too long. According to the Special Rapporteur of the ILC, 'the time to decide on an offer of humanitarian assistance cannot be extended unjustifiably. The expediency with which relief is provided is crucial. It is in the interest of all parties involved to know as soon as possible what the affected State decides regarding the external assistance or the offer thereof.'[112]

The rapid developments in means of transportation and communication techniques make that many responders are usually ready to act; sovereignty might then become a 'bottleneck' for aid, which must not necessarily be seen as a negative

---

[108] Prompting the Ecuadorian President Correa to comment on 'imperialism among the donors'; Hans-Joachim Heintze, 'Humanitarian Assistance and Failed States: Still an Issue of Sovereignty? The Case Study of Haiti' in Andrej Zwitter *et al* (eds), *Humanitarian Action: Global, Regional and Domestic Legal Responses* (Cambridge University Press, Cambridge 2014) 438.

[109] Heintze (n 108) 426. Following Heintze's arguments, the fact that Haiti is a failed state means that it forms a threat to the peace and security within the region. For years, an ongoing UN mission has been present on the territory but an interesting point in the context of this research is whether the mandate of such a mission could be used in case the 'host' state refuses aid.

[110] As argued by Fisher, 'Desk Study' (n 5) 91.

[111] See ibid, 92; Heintze (n 108) 438.

[112] Valencia-Ospina, 'Fourth Report' (n 3) para 75.

effect because in this way it can be prevented that too much aid flows in.[113] Yet, having to wait for consent means that the providing-side has to wait for something to happen, and this can be abused by the accepting-side.[114] The problems resulting from delays in giving consent became visible in the context of the Indian Ocean tsunami. Because of the scale of the disaster, many international actors responded in bringing relief and this massive response laid some problems bare. Due to delays in accepting relief goods, 'perishable items rotted, medicines expired, and emergency relief items like clothes, tents, blankets and surgical equipment, which were essential at the start of the relief effort, were redundant by the time they were cleared months later'.[115] Indonesia, for example, claimed to accept aid, but a year after the tsunami much relief goods were still not cleared to enter Indonesia: 'an estimated 217 containers of tsunami relief aid were reportedly still with customs authorities in Tanjung Priok Port outside Jakarta and a further 232 containers and 58 vehicles were in a similar predicament in Belawan Port, Medan'.[116]

Delays in consent can be manifested through all kinds of practical barriers (like tax and import requirements). In Eritrea, for example, 'hundreds of tonnes of UN food aid was held up as a result of governance tax demands and were not released to drought victims for over a month'.[117] In the context of Hurricane Katrina, import barriers formed the delay: 'nearly 400,000 'meals ready to eat' flown to Little Rock by the UK in response to Hurricane Katrina were quarantined in a warehouse because they contained British beef, banned by American health regulations'.[118] These delays can in part be solved by implementing the IDRL Guidelines, making national legal systems ready for accepting international assistance when necessary. Still, not all states are willing to remove barriers for all situations, especially when considering that not all international actors provide the same quality as such 'suggesting that the issue of initiation, access, and facilitation are in fact inextricably linked to the quality and accountability of humanitarian assistance'.[119]

---

[113] David P. Fidler, 'Disaster Relief and Governance after the Indian Ocean Tsunami: What Role for International Law?' (2005) 6 Melbourne Journal of International Law 458, 471.

[114] Bannon, 'International Disaster Response Law' (n 45) 850.

[115] Victoria Bannon *et al.*, 'Legal Issues from the International Response to the Tsunami in Indonesia' (IFRC, Geneva 2007) 22 cited by Bannon, 'International Disaster Response Law' (n 45) 850; Victoria Bannon & David Fisher, 'Legal Lessons in Disaster Relief from the Tsunami, the Pakistan Earthquake and Hurricane Katrina' (2006) 10 ASIL Insight [6] at fn 2.

[116] Bannon & Fisher (n 115).

[117] ——, 'Food Aid Held for Taxes to be Released Says Government Official' *IRIN* 16 August 2005 cited by Bannon, 'International Disaster Response Law' (n 45) 850.

[118] Cecil Connolly, 'Katrina Food Aid Blocked by U.S. Rules' *Washington Post* 14 October 2005 cited by Bannon & Fisher (n 115) at fn 4.

[119] Fisher, 'Desk Study' (n 5) 133 cited by Bannon, 'International Disaster Response Law' (n 45) 852.

*4.3.3 No authority to give consent*

It was already pointed out in the foregoing that there is not always an authority present that is capable to give its consent. One example addressed above is that of South Somalia when the drought hit its peak in 2011, but already during the humanitarian crisis of 1992 and 1993 this was a problem. At this time, '(c)ivil order there had collapsed to such a degree that there was no government in place to either grant or deny consent'.[120] Another example already mentioned is that of Haiti. After the earthquake of 2010, the government's capacity to respond and coordinate was limited and making a needs-assessment took time. In these situations, it may be wondered how long the UN and international community have to await consent from a state unable to respond.[121] A partial solution can be found in making use of the assistance from organisations like OCHA and the IFRC, and the UN Emergency Relief Coordinator has been given the task of negotiating humanitarian access.[122] However, tensions remain between time consuming negotiations and immediate needs of disaster survivors and especially when there is a lack of authority the question remains whether and how long international actors must await consent.

*4.3.4 Not giving consent for valid reasons*

Refusal of aid (not giving consent to assistance) can occur based on valid reasons. Such reasons are for example the necessity of goods, quality of aid or of those providing it, motives with which aid is provided, and political ties between the offering state and accepting state. If a state made a needs-assessment, it can clearly indicate what items it needs and refuse those items which are not required. Also, some goods are not necessary in certain situations, like the summer clothes delivered to survivors of the 2005 Pakistan earthquake or pork delivered in Muslim populations.[123] It also happens that aid providers do not meet certain quality standards and are in need of assistance themselves, or provide poor-quality aid, for example demand religious conversion in exchange for assistance.[124] The standards of the humanitarian principles help in determining whether humanitarian assistance and actors are providing sufficient quality or whether a state has a valid reason to refuse.[125] When assistance meets the humanitarian principles, there is also less chance that the offer is a form of 'tied aid' or in another way conditional. It is generally recognized that

[120] George Kent, 'Disasters and 'Responsibility to Protect': Should Nations Force Aid on Others? Rights and Obligations' (2010) 34 Natural Hazards Observer [3] 19.

[121] Linda A. Malone, 'The Responsibility to Protect Haiti' (2010) 14 ASIL Insights [7], 3.

[122] Bannon, 'International Disaster Response Law' (n 45) 848.

[123] Bannon & Fisher (n 115).

[124] Ibid.

[125] As also explicitly included in the Draft Articles on the Protection of Persons in the Event of Disasters, ILC Drafting Committee 'Protection of Persons in the Event of Disasters: Text and titles of draft articles 6, 7, 8, and 9 provisionally adopted by the Drafting Committee' (UN Doc. A/CN.4/L.776 of 14 July 2010), draft article 6.

> Humanitarian assistance could be a way of achieving other foreign policy or national security objectives. The prospect that assistance could be a cover for ulterior, power-political objectives highlighted the importance for the victim state to retain sovereign control over whether and how such assistance would be accepted.[126]

Nevertheless, the difficulty remains to determine when a state is 'rightfully' refusing an offer of assistance and when the withholding of consent is arbitrary. This difficulty is not helped by the lack of clear legal definition of 'arbitrariness' apart from the indications that 'valid' reasons are required, not 'capricious ones' and that offers meeting the humanitarian principles should be sooner accepted than offers that are not meeting these principles. In practice, no solution can be found to determine which reasons are valid.

### 4.4 Conclusion

What follows from practice is that consent is indeed awaited before international assistance is delivered and that there is clearly room for affected states to withhold their consent to international humanitarian assistance. Given the importance of consent for the terms and conditions of humanitarian operations, the requirement of consent is a valuable practical feature yet which can at the same time stand in the way of essential relief operations. What has become clear is that especially when offers do not meet the humanitarian principles (humanity, neutrality, impartiality and independence), the affected state has a valid reason for refusing to give consent. On the other hand, the limits of the state's freedom to withhold consent cannot be clearly or explicitly found in practice. Although the reasons for withholding consent are in some cases valid, it is not clear what 'arbitrary' reasons are and there is no reference to the violation of any rules of international (human rights) law by not giving consent. In some situations however the refusal to give consent is not accepted by international actors. In these – rather rare – cases, discussions take place on ways to move forward without obtaining consent of the affected state. In section 6 below such situations will be addressed in more detail. First, to complete the cycle, the provision of assistance and termination of operations will be discussed.

## 5 Provision of Assistance and Termination of Operations

The issues relating to the actual provision of international assistance are less relevant for this research than the questions surrounding requests, offers, and acceptance, since at the stage of provision the affected state already accepted aid. Nonetheless, problems arising when aid is being provided by international actors could cause reluctance to accept international assistance in the first place and help to gain insight in affected states' decisions to refuse. Therefore, provision of aid and

[126] Fidler (n 113) 461.

termination of operations will be discussed in short. First, it must be noted that as is the case with offering aid, it is very doubtful whether a duty to provide aid exists.[127] Only in specific agreements, like bilateral agreements on disaster response, it is possible to find somewhat obligatory language encouraging states to provide assistance when requested to do so.[128] International organisations specifically mandated to respond in emergencies have different types of obligations, as the requirement to respond forms part of the organisations' constitution.[129]

In their operations, those supplying humanitarian assistance must adhere to the humanitarian principles and other standards as laid down in various instruments. When not complying, the assistance can even be counterproductive and can make it more difficult in the future to obtain consent for operations. When Indonesia for example decided to grant access to the usually closed area of Aceh, many aid organisations started working there, not always keeping to agreements on coordination. The organisation *Médecins du Monde* arrived at a village near Banda Aceh and 'found that an unknown NGO had vaccinated some of the children there leaving no records and no sure way to determine who had and had not already been served'.[130] Often the content of the consent given in terms of conditions already tries to prevent such situations. In addition, national laws may contain requirements and restrictions for relief providers. Personnel may require visa, certain diplomas or certificates of, for example, doctors must be recognized in the national system, relief organisations may need to be registered in the affected state, etcetera. These special requirements are addressed in the IFRC IDRL Guidelines in order to make the provision of relief more effective.[131]

The phase in which humanitarian assistance is provided is always temporary and must be followed by a state of 'normality' or must be transferred into a development assistance-operation. For those delivering assistance, this means that '(a)t a certain point, international disaster responders must either go home or the nature of their status must change (or revert) to that of a development actor. The management of this transition is not always as smooth as might be hoped'.[132] In some cases, the affected state sets a date by which the humanitarian assistance mandate expires. In other cases, aid agencies terminate their own operations, for example when funds are depleted. Some do this without any coordination or consultation.

Upon the change of nature of operations, some practical issues arise. Where emergency relief can be based on less strict visa and tax requirements, the recovery

---

[127] ILC Memorandum (n 1) para 61.

[128] See the examples provided by the ILC, ILC Memorandum (n 1) paras 61 and 62.

[129] For example the International Atomic Energy Agency which 'shall respond (...) to a (...) request for assistance in the event of a nuclear accident or radiological emergency'; ILC Memorandum (n 1) para 63.

[130] Bannon & Fisher (n 115).

[131] IDRL Guidelines (n 1) Part V on Legal Facilities for Entry and Operations.

[132] Fisher, 'Desk Study' (n 5) 89.

or development assistance may again be bound by 'normal' requirements to which workers must adapt. The transition from one phase to another is not always easy to make.

## 6 INTERNATIONAL HUMANITARIAN ASSISTANCE WITHOUT CONSENT

### 6.1 Introduction

The rule that consent is required before international assistance can be delivered to an affected state leads to complicated situations in practice. It is not only possible that a state takes a long time to give its consent, there are also situations in which a state chooses not to give consent or where consent cannot be obtained because there is no right authority to give it. Since the affected state has the principal responsibility to respond to a disaster, there is no problem with refusing to give consent as long as the individual response is adequate and sufficient. However, when the affected state's 'individual response is inadequate for whatever reason and, as a consequence, the duty falls upon a state to seek international assistance, the failure to obtain consent becomes a problem. Especially in large-scale humanitarian emergencies with much media attention, the international community wonders whether consent should be awaited or whether it should undertake action without consent.

In one disaster in particular it was extensively debated whether humanitarian assistance should be forced upon the affected state. The state in question, Myanmar, did not respond effectively after cyclone Nargis hit the country in 2008. However, the military regime of Myanmar also refused to give its consent to offers of foreign assistance. In response, the international community started to debate whether an intervention in the framework of the Responsibility to Protect (RtoP) should be undertaken here. This debate is essential for understanding the difficulties that still exist when a state refuses to accept aid in the aftermath of a natural disaster and will therefore be rather extensively discussed in section 6.2. As will become clear, there is no genuine solution for situations in which a state is uncooperative while a humanitarian emergency is occurring on its territory. The gaps that persist will be analysed in section 6.3.

### 6.2 Action when consent cannot be obtained

#### *6.2.1 Introduction*

Myanmar knows a history of single party politics, suppression and has generally a poor reputation when it comes to human rights.[133] In 2003 the leading military

[133] See for an overview of Myanmar's history Paulo Sérgio Pinheiro & Meghan Barron, 'Burma (Myanmar)' in Jared Genser & Irwin Cotler, *The Responsibility to Protect: The Promise of Stopping Mass Atrocities in Our Time* (Oxford University Press, Oxford 2012) 260-263. In this

powers presented a 'roadmap to democracy', according to which a constitution was to be drafted and a referendum was to be held to approve a new constitution. This referendum was scheduled for 10 May 2008.[134] However, on 8 May 2008 a devastating cyclone hit Myanmar, killing 138,366 people and affecting almost 2.5 million people.[135]

Cyclone Nargis made landfall in the Irrawaddy Delta causing devastation with strong winds and floods, wiping away entire villages.[136] Even though the government of Myanmar was aware of the approaching cyclone, it did not warn its people, nor did it respond in the immediate aftermath by providing food, water and shelter.[137] Moreover, the military regime did initially not accept any foreign assistance and it was further delaying the provision of aid:

> Humanitarian organizations that were already present in the country were able to get small numbers of aid workers into the region but reported tightening restrictions, while other NGOs, UN agencies and states that offered assistance were hindered by slow visa approvals as the junta rejected offers of aid personnel and insisted on distributing the aid itself.[138]

The regime did not, however, do a good job doing this. In distributing the little aid that they did, the military discriminated against ethnic and religious minority Karen, it forcibly displaced refugees from camps to military shelters and even to the devastated villages, without means for reconstruction. The military also used survivors, including children as forced labour for reconstruction.[139]

According to OCHA and Oxfam, ten days after Nargis struck only a quarter of the required aid was being allowed into the country.[140] Even when after long waiting times permission was granted to enter the country, access was not granted

---

research, the country is referred to as Myanmar, not Burma. There is no particular intention behind this choice.

[134] Alex J. Bellamy, 'Disasters and 'Responsibility to Protect': Should Nations Force Aid on Others? A Cyclone is Not Enough' (2010) 34 Natural Hazards Observer [3] 1, 9. The scheduled referendum has played a major role in the debate on Myanmar's decision to refuse humanitarian assistance after cyclone Nargis hit. It was claimed that the government was afraid that interference from outside would affect the outcome of the referendum and influence the elections planned for 2010. Also, the government was criticised for proceeding with the referendum (although in the hardest-hit areas the voting was postponed until 24 May) while so many people died or were not in a position or mind-set to vote.

[135] EM-DAT <http://www.emdat.be/> accessed 16 July 2012.

[136] Johns Hopkins Bloomberg School of Public Health Center for Public Health and Human Rights, 'After the Storm: Voices from the Delta' (2nd ed., 2009) ('After the Storm') 24-26.

[137] Pinheiro & Barron (n 133) 266.

[138] Mely Caballero-Anthony & Belinda Chng, 'Cyclones and Humanitarian Crises: Pushing the Limits of R2P in Southeast Asia' (2009) 1 Global Responsibility to Protect 135, 139 referring to ——, 'World Fears for Plight of Myanmar Cyclone Victims', *New York Times* 13 May 2008.

[139] Pinheiro & Barron (n 133) 267; 'After the Storm' (n 136) 40-7.

[140] Bellamy (n 134) 9.

to the hardest-hit areas.[141] Moreover, aid which was being distributed was at a large scale limited and confiscated by government representatives, and some relief workers were obstructed and arrested. Information was being distorted, collecting data was forbidden, and coordination between groups as such became impossible.[142]

The question raised on the international level was whether the actions of Myanmar's government constitute a situation in which the international community should intervene according the framework of the concept of RtoP.[143] The surviving disaster victims 'faced severe threats to life as a result of injury, hunger, and diseases, among other things'[144] and the military regime did not come to the aid of these victims and was moreover 'refusing the entry of humanitarian assistance during the crucial period when relief was most needed resulting in a humanitarian crisis of massive proportions'.[145]

As explained in Chapter II, the concept of RtoP departs from the idea that a state is responsible for the well-being of its population. If the state fails to protect its people, the responsibility is transferred to the wider international community:

> It is foremost the responsibility of the Government of Myanmar to address the problem of gross and systematic human-rights violations by all parties, and to end impunity (...). If the Government fails to assume this responsibility, then the responsibility falls to the international community.[146]

It has also been explained above that RtoP can be invoked when gross human rights violations amount to one of four predetermined crimes: genocide, ethnic cleansing, war crimes, and crimes against humanity. Some argue that 'the refusal to allow humanitarian assistance where it was most needed and neglecting the plight of helpless victims whose lives were threatened essentially constituted a crime against humanity'.[147]

The proponents of invocation of RtoP were mostly European and North American government representatives, former government officials and analysts.[148] Strong proponents of invoking RtoP were Bernard Kouchner (at that time French Minister of Foreign Affairs) and Javier Solana (EU High Representative for the

---

[141] Pinheiro & Barron (n 133) 266-7 referring to Emergency Assistance Team (Burma) and 'After the Storm' (n 136).

[142] Pinheiro & Barron (n 133) 267; 'After the Storm' (n 136) 29ff.

[143] The concept of the Responsibility to Protect is discussed in section 4.3 of Chapter II.

[144] Caballero-Anthony & Chng (n 138) 136.

[145] Ibid, 137. For the discussion, Caballero-Anthony and Chng refer to Peter McKenna, 'Should the World Force Aid on Burma?' *Centre for International Governance Initiative* 15 May 2008 and Ivo Daalder & Paul Stares, 'The UN's Responsibility to Protect' *International Herald Tribune* 13 May 2008.

[146] Tomás Ojea Quintana, 'Report of the Special Rapporteur on the Situation of Human Rights in Myanmar' (UN Doc. A/65/368 of 15 September 2010) paras. 67-68, cited by Pinheiro & Barron (n 133) 276.

[147] Caballero-Anthony & Chng (n 138) 137.

[148] Ibid, 140.

Common Foreign and Security Policy). Also Lloyd Axworthy (Canadian Minister of Foreign Affairs) supported the use of RtoP based on the argument that 'there is no difference between an innocent person being killed by machete or (…) dying in a cholera pandemic that could be avoided by proper international responses'.[149] The goal of RtoP would then be to deliver aid 'without the consent of the Myanmar government'.[150] It was also discussed whether undertaking action in the RtoP framework would mean the possibility to bypass the UN Security Council, referring to the humanitarian action undertaken in 1991 by the UK, France and the US to protect Kurds from Iraq and the action of NATO taken in Kosovo in 1999, both without Security Council permission.[151]

In the discussion on whether RtoP could and should be invoked in the situation of Myanmar, three different questions are generally mixed up. In the first place, it is debated whether a situation such as Myanmar (i.e. a situation where the population suffers hardship as a result of actions or omissions by the government after a natural disaster) could constitute one of the four crimes falling under RtoP. In this discussion a second question is often raised as an answer to the first question, namely whether RtoP can be used in disaster situations at all. Finally, a third question often included in answering the first two, is whether an intervention to bring international assistance into a state is actually meaningful. It is striking to see that many confused these three different issues, like for example Kouchner did: '(i)nstead of cogently linking the Burmese military regime's refusal to accept aid to one of the enumerated crimes that triggers the application of RtoP, Kouchner instead equated RtoP to the right to intervene to provide humanitarian assistance'.[152] Each of the three questions will be discussed separately below.

### *6.2.2 Poor disaster response as a crime against humanity*

According to the World Summit Outcome of 2005, one of four crimes (i.e. genocide, ethnic cleansing, war crimes and crimes against humanity) must occur before RtoP can be invoked.[153] Although the military junta knows a history of discriminatory treatment of the many ethnic groups living in Myanmar,[154] it cannot be said that the actions and omissions of the junta were targeted against one specific group with an aim to destroy that group. The refusal of aid and lack of response did therefore not

---

149 ——, *Edmonton Journal* 4 June 2008 cited by Caballero-Anthony & Chng (n 138) 140.

150 Bellamy (n 134) 9.

151 Ibid, 9-10 referring to Andrew O'Neil, 'Kosovo Aid the Model' (Your Say blog, The Australian, 14 May 2008).

152 Pinheiro & Barron (n 133) 268-9.

153 UNGA, '2005 World Summit Outcome' (UN Doc. A/Res/60/1 of 16 September 2005), paras 138 and 139.

154 The largest ethnic group is represented by the military government, the Burman. Other major ethnic groups, of which the majority has over time taken up arms against the government and each other, are the Karen, Kachin, Karenni, Chin, Mon, Rhakine, Shan, Wa and Rohingya. ——, 'Briefing: Myanmar's Ethnic Problems' *IRIN* 29 March 2012 <http://www.irinnews.org/report/95195/briefing-myanmar-s-ethnic-problems> accessed 6 January 2015.

constitute genocide (i.e. having the intention of destroying a national, ethnic, racial or religious group)[155] or ethnic cleansing (i.e. without special intent to destroy a group but still targeting to forcibly remove a group).[156] Moreover, even though the country was not free from violence and aggression at the time of the cyclone, it would go too far to speak of an armed conflict, as such excluding war crimes.[157] The discussion therefore focused on the question whether the refusal of aid and lack of individual response could constitute a crime against humanity.

The Rome Statute of the International Criminal Court (Rome Statute) provides a definition of 'crime against humanity'. This definition is used here as it is 'generally regarded as crystallizing, for the most part, notions that already existed in customary international law'.[158] According to article 7 of the Rome Statute, a crime against humanity is a certain act (or omission) 'committed as part of a widespread or systematic attack directed against any civilian population, with knowledge of the attack'.[159] A number of 'acts' are described in article 7, including murder, extermination, enslavement, and also the category 'other inhumane acts of a similar character intentionally causing great suffering or serious injury to body or to mental or physical health'.[160] The phrase 'attack against any civilian population' refers to a 'course of conduct involving the multiple commission of acts referred to in paragraph 1 against any civilian population, pursuant to or in furtherance of a State or organizational policy to commit such attack'.[161] In other words, for a crime against humanity to exist there must be an act (or omission) which falls under one of the categories of crimes against humanity, which was part of a widespread or systematic attack and of which there was knowledge (subjective element of the crime).[162]

---

[155] International Criminal Court, 'Elements of Crimes' (ICC 2011) 2.

[156] Robert Cryer *et al*, *An Introduction to International Criminal Law and Procedure* (Cambridge University Press, Cambridge 2009) 165, 175. The question whether or not ethnic cleansing falls under the concept of genocide is not addressed here. Compare the cases of ICTY *Karadzic and Mladic* (ICTY T. Ch. I 11.7.1996) arguing that ethnic cleansing can be seen as genocide and the Jerusalem District Court case *A-G of Israel v. Eichmann* (1968) where the opposite is argued.

[157] This opinion is not shared by all. For example Pinheiro and Barron are of the opinion that an internal armed conflict existed (or perhaps still exists) in Myanmar and they therefore do not exclude the possible existence of war crimes. Pinheiro & Barron (n 133) 272.

[158] Anthony Cassese, *International Criminal Law* (2003) 74 cited by Rebecca Barber, 'The Responsibility to Protect the Survivors of Natural Disaster: Cyclone Nargis, a Case Study' (2009) 14 Journal of Conflict & Security Law 3, 18.

[159] Article 7(1) Rome Statute.

[160] The other acts are: murder, extermination, enslavement, deportation or forcible transfer of population, imprisonment or other severe deprivation of physical liberty, torture, rape or other forms of sexual violence, persecution against a group, enforced disappearances, and apartheid.

[161] Article 7(2) under (a) Rome Statute.

[162] Barber, 'The Responsibility to Protect' (n 158) 19. Apart from 'an act', there can also be an omission. See Article 15 of the Draft Articles on Responsibility of States for Internationally Wrongful Acts and ICTY *Mrksic* (IT-95-13/1-T) 'Vukovar Hospital' (27 September 2007) para 553ff where it is recognized that a crime can be committed through an omission

Before a crime against humanity can exist, it must be established that the 'act' is severe enough. Therefore, 'the conduct must be comparable in nature and gravity to the broad categories of crimes listed in Article 5, and must compare also – in nature and gravity – to the crimes already specified in Article 7'.[163] Subsequently, if an act is severe enough to constitute an 'other inhumane act', it must still be part of a widespread or systematic attack directed against a civilian population. In the ICTR-case *Prosecutor v. Akayesu,* 'widespread' is defined as 'massive, frequent, large-scale action, carried out collectively and with considerable seriousness and directed against a multiplicity of victims'.[164] In the same case, 'systematic' is described as meaning 'thoroughly organised and following a regular pattern on the basis of a common policy involving substantial public or private resources'.[165] As such,

> It is required that a single crime be an instance of a repetition of similar crimes or be part of a string of such crimes (widespread practice), or that it be the manifestation of a policy or a plan drawn up, or inspired by, State authorities or by the leading officials of a de facto state-like organization, or of an organised political group (systematic practice).[166]

Pinheiro and Barron define 'widespread' as 'a large-scale attack with numerous victims' and 'systematic' as 'highly organized, often as part of a pattern or methodical plan'.[167]

Finally, there must be knowledge of the attack; 'there must be an intention to bring about a certain result; that the perpetrator must be aware of the risk that his action might bring about serious consequences for the victims; and that the perpetrator must be cognisant of the link between his misconduct and a policy or systematic practice'.[168]

In theory, based on these elements, it would be possible to determine if the inadequate response and the refusal of international aid by the military junta after cyclone Nargis is in fact a crime against humanity. However, when applying these elements on the case of Myanmar, it becomes clear that a conclusion cannot be easily drawn. The last element is perhaps the clearest requirement in this particular case. The regime could not but have known about the consequences of the disaster, must have been aware of the lack of food, water, shelter and access to healthcare, and must have known that not responding would make the situation worse. Whether not responding to the disaster can be considered an 'act' or in this case rather 'omission' severe enough to constitute an 'other inhuman act' and whether the 'act' was part of a widespread or systematic attack remains, however, debatable. Some

[163] Barber, 'The Responsibility to Protect' (n 158) 20.
[164] ICTR *Prosecutor v. Akayesu* (Trial Chamber) Case No ICTR 96-4-T (2 September 1998) (Judgement) cited by Barber, 'The Responsibility to Protect' (n 158) 22.
[165] Ibid.
[166] Cassese (n 158) 64 cited by Barber, 'The Responsibility to Protect' (n 158) 23.
[167] Pinheiro & Barron (n 133) 271.
[168] Cassese (n 158) 82 cited by Barber, 'The Responsibility to Protect' (n 158) 24.

see the lack of response after Nargis in the light of other problems in Myanmar: 'the Burmese military regime has a long history of perpetrating, and continues to perpetrate, severe, widespread, and systematic human rights abuses against its people'.[169] It is, in this line of thought, argued that '(t)hese atrocities (...) in some cases rise to the level of both crimes against humanity and war crimes under the Rome Statute'.[170] Crimes committed by the military regime which can be taken into the equation are the forcible transfer of population, mainly focussing on 3,600 villages which were destroyed between 1996 and 2007,[171] murder and torture,[172] rape and sexual violence,[173] and the detention of political prisoners.[174] If the flawed disaster response can indeed be seen in the light of these other crimes, it can be argued that the act was part of widespread and systematic attacks and that there is a crime against humanity.

On the other hand, it can also be argued that the junta was not refusing all aid and that the regime did not completely prevent aid agencies already working in the country from doing their work. Moreover, it can be argued that there 'was no evidence of widespread intent by the authorities to cause suffering'.[175] In this line, it may be wondered '(a)t what point does the junta's intransigence create a death toll among the innocent Burmese population so high that it amounts to a 'crime against humanity'?'[176]

It therefore depends on the arguments used (and the interpretations of the facts of the case), the severity of the humanitarian situation and the context of the affected state whether inadequate disaster response in combination with the refusal of international assistance can be regarded as a crime against humanity. In this research, the stance is taken that *in theory*, when the response to a disaster like that of Myanmar takes place in a context of severe crimes already committed against a population, it *can* constitute a crime against humanity. Whether or not a crime against humanity was in fact committed in Myanmar by refusing international humanitarian assistance is difficult to determine without a more extensive study into the 'systematic' (other) crimes committed against the civilian population, but it is assumed here that the level of being 'highly organized, often as part of a pattern or methodical plan' cannot be demonstrated here.[177] Nonetheless, the further line of argumentation in this section departs from the consideration that an extreme

[169] Pinheiro & Barron (n 133) 263.
[170] Ibid (footnote omitted).
[171] Ibid, 272-3.
[172] Ibid, 273-4.
[173] Ibid, 274.
[174] Ibid, 275.
[175] Bellamy (n 134) 12.
[176] Dan Whipple, 'Wrestling with Generals: Pinning Down the 'Responsibility to Protect' (2010) 34 Natural Hazards Observer [3] 17.
[177] Which is the description of 'systematic' according to Pinheiro & Barron as provided above (n 133).

situation like as seen in Myanmar *could in theory* constitute a crime against humanity. In that case, RtoP could be invoked.

*6.2.3 Applicability of RtoP in disaster situations*

Even though the refusal to accept international humanitarian assistance can in extreme situations be a crime against humanity, it is claimed by many that RtoP cannot be used in disaster situations.[178] The origins of this discussion can be found in the ICISS-report.[179] According to this report, natural disasters may provide a reason to invoke RtoP: when discussing in which situations military intervention for human protection purposes is justified, i.e. in situations of large scale loss of life, the ICISS explicitly includes 'overwhelming natural or environmental catastrophes, where the state concerned is either unwilling or unable to cope, or call for assistance, and significant loss of life is occurring or threatened'.[180] In the World Summit Outcome of 2005, there is no mentioning of disasters; only in the case of one of the four earlier mentioned crimes RtoP can be invoked.

When European and North American voices started to argue in favour of using RtoP in Myanmar, China and other states in the South East of Asia argued that RtoP did not apply. This opinion was shared by UK's Secretary of State for International Development Douglas Alexander and Britain's UN ambassador John Sawers, who agreed that RtoP should not be invoked to justify the forcible delivery of aid or to coerce the government of Myanmar.[181] Also Ban Ki-moon, Secretary-General of the UN, argued in his report on the implementation of RtoP that it should not be applied in situations of natural disasters until Member States decide otherwise. He followed the stance of a number of scholars[182] in arguing that application in situations like Myanmar would 'undermine the 2005 consensus and stretch the concept beyond recognition or operational utility'.[183]

The main argument used is that the vast majority of states agreed on a rather limited version of RtoP as laid down in the World Summit Outcome of 2005. In the three paragraphs of the Outcome Document dealing with RtoP, the four crimes are used as the point of departure, but the larger framework is by far not as extensive as

---

[178] The political resistance against extending RtoP to disasters is depicted by the discussion on inclusion of RtoP in the ILC's work on the Protection of Persons in the Event of Disasters. See for an overview of the discussion J. Benton Heath, 'Disasters, Relief, and Neglect: The Duty to Accept Humanitarian Assistance and the Work of the International Law Commission' (2010) 43 Journal of International Law & Politics 419, 432-6.

[179] For background information on the development of RtoP and the report of the International Commission on Intervention and State Sovereignty see Chapter II section 4.3.

[180] ICISS, 'The Responsibility to Protect' (International Development Research Centre, Ottowa 2001) 32-3, paras 4.19 and 4.20.

[181] Bellamy (n 134) 10, citing Julian Borger & Ian MacKinnon, 'Bypass Junta's Permission for Aid, US and France Urge' *The Guardian* 9 May 2008.

[182] See e.g. Bellamy (n 134) 10, Caballero-Anthony & Chng (n 138) 144.

[183] UNGA, 'Implementing the Responsibility to Protect: Report of the Secretary-General' (UN Doc A/63/677 of 2009), para 10(b).

that of the ICISS. Nonetheless, it can be questioned how relevant it is that natural disasters are not mentioned in the Outcome Document. In the Outcome Document, states pledge that they accept the responsibility to protect their populations from, amongst others, crimes against humanity.[184] The international community has the responsibility to help to protect populations through appropriate diplomatic, humanitarian, and other peaceful means or through action in accordance with Chapter VII of the UN Charter when national authorities are manifestly failing to protect their populations from, amongst others, crimes against humanity.[185] When following the Outcome Document, it must therefore be established that international action is required when a state cannot protect or is not protecting its population from crimes against humanity; whether or not these crimes take place in a disaster situation is not relevant.

Situations like Myanmar, in which the flawed response to a natural disaster taken together with crimes committed against the civilian population could possibly constitute a crime against humanity, are rare. While the mere occurrence of a natural disaster is not enough to invoke RtoP, disaster situations cannot be excluded from RtoP per se: 'the construction of the doctrine does not, on its face, preclude such an application should a government's actions following a natural disaster rise to the level of genocide, war crimes, ethnic cleansing, or crimes against humanity'.[186] However, coming to the final question, it must be asked whether RtoP is useful in cases like Myanmar.

### *6.2.4 Usefulness of RtoP in disaster response*

The World Summit Outcome of 2005 clearly distinguishes between peaceful means of international assistance and methods of intervention. The calls for invocation of RtoP described above generally referred to rather intrusive measures, for example the airdrop of supplies[187] or to force the passage of humanitarian assistance through the SC.[188] Sir John Holmes, UN Emergency Relief Coordinator, was requested by France to brief the SC and proposed a resolution calling on Myanmar to allow unhindered humanitarian access.[189] The request was rejected by several countries. Moreover, several countries rejected the idea to apply RtoP on a natural disaster situation and even Sir Holmes described Kouchner's call as unnecessarily confrontational.[190] In the past, rather forceful measures have indeed been taken in humanitarian emergencies, like the humanitarian missions in Somalia in the early

---

[184] UNGA, '2005 World Summit Outcome' (n 153) para 138.
[185] Ibid, para 139.
[186] Pinheiro & Barron (n 133) 270.
[187] Embassy of France in the UK, 'Burma-Joint Press Briefing Given By M. Bernard Kouchner, Minister of Foreign Affairs, and M. Jean-Pierre Jouyet, Minister of State Responsible for European Affairs' of 13 May 2008, cited by Pinheiro & Barron (n 133) 268.
[188] Embassy of France in the UK, 'Burma-Article by M. Bernard Kouchner, Minister of Foreign and European Affairs' *Le Monde* 20 May 2008 cited by Pinheiro & Barron (n 133) 269.
[189] Caballero-Anthony & Chng (n 138) 141.
[190] Borger & MacKinnon (n 181); Bellamy (n 134) 10.

1990s, in Haiti in 1993, and the humanitarian relief efforts for Iraqi Kurds in the 1990s, although except for Haiti these actions took place in a context of armed conflict. [191] It can, however, be questioned whether forcefully providing humanitarian assistance into Myanmar would have been productive, as it would further polarise the position of the military regime.

Even those who argue that RtoP is applicable in the situation of Myanmar do not necessarily endorse forceful measures. Former UN Special Rapporteur on Myanmar Paulo Sérgio Pinheiro argues for example that intervention (either under the framework of RtoP or otherwise) would not address any root causes, and would therefore only be a temporary solution.[192] Attempting to seek Security Council authorization would lead to no result, as China and Russia held the position that forcing humanitarian aid would not be the best solution. Action without authority of the Security Council could lead to political tensions.[193] Within the framework of the ICISS-version of RtoP, six criteria are formulated to test whether military intervention is an acceptable option for human protection purposes.[194] In the case of Myanmar, not all these criteria would have been met: negotiations were still ongoing, especially with the support of ASEAN, and there is no certainty that the civilian population would have benefited from a military operation, possibly they would have suffered more as a result.[195]

Instead, many supported the road that was actually taken. Through the platform provided by the ASEAN Agreement on Disaster Management and Emergency Response, the ASEAN Secretariat and Member States could send a joint assessment team and negotiate access of humanitarian relief.[196] Also, the US tried to stimulate dialogue between Myanmar and its partners, ASEAN, China and India so that these parties could 'convince the regime to accept assistance from the international community'.[197] In the end, Myanmar started to accept international assistance, but it took a relatively long time before negotiations achieved this. In the three weeks that Myanmar refused aid, the delay 'led to unnecessary suffering and hardship for the victims at the very least and, at the worst, contributed to a higher number of deaths and casualties'.[198]

---

[191] Malone (n 121).
[192] See Pinheiro & Barron (n 133) 276.
[193] Ibid, 277.
[194] These criteria are right authority (who can authorize military action?), just cause (i.e. halting or averting large scale loss of life or ethnic cleansing), right intention, last resort, proportional means, and reasonable prospects. ICISS Report (n 180) 32-37.
[195] See Barber, 'The Responsibility to Protect' (n 158) 24-33.
[196] Bannon, 'International Disaster Response Law' (n 45) 847.
[197] Scot Marciel, 'Burma in the Aftermath of Cyclone Nargis: Death, Displacement, and Humanitarian Aid' (Statement before the Subcommittee on Asia, the Pacific, and the Global Environment of the House Committee on Foreign Affairs, Washington 20 May 2008) cited by Caballero-Anthony & Chng (n 138) 142.
[198] Caballero-Anthony & Chng (n 138) 144.

Therefore, one very important question that has been asked throughout this Chapter remains: does the international community have to await consent at all times or is it possible to intervene? As seen above, even in an extreme case like Myanmar it was impossible to come to an agreement on action. Possibly, RtoP will be applied sooner when there is an underlying situation of armed conflict, but recent cases once again illustrate that RtoP is still depending on the willingness of states to apply it. Accordingly, as will be illustrated in the next section, there is no effective answer to humanitarian emergencies in which consent cannot be obtained.

### 6.3 The persisting gap in providing humanitarian assistance

Myanmar is not the only example in which consent could not be obtained. The drought in Somalia of 2011 was already mentioned as another case, just as the L'Aquila and Sichuan earthquakes, and, partly, hurricane Katrina in US. The problems of humanitarian access also exist in armed conflict situations. In 2013, Blue Nile State in Sudan is the stage of a conflict while access of humanitarian agencies is denied, resulting in many IDPs throughout the region with no access to assistance. Throughout the conflict in Syria, humanitarian access has been a problem, now addressed by the Security Council through resolutions 2165 and 2191 in which the Security Council grants access to Syria for (UN affiliated) humanitarian organisations in the state's stead.[199] Yet whether this solution by the Security Council will be applied in other situations remains to be seen.

These examples make clear that when during a humanitarian emergency access is being denied, whether by a government, a party to an internal conflict, or a *de facto* leading power, there is no clear response from the international community other than trying to negotiate access. The rules and principles as described in the previous Chapter are not always followed in practice, and there is no answer when an affected state decides to refuse assistance. While it is often argued that state sovereignty stands in the way of action, the problems cannot be blamed on state sovereignty alone. Discussions on the 'forfeiture of sovereignty', 'theory of conditional sovereignty' or 'temporary surrender of sovereignty' appear interesting in theory, but cannot lead to practical results due to sovereignty itself.[200] Requiring states to 'temporarily forfeit their sovereignty when it allows gross violations of human rights to occur' implies a higher authority to forfeit sovereignty to.[201] In Chapter II the idea of sovereignty as responsibility has been discussed, where sovereignty does not cease to exist, but brings responsibilities for the state and for the wider international community. This idea lies at the basis of RtoP, but has not, as seen in this section, led to clear results.

---

[199] See section 4.3 of Chapter II.
[200] Saechao (n 40) 672, citing Mohamad Y. Mattar, 'State Responsibilities in Combating Trafficking in Persons in Central Asia' (2005) 27 Loy. L.A. International and Comparative Law Review 145, 212-3.
[201] Ibid.

## 7 Conclusion

The three steps of the legal framework on accepting external assistance after a disaster and the three rules directing states in their decision when they must seek and when they must accept such assistance have gained detail by looking at their applicability in practice. The primary role of the affected state is firmly established and forms the point of departure for relief operations. Due to the primary role, the affected state must make a needs-assessment to determine what it can deliver itself and what is needed from other actors. If the affected state decides that international assistance is required, it can initiate this process by requesting assistance or by responding to offers already made. Before relief can be delivered to an affected state, the consent of that state is needed and in practice always awaited. The limitations that were found on the state's freedom to withhold consent appear, however, to not have great practical value.

If an affected state comes to the conclusion that its own response is inadequate (or is likely to be inadequate), it must give its consent to international assistance. The problem is that it is up to the affected state to decide that its capacity is overwhelmed. Moreover, it is very difficult to determine when a state's response is inadequate. Often this is a matter of opinion and a state may be successful in certain aspects but fail to address other aspects.

In the second place, the affected state may not withhold its consent if it results in a violation of a norm of international law. There are no clear appeals on a certain norm that would be violated, although in extreme cases the state is reminded of its duties towards its own population. Under human rights law, these duties are most clearly and elaborately established. In situations like that of Myanmar, the refusal of aid can – when seen in the context of other acts directed against the population – constitute a crime against humanity, but circumstances must be extreme before poor disaster response can be considered as such.

The third rule that helps a state to determine whether international assistance must be sought or accepted – the rule that consent may not be withheld arbitrarily – has become a bit clearer by looking at practical application. Humanitarian assistance offered by external parties must be of good quality and must meet the humanitarian principles. When meeting these principles, there is less ground for an affected state to refuse the offer. In practice there are some examples in which a refusal of assistance is considered tolerable because of the quality of the offer (conditional, culturally inappropriate, in violation of national legislation). In addition, it can be argued that a state must have very good reasons for withholding consent when the national capacity is overwhelmed or when a norm of international law will be violated by not giving consent. Still, how much room a state has exactly for valuing offers of assistance and refusing when the offer meets the humanitarian principles does not become completely clear from looking at the practical application.

Although not being the main focus of the present study, it has been explored what happens in situations where international humanitarian assistance is refused and where there is broad consensus that the state should give its consent. There is no solution to situations in which a civilian population suffers from the consequences of a disaster and in which the assistance delivered by the state is inadequate. Disaster situations are excluded from RtoP, although in rare cases the refusal of aid can be considered as a crime against humanity. In most situations though, this threshold cannot be reached and the question remains what the international community can do when the state refuses to give consent. This question will not be further addressed here: this research focuses on the preceding question - in which situations a state has an obligation to give consent.

# Preliminary Conclusions

The goal of the present research is to find out to what extent public international law contains standards for affected states determining whether that state must accept international humanitarian assistance after the occurrence of a disaster. A legal framework has been identified based on the legal sources relating to humanitarian assistance and disaster response. This legal framework consists of three steps or sequences.

Point of departure is the primary role of the affected state. It is not the occurrence of a disaster that instigates the existence of the primary role: responsibilities towards the own population follow from sovereignty and are also present when there is no disaster. The aspects of the responsibilities a state has towards its own population that are prompted by the occurrence of a disaster relate to humanitarian assistance. As a first step the affected state makes a needs-assessment within the first seventy-two hours and determines whether it has the capacity to answer to these needs or whether additional assistance is required.

The second step is to trigger international humanitarian assistance if necessary, which must follow from the needs-assessment. International humanitarian assistance is necessary when the national capacity is overwhelmed or when a rule of international law is violated by withholding consent. At this stage, there is no obligation to actually *accept*: affected states only have a duty to *seek* assistance by actively making requests or by going through the offers already made. The goal at this stage is to value the offers made to the affected state to see whether they are acceptable. This is determined by the content of the offer (is what is being offered needed in the affected state according to the needs-assessment? Is what is being offered useful for the particular situation at hand?) and by the form of the offer (does the offer meet the humanitarian principles?). Considering each individual offer and accepting what is needed can take much time. It is more efficient to issue a concrete request or multiple requests for the relief the affected state needs, based on the needs-assessment. In either case it is necessary to make the moment of acceptance explicit and foresee the acceptance of the necessary detail. This is the third step.

Consent to international humanitarian assistance has major legal implications. Consent makes acts that would otherwise violate principles of sovereignty and territorial integrity legal. Given this function, certain details must be arranged, like the subject of consent (items, staff, transportation), the period during which relief may be provided, the areas to which access is granted, et cetera. After this, international actors deliver humanitarian assistance while the affected state retains control and at a certain point operations are ended.

Although the affected state is in principle free to withhold its consent to offers that are not needed or which do not meet the humanitarian principles, this freedom is limited if one of the following three situations occurs. First, if the capacity of the affected state is overwhelmed by the occurrence of a disaster, there is an obligation to accept assistance. Second, if the affected state is violating a norm of international (human rights) law by not accepting international humanitarian assistance, it must give its consent. Third, consent may not be withheld for arbitrary reasons. If what is being offered is needed according to the needs-assessment, is suitable for the situation at hand and meets the humanitarian principles, there is less ground – if any – for the affected state to refuse the offer.

To a certain extent, the main research question can be answered through this legal framework: based on international law a framework is identified that contains the three main steps of the process of accepting international humanitarian assistance along with the standards that determine at what points the affected state must move to the next step in the legal framework, as such providing when the state must accept international humanitarian assistance. However, after placing the legal framework in the light of practice it became clear that the rules in that case prove too generally formulated to constitute concrete standards. Ending at this point therefore is quite unsatisfactory. Rather, something is needed that gives the rules found so far more detail, so that they can constitute concrete standards. What is needed is a way in which the needs-assessment can objectively and concretely set out what is required and based on which it can be determined whether the capacity of the affected state is adequate. Departing from this needs-assessment with more concrete standards, it would also become more easy to determine whether an offer is suitable and whether a refusal of assistance arbitrary or valid. In Chapter II, the ICESCR has already been identified as a very promising candidate for this purpose and throughout Chapters II and III it has been implied that human rights obligations could provide the standards of international law that co-determine whether assistance must be accepted or not.

In Chapter II it has been more generally acknowledged that the standards set by human rights law can be a useful tool for setting disaster policy. With the help of human right indicators, it is possible to determine what a state must achieve (or aim to achieve) after a disaster. Looking at human rights instruments, in particular the ICESCR emerges as a very topical treaty. The ICESCR contains the rights to housing, food, water and health, rights that are of special importance in disaster settings. In addition, the ICESCR contains a provision on general obligations stating that apart from working on human rights realization individually, international assistance and cooperation must be used as well. Also, states must use, according to the general obligations, the maximum of its available resources, which could refer to assistance available internationally.

The next part of the research will aim at making the findings of this research so far more concrete by identifying standards under the ICESCR that tell states when to accept international humanitarian assistance.

# Part II

# Chapter IV
# The Content and Meaning of Article 2(1) ICESCR

## 1 Introduction

When analysing the instruments and documents that potentially contain rules on accepting international humanitarian assistance in response to disasters in Chapter II, it was explored how human rights standards could play a role in disaster response. At that point the question has been addressed to what extent human rights standards in disaster settings have correlative obligations for states eventually resulting in an obligation to accept humanitarian assistance if the state is unable to realize the human rights standards. In general, the standard-setting function of human rights law can help to concretize obligations for state parties immediately after a disaster, but in particular the ICESCR appears to give direction on accepting humanitarian assistance. The ICESCR contains a provision on the general obligations for state parties that could help to answer the question at what point an affected state is under an obligation to accept. Article 2(1) of the ICESCR tells state parties to come to the full realization of the rights 'individually and through international assistance and cooperation'. In addition, each state party must use 'the maximum of its available resources'. These general obligations must be read in conjunction with substantive rights, of which the ICESCR contains a number highly relevant in disaster settings, like the rights to housing, food, water and health.

With the help of the ICESCR, it will be considered whether the legal framework as identified in the previous Chapters can be foreseen of more concrete standards. Possibly, the inclusion of the ICESCR will result in a clearer delineation of the primary role of the affected state, indicating when the affected state should move on to triggering international humanitarian assistance. Moreover, the obligations stemming from the ICESCR may be useful for determining when the point is reached at which the affected state must give its consent to international assistance, for example by giving standards to determine when the national capacity is exceeded, or by giving concrete obligations that can be violated by refusing to accept assistance. Accordingly, the ICESCR will be used to formulate a more complete answer to the main research question.

To achieve this it must first be determined what exactly the content is of the obligations of article 2(1) ICESCR. After this, these obligations must be considered in the context of disaster settings, resulting in an overview of general expectations of state parties in the aftermath of disasters. These findings will be taken together with the aforementioned substantive rights (i.e. the rights to housing, food, water and health) to establish standards for affected states on accepting assistance. The obligations following the ICESCR are in the first place directing the 164 state parties to the Covenant in their actions.[1] To what extent non-party states are also bound by the findings below is subject to debate. Using arguments of obligations *erga omnes*, customary law (or at least the view that almost all rights in the Universal Declaration of Human Rights, so also ESC-rights, have a core that is recognized as customary law), the 'do no harm'-principle and by looking at repeated recognition of extraterritorial aspects of economic, social and cultural rights, the position can be defended that also non-party states have certain obligations in this respect.[2] Here, the position is taken that the existence of positive obligations for non-party states is a bridge too far, but that such states have at least a duty not to violate the rights of the ICESCR (which is in line with the 'do no harm'-principle).[3] The present Chapter will start with identifying the general obligations of article 2(1). The next Chapter will place these findings in a disaster-context. To find the exact content and meaning of article 2(1), the methodology of treaty interpretation as described in the Vienna Convention on the Law of Treaties (VCLT) will be used.[4]

---

[1] According to the UN Treaty Collection's Database, consulted on 21 April 2015. An additional five states has signed the ICESCR, meaning that they may not act in violation of the object and purpose of the treaty <https://treaties.un.org/pages/viewdetails.aspx?chapter=4&lang=en&mtdsg_no=iv-3&src=treaty>.

[2] See for a discussion of these concepts and ideas Malcolm Langford, Fons Coomans & Felipe Gómez Isa, 'Extraterritorial Duties in International Law' in Malcolm Langford, Wouter Vandenhole, Martin Scheinin & Willem J.M. van Genugten (eds), *Global Justice, State Duties: The Extraterritorial Scope of Economic, Social and Cultural Rights in International Law* (Cambridge, Cambridge University Press 2013) 68-9. In section 3.3 of Chapter II it has already been argued that ESC-rights do (probably) not constitute customary law, yet that possible the core of these rights could crystallize into customary law more easily, which is in line with the customary-core idea.

[3] The 'do no harm'-principle is a well-established norm in international environmental law and has been connected to human rights to define extraterritorial obligations. See Langford *et al* (n 2) 69 referring to Sigrun I. Skogly, *Beyond National Borders: States' Human Rights Obligations in International Cooperation* (Intersentia, Antwerp 2006) 165 and Fons Coomans, 'Some Remarks' in in Fons Coomans & Menno T. Kamminga (eds), *Extraterritorial Application of Human Rights Treaties* (Intersentia, Antwerp 2004).

[4] The VCLT was adopted at the Vienna Conference in 1969 and entered into force in 1980. It contains three articles on treaty interpretation that are widely used and cited. For more background on the debate surrounding and leading up to the development of the rules on interpretation, see Alexander Orakhelashvili, *The Interpretation of Acts and Rules in Public International Law* (Oxford University Press, Oxford 2008), Sir Gerald Fitzmaurice, 'The Law and Procedure of the International Court of Justice: Treaty Interpretation and Certain Other Treaty Points' (1951) 28 B. Yearbook of International Law 1; Francis G. Jacobs, 'Varieties of Approach to Treaty Interpretation: With Special Reference to the Draft Convention on the Law of Treaties Before the Vienna Diplomatic Conference' (1969) 18 International and Comparative Law Quarterly 318; ILC, 'Draft Articles on the Law of Treaties with Commentaries' (Yearbook of the International Law Commission 1966 Vol. II).

The idea behind using the rules on treaty interpretation is to make the outcome of interpretation more predictable and less arbitrary (enhancing legal certainty), so that parties to a treaty can foresee and anticipate on what is expected in terms of obligations.[5] Using the rules therefore gives the impression that applying them will 'place the "decision-maker" on a sort of conveyor belt which will lead him, as it were painlessly, if not always to the right spot precisely, then to some haven very close to it'.[6] Yet, when considering the model and its practical functionality, it becomes clear that this very optimistic idea is not necessarily true and a few adjustments are made accordingly.[7]

Article 31 VCLT on the 'general rule of interpretation' states that '(a) treaty shall be interpreted in good faith in accordance with the ordinary meaning to be given to the terms of the treaty in their context and in the light of its object and purpose'. Article 32 continues by providing that supplementary means (like preparatory work or circumstances of conclusion) may be used when the outcome of applying article 31 'leaves the meaning ambiguous or obscure' or 'leads to a result which is manifestly absurd or unreasonable'.[8] Because interpretation exists of the ordinary meaning of words considered in context and in the light of object and purpose, with the inclusion of various sources, interpretation is a process rather than a single act.[9] Within this process, '(e)lements can only be taken up one at a time, but they are to be evaluated together. Thus interpretation may require going round the circle more than once if a factor presents itself under an element of the rules

[5] Ch. de Visscher, *Problèmes d'Interpretation Judiciaire en Droit International Public* (1963) 17 cited by Orakhelashvili, *The Interpretation of Acts and Rules* (n 4) 306.

[6] Sir Gerald Fitzmaurice, '*Vae Victis* or Woe to the Negotiators! Your Treaty or our "Interpretation" of it?' (1971) 65 American Journal of International Law 358, 359.

[7] The main problem lies in making visible which choices the interpreter has made. See for example Alexander Orakhelashvili, 'Restrictive Interpretation of the Human Rights Treaties in the Recent Jurisprudence of the European Court of Human Rights' (2003) 14 European Journal of International Law 529, in which the author explains the methodology of interpretation in some detail on page 533ff but does not illustrate how these features are applied while interpreting; only the – very interesting – outcomes are discussed.

[8] 'The word "supplementary" emphasizes that article 28 (now article 32) does not provide for alternative, autonomous, means of interpretation but only for means to aid an interpretation governed by the principles contained in article 27 (now article 31). The Commission considered that the exception must be strictly limited, if it is not to weaken unduly the authority of the ordinary meaning of the terms'. ILC, 'Draft Articles on the Law of Treaties' (n 4) 'Commentary to draft articles 27 and 28', para 19.

[9] Torres Bernárdez, 'Interpretation of Treaties by the International Court of Justice following the Adoption of the 1969 Vienna Convention on the Law of Treaties' at 726 para 11, cited by Richard K. Gardiner, *Treaty Interpretation* (Oxford International Law Library, Oxford University Press 2008) 30. This is confirmed in the ILC, 'Draft Articles on the Law of Treaties' (n 4) 'Commentary to draft articles 27 and 28', para 8. This idea is also taken up by, for example, the ECtHR, which said in the Golder-case that 'the process of interpretation of a treaty is a unity, a single combined operation'. ECtHR *Golder v. United Kingdom* (App no 4451/70) (1975) Series A no 18, 1 EHRR 524, para 30.

later in the list and which appears to outweigh one already taken up'.[10] For this reason, before describing the content and meaning of article 2(1), first the immediate context will be discussed, followed by the object and purpose.

What must finally be noted is that the goal here is to find the meaning in the light of present-day circumstances.[11] Human rights standards may change over time, which is in the context of the ECHR referred to as the 'living instrument'-doctrine. The notion 'living instrument' is generally attributed to the ECtHR-case of Tyrer v. United Kingdom, in which the Court stated that 'the Convention is a living instrument which, as the Commission rightly stressed, must be interpreted in the light of present-day conditions'.[12] From the Commission's reasoning it becomes clear that the fact that a certain interpretation of a right or freedom was not recognized at the time of adoption does not mean that that interpretation cannot be read into a treaty at a later stage. Even though this reasoning is used in the context of the ECHR, the idea is based on the character of human rights instruments in general, so also the ICESCR must be considered in the light of present-day circumstances, for which the work of the Committee on Economic Social and Cultural Rights (CESCR) can be helpful.[13]

The Committee on Economic, Social and Cultural Rights is the treaty body created for the supervisory tasks foreseen in the ICESCR. Being the main authority for this Covenant, the CESCR is responsible for interpreting the rights and obligations of the ICESCR. Although not being able to give binding decisions like a court does – apart from the Optional Protocol's individual complaint mechanism as

---

[10] Gardiner (n 9) 7, 30, after recognizing that '(t)he rules are not a set of simple precepts that can be applied to produce a scientifically verifiable result. More guidance is needed to set the ground for a 'correct' result, or at least one which has been correctly ascertained'.

[11] Soren C. Prebensen, 'Evolutive Interpretation of the European Convention on Human Rights' in Paul Mahoney *et al* (eds), *Protection des droit de l'homme: la perspective europeenne* (Carl Heymanns Verlag, 2000) 1131.

[12] ECtHR *Tyrer v. United Kingdom* (App no 5856/72) (1978) Series A no 26; (1979-80) 2 EHRR 1, para 31. The Tyrer-case concerned the question whether judicial corporal punishment for juveniles (in this case three strokes of the birch on the bare behind) can be considered as 'degrading treatment or punishment' in the sense of article 3 ECHR. This reasoning has been used in various subsequent cases, where usually the Tyrer-case is cited. See generally Alastair Mowbray, 'The Creativity of the European Court of Human Rights' (2005) 5 Human Rights Law Review 57, 61ff. Examples of cases are: Soering v. United Kingdom A 161 (1989); Sigurdur A Sigurjonsson v. Iceland A 264 (1993) (1993) 16 EHRR 462, Loizidou v. Turkey (Preliminary Objections) A 310 (1995) (1995) 20 EHRR 99; Matthews v. United Kingdom 1999-I 251 (1999) 28 EHRR 361; Selmouni v. France 1999-V 149 (2000) 29 EHRR 403, ECtHR Bayatyan v. Armenia (app. No. 23459/03) judgement of 27 October 2009 para 62. When closely considering the Court's reasoning, it becomes clear that the Court does not provide any additional information for its living instrument-approach apart from the reference to the Commission ('as the Commission rightly stressed'), but within the treatment of the case by the Commission no reference to 'living instrument' is made.

[13] Whereby it is emphasized that the goal of this research is establishing *lex lata* and not *lex ferenda*.

will be discussed below – the CESCR clarifies what is expected from state parties. Within General Comments, the CESCR has explained how various provisions and topics must be understood and be realized. These General Comments are widely cited when discussing the scope, nature and content of ESC-rights and the CESCR's views will play a dominant role in the interpretation below.[14]

## 2 Context: Article 2(1) in the Immediate Context of the ICESCR

Before going into concrete obligations stemming from article 2(1) and later from the substantive rights of the ICESCR, a preliminary question will first be addressed: to what extent does the ICESCR contain obligations for its state parties concrete enough to be justiciable? The first element of treaty interpretation, context, will be used to answer this question by looking at the place of article 2(1) within the ICESCR.[15]

Part II of the ICESCR describes general expectations from state parties, so the 'way in which States Parties must behave in order to implement and guarantee the substantive rights contained in the Covenant'.[16] The fact that article 2(1) can be found in part II of the ICESCR does not only confirm the general nature of the provision, but at the same time implies that what is written in article 2(1) is valid for the whole treaty. Moreover, there does not appear to be room for negotiation in the articles of Part II: they are rules of engagement states must adhere to, and it would seriously damage the function of these articles when states have too much discretionary freedom: '(i)ndeed, Part II imposes obligations on States parties with regard to each of the substantive rights contained in Part III. Provisions in Part II have a dynamic relationship with all substantive rights and the latter cannot be interpreted without taking into account Part II provisions'.[17] The substantive rights

[14] By becoming a party to a treaty, the state commits itself to 'perform the treaty in good faith', as laid down in article 26 VCLT. Although the General Comments are not legally binding instruments per se, the CESCR has obtained the task through the ECOSOC to explain to state parties how they must perform the treaty in good faith, and are therefore authoritative documents.

[15] What context is, is explained in article 31(2), (3) and (4) VCLT.

[16] Magdalena Sepúlveda, *The Nature of the Obligations under the International Covenant on Economic, Social and Cultural Rights* (Intersentia, Antwerp 2002) 16. Part I of the ICESCR is not mentioned because it contains only one provision (on self-determination) which is not relevant for the understanding of article 2(1). Part II contains general obligations, the equality of women and men, a limitation clause and the determination that the ICESCR may not be abused or misinterpreted to limit already existing rights.

[17] Magdalena Sepúlveda, 'Obligations of 'International Assistance and Cooperation' in an Optional Protocol to the International Covenant on Economic, Social, and Cultural Rights' (2006) 24 Netherlands Quarterly of Human Rights 271, 295. This is confirmed when considering the topics of the General Comments; article 2(1) is discussed in General Comment 3 under the title 'The Nature of States Parties Obligations'. This General Comment is preceded by a Comment on 'Reporting by States Parties' and one on 'International Technical Assistance Measures'. The Comments following General Comment 3 are all considering substantive rights. Assuming a logical sequence, it is arguable that the Committee first dealt with more general issues, before

of the ICESCR are laid down in Part III. These articles contain 'a complex range of correlative duties, often divided into duties to respect, to protect and to fulfil'.[18]

In the past, it used to be argued by some that when comparing economic, social and cultural rights (ESC-rights) to civil and political rights (as laid down in the ICCPR) ESC-rights constitute fewer obligations, if any. Instead, ESC-rights were at times considered not as rights but as goals of economic and social policy.[19] These ideas can be traced back to the origins of the ICESCR. To be modelled after the UDHR, a single treaty was supposed to be adopted containing civil and political rights as well as ESC-rights. However, instead of adopting one text, two Covenants were created, which is 'largely a reflection of the perception developed during the drafting of the Covenants that the two categories of rights were different in nature, origin, and significance'.[20] No matter the reason for separating the Covenants, the mere existence of two instruments each containing a different set of rights has fed the assumption that the nature of the rights, and thus the nature of obligations, is essentially different.[21] Civil and political rights used to be considered to constitute primarily negative obligations suitable for immediate application. ESC-rights, on the other hand, were deemed to have mostly a positive character, requiring long-term planning, investments, and other efforts of states.[22]

Truly, for some provisions of the ICESCR the drafters did not intend to create any obligations and they made this explicitly clear, but for most articles such a statement has not been made and already quite early in the ICESCR's existence it was acknowledged that '(i)t cannot be assumed that the Covenant's provisions do not possess legal force unless there are overriding indications otherwise'. [23] The variety in terminology indicating what is expected of state parties is not consistent (e.g. 'respect', 'ensure', 'should', 'guarantee', or omission of the word 'right') but

---

going into the actual rights. Article 2(1) would in that case be a provision applicable to all substantive rights.

[18] Sepúlveda, *The Nature of the Obligations* (n 16) 16.

[19] See Philip Alston & Gerard Quinn, 'The Nature and Scope of State Parties' Obligations under the International Covenant on Economic, Social and Cultural Rights', (1987) 9 Human Rights Quarterly 156, 158. See also See Sepúlveda, *The Nature of the Obligations* (n 16) 312.

[20] Matthew C.R Craven, *The International Covenant on Economic, Social and Cultural Rights: A Perspective on its Development* (Oxford Monographs in International Law, Clarendon Press, 1995) 7. The distinction between the two sets of rights can be partly retraced to the disagreements between East and West: '(t)he Soviet States, on the one hand, championed the cause of economic, social, and cultural rights, which they associated with the aims of the socialist society. Western States, on the other hand, asserted the priority of civil and political rights as being the foundation of liberty and democracy in the 'free world'.' H. Gros Espiel, 'The Evolving Concept of Human Rights: Western, Socialist and Third World Approaches' in B. Ramcharan (ed.), *Human Rights Thirty Years After the Universal Declaration* (1979) 41 cited by Craven at p. 9.

[21] Craven (n 20) 9.

[22] See *inter alia* Alston & Quinn (n 19) 159.

[23] Of article 15 it is described in the preparatory work that no obligations were intended. Alston & Quinn (n 19) 186. R. Bernhardt, 'Treaties' in *Encyclopaedia of Public International Law* (Vol. 7, 1984) 459, 460 cited by Craven (n 20) 135.

this must not be considered as indicating the non-existence of an obligation.[24] The fact that article 10, for example, does not contain the word 'right' does not mean that it has a different nature than other rights: '(t)he Committee has considered it appropriate to infer the existence of a 'right' from the terms'.[25]

The Committee on Economic, Social and Cultural Rights (CESCR) – created in 1985 through the adoption of a resolution by ECOSOC for the monitoring of state parties' compliance with the ICESCR – has further stressed that a number of rights of the ICESCR are readily applicable in courts. It explained in relation to the justiciability of the ICESCR as 'those matters which are appropriately resolved by the courts') and most rights are self-executing, (meaning that they are capable of being applied 'by courts without further elaboration').[26] The adoption of the Optional Protocol (OP) to the ICESCR in 2008, establishing an individual complaint procedure as is also existing for the ICCPR, is a further confirmation of the justiciability of ESC-rights. Through this mechanism the CESCR has obtained the position to give its views on concrete cases of potential rights violations in the state parties that ratified the Optional Protocol.[27] During the drafting process of the OP to the ICESCR, the nature of obligations under the ICESCR and the justiciability of the rights of that Covenant were debated. Several delegations argued that the open-ended or vague formulation of rights make that the rights are unsuitable for an individual complaint mechanism.[28] Yet the adoption of the OP shows that the general understanding of the ICESCR is that it contains concrete obligations which states could possibly violate and which would result in a certain claim for individuals. Through the General Comments and especially by defining for each right the minimum core obligations, the CESCR has started defining

[24] Alston & Quinn place 'guarantee' and 'respect' on the same level. However, 'respect' does have a certain connotation to abstention; 'respecting one's privacy' means not to intrude, so to abstain. Alston & Quinn (n 19) 186.

[25] Reporting Guidelines UN Doc. E/1991/23, Annex IV 98-9, UN ESCOR, Supp. (No 3) (1991) cited by Craven (n 20) 135.

[26] CESCR, General Comment 9 on 'The Domestic Application of the Covenant' (UN Doc. E/C.12/1998/24 of 3 December 1998) para 10. This view is shared by Alston & Quinn (n 19) 159. The resolution creating the CESCR is ECOSOC Res. 1985/17 of 28 May 1985.

[27] The Optional Protocol was adopted by the UN GA on 10 December 2008 (UN Doc. A/RES/63/117) and entered into force on 5 May 2013 upon deposit of the tenth instrument of ratification (*ex* article 18(1) OP). According the UN Treaty database, by April 2015, 20 states ratified or acceded to the Optional Protocol (and 45 states signed the Optional Protocol). <https://treaties.un.org/pages/ViewDetails.aspx?src=TREATY&mtdsg_no=IV-3-a&chapter=4&lang=en> accessed 21 April 2015). By April 2015, only three cases are pending, two coming from Spain and one from Equador. See the Statistical Survey of the CESCR at <http://www.ohchr.org/EN/HRBodies/CESCR/Pages/PendingCases.aspx> accessed 21 April 2015.

[28] See for a summary of the arguments used: Commission on Human Rights, 'Economic, Social and Cultural Rights: Report of the Open-Ended Working Group to Consider Options Regarding the Elaboration of an Optional Protocol to the International Covenant on Economic, Social and Cultural Rights on its First Session' UN Doc. E/CN.4/2004/44 of 15 Marc 2004, paras 52-66.

obligations in detail.[29] The CESCR also affirms that the nature of general legal obligations must indeed be based on article 2(1) ICESCR.[30] Consequently, 'among the principle obstacles to reasoned discussion of the Covenant (...) are various propositions that have been attributed by some commentators to the Covenant but that, on closer inspection, exist more in the eye of the beholder than in the text of the Covenant'.[31]

## 3 Object & purpose: the nature of obligations stemming from article 2(1)

### 3.1 Purpose

Now that it is clear that art. 2(1) ICESCR contains certain obligations, it must be established what the nature of these obligations is through the object and purpose, but first it will be explained what is meant with these words. 'Object' and 'purpose' could be used as synonyms but the French version of the VCLT, speaking of '*l'objet et le but*', explains the difference.[32] According to the doctrine underlying these terms a distinction must be made between '*objet ou effet direct et immédiat de l'acte*' and '*but ou résultat de l'effet juridique produit par l'acte*'.[33] The object of a treaty provision is 'the situation which the author of the act has envisaged or the effect he is striving for'.[34] The purpose is the reason why the object exists because it explains what it is that must be achieved in the end.[35] So 'object' indicates 'the substantial content of the norm, the provisions, rights and obligations created by the norm'.[36] The purpose is 'the general result which the parties want to achieve by the treaty'.[37]

Article 2(1) is a 'programmatic article' which commonly contains the purpose of an instrument and it proposes the idea that the purpose of the ICESCR is the full realization of rights.[38] This, as a purpose, has explicitly been addressed by the

[29] This development started in CESCR, General Comment 3 on 'The Nature of States Parties Obligations' of 14 December 1990.
[30] CESCR, GC 3 (n 29) para 1.
[31] Alston & Quinn (n 19) 220.
[32] Isabelle Buffard & Karl Zemanek, 'The Object and Purpose of a Treaty: An Enigma?' (1998) 3 Austrian Review of International & European Law 311, 325.
[33] Ch. Rousseau, *Droit International Public* (Vol. 1, Paris 1970) 272 cited by Buffard & Zemanek (n 32) 325.
[34] P. Weckel, *La concurrence des traités internationaux,* Thèse Strasbourg III 1989, 26, n 10 cited by Buffard & Zemanek (n 32) 325.
[35] Ibid.
[36] Ibid, 326.
[37] Ibid.
[38] Besides this reference to the purpose, article 2(1) contains some indications as to the object, especially when read together with the substantive articles of Part III of the ICESCR.

CESCR.[39] The preamble of the ICESCR confirms that the full realization of rights is indeed the purpose. It connects the ICESCR to the UN Charter: '(c)onsidering the obligation of States under the Charter of the United Nations to promote universal respect for, and observance of, human rights and freedoms'. The preamble further refers to the UDHR: 'in accordance with the Universal Declaration of Human Rights, the ideal of free human beings enjoying freedom from fear and want can only be achieved if conditions are created whereby everyone may enjoy his economic, social and cultural rights, as well as his civil and political rights'. Apparently, the ideal of the UDHR is translated into the ICESCR and ICCPR, and concerns the conditions in which people can fully enjoy their rights. Taking together the references to the UN Charter and the ideals of the International Bill of Rights, it appears that the purpose of the ICESCR is directly connected to these ideals. From the preambles of the instruments of the International Bill of Rights it follows that a common goal is being pursued, namely the full and universal realization of human rights.[40] As such, the purpose of 'full realization' is confirmed by the preamble, although the scope is widened from only ESC-rights to all types of human rights.

### 3.2 Object

The object determines how state parties to the ICESCR must achieve the purpose. Without any object states would be free in determining how they would achieve the purpose, as long as they achieve it in the end. From the title of article 2(1) it follows that state parties are directed in how they must achieve the purpose, so article 2(1) must contain the object of the ICESCR. The CESCR has provided clarity on the object through its General Comments, in which mainly the 'minimum core obligations' constitute clear duties.[41] Also on other occasions does the CESCR use

[39] CESCR, GC 3 (n 29) para 9.

[40] The CESCR has repeatedly confirmed the idea that the ICESCR, ICCPR and UDHR are inextricably connected and have therefore a shared purpose. Consequently, 'efforts to promote one set of rights should also take full account of the other'. See *inter alia* CESCR, General Comment 2 on 'International Technical Assistance Measures' of 2 February 1990, para 6; CESCR, GC 3 (n 29) para 8. This has also been recognized with respect to individual rights: CESCR, General Comment 4 on 'The Right to Adequate Housing' of 13 December 1991, para 9, and also in CESCR, GC 9 (n 29) para 10; CESCR, General Comment 11 on 'Plans of Action for Primary Education' (UN Doc. E/C.12/1999/4 of 10 May 1999), para 2; CESCR, General Comment 12 on 'The Right to Adequate Food' (UN Doc. E/C.12/1999/5 of 12 May 1999) para 4.

[41] The CESCR provided initially the example where 'any significant number of individuals is deprived of essential foodstuffs, of essential primary health care, of basic shelter and housing, or the most basic forms of education is, prima facie, failing to discharge its obligations under the Covenant'; CESCR, GC 3 (n 29) para 10. Minimum core obligations can also be found in CESCR, General Comment 13 on 'The Right to Education' (UN Doc. E/C.12/1999/10 of 8 December 1999) para 57; CESCR, General Comment 14 on 'The Highest Attainable Standard of Health' (UN Doc. E/C.12/2000/4 of 11 August 2000) para 43; CESCR, General Comment 15 on 'The Right to Water' (UN Doc. E/C.12/2002/11 of 20 January 2003) para 37; CESCR, General

strong and unequivocal phrases to refer to obligations (for example in the General Comment on the right to food: '(e)very State is obliged to ensure for everyone under its jurisdiction access to the minimum essential food which is sufficient, nutritionally adequate and safe, to ensure their freedom from hunger'),[42] yet there are also many examples in which the Committee remains quite vague in its terminology ('States parties should recognize the essential role of international cooperation').[43]

At one instance the CESCR is using very remarkable and somewhat confusing terminology in connection to obligations: '(t)he equal right of men and women to the enjoyment of economic, social and cultural rights is a *mandatory* and immediate obligation of States parties'.[44] On first sight this remark appears to indicate by explicitly referring to 'mandatory obligations' that there must be such a thing as 'optional' or 'discretionary' obligations, which is a contradiction in terms. However, the CESCR made this comment with article 4 ICESCR in mind, which contains a limitation clause, making it possible for states to limit certain rights of the ICESCR. With the phrase cited above the Committee indicates that some obligations cannot be limited by article 4.[45] The CESCR explains this in the following words: article 3 ICESCR sets 'a non-derogable standard for compliance with the obligations of States parties as set out in articles 6 through 15 of ICESCR'.[46] It does not become clear whether this special status of article 3 is based on its place within the ICESCR (i.e. Part II) – which would mean that limitation of article 2(1) is not possible either – or whether the special status is attributed based on other reasons.

The language in which the CESCR defined obligations has evolved over time, of which the temporary end is found in General Comment 21. In this General Comment, a summary can be found of what is expected from state parties in terms of obligations:

Comment 17 on 'The Right of Everyone to Benefit From the Protection of the Moral and Material Interests Resulting From Any Scientific, Literary or Artistic Production of Which He is the Author' (UN Doc. E/C.12/GC/17 of 12 January 2006) para 39; CESCR, General Comment 18 on 'The Right to Work' (UN Doc. E/C.12/GC/18 of 6 February 2006) para 31; CESCR, General Comment 19 on 'The Right to Social Security' (UN Doc. E/C.12/GC/19 of 4 February 2008) para 59; and CESCR, General Comment 21 on 'The right of everyone to take part in cultural life' (UN Doc. E/C.12/GC/21 of 21 December 2009) para 55.

[42] CESCR, GC 12 (n 40) para 14.

[43] CESCR, GC 14 (n 41) para 38; the same words have been used in CESCR, GC 15 (n 41) para 30; CESCR, GC 17 (n 41) para 36; CESCR, GC 18 (n 41) para 29; CESCR, GC 19 (n 41) para 52; CESCR, GC 21 (n 41) para 56.

[44] CESCR, General Comment 16 on 'The Equal Right of Men and Women to the Enjoyment of All Economic, Social, and Cultural Rights' (UN Doc. E/C.12/2005/4 of 11 August 2005) para 16 (emphasis added). The CESCR refers here to CESCR, GC 3 (n 29).

[45] The obligation indicated here is equality between women and men as provided in article 3 ICESCR.

[46] CESCR, GC 16 (n 44) para 17.

> To demonstrate compliance with their general and specific obligations, States parties must show that they have taken appropriate measures to ensure the respect for and protection of cultural freedoms, as well as the necessary steps towards the full realization of the right to take part in cultural life within their maximum available resources.[47]

Here, the CESCR uses two categories of obligations: obligations of conduct (comparable to object or *l'objet*) and obligations of result (comparable to purpose or *le but*). The International Law Commission, which also uses the distinction, describes the obligation of conduct as an obligation 'where an organ of the State is obliged to undertake a specific course of conduct, whether through act or omission, which represents a goal in itself'.[48] 'Obligation of result' is described as requiring a 'State to achieve a particular result through a course of conduct (...), the form of which is left to the State's discretion'.[49] Eide uses similar terms to define the two categories of obligations: 'an obligation of conduct (active or passive) points to behaviour which the duty holder should follow or abstain from. An obligation of result is less concerned with the choice of the line of action taken, but more concerned with the results which the duty-holder should achieve or avoid'.[50] In defining the obligations, the CESCR has made the distinction: there is first a basic level which must be achieved, constituting immediate obligations ('appropriate measures to ensure the respect for and protection of'). Next, there are obligations of conduct ('the necessary steps towards full realization') and finally the obligations of result ('full realization of the right to take part in cultural life'). For each right of the ICESCR it would be possible to identify these obligations, yet the set of obligations of conduct would differ from right to right, also depending on the circumstances within a state.

References to 'progressive realization' and the debate on the nature of ESC-rights made that the 'full realization of rights' was not considered as an obligatory goal. If the purpose is not understood as obligatory, the whole set of 'obligations' of the ICESCR would aim to realise a vague aspiration, making it even more difficult to pinpoint the exact obligations of the ICESCR. Likewise, having only obligations of result (or purpose) would deprive the Covenant of 'any serious content': '(a)s the terms of article 2(1) make clear, the result, namely the full realization of the rights, only has to be achieved in a progressive manner. If States had total discretion as to the means employed to that end, there would be little basis upon which to judge whether or not they were acting in good faith'.[51] When the purpose of the ICESCR

---

[47] CESCR, GC 21 (n 41) para 60.
[48] Craven (n 20) 107.
[49] Report of the ILC (1977) 2 Yrbk ILC 20, para 11-30 cited by Craven (n 20) 107.
[50] Asbjorn Eide, 'Realization of Social and Economic Rights and the Minimum Threshold Approach' (1989) 10 Human Rights Law Journal 35, 38 cited by Maria Green, 'What We Talk about When We Talk about Indicators: Current Approaches to Human Rights Measurement' (2001) 23 Human Rights Quarterly 1062, 1075.
[51] Craven (n 20) 107.

is understood as the full realization of rights, the set of obligations must be understood as concrete, hard and measurable legal norms, since it would otherwise become difficult to achieve that purpose. Consequently, article 2(1) is the bridge between the object and purpose, as it contains the final goal, and also in general terms what the general obligations are to achieve this final goal (further specified by the substantive articles).

That both object and purpose can be found within article 2(1) is confirmed by Craven: '(a)lthough emphasis is placed on the result, namely 'the full realization of the rights', there are plenty of indications within article 2(1) and the substantive articles themselves as to what steps are to be taken'.[52] According to Craven, 'the objective of the State obligations is clearly stated in article 2(1), namely the 'full realization of the rights recognized' in the Covenant'.[53] Article 2(1), consequently, is a rather ambiguous provision. It contains the formulation of the purpose of the treaty, it contains certain indications of the object and it is not a substantive article. Rather, article 2(1) is a programmatic article, making it not uncommon to contain both the purpose and the object of the treaty. In fact, 'a closer examination shows that the difference between the two forms of obligations is not as great as first appears'.[54] The object must be aimed at achieving the purpose and the purpose can be determined through assessing the direction of the objects.[55]

If article 2(1) were understood as constituting a provision so vague as to amount to an aspiration without creating obligations it would completely undermine the ICESCR: 'the overall objective, indeed the *raison d'être*, of the Covenant (...) is to establish clear obligations for States Parties in respect of the full realization of the rights in question'.[56] In other words, interpreting article 2(1) as not containing legally binding obligations would undermine the object and purpose of the Covenant.[57]

## 4 Ordinary meaning of words: the legal content and meaning of article 2(1)

### 4.1 Introduction

Considering and defining each individual word of article 2(1) separately would result in having so much information that further analysis would become

---

[52] Ibid.
[53] Ibid, 109.
[54] Ibid, 107.
[55] When describing obligations of conduct, it is not uncommon to also find mention of 'an objective towards which that conduct is aimed'. Ibid.
[56] CESCR, GC 3 (n 29) para 9 cited by Sepúlveda, *The Nature of the Obligations* (n 16) 312.
[57] According to Sepúlveda, *The Nature of the Obligations* (n 16) 311, citing CESCR, GC 3 (n 29) para 9.

impossible.[58] Some of the words used in article 2(1) have dozens of possible meanings, many of which could immediately be eliminated in the light of the text. The provision will therefore be divided in 'phrases' to be able to make use of the immediate context of that phrase. The 'phrases' to be discussed here are deemed to be the most relevant for the question to what extent article 2(1) contains a duty to accept humanitarian assistance: 'undertakes to take steps'; 'individually and through international assistance and cooperation'; 'to the maximum of its available resources'; 'with a view to achieving progressively the full realization'; and 'by all appropriate means'. Although this section depicts what in the methodology has been referred to as 'ordinary meaning of words', a complete overview of the content and meaning is given to which end a variety of sources is included along with the findings of the previous two sections.

### 4.2 Undertakes to take steps

According to the CESCR, the phrase 'undertakes to take steps' refers to an immediate obligation, meaning that it is an obligation that must be adhered to from the moment of becoming a party to the treaty.[59] The obligation of taking steps is directly linked to the idea of progressive realization (also laid down in article 2(1)). In the words of the Committee: 'full realization of the relevant rights may be achieved progressively; steps towards that goal must be taken within a reasonably short time after the Covenant's entry into force'.[60] Suggested alternatives to 'take steps towards full realization' were 'to guarantee' or 'ensure' the rights.[61] Even though the requirement to 'guarantee' achievement of a certain goal seems more definite than 'taking steps' towards that goal, it does not mean that 'taking steps' cannot be considered a 'hard' legal norm. The formulation is also used in the ICCPR (where the phrase is used in article 2) and the CAT (also in article 2), which are considered to constitute legal obligations.

The CESCR makes a distinction between obligations of conduct and obligations of result, the first category indicating obligations of action and the other category is

---

[58] The text of article 2(1) ICESCR is: 'Each State Party to the present Covenant undertakes to take steps, individually and through international assistance and co-operation, especially economic and technical, to the maximum of its available resources, with a view to achieving progressively the full realization of the rights recognized in the present Covenant by all appropriate means, including particularly the adoption of legislative measures.'

[59] Others understand 'taking steps' in the same way: 'an immediate and readily identifiable obligation upon states parties'. Alston & Quinn (n 19) 166. In all five authentic languages of the ICESCR, the understanding is reflected that 'to take steps', although translated in different ways, indicates taking immediate action.

[60] CESCR, GC 3 (n 29) para 2.

[61] UN Doc. E/CN.4/L.73 (1952) cited by Alston & Quinn (n 19) 165. Another proposal deemed unacceptable was 'to pledge themselves'; 8 UN ESCOR C.4 (270th mtg.) at 11, UN Doc. E/CN.4/SR.270 (1952) and 7 UN ESCOR C.4 (231st mtg.) at 18-9, UN Doc. E/CN.4/SR.231 (1951), cited by Alston & Quinn (n 19) 165.

referring to the obligations of what must be achieved through this action. Taking steps would constitute an obligation of conduct 'to take the necessary action to execute the provisions of the Covenant'.[62] The nature of the obligation 'to take steps' is considered to be of such importance that it cannot be subjected to limitation.[63] Accordingly, there is a strong indication that the limitation-clause of article 4 ICESCR cannot be applied on article 2(1). However, it has not been clarified whether the impossibility of limitation includes 'limitation' due to limited available resources.[64]

The CESCR elaborated on its understanding of 'steps': these 'should be deliberate, concrete and targeted as clearly as possible towards meeting the obligations recognized in the Covenant'.[65] The word 'undertakes' indicates a commitment to start doing something (and then to actually do it).[66] In the context of this phrase, the commitment would be to 'taking steps' towards the full realization of rights.

Through the state reporting procedure of article 16 ICESCR, states must explain the steps which they will take. According to the CESCR there is an obligation for parties to 'work out and adopt a detailed plan of action for the progressive implementation of each of the rights of the Covenant', a duty which is explicitly laid down in article 14 ICESCR.[67] States can quite clearly explain their plans in the state reports, which makes it possible for the CESCR to examine the plans and thus the steps taken (or the steps that states intend to take). Yet, the Committee acknowledges that it is extremely difficult to do this, because the socio-economic situation in each state party is different and therefore the steps required for the full realization of the rights also differ. The CESCR therefore needs detailed

---

[62] Craven calls this 'a general rule of international law' which he bases on PCIJ, *The Case Relative to the Exchange of Greek and Turkish Populations under the Lausanne Convention VI* (1925) Series B, No 10 at 20, Craven (n 20) 114. This is also concluded by Alston & Quinn (n 19) 165.

[63] Sepúlveda, *The Nature of the Obligations* (n 16) 313, basing the statement on the General Comments and the Limburg Principles (Principle 16).

[64] The phrase 'to the maximum of its available resources' will be discussed in section 3.4.

[65] CESCR, GC 3 (n 29) para 2; CESCR, GC 13 (n 41) para 43, 52; CESCR, GC 14 (n 41) para 30; CESCR, GC 15 (n 41) para 17; CESCR, GC 18 (n 41) para 19; CESCR, GC 19 (n 41) para 40. Also according the dictionary, 'steps' refers to something as part of a sequence, although achieving a final goal is not necessarily part of the definition; Oxford Advanced Learner's Dictionary (7th edition 2007) 1503. This is in line with the referral to the phrase as an obligation of conduct, and not an obligation of result.

[66] An alternative meaning of undertake is 'to agree or promise that you will do something', where the actual action is not included. That here the actual taking of action is included follows from the meaning of 'take' ('somebody is doing something, performing an action, etcetera'); Oxford Advanced Learner's Dictionary (7th edition 2007) 1667 resp. 1563. The word 'undertakes' is not in itself explained by the CESCR in any of the General Comments.

[67] CESCR, General Comment 1 on 'Reporting by State Parties' of 24 February 1989, para 4; these words are according to the CESCR a reflection of the phrases 'to take steps' and 'by all appropriate means'.

information from the state reports and, where possible, other sources to have a proper check on the steps taken by states.

### 4.3 Individually and through international assistance and cooperation

There are two ways in which 'individually and through international assistance and cooperation' can be understood in terms of obligations. It is on the one hand possible to understand 'international assistance and cooperation' as an obligation to be used next to individual action, meaning that states are obliged to make use of international assistance and cooperation and that they violate the ICESCR when they only act individually. On the other hand, the phrase can also be understood as a means to achieve certain goals (or to fulfil certain obligations), like the full realization of the rights of the ICESCR. In that case, it could be considered as not constituting an obligation to cooperate internationally or to use international assistance: it is then merely a suggested alternative way of working (besides acting individually) in order to meet certain obligations. The CESCR is not taking a clear line in subscribing either of the two possible meanings.

In the first General Comment, the language used regarding international assistance and cooperation is quite casual. The first General Comment aims at clarifying what is expected of states in the reporting mechanism, and the CESCR explains that it

> Is aware that this process of monitoring and gathering information is a potentially time-consuming and costly one and that international assistance and cooperation (...) may well be required in order to enable some States parties to fulfil the relevant obligations. If that is the case, and the State party concludes that it does not have the capacity to undertake the monitoring process (...) it may note this fact in its report to the Committee and indicate the nature and extent of any international assistance that it may need.[68]

Here 'international assistance and cooperation' is not, in itself, considered to be an obligation. Instead, states are required to 'fulfil the relevant obligations', and to do so international assistance and cooperation 'may' be required. This – for legal purposes – soft language does not change much in the years following the first General Comment,[69] although the third General Comment contains elements in which another view becomes somewhat visible. The line of reasoning that '(w)ithout an active programme of international assistance and cooperation, the full

[68] Ibid, para 3.

[69] General Comment 2 provides in relation to the debt crisis of many (developing) countries that 'international measures to deal with the debt crisis should take full account of the need to protect economic, social and cultural rights through, inter alia, international cooperation'. CESCR, GC 2 (n 40) para 9 (the underlining from the original is omitted). In General Comment 3, the CESCR acknowledges 'the essential role of such [international] cooperation in facilitating the full realization of the relevant rights'. CESCR, GC 3 (n 29) para 13.

realization of economic, social and cultural rights will remain an unfulfilled aspiration', with which the Committee is indicating that 'international assistance and cooperation is only a means to realize the rights of the Covenant',[70] can also be found in General Comment 4 on article 11(1) ICESCR. In this article it is worded that states should recognize the 'essential importance of international cooperation based on free consent'. The noncommittal language of 'recognize' and 'free consent' is not addressed or clarified in any way.

Using stronger language compared to the previous Comments and to other paragraphs within the same Comment, General Comment 3 provides that 'international cooperation for development and thus for the realization of economic, social and cultural rights is an *obligation* of all States', especially for those that are in a position to assist others.[71] Consequently, the Committee understands 'international assistance and cooperation' as a concrete obligation, and while still aimed at achieving a certain goal, it is not a policy choice between merely acting individually or using international assistance and cooperation. Moreover, the CESCR makes a distinction between states that are in a position to give assistance, and those who receive it. The states in the position to assist are especially under an obligation to do so. Whether or not other states are as a result under a duty to receive is not made clear. In the other General Comments, the CESCR continues with the rather confusing line on 'international assistance and cooperation', although it must be noted that language establishing an obligation has not been used in General Comments after number 17.[72]

One way of achieving more clarity which has (perhaps unintentionally) been attempted by the CESCR is distinguishing between states that are offering or

---

[70] CESCR, GC 3 (n 29) para 14. With this phrase, the CESCR is arguing that a state party is not capable of realizing the rights of the ICESCR only by acting individually.

[71] CESCR, GC 3 (n 29) para 14 (emphasis added); these words are repeated in CESCR, GC 21 (n 41) para 58.

[72] Although the General Comments after number 17 still mention 'international assistance and cooperation, only in weaker language: 'States parties should recognize the essential role of international cooperation', CESCR, GC 18 (n 41) para 29; CESCR, GC 19 (n 41) para 52; CESCR, GC 21 (n 41) para 56. The same words have been used in CESCR, GC 14 (n 41) para 38; CESCR, GC 15 (n 41) para 30 and in CESCR, GC 17 (n 41) para 36. Other examples of weaker formulations are '(i)nternational cooperation requires States parties to refrain from actions that interfere, directly or indirectly, with the enjoyment of the right to water in other countries' (a negative formulation), CESCR, GC 15 (n 41) para 31; '(i)f necessary, they should avail themselves of international cooperation and technical assistance in line with article 2, paragraph 1, of the Covenant' and '(w)hen examining the reports of States parties and their ability to meet the obligations to realize the right to social security, the Committee will consider the effects of the assistance provided by all other actors', CESCR, GC 19 (n 41) paras 41, 68 and 84. Examples of reference to 'international assistance and cooperation' as an obligation can also be found: 'international cooperation for development and thus for the realization of economic, social and cultural rights is an obligation of all States parties (...)' and 'their obligations under the Covenant, in particular the obligations contained in articles 2 paragraph 1, (...) concerning international assistance and cooperation', CESCR, GC 17 (n 41) paras 37 and 56.

providing assistance on the one hand and those states seeking or receiving it on the other, as was mentioned above in connection to General Comment 3. In General Comment 11 it is provided that 'in appropriate cases, the Committee encourages States parties to seek the assistance of relevant international agencies'.[73] Here, the CESCR is directing the suggestion to states 'seeking' assistance and not those offering it. The 'obligation' to international assistance as seen in General Comment 3 was especially directed to states in a position to assist. It accordingly appears as if offering assistance has a stronger obligatory connotation than seeking assistance.[74] It has been acknowledged by others that this distinction exists, although no clear indicators on legal obligations can be found.[75] At the very least, it is accepted that there is no right to do nothing.[76]

One other quite interesting way of determining the obligations of state parties can be found in General Comment 12. In this Comment, the distinction is made between on the one hand violation of obligations due to inability of the state to do otherwise and on the other hand violation due to unwillingness to realize the rights

[73] CESCR, GC 11 (n 40) para 11.

[74] Also in General Comments 8, 12, 13 14, 15 and 17 the CESCR refers to the providing-side in more obligatory wordings: 'external entities' have 'an obligation 'to take steps, individually and through international assistance and cooperation, especially economic and technical' in order to respond to any disproportionate suffering experienced by vulnerable groups within the targeted country' in CESCR, General Comment 8 on 'The Relationship between Economic Sanctions and Respect for Economic, Social and Cultural Rights' (UN Doc. E/C.12/1997/8 of 12 December 1997) para 14. 'States parties should take steps to respect the enjoyment of the right to food in other countries, to protect that right, to facilitate access to food and to provide the necessary aid when required' in CESCR, GC 12 (n 40) para 36. General Comment 13 (n 41) provides a list of instruments referring to international assistance and cooperation, which 'all reinforce the obligation of States parties in relation to the provision of international assistance and cooperation', para 56. General Comments 14 and 15 provide that: '(d)epending on the availability of resources, States should facilitate access to essential health facilities, goods, and services in other countries, wherever possible and provide the necessary aid when required'. CESCR, GC 14 (n 41) para 39; CESCR, GC 15 (n 41) para 34. Finally, 'it is particularly incumbent on States parties and other actors in a position to assist, to provide "international assistance and cooperation".' CESCR, GC 14 (n 41) para 45; CESCR, GC 15 (n 41) para 38; CESCR, GC 17 (n 41) para 40. With regard to 'seeking assistance', the CESCR merely argues that a state must do so when it does not have sufficient resources to realize the rights of the ICESCR.

[75] Alston & Quinn explain that the soft language for the seeking-side follows from the drafting of the ICESCR: UN Doc. E/CN.4/SR.233 (1951) 8, cited by Alston & Quinn (n 19) 187. Although this explicitly constitutes a 'duty' to request or seek assistance, it also implies a duty to accept at the same time; otherwise the request would be futile as it would do nothing to supplementing the requesting state's resources. See further Judith Bueno de Mesquita, Paul Hunt & Rajat Khosla, 'The Human Rights Responsibility of International Assistance and Cooperation in Health' in Mark Gibney & Sigrun I. Skogly (eds), *Universal Human Rights and Extraterritorial Obligations* (University of Pennsylvania Press, Philadelphia 2010) 113.

[76] Based on W. Verwey, *The Establishment of a New International Economic Order and the Realization of the Right to Development and Welfare* (1980) 22 and F. van Hoof, 'Problems and Prospects with Respect to the Right to Food' in P. van Dijk *et al.* (eds.) *Restructuring the International Economic Order: The Role of Law and Lawyers* (1987) 107, 117. Craven (n 20) 146.

of the ICESCR. When a state claims that it could not carry out its obligations for reasons beyond its control (i.e. being unable to do so), the state has the 'burden of proving that this is the case and that it has unsuccessfully sought to obtain international support to ensure the availability and accessibility of the necessary food'.[77] Here, the duty to justify why a state did not fulfil its obligations under the right to food implies a duty to seek international assistance and cooperation, because proof that such assistance has been sought illustrates that the state was in fact willing to meet its obligations, yet unable to do so.

Finally, some remarks on the meaning of 'cooperation' and 'assistance' as used by the CESCR are in place. In the understanding of the CESCR, 'assistance' is a specific kind of 'cooperation', where 'cooperation' must not be considered as development cooperation only.[78] 'Assistance' would refer to the transfer of 'funds, goods, and services', as such indicating a one-way direction.[79] Apparently, it was not at first the intention to include the word 'assistance', as illustrated by early drafts of article 2(1) that merely speak of 'cooperation'.[80] In general, states responded negatively on the inclusion of 'international assistance'. According to many states, 'assistance' can never be regarded as an obligation since it must be given out of free will (as such acknowledging that this part of article 2(1), at least, constitutes obligations).[81] Even so, the mere fact that in the drafting process obligations to international assistance and cooperation were not foreseen is not enough to conclude that no such obligations exist:

> On the basis of the preparatory work it is difficult, if not impossible, to sustain the argument that the commitment to international cooperation contained in the Covenant can accurately be characterised as a legally binding obligation upon any particular state to provide any particular form of assistance. It would, however, be unjustified to go further and suggest that the relevant commitment is meaningless.[82]

What has been seen is so far is that the CESCR is not consistent nor fully clear in its understanding of 'international assistance and cooperation', on the one hand seeing it as a noncommittal option out of a number of other possibilities to realize the rights of the ICESCR and on the other hand as an obligation in the sense that it must necessarily be used to realize the rights of the ICESCR. Only where the Committee distinguishes between offering/providing and seeking/accepting international assistance and cooperation, some clarity is achieved, where the

---

[77] CESCR, GC 12 (n 40) para 17.

[78] Craven (n 20) 147 cited by Rolf Künnemann, 'Extraterritorial Application of the International Covenant on Economic, Social and Cultural Rights' in Fons Coomans & Menno T. Kamminga, *Extraterritorial Application of Human Rights Treaties* (Intersentia, Antwerp 2004) 203, 204. Künnemann bases this conclusion on the General Comments.

[79] Künnemann (n 78) 203.

[80] Ibid.

[81] Alston & Quinn (n 19) 190-1.

[82] Ibid, 191.

CESCR is more inclined to acknowledge the existence of an obligation to offer assistance than an obligation to accept (or seek) assistance. However, 'there should be no doubt that the Committee considers that there are 'legal' obligations in regard to international assistance and cooperation'.[83] This view is shared by Paul Hunt, former Special Rapporteur on the Right to Health:

> If there is no legal obligation underpinning the human rights responsibility of international assistance and cooperation, inescapably all international assistance and cooperation fundamentally rests upon charity. While such a position might have been tenable in years gone by, it is unacceptable in the twenty-first century.[84]

The exact 'scope and content of international obligations still needs to be determined' but other instruments of international law also refer to 'international cooperation'.[85] For example, the UN Charter – to which the ICESCR refers in its preamble – describes as one of the purposes of the UN 'to achieve international co-operation in solving international problems of an economic, social, cultural, or humanitarian character and in promoting and encouraging respect for human rights'.[86] In addition, article 55 explains that certain conditions are required for international stability and peace, like higher standards of living, international cultural and educational cooperation, and universal respect for human rights. These purposes must be achieved, according to article 56, through joint and separate action of states in cooperation with the UN. Here again the articles do not provide any details with regard to what is expected from states and it is therefore very difficult to determine which parts constitute obligations, and what exactly these obligations would entail.[87] The OAS does provide some details on obligations: 'Member States have obligations to work together for economic, social, and cultural

[83] Sepúlveda, 'Obligations of 'International Assistance and Cooperation' (n 17) 278. Sepúlveda refers to other sources where the same conclusion is drawn, for example the Limburg Principles. Even so, she also acknowledges that in the years between the CESCR's start with clarifying the scope and meaning of obligations and the time of her research more than ten years later, the meaning of the phrase has not become much clearer.

[84] Report of the Special Rapporteur on the Right of Everyone to the Enjoyment of the Highest Attainable Standard of Physical and Mental Health, Paul Hunt, Addendum: Missions to the World Bank and International Monetary Fund in Washington, DC (20 October 2006) UN Doc. A/HRC/7/11/Add.2 of 5 March 2008, para 133 cited by Bueno de Mesquita, Hunt & Khosla (n 75) 112.

[85] Sepúlveda, 'Obligations of 'International Assistance and Cooperation' (n 17) 275 & 278.

[86] Article 1(2) and (3) UN Charter. A comparable purpose can also be found for the OAS: '(a)mong the core purposes of the OAS is the promotion, through cooperative action, of economic and social development'; Brian Concannon Jr. & Beatrice Lindstrom, 'Cheaper, Better, Longer-Lasting: A Rights-Based Approach to Disaster Response in Haiti' (2011) 25 Emory International Law Review 1145, 1154 (footnotes omitted), referring to article 2(f) OAS Charter.

[87] Alston & Quinn (n 19) 187.

rights, particularly when a state is seriously affected by conditions it cannot remedy alone'.[88]

In Chapter II it has already been said that also the Convention on the Rights of the Child contains references to international assistance and cooperation. The CRC refers in article 4 to international assistance and cooperation and to using the maximum of available resources.[89] The importance of international cooperation is also reiterated in the CRC's preamble, in article 23 on rights of disabled children, in article 28 on the right to education and in article 45 on implementation of the CRC.[90] The Committee on the Rights of the Child has frequently assessed when assessing state reports 'whether 'international assistance is needed' for the fulfilment of the rights contained therein'.[91] In the Concluding Observations the Committee on the Rights of the Child time and again recommends a state party to 'increase international assistance and to use the principles and provisions of the Convention as a framework for its programme of international development assistance'.[92]

For now, it is only possible to give some general indications of obligations in the context of international cooperation and assistance, a conclusion that others also arrived at: '(i)n the context of the human rights responsibility of international assistance and cooperation, the devil is *not* in the detail, but in sweeping generalizations of an entirely abstract nature'.[93] More detail can be found in the substantive articles of the ICESCR: '(i)n the context of a given right it may, according to the circumstances, be possible to identify obligations to cooperate internationally that would appear to be mandatory on the basis of the undertaking contained in Article 2(1) of the Covenant'.[94] In other words, to determine whether an obligation regarding international cooperation and assistance exists, it must be considered what the circumstances are in individual cases for separate rights: '(i)n our view, the way forward is to look at this human rights responsibility in relation to specific sectors, issues, and rights'.[95]

---

[88] Concannon & Lindstrom (n 86) 1154 (footnotes omitted), referring to articles 37 of the OAS Charter.

[89] The text reads: 'with regard to economic, social and cultural rights, States parties shall undertake such measures to the maximum extent of their available resources and, where needed, within the framework of international co-operation'.

[90] In addition, the CRC refers in articles 24 and 28 to 'progressive realization', and in article 23 to 'available resources'.

[91] Sepúlveda, 'Obligations of 'International Assistance and Cooperation' (n 17) 276. Sepúlveda cites the example of the List of Issues Trinidad and Tobago (UN Doc. CRC/C/Q/TRI/1 of 13 June 1997).

[92] Concluding Observations Australia (UN Doc. CRC/C/15/Add.79) para 25, cited by Sepúlveda, 'Obligations of 'International Assistance and Cooperation' (n 17) 276.

[93] Bueno de Mesquita, Hunt & Khosla (n 75) 128-9 (emphasis in original).

[94] Alston & Quinn (n 19) 191.

[95] Bueno de Mesquita, Hunt & Khosla (n 75) 128. This will be done in the next Chapter.

## 4.4 To the maximum of its available resources

As was the case with the phrase 'individually or through international assistance and cooperation', the phrase 'to the maximum of its available resources' can be understood in two ways. First, it can be an obligation stating that as many resources as possible must be obtained for the realisation of the ICESCR (making it part of the whole set of obligations stemming from article 2(1)). In the second place, it could also be understood as a justification for non-compliance: when the state does not meet certain obligations, it can argue that it did not have the resources to comply. For this research it is crucial what the meaning of the phrase is. In the first option states appear to have a duty to seek assistance if their own resources are insufficient (which is not uncommon in disaster situations). The second option means that states can use the occurrence of a disaster – and consequently not having sufficient resources – as a justification for non-compliance.

In the *travaux préparatoires* of the ICESCR it has been stressed on various occasions that having insufficient resources should not be considered as a ground to circumvent obligations.[96] To prevent abuse it has been argued that 'real' resources should be taken into account instead of only considering allocations made by the government. [97] Furthermore, 'resources' were meant 'to include whatever international as well as national resources were available', so that states were not free to 'arbitrarily and artificially determine for themselves the level of commitment required by the Covenant'.[98] Any discretion granted to states 'cannot be entirely open-ended or it would have the *de facto* effect of nullifying the existence of any real obligation'.[99] 'To the maximum of its available resources' therefore includes those resources available internationally and using the maximum of available resources is an obligation, giving ground for the related obligation to seek international assistance if insufficient resources are available.[100]

Notwithstanding the intentions of the drafters, it appears that the CESCR considers the phrase to be a justification for non-compliance, but with some limitations. These limitations lie in certain obligations a state has at all times, also when little resources are available. States should always, at the very least, continue

---

[96] It must be noted that although 'resources' has a connotation to consists of monetary resources, it can also include material items like 'equipment'. See Oxford Advanced Learner's Dictionary (7th edition 2007) 1293.

[97] Alston & Quinn (n 19) 178.

[98] Ibid, 179.

[99] Ibid, 177.

[100] The CESCR too recognized the phrase as 'intended by the drafters of the Covenant to refer to both the resources existing within a State and those available from the international community through international cooperation and assistance'. CESCR, GC 3 (n 29) para 13. This was repeated in General Comment 4: 'To the extent that any such steps are considered to be beyond the maximum resources available to a State party, *it is appropriate* that a request be made as soon as possible for international cooperation'; CESCR, GC 4 (n 40) para 10 (emphasis added to illustrate the 'soft' language used here). See further CESCR, GC 11 (n 40) para 9.

to monitor and to make strategies and plans (which is in line with 'undertakes to take steps'),[101] and in times of 'severe resources constraints' the state must at least take care of the most vulnerable groups through 'relatively low-cost targeted programmes'.[102] Moreover, the minimum core obligations of each right must also be realized at all times. A minimum core obligation – or the core content of a right – must

> Ensure the satisfaction of, at the very least, minimum essential levels of each of the rights is incumbent upon every State party. Thus, for example, a State party in which any significant number of individuals is deprived of essential foodstuffs, of essential primary health care, of basic shelter and housing, or of the most basic forms of education is, prima facie, failing to discharge its obligations under the Covenant. If the Covenant were to be read in such a way as not to establish such a minimum core obligation, it would be largely deprived of its raison d'être.

While the core contents must at all times be realized (by General Comment 17 it is even explicitly stated that the core contents are non-derogable), the CESCR did however leave an opening for situations of resource constraints:

> It must be noted that any assessment as to whether a State has discharged its minimum core obligation must also take account of resource constraints applying within the country concerned. (...) In order for a State party to be able to attribute its failure to meet at least its minimum core obligations to a lack of available resources it must demonstrate that every effort has been made to use all resources that are at its disposition in an effort to satisfy, as a matter of priority, those minimum obligations.[103]

Consequently, not having sufficient resources to realize certain rights of the ICESCR can be used as a justification for non-compliance, but not for all

---

[101] 'A State party cannot escape the unequivocal obligation to adopt a plan of action on the grounds that the necessary resources are not available. If the obligation could be avoided in this way, there would be no justification for the unique requirement contained in article 14 which applies, almost by definition, to situations characterized by inadequate financial resources'. CESCR, GC 11 (n 40) para 9.

[102] CESCR, GC 3 (n 29) para 11-2. Also in General Comment 5 it is stated that 'the duty of States parties to protect the vulnerable members of their societies assumes greater rather than less importance in times of severe resource constraints; CESCR, General Comment 5 on 'Persons with disabilities' of 9 December 1994, para 10; see also CESCR, General Comment 6 on 'The Economic, Social and Cultural Rights of Older Persons' of 8 December 1995, para 17, CESCR, GC 15 (n 41) para 13; CESCR, CESCR, GC 17 (n 41), para 20; CESCR, GC 21 (n 41) para 23.

[103] CESCR, GC 3 (n 29) para 10. This is also confirmed by others. See inter alia Craven (n 20) 141, citing A. Eide, 'Realization of Social and Economic Rights and the Minimum Threshold Approach' (1989) 10 Human Rights Law Journal 35, 43-7, Mratchkov E/C12/1990/SR.46, at 8 para 37, Alston E/C.12/1987/SR.19 at 8, para 40, Taya E/C.12/1990/SR.46 at 9 para 42.

obligations,[104] and not when a state has failed to seek additional resources through international assistance and cooperation. Here, the difference between an unable and unwilling state becomes clear. An unable state has tried to obtain additional resources, an unwilling state is either not using the maximum of its available resources or has not tried to obtain additional resources internationally.[105] To monitor the use of resources, the CESCR had to overcome some practical hurdles. Allocation of resources is a matter of the state and the Committee cannot easily judge on compliance and it cannot dictate how each state must allocate its resources.[106] Therefore, only in case of non-compliance with other obligations the use of resources is checked: 'the question of resources enters into the discussion at the point of determining whether or not the minimum core obligation has been satisfied'.[107] Not fulfilling certain obligations results in a violation of the Covenant,[108] on which the Committee assesses the budgetary decisions and claims on resources made by the state party and gives its opinion on it.[109] This approach appears to solve a number of difficulties the CESCR would have in monitoring:

> As far as the Committee is concerned, it avoids the problems of measuring progress against resources availability, of speculating as to alternate courses of action, or of acquiring evidence of State responsibility. In cases where significant numbers of

[104] As inter alia depicted in GC 14: 'If resource constraints render it impossible for a State to comply fully with its Covenant obligations, it has the burden of justifying that every effort has nevertheless been made to use all available resources at its disposal in order to satisfy, as a matter of priority, the obligations outlined above.' CESCR, GC 14 (n 41) para 47; the same words are used in CESCR, GC 15 (n 41) para 41 and in CESCR, GC 17 (n 41) para 41.

[105] See for example CESCR, GC 14 (n 41) para 47: '(a) State which is unwilling to use the maximum of its available resources for the realization of the right to health is in violation of its obligations under article 12'. Notably, the CESCR argues that this is a violation of article 12, and not of article 2(1) which contains the phrase 'maximum of its available resources'. The same terminology is used in CESCR, GC 15 (n 41) para 41, only ending the phrase with 'is in violation of its obligations under the Covenant'. In GC 17 also the same terminology is used, but then ending the phrase with reference the particular right under discussion; CESCR, GC 17 (n 41) para 41; see further CESCR, GC 18 (n 41) para 32 with explicit referral to article 6 ICESCR.

[106] Although states have certain obligations of realizing minimum core obligations, limiting the freedom of resource allocation slightly as it is directed by the obligations stemming from the ICESCR. Sepúlveda, *The Nature of the Obligations* (n 16) 315. Alston & Quinn (n 19) 181. As an extra check, the Committee recommends the involvement of national courts in the allocation of resources; CESCR, GC 9 (n 29) para 10.

[107] Craven (n 20) 143.

[108] Ibid, 142.

[109] Ibid, 137. Resources allocated to a certain goal must be used for that goal, through which a state has the duty to prevent corruption and to make sure that resources are used properly: Concluding Observations Nigeria (UN Doc. E/1999/22 paras 97 and 119), Concluding Observations Mexico (UN Doc. E/2000/22 paras 381 and 394) and Concluding Observations Colombia (UN Doc. E/ 1996/22 para 181), cited by Sepúlveda, *The Nature of the Obligations* (n 16) 315.

> people live in poverty and hunger, it is for the State to show that its failure to provide for the persons concerned was beyond its control.[110]

The burden of proof is transferred to the state, yet it must first be determined whether or not a certain obligation has been fulfilled, which is challenging enough.[111] If a situation of non-compliance is found in which it is concluded that insufficient resources were available, it does not automatically mean that the problem of non-compliance would indeed have been resolved by using more resources.[112]

In the context of the the Optional Protocol to the ICESCR – creating room for individual complaints – the evaluation of complaints regarding the obligation to use the maximum of available resources has been explained following this line. In the words of the CESCR:

> The "availability of resources", although an important qualifier to the obligation to take steps, does not alter the immediacy of the obligation, nor can resource constraints alone justify inaction. Where the available resources are demonstrably inadequate, the obligation remains for a State party to ensure the widest possible enjoyment of economic, social and cultural rights under the prevailing circumstances. The Committee has already emphasized that, even in times of severe resource constraints, States parties must protect the most disadvantaged and marginalized members or groups of society by adopting relatively low-cost targeted programmes.
>
> The undertaking by a State party to use "the maximum" of its available resources (…) entitles it to receive resources offered by the international community. (…)[113]

For evaluating individual complaints on this ground, the CESCR explicitly stated that if a country is recovering from a disaster, that particular circumstance will be taken into account. In addition, whether or not the state has rejected offers of assistance will also be taken into account.[114] Using the maximum of available resources is therefore an obligation of conduct, including seeking additional resources internationally, only to be measured in case of non-compliance.

---

[110] Craven (n 20) 143.

[111] The core obligations can be useful here, as they are somewhat easier to measure due to the relatively concrete formulation.

[112] As already issued by the US; Restatement of the Foreign Relations Law of the United States para 701, reporters' note 8, 467 (Tent. Draft No. 6, 1985) cited by Alston & Quinn (n 19) 178.

[113] CESCR, 'Statement by the Committee: An Evaluation of the Obligation to Take Steps to the "Maximum of Available Resources" under an Optional Protocol to the Covenant' (UN Doc. E/C.12/2007/1 of 21 September 2007) paras 4 and 5.

[114] Ibid, para 10 under (d) and (f).

## 4.5 With a view to achieving progressively the full realization

Perhaps the most controversial and ambiguous phrase of article 2(1) ICESCR is that of 'progressive realization', as it seems to make the existence of any direct obligations under the ICESCR impossible. 'Progressive realization' has been referred to as the 'linchpin of the whole Covenant' because the meaning and nature of state obligations turns on this phrase.[115] Since 'progressive realization' is not found within the ICCPR, it is often assumed that the ICCPR contains immediate obligations and the ICESCR does not. Yet even in the context of civil and political rights it is impossible to claim that all rights are suitable for immediate implementation.[116] For some rights, certain efforts and plans are required, making progressive realization the only option.[117] In the preparatory phase, this was acknowledged by looking at categories of rights that can be realized immediately, or those that would require long-term planning and programming.[118]

The CESCR responded to the difficulties of the phrase at an early stage:

> The fact that realization over time, or in other words progressively, is foreseen under the Covenant should not be misinterpreted as depriving the obligation of all meaningful content. It is on the one hand a necessary flexibility device, reflecting the realities of the real world and the difficulties involved for any country in ensuring full realization of economic, social and cultural rights. On the other hand, the phrase must be read in the light of the overall objective, indeed the raison d'être, of the Covenant which is to establish clear obligations for States parties in respect of the full realization of the rights in question.[119]

What 'progressive realization' means in terms of obligations has been explained in the same paragraph: to 'move as expeditiously and effectively as possible' towards realizing the rights of the ICESCR.[120]

It has been confirmed by the CESCR that immediate as well as long-term obligations follow from the ICESCR.[121] The phrase 'achieving progressively the full realization' indicates long-term obligations (to achieve in the end full

---

[115] Alston & Quinn (n 19) 172.
[116] Craven (n 20) 130.
[117] See e.g. Van Hoof (n 76), cited by Alston & Quinn (n 19) 172.
[118] 6 UN GAOR C.3 (565th mtg.) para 9, UN Doc. A/C.3/565 (1952) cited by Alston & Quinn (n 19) 173.
[119] CESCR, GC 3 (n 29) para 9.
[120] Ibid. The same words have also been used in CESCR, GC 13 (n 41) para 44; CESCR, GC 17 (n 41) para 26; and CESCR, GC 18 (n 41) para 20. This interpretation is in line with the general meaning of the words, where 'progressive' means 'steadily and continuously'. Oxford Advanced Learner's Dictionary (7th edition 2007) 1207.
[121] See CESCR, GC 12 (n 40) para 16; see also CESCR, GC 13 (n 41) para 43: 'While the Covenant provides for progressive realization and acknowledges the constraints due to the limits of available resources, it also imposes on States parties various obligations which are of immediate effect'.

realization), but even so there is an immediate obligation to start taking steps:[122] 'the implementation of the rights in question should be pursued without respite'.[123] 'Undertake to take steps' and 'progressive realization' are consequently inextricably linked to each other: 'to promote progressive realization of the relevant rights to the maximum of their available resources clearly requires Governments to do much more than merely abstain from taking measures which might have a negative impact on persons with disabilities'.[124]

'The ultimate objective of the Covenant [namely] the 'full realization' of the rights' is what must be achieved progressively.[125] Using 'full realization' was preferred over 'implementation', as this would 'strengthen rather than to weaken the objective set before future contracting parties'.[126] However, in combination with 'progressive', this phrase 'introduced a dynamic element, indicating that no fixed goal had been set',[127] and that 'the realization of those rights did not stop at a given level'.[128] In each individual state party ESC-rights are in different stages of realization and that the further realization strongly depends on the economic and social circumstances in each state. Obligations imposed on state parties could therefore not be phrased in absolute terms.[129] Consequently, the obligation of result leaves room for individual state circumstances, but making it difficult to measure compliance.

A consequence of 'progressive realization' is that taking retrogressive measures can in principle not be allowed. 'Progressive realization' indicates 'a continuous improvement of conditions over time without backward movement of any kind – in what may be described as a form of 'ratchet effect'.'[130] It can be argued that it is

---

[122] CESCR, GC 14 (n 41) para 30, which is repeated in CESCR, GC 15 (n 41) para 17 and in CESCR, GC 17 (n 41) para 25.

[123] 7 UN ESCOR C.4 (233rd mtg.) at 8, UN Doc. E/CN.4/SR.233 (1951) (Mr. Azmi Bey, Egypt) cited by Alston & Quinn (n 19) 175.

[124] CESCR, GC 5 (n 102) para 9. See also CESCR, GC 12 (n 40) para 14: the 'principal obligation is to take steps to achieve *progressively* the full realization of the right to adequate food' (italics in original).

[125] Craven (n 20) 128.

[126] Cassin (France) E/CN.4/SR.223, at 8 (1951) cited by Craven (n 20) 128.

[127] Sørensen (Denmark) E/CN.4/SR.236 at 21 (1951) cited by Craven (n 20) 129.

[128] Mr Whitlam (Australia) E/CN.4/SR.237 at 5 (1951) cited by Craven (n 20) 129.

[129] 8 UN ESCOR C.4 (271st mtg.) at 12, UN Doc. E/CN.4/SR.271 (1952) (Mr. Azkoul, Lebanon) cited by Alston & Quinn (n 19) 174.

[130] Craven (n 20) 131 (also citing the Committee's repetitive formulation on retrogressive measures); Sepúlveda, *The Nature of the Obligations* (n 16) 319-20. The obligation of 'continuous improvement' can be found in article 11 ICESCR, where it is provided that there must be a 'continuous improvement of living conditions'. Retrogressive measures are mentioned in CESCR, GC 3 (n 29) para 9; CESCR, GC 13 (n 41) para 45; CESCR, GC 14 (n 41) para 32 and 48; CESCR, GC 15 (n 41) para 19 and 42; CESCR, GC 16 (n 44) para 42; CESCR, GC 17 (n 41) para 27 and 42; CESCR, (n 41) para 21; CESCR, GC 19 (n 41) para 42 and 64 (where in para 42 criteria have been formulated); and CESCR, GC 21 (n 41) para 46 (speaking of 'regressive measures') and 65.

possible for states to violate their obligations by not acting.[131] If a deterioration of the level of rights takes place and the state does not undertake action, it would violate the ICESCR.[132] Retrogressive measures are not violations of obligations per se, but when such measures are taken it is provided that such measures 'require the most careful consideration and would need to be fully justified by reference to the totality of the rights provided for in the Covenant and in the context of the full use of the maximum available resources'.[133] The CESCR provides two justifications for taking a retrogressive measure: 'for the purpose of improving the situation with regard to the 'totality of the rights in the Covenant' and an economic crisis which makes progression impossible even if all available resources are used.[134]

In their reports states are expected to show progress over time with respect to effective realization of the rights, including quantitative and qualitative data.[135] Through the reports containing the plans made by the state parties, the CESCR is able to monitor progress made.[136] Progressive realization does not preclude the obligation of immediate realization where this is possible, but the CESCR assumes that also developed states work on realizing the rights progressively and it has, at times, 'been unwilling to accept statements of government representatives claiming that the rights are fully implemented in their country'.[137] It remains difficult to determine exactly what 'progression' is, how much progression is possible in an individual country, and to what extent non-realization is attributable to the state.[138] It must be assessed on a case-by-case basis whether and to what extent a state has done all it can to realize the rights of the Covenant.

---

[131] See for a more detailed overview of the evolution in case law Sepúlveda, *The Nature of the Obligations* (n 16) 320, n 46.

[132] Sepúlveda, *The Nature of the Obligations* (n 16) 321. Examples of this view can be found in Concluding Observations (threats to natural environments in the Solomon Islands affecting article 11, Concluding Observations Solomon Islands UN Doc. E/2000/22 paras 204 and 209; increase of HIV infections in the Russian Federation, Concluding Observations Russian Federation UN Doc. E/1998/22 paras 113 and 126; protection against sexual exploitation of children in Sri Lanka, CO Sri Lanka UN Doc. E/1999/22 paras 76 and 90. These examples are derived from Sepúlveda, *The Nature of the Obligations* (n 16) 322.

[133] CESCR, GC 3 (n 29) para 9. See Craven (n 20) 132.

[134] Craven (n 20) 132.

[135] CESCR, GC 1 (n 67) para 7.

[136] The General Comment on the right to education illustrates this: within two years state parties must work out and adopt a detailed plan of action for the progressive realization within a reasonable number of years to achieve free and compulsory primary education (paras 1 & 8). The number of years deemed reasonable by the state party must be fixed in the plan of action. CESCR, GC 11 (n 40) para 10.

[137] The example mentioned by Craven is the reaction to the Austrian representative's statement that its domestic situation was fully in conformity with the Covenant: E/C.12/1988/SR.4 at 2 para 3, Craven (n 20) 133.

[138] Craven mentions the example of homeless persons: it is difficult to determine whether a person is homeless due to his or her own actions or whether it is a result of state policy. Craven (n 20) 133-4.

## 4.6 By all appropriate means

The phrase 'by all appropriate means' is not widely discussed in the General Comments apart from the explanation by the CESCR that it is a means to satisfy the obligation 'to take steps'.[139] Because article 2(1) ICESCR mentions 'particularly the adoption of legislative measures' to be included in 'all appropriate means', the CESCR provides some further clarification on this. 'All appropriate means' should not be limited to legislative measures only, but instead the phrase must be given its 'full and natural meaning'.[140] From the *travaux préparatoires* it follows that 'legislative measures' were indeed not meant as an obligatory element in the realization of ESC-rights, but merely as one out of many examples of means to fully realize the rights.[141] Also according to the ILC, legislative measures are 'the most normal and appropriate for achieving the purposes of the Covenant in question', yet not the sole means.[142] Appropriate means are for example judicial, administrative, financial, educational or social measures.[143]

The CESCR has addressed the question what 'appropriate' is and determined that while the state must decide which means it finds appropriate, 'the ultimate determination as to whether all appropriate measures have been taken remains one for the Committee to make'.[144] The measures taken are required to be 'reasonable' and 'effective', and they must produce results compatible with the obligations under the Covenant.[145] Through plans for full realization, including the identification of certain benchmarks to monitor progress, it is possible for the CESCR to determine what constitutes 'appropriate means'.[146]

Consequently, 'all appropriate means' are considered to be a means to an end and an open-ended indication of obligations of conduct aimed at the full realization of the rights. How this must be achieved is not precisely defined. Yet, at the same time states must act in good faith when deciding which means would be appropriate for their specific context. In the ICCPR an equal phrase can be found. In this context, the meaning of the phrase has been described as imposing a ''conditional' obligation of conduct'.[147] This description strokes with the meaning found in ICESCR-context.

---

[139] CESCR, GC 3 (n 29) para 3.

[140] Ibid, para 4. The CESCR is at one point explicit in an example: creating effective remedies, which is also emphasized in the ICCPR, is an appropriate means of immediate effect; ibid, para 5. 'Means' in its 'natural meaning' refers to 'an action, an object or a system by which a result is achieved; a way of achieving or doing something', or 'the money that a person has'.

[141] UN Doc E/CN.4/SR.427 at 10 (1954) cited by Craven (n 20) 125.

[142] ILC (1977) 2 Yearbook ILC 20, para 8 cited by Craven (n 20) 117.

[143] CESCR, GC 3 (n 29) para 7 cited by Sepúlveda, *The Nature of the Obligations* (n 16) 336.

[144] CESCR, GC 3 (n 29) para 4.

[145] Sepúlveda, *The Nature of the Obligations* (n 16) 337.

[146] Craven (n 20) 118.

[147] For example article 23(4) ICCPR, providing 'States Parties to the present Covenant shall take appropriate steps (...)'. Craven (n 20) 117, footnote omitted.

### 4.7 Conclusion

What has been done in this section is analysing the ordinary meaning of words, yet in the broadest meaning possible. To find the legal content of each of the phrases of article 2(1) discussed above, a wide variety of sources has been included. This has resulted in a preliminary overview of general obligations stemming from article 2(1). At certain points it has already been concluded that these phrases must be considered together, which is done here. The main findings will be reiterated in short before moving on the final conclusions in which all elements of the interpretation are taken together.

State parties to the ICESCR must from the moment of becoming a party to the Covenant take steps that are targeted at the full realization of the rights of the ICESCR. Although there is room for full realization in steps and therefore for progressive realization, it does not mean that states can stand still in human rights achievements. For the progression states must use all available resources, also those available internationally. If a state's own resources are inadequate, states must seek additional resources from the international community. This is one clear element of the duty to international assistance and cooperation; otherwise the reference to international assistance and cooperation remains rather unclear as to which exact obligations follow from it.[148]

## 5 Considering Context, Object and Purpose and Ordinary Meaning Together: Conclusions

Based on the findings of this Chapter – consisting of the context, object and purpose and ordinary meaning of article 2(1) ICESCR – it is possible to construct the article's content and meaning in terms of obligations. The CESCR formulated obligations stemming from article 2(1) in terms of obligations of conduct ('object') and obligations of result ('purpose'), and in immediate obligations and long-term obligations. The long-term obligation of result is the full realization of rights; the obligations of conduct (immediate as well as long-term) follow from the phrases of article 2(1). Although the obligations formulated by the CESCR are directed at the state parties to the ICESCR, certain obligations to respect (and other obligations acquiring abstention from states to meet that obligation) can be clearly adhered to by non-state parties under the 'do no harm'-principle. The nature of these obligations are primarily formulated in the context of substantive rights and will therefore be mentioned in the next Chapter.

[148] The obligatory nature of international assistance and cooperation in case of insufficient resources has been explicitly recognized during the drafting of the Optional Protocol to the ICESCR. Commission on Human Rights, 'Elements of an Optional Protocol to the International Covenant on Economic, Social and Cultural Rights - Analytical Paper by the Chairperson-Rapporteur Catarina de Albuquerque' UN Doc. E/CN.4/2006/WG.23/2 of 30 November 2005, para 51.

The phrase 'undertakes to take steps' is in terms of obligations inextricably linked to the phrase 'with a view to achieving progressively the full realization'. State parties are obliged to take action to achieve the purpose of the treaty from the moment of becoming a party to the ICESCR. The steps taken should be deliberate, concrete and targeted towards the purpose, although circumstances may dictate the size of the steps taken. Through these steps, rights are being realized progressively. Progressive realization indicates the steady and continuous movement (as expeditiously and effectively as possible) towards a certain goal, in this case the full realization of rights, where there is no room for a state to do nothing: progression does not mean a standstill. Since 'with a view to' is part of this phrase, states must have the intention to actually realize the rights, something that has also become clear from 'undertakes'. Consequently, 'undertakes to take steps with a view to achieving progressively the full realization' constitutes immediate obligations of conduct to take action and to continue this action, which must be aimed at the long-term obligation of full realization of rights. Retrogressive measures, which include deterioration of the level of rights enjoyment through passiveness of the state, cannot be allowed, but if they are nonetheless taken they must be fully justified.

The phrases 'individually and through international assistance and cooperation' and 'to the maximum of its available resources' must also be considered together. Being obligations of conduct, these phrases explain how the full realization of rights must be achieved. Apart from taking steps individually, states should or could make use of international assistance and cooperation. The extent to which this is an obligation is not entirely clear but a few indicators have been found. Distinguishing between offering/providing states on the one hand and requesting/accepting states on the other, the CESCR is more inclined to assume a duty to offer or provide than to request or accept. Possibly, obligations to international assistance and cooperation may be found within the context of substantive rights, but more detail is needed before this can be confirmed or refuted. Only when looking at the phrase 'maximum of its available resources' a clear obligation to use international assistance and cooperation can be found. When a state has insufficient resources to take steps towards full realization, and therefore to make sufficient progression, there is an obligation to use those resources available internationally. This is in line with the legal framework on accepting international humanitarian assistance where the needs-assessment must demonstrate whether the affected state's capacity is sufficient and, if not, the affected state must trigger the process of obtaining international humanitarian assistance. Nonetheless, within the ICESCR not having sufficient resources can be used as a justification for non-compliance, but only if the state has tried to obtain additional resources internationally and not for the obligations that are non-derogable, like the non-discrimination provision or the core obligations of each right. This can be compared to the evaluation of offers during the second stage of the legal framework on accepting assistance where the affected state must seek international assistance but also has discretionary space to determine whether offers by international actors are needed, suitable and in line with the humanitarian principles.

'By all appropriate means' refers to an open-ended obligation of conduct that state parties must use any means available to achieve the full realization of rights. It will differ from case-to-case which means are suitable, acceptable, and/or correct for the circumstances. Basically, this phrase is an extra confirmation of 'undertakes to take steps', leaving open which steps must be taken.

Consequently, state parties to the ICESCR are under the obligation to achieve the full realisation of rights. They must start to work towards this goal continuously from the moment they have become a party to the ICESCR. Working towards the final goal occurs in steps or stages without deterioration of the level of rights enjoyment. State parties are obliged to make use of their maximum available resources which they have to obtain – if necessary – internationally. Whether making use of international assistance and cooperation is an obligation outside situations in which insufficient resources are available does not become clear because the CESCR is not consistently taking a line and because more detail is required to determine the exact scope of the phrase. Based on the location of article 2(1) in the ICESCR it can be concluded that the general obligations found here are applicable on each individual right as provided in Part III of the treaty and the substantive rights may provide the context that is needed to formulate more precise obligations.

At this point, the obligations found in article 2(1) provide a general idea of what the duties are of an affected state, but only when these general obligations are placed in the light of disaster response it is possible to give a more detailed description of what these obligations mean for the affected state when it comes to accepting international humanitarian assistance. To give even more detail to the obligations article 2(1) must be considered together with concrete rights, in this case the rights most often affected by disasters: housing, food, water and health. This will be done in the next Chapter.

# CHAPTER V
# APPLYING THE ICESCR ON DISASTER SITUATIONS: SPECIFIC OBLIGATIONS

## 1 INTRODUCTION

To be able to place the findings of the previous Chapter in the light of disaster response, the framework as described in the first Part of this research will be included. This allows to see the obligations found for article 2(1) in the broader context of obligations on accepting humanitarian assistance. The three steps of the legal framework are the primary role of the affected state, the initiation or triggering of international humanitarian assistance, and the acceptance of international humanitarian assistance. The obligations of article 2(1) are placed in this framework to see how much room individual state parties receive to fulfil their obligations individually and when article 2(1) prescribes that states must look for international assistance and cooperation. As the last step, it will be considered how article 2(1) sets standards on accepting international assistance.

Apart from placing the findings of the previous Chapter in the light of disaster response and applying them on the substantive rights of the ICESCR, this Chapter will address a question that has remained unanswered so far. In Chapter II it was explained that derogation from human rights obligations is possible during the existence of a 'state of emergency', at least under the ICCPR. Before looking at disaster-specific obligations for state parties to the ICESCR, it would not be superfluous to first establish to what extent state parties to the ICESCR may derogate from their obligations in (post-) disaster obligations. Section 2 will provide an answer to this question. Next, in section 3, the findings of the previous Chapter will be considered in the context of disaster response resulting in an overview of the general obligations that states must adhere to immediately after a disaster. With these results, the rights to housing, food, water and health will be analysed in section 4 to find out whether any concrete standards can be identified that dictate the behaviour of state parties in the response to a disaster.

## 2 Derogation during the State of Emergency

### 2.1 Introduction

Article 4 of the ICCPR contains an option to derogate from certain obligations under that treaty in case of an emergency.[1] The ICESCR does not contain a similar derogation clause, but still it is at times questioned whether it is possible to derogate from the obligations stemming from the ICESCR in times of an emergency. The answer to this question is of particular importance in this research. If the option to derogate would indeed exist, it would be no use to look at disaster-specific obligations of states since these could be set aside. Therefore, this section will establish to what extent states have an option to derogate during emergencies under the ICESCR.

The function of a derogation-clause is to temporarily stop the working of a certain right due to an exceptional situation.[2] Consequently, people cannot appeal to that right during the time of derogation. To protect people against abuse of derogation, there are some criteria and requirements before states can derogate from their obligations. Looking at the text of article 4 ICCPR, a number of safeguards can be identified.[3] Moreover, a number of provisions are excluded from derogation, like the right to life of article 6.[4]

The drafters of the ICESCR apparently considered the option of limitation of the rights since in article 4 ICESCR a limitation-clause is included, yet did apparently not consider it necessary to include a derogation-clause in the ICESCR. When considering the preparatory work of the ICESCR, no specific discussion can be found 'on the issue of whether or not a derogation clause was considered necessary, or even appropriate, in the context of a covenant dealing with economic, social, and

---

[1] Article 4 ICCPR provides 'In time of public emergency (...) the States Parties to the present Covenant may take measures derogating from their obligations under the present Covenant (...)'. Comparable derogation-clauses can be found in article 15 of the European Convention on Human Rights, article 30 of the European Social Charter, and article 27 of the American Convention on Human Rights.

[2] Jan-Peter Loof, *Mensenrechten en staatsveiligheid: verenigbare grootheden? Opschorting en beperking van mensenrechtenbescherming tijdens noodtoestanden en andere situaties die de staatsveiligheid bedreigen* (Wolf Legal Publishers, Nijmegen 2005) 378; Jaime Oraá, *Human Rights in States of Emergency in International Law* (Clarendon Press, Oxford 1992) 9-10.

[3] According to article 4, the emergency must threaten the life of the nation, the existence of the state of emergency must be officially proclaimed, derogation is allowed to the extent strictly required by the exigencies of the situation, the measures may not be inconsistent with other obligations under international law and may not be discriminatory. In addition, the state declaring the state of emergency must immediately inform the other States Parties of the provisions from which it has derogated and of the reasons by which it was actuated and of the date of ending the state of emergency.

[4] The articles mentioned are articles 6, 7, 8 (paragraphs 1 and 2), 11, 15, 16 and 18.

cultural rights'.[5] If the drafters discussed or considered the inclusion of a derogation-clause, it must either be recorded in the drafting history or a derogation-clause would have been included in the ICESCR.[6]

The mystery of the missing derogation clause has led to different opinions on the implications. Roughly, these opinions can be divided into two positions that appear to arrive at different conclusions but at closer scrutiny are in line with each other. Here, the opinions will be presented as different positions after which their overlap is clarified, which forms the basis for the position on derogation taken here. The first position argues that due to the nature of the ICESCR derogation is not possible. The second position contends that the option to derogate is implied in the obligations of the ICESCR.

## 2.2 Position 1: Derogation is not possible in the context of the ICESCR

The obsolete idea that the ICESCR does not contain concrete obligations but merely policy indicators makes the existence of a derogation-clause superfluous. In that case it is argued that without obligations there is no need to have an option to derogate and that derogation even becomes impossible.[7] When considering the earlier discussion on the obligations stemming from article 2(1) though, it is clear that this position is not supported here.

Another argument supporting the position that derogation from obligations under the ICESCR is not possible is founded on the words 'progressive realization' as used in article 2(1). When understanding progressive realization as allowing a state to bring progression at a standstill in exceptional situations, it is not possible to derogate from obligations. The formulation of progressive realization stands in the way of derogation. This argument is also refuted here. In the first place it has already been established that progressive realization cannot be used in this way, although available resources and special circumstances may determine the amount of progression that can be expected. In addition, it is determined that absolute standstill is not acceptable: for example the non-derogable core obligations that the CESCR identified for most rights must be realized at all times and there is an obligation of continuous improvement.[8] As will also be argued further below, even

[5] Philip Alston & Gerard Quinn, 'The Nature and Scope of State Parties' Obligations under the International Covenant on Economic, Social and Cultural Rights', (1987) 9 Human Rights Quarterly 156, 217.

[6] See for example Alston & Quinn (n 5) 217 and Rebecca J. Barber, 'Protecting the Right to Housing in the Aftermath of Natural Disaster: Standards in International Human Rights Law' (2008) 20 International Journal of Refugee Law 432, 441.

[7] See for example Oraá who excluded ESC-rights from the scope of his research because of the programmatic nature of the rights: Oraá (n 2) 2.

[8] The problem with non-derogable core contents is that the term prompts some to argue that the rest of a right is 'derogable', so can be derogated from. See Michael J. Dennis, 'Application of Human Rights Treaties Extraterritorially in Times of Armed Conflict and Military Occupation' (2005) 99 American Journal of International Law 119, 140.

in times of severe resources constraints, it cannot be accepted that a state violates its core obligations.[9]

### 2.3 Position 2: Even in the absence of an explicit clause, derogation is possible

There are those who argue that derogation from the rights of the ICESCR is possible despite the absence of a derogation-clause. Two views supporting this position are mentioned here.

First, some argue that article 4 ICCPR constitutes customary international law. Because of this status, the provision, including its conditions, can be applied in situations outside the scope of the ICCPR, so also in the context of the ICESCR. The lack of a derogation-clause in a human rights instrument would then not necessarily stand in the way of derogation.[10] For this position quite a bit of support can be found. The former Special Rapporteur on the state of emergency collected many reports of states that proclaimed the state of emergency, including states that were not a party to the ICCPR.[11] Based on these reports, the Special Rapporteur identified certain principles commonly valued during states of emergency, which potentially are applicable in all emergency situations.[12] These principles are, amongst others, non-derogability of certain rights, the proclamation of the state of emergency, legality, notification, exceptional threat, proportionality, temporariness and non-discrimination.[13] Still, this does not conclusively prove that article 4 ICCPR can be considered as customary law and practice shows only few examples of actually using article 4 in this way. One is the International Labour Organisation (ILO) which refers to the derogation clause of the ICCPR when there is a situation of emergency, because no derogation clauses are present in its own instruments.[14] Moreover, the ICJ has also considered this option in the Wall-case, where the Court argued that article 10 of the ICESCR remains applicable in the situation of occupation because Israel 'was not entitled to derogate from the provisions of the

---

[9] See section 4.2 below.

[10] Alston & Quinn (n 5) 219. Dennis argues that derogation is allowed as there is no article that says the contrary. Dennis (n 8) 140.

[11] In 1985, the UN sub-commission on Prevention of Discrimination and Protection of Minorities appointed a special rapporteur to research derogation of rights during the state of emergency. The sub-commission already did some work on derogation during the state of emergency, and the UN Commission on Human Rights urged the sub-commission to continue and take further steps. Therefore special rapporteur Mr Leandro Despouy worked in the framework of a sub-commission. UN Commission on Human Rights Res. 1985/23; Jaime Oraá, 'The Protection of Human Rights in Emergency Situations under Customary International Law' in Guy S. Goodwin-Gill & Stefan Talmon, *The Reality of International Law: Essays in Honour of Ian Brownlie* (Clarendon Press, Oxford 1999) 423-4.

[12] Oraá mentions *inter alia* the idea that some rights are non-derogable and that states of emergency must be officially proclaimed; Oraá (n 11) 423.

[13] Ibid. Oraá is referring to UN Doc. E/CN.4/Sub.2/1985/19 (17 June 1985).

[14] Alston & Quinn (n 5) 218.

ICESCR because the 'protection offered by human rights conventions does not cease in case of armed conflict, save through the effect of provisions for derogation from the kind found in article 4 of the (ICCPR)'.'[15] This reasoning by the ICJ can be understood in different ways. One way is as a statement that derogation from the ICESCR is not possible, as it does not contain a clause as in article 4 ICCPR. Another way of reading this dictum is to regard it as an opening for applying the rules of article 4 ICCPR in the ICESCR-context. Although there are some indicators to argue that article 4 ICCPR can be applied outside the ICCPR, the position is taken here that there remains sufficient uncertainty to not understand the provision as customary international law.

The second line of thought comes close to what has been argued in the second line of thought for the first position: the words used in article 2(1) make derogation possible even in the absence of a derogation-clause. If a state has tried everything in its power to follow-up on its obligations stemming from article 2(1) (especially using the maximum of its available resources and seeking additional resources internationally) but still cannot make sufficient progression, the breach of obligations would be excused. The conditions for derogation are in this case not those of article 4 ICCPR, but follow from article 2(1).

## 2.4 To derogate or not to derogate?

From the foregoing it becomes at the very least clear that there are strong indicators to accept that derogation during an emergency would somehow be possible under the ICESCR. The way in which article 2(1) ICESCR is phrased leaves room for flexibility in progression made after a disaster, at least when certain conditions are met. In this respect it has already become clear that states have an obligation to seek international assistance when insufficient resources are available for fulfilling the obligations of the ICESCR. Consequently, the obligation to seek international assistance remains intact even if an option for derogation exists. The flexibility that the option to derogate entails is most relevant for the amount of progression that can be expected. How this will influence the obligations under the ICESCR in disaster contexts and ultimately the obligation to accept international humanitarian assistance will be considered below.

[15] ICJ Legal Consequences of the Construction of a Wall in the Occupied Palestinian Territory 131 para 106, see Barber (n 6) 438. It was furthermore provided by the Court that Israel was not able to use the limitation clause of article 4 ICESCR as 'the restrictions on the enjoyment by the Palestinians living in the territory occupied by Israel of their economic, social and cultural rights' were not 'solely for the purpose of promoting the general welfare in a democratic society'.' Consequently, as Israel could not invoke the limitation clause of the ICESCR, it would have to seek recourse in an option to derogate, opened here by the ICJ when it does not exclude the applicability of derogation clauses in the context of the ICESCR.

## 3 POST-DISASTER OBLIGATIONS FOLLOWING FROM ARTICLE 2(1)

### 3.1 Introduction

In this section, the findings of the previous Chapter will be placed in the light of disaster-contexts. To specify the obligations that follow from article 2(1) ICESCR further, the tripartite typology (consisting of the duty to respect, protect and fulfil).[16] The CESCR divided the obligation to fulfil further into a duty to facilitate, provide and promote.[17] With 'facilitating' the CESCR indicates the requirement of the state to be active in making sure that individuals can enjoy their rights.[18] 'Providing' relates to situations in which (groups of) individuals are unable to realise their rights by themselves by the means at their disposal due to reasons beyond their control.[19] It hardly needs pointing out that this obligation is specifically relevant in disaster situations. 'Promoting' relates to supporting the further development and promotion of human rights in their territory. [20] General Comments and Concluding Observations by the CESCR will be used insofar they provide any insight in obligations in disaster settings, along with the work of scholars and interpretations like the Maastricht Guidelines on Violations of Economic, Social and Cultural Rights[21] and Maastricht Principles on Extraterritorial Obligations of States in the Area of Economic, Social and Cultural Rights.[22] This research focuses on the

---

[16] The tripartite typology in terms of obligations to respect, protect and fulfil can be ascribed to Asbjorn Eide and his work as Special Rapporteur on the Right to Food, although Eide based his version of the tripartite typology on Henry Shue, *Basic Rights: Subsistence, Affluence, and U.S. Foreign Policy* (Princeton University Press 1980). See generally A. Eide, 'The Right to Adequate Food as a Human Right' UN Doc. E/CN.4/Sub.2/1987/23 of 7 July 1987, see also Magdalena Sepúlveda, *The Nature of the Obligations under the International Covenant on Economic, Social and Cultural Rights* (Intersentia, Antwerp 2003) 161ff for a more extensive analysis on the development of the tripartite typology. The obligations to respect, protect, and fulfil each contains elements of obligations of conduct and obligations of result; Asbjorn Eide, 'State Obligations Revisited' in Wenche Barth Eide & Uwe Kracht (eds), *Food and Human Rights In Development: Volume II – Evolving Issues and Emerging Applications* (Intersentia, Antwerp 2007) 147.

[17] See also Chapter IV above.

[18] Sepúlveda, *The Nature of the Obligations* (n 16) 199.

[19] Ibid.

[20] Ibid.

[21] The Maastricht Guidelines were adopted in 1997 as the follow-up of the Limburg Principles on the Implementation of the International Covenant on Economic, Social and Cultural Rights. The Maastricht Guidelines are recognized by the UN and published as an official UN document (ECOSOC, UN Doc. E/C.12/2000/13 of 2 October 2000).

[22] The Maastricht Principles (2013) contain the interpretation of extraterritorial elements of ESC-rights by experts in the field of international (human rights) law and who are or were members of various human rights treaty bodies. The Principles are therefore an authoritative authorization not purporting 'to establish new elements of human rights law. Rather, the Maastricht Principles clarify extraterritorial obligations of States on the basis of standing international law' (Introduction to the Principles). ETO Consortium, 'Maastricht Principles on Extraterritorial

immediate post-disaster phase (including the disaster-proper phase) and not immediately on the preparedness and recovery phases. However, the phases together are seen as a full 'cycle of protection' where it is not always possible to exclude the other phases.[23]

### 3.2 Undertakes to take steps

The obligation to 'take steps' has been described in the previous Chapter as an immediate obligation, or at least an obligation which must be fulfilled within a reasonably short time after becoming a party to the Covenant. The steps to which article 2(1) refers must be deliberate, concrete and targeted, making this an obligation of conduct. Whether or not states comply with this obligation can be assessed through the state reports in which states are expected to work out and adopt a detailed plan of action.

The occurrence of a disaster only affects these obligations in part. Certain obligations remain intact. Also immediately after a disaster, steps can be taken towards full realization. At the very least, states can make plans of action. That scarcity of resources is in principle not standing in the way of this obligation, follows *inter alia* from Concluding Observations made with regard to the state report of Iraq. This state had difficulties to realize the rights of the ICESCR due to sanctions imposed against it. The CESCR stated that Iraq nonetheless had to work on realizing the rights to food and health to the maximum of its available resources, or in other words, by taking steps.[24] The scope of the obligation to take steps is, however, determined by the availability of resources. In this way the basis of the obligation remains intact, but what can be expected from states exactly is determined by the availability of resources. Consequently, not having sufficient resources due to a disaster can limit the 'steps' a state party makes after that disaster without violating the ICESCR while the obligation to take steps remains intact.

Nonetheless, the CESCR stresses the existence of the obligation to take steps also in relation to disasters, for example in connection to the right to social services: '(p)articular attention should be paid in this regard to persons (...) living in remote or disaster-prone areas, (...) so that they, too, can have access to these services'.[25] This appears to be of special importance in the preparedness-phase, yet logic dictates that it certainly must also be applicable in the immediate post-disaster

Obligations of States in the Area of Economic, Social and Cultural Rights' (FIAN International, Heidelberg 2013).

[23] Walter Kälin, 'Report of the Representative of the Secretary-General on the Human Rights of Internally Displaced Persons: Addendum on Protection of Internally Displaced Persons in Situations of Natural Disasters' UN Doc. A/HRC/10/13/Add.1 of 5 March 2009, para 21.

[24] Sepúlveda, *The Nature of the Obligations* (n 16) 314, referring to Concluding Observations Iraq UN Doc. E/1998/22.

[25] CESCR, General Comment 19 on 'The Right to Social Security' (UN Doc. E/C.12/GC/19 of 4 February 2008), para 27.

phase. In the same General Comment, the CESCR further provides that 'States parties should also consider schemes that provide social protection to individuals belonging to disadvantaged and marginalized groups, for example crop or natural disaster insurance for small farmers (...)'[26] and '(s)pecial attention should be given to ensuring that the social security system can respond in times of emergency, for example during and after natural disasters, armed conflicts and crop failure'.[27] State parties to the ICESCR therefore have obligations to take steps right after a disaster although these steps can be influenced by the availability of resources.

### 3.3 International assistance and cooperation

In the previous Chapter it has been explained that the nature of the obligation of international assistance and cooperation is rather ambiguous. Nevertheless, of at least one element of the phrase it was found that it constitutes an obligation: when the national capacity in terms of available resources of a state is overwhelmed, the state should accept international assistance and cooperation. A similar duty followed from the general legal framework where it was argued that the limit of a state's freedom to withhold consent can be co-determined by the national capacity of the affected state. Another major point that followed from the analysis of 'international assistance and cooperation' is that there is a stronger obligation on the offering parties to offer assistance than on the accepting-side to seek or accept assistance.[28] Even more so, it is often emphasized that international assistance may be requested but that there is no legal right to claim or receive assistance.[29] Article 11 ICESCR emphasizes this by providing that international cooperation should be based on free consent.[30]

---

[26] Ibid, para 28.

[27] Ibid, para 50.

[28] Although it must be stressed that the General Comments have not been consistent in the language used. General Comment 12, for example, refers to a 'responsibility' to provide disaster relief and humanitarian assistance. CESCR, General Comment 12 on 'The Right to Adequate Food' (UN Doc. E/C.12/1999/5 of 12 May 1999) para 38.

[29] Craven mentions in this respect para 33 of the Limburg Principles. Matthew C.R. Craven, *The International Covenant on Economic, Social and Cultural Rights: A Perspective on its Development* (Oxford Monographs in International Law, Clarendon Press, 1995) 149. Sepúlveda has also considered international obligations in the light of the tripartite typology and comes to the same conclusions as Craven, but she also emphasizes that the CESCR created an opening in the duty to fulfil: the General Comment on the right to health provides that 'states should facilitate access to essential health facilities, goods and services in other countries'. CESCR, General Comment 14 on 'The Highest Attainable Standard of Health' (UN Doc. E/C.12/2000/4 of 11 August 2000) para 39 cited by Sepúlveda, *The Nature of the Obligations* (n 16) 374.

[30] Craven (n 29) 149. The clause in article 11(1) 'based on free consent' should 'not be seen as restricting the obligatory nature of international co-operation'; Rolf Künnemann, 'Extraterritorial Application of the International Covenant on Economic, Social and Cultural Rights' in Fons Coomans & Menno T. Kamminga, *Extraterritorial Application of Human Rights Treaties* (Intersentia, Antwerp 2004) 205.

When considering this finding in the light of the entire legal framework and in the context of the rest of article 2(1), it cannot but be concluded that the emphasis on the offering-side makes sense. Due to the fundamental concepts of sovereignty and territorial integrity and because of the danger of too much assistance hampering humanitarian operations it is understandable that the accepting-side cannot be under an unlimited obligation to accept offers of assistance: 'the recipient State should not be obliged to accept aid if the aim of the donor country was to exploit the relationship to its own advantage'.[31] There must always be a certain room for discretion. Yet, when the state does not have sufficient resources to fulfil its obligations, it has a duty to seek international assistance. On the other hand, the same arguments can be used for the providing-side: 'it would be a breach of sovereignty on the part of the wealthy state to be required to provide aid to a particular country'.[32]

Compared to the General Comments more emphasis on a duty to seek or accept international assistance can be found in several Concluding Observations to state reports. Developing states are often found to be under an obligation to actively seek assistance and to request this assistance from wealthier states, UN Specialized Agencies (e.g. ILO, UNESCO, WHO, FAO), or intergovernmental or non-governmental organisations, including the World Bank and IMF.[33] The difference between the tone in General Comments and that in Concluding Observations may be explained through the specifics of the case. Apparently, the CESCR finds a general obligation for the receiving-side to use international assistance too farfetched, but is willing, when taking the circumstances of a certain state into account, to acknowledge the existence of an obligation to accept assistance based on the specifics of that particular case.[34]

When developing states receive assistance, they have further obligations to 'refrain from obstructing international organisations in their legitimate efforts to gain access to individuals under the jurisdiction of the State in order to assist them

[31] This point was made by the representative of the Congo during the drafting of the Covenant. UNGA Third Committee, Meetings 1181 to 1185 (UN Doc. A/C.3/SR.1181 of 13 November 1962), at 237 para 30; Craven (n 29) 149.

[32] Ibid.

[33] Sepúlveda, *The Nature of the Obligations* (n 16) 376.

[34] This can also be seen in the work of the ILC. 'The matter of international cooperation and assistance was considered in relative detail by the ILC Special Rapporteur in his past reports, putting forward that obligations of assistance and cooperation exist, both on the part of the international community and the affected State – although some matters might still require further elaboration.' ILC 'Fourth Report on the Protection of Persons in the Event of Disasters by Eduardo Valencia-Ospina, Special Rapporteur' (UN Doc. A/CN.4/643 of 11 May 2011); ILC 'Fifth Report on the Protection of Persons in the Event of Disasters by Eduardo Valencia-Ospina, Special Rapporteur' (UN Doc. A/CN.4/652 of 9 April 2012)..

in the enjoyment of economic, social and cultural rights',[35] to use the assistance for realising the rights of the ICESCR,[36] to make sure that there is a check on the proper use of assistance[37] and to give priority to the most vulnerable and disadvantaged groups.[38] Most of these elements were also found above, yet in specific disaster context the primary role of the affected state was emphasized including the control that the affected state retains over humanitarian operations. Through the CESCR's observations made in response to state reports the CESCR has to a certain extent given grounds to limit this control of the affected state (e.g. by stating that international organisations may not be obstructed in their legitimate efforts to gain access to individuals). This is quite remarkable considering the way that the primary role of the affected state is respected and adhered to in practice. The CESCR gives direction to affected states on how they should execute their role and in this way the primary role of the state gains content.

In terms of the duty to fulfil – and the three components to facilitate, to provide and to promote – the difference between the offering and accepting-sides can be defined further. The duty to facilitate implies that states must make sure that through development programmes, facilitation of rights is made possible.[39] The duty to provide is closely linked to the pledge of developed states to spend 0.7% GNP on development assistance and 'this level entails the duty of developed states to provide, subject to the availability of resources, a specific type of international assistance for the satisfaction of Covenant rights in other States'.[40] In the Maastricht

---

[35] See for example the Concluding Observations El Salvador (UN Doc. E/1997/22) paras 171 and 185; Concluding Observations Mexico (UN Doc. E/2000/22) para 387; CESCR, GC 12 (n 28) para 19; Sepúlveda, *The Nature of the Obligations* (n 16) 376.

[36] See for example Concluding Observations Guatemala (E/1997/22) para 137; Concluding Observations Colombia (E/1996/22) para 202; CESCR, GC 14 (n 29) para 45; Sepúlveda, *The Nature of the Obligations* (n 16) 377.

[37] See for example Concluding Observations Sri Lanka (UN Doc. E/1999/22) para 86; Concluding Observations Ukraine (UN Doc. E/1996/22) para 271; Concluding Observations Colombia (UN Doc. E/1996/22) para 202; CESCR, General Comment 4 on 'The Right to Adequate Housing' of 13 December 1991, para 19; Sepúlveda, *The Nature of the Obligations* (n 16) 377.

[38] See e.g. Concluding Observations Sri Lanka (E/1999/22) para 86; CESCR, GC 12 (n 28) para 38; Sepúlveda, *The Nature of the Obligations* (n 16) 377.

[39] This is explained in the words: 'any international assistance and cooperation programme should provide for the institutional machinery that will facilitate the enjoyment of economic, social and cultural rights in the recipient country, and developed states must ensure that economic, social and cultural rights form an integral part of any existing international assistance programme'. Concluding Observations Slovakia, UN Doc. E/C.12/1/Add. 81, para 21 cited by Magdalena Sepúlveda, 'Obligations of 'International Assistance and Cooperation' in an Optional Protocol to the International Covenant on Economic, Social, and Cultural Rights' (2006) 24 Netherlands Quarterly of Human Rights 271, 285.

[40] Sepúlveda, 'Obligations of 'International Assistance and Cooperation' (n 39) 286-7. Sepúlveda concludes that this pledge does not constitute a general obligation. The CESCR indeed refers to the 0.7%-pledge in Concluding Observations: when the state's spending on development assistance has decreased, the Committee expresses its regret and recommends that the state

Principles, the duty to provide is described as follows: '(a)s part of the broader obligation of international cooperation, States, acting separately and jointly, that are in a position to do so, must provide international assistance to contribute to the fulfilment of economic, social and cultural rights in other States (...)'.[41] Through this, the (non-legally binding) Maastricht Principles establish a duty to provide assistance as a part of the broader obligation of international cooperation, albeit in a more general context and not for the specific case of the occurrence of a disaster. The duty to promote, finally, would refer to a duty to assist the recipient state in implementing its treaty obligations, a duty not (yet) explicitly recognized by the CESCR.[42]

The Maastricht Principles add the obligation to *seek* international assistance to the duty to fulfil: '(a) State has the obligation to seek international assistance and cooperation on mutually agreed terms when that State is unable, despite its best efforts, to guarantee economic, social and cultural rights within its territory (...)'.[43] This is in line with the second step of the legal framework on accepting humanitarian assistance: at first, there is an obligation to seek assistance, and the third step concerns the *obligation* to accept. The Principles explain how states must respond to a request for international assistance and cooperation: 'States that receive a request to assist or cooperate and are in a position to do so must consider the request in good faith, and respond in a manner consistent with their obligations to fulfil economic, social and cultural rights extraterritorially (...)'.[44] Consequently, the Maastricht Principles acknowledge the obligation to seek international assistance and a corresponding obligation (therefore indicating the use of targeted requests) to consider the request and to respond to the request in line with extraterritorial obligations to fulfil ESC-rights.

Various treaty bodies have commented on a possible obligation to make use of international assistance and cooperation,[45] the conclusions of which the ILC summarized as follows: 'the bodies have currently referred to obligations to request

achieves the 0.7%: Concluding Observations France, UN Doc. E/C.12/1/Add.72, paras 14 and 24; Concluding Observations Sweden, UN Doc. E/C.12/1/Add.70, para 7, Concluding Observations Luxembourg, UN Doc. E/2004/22, para 67; Sepúlveda, 'Obligations of 'International Assistance and Cooperation' (n 39) 287-8.

[41] Principle 33.

[42] Sepúlveda, 'Obligations of 'International Assistance and Cooperation' (n 39) 289.

[43] Principle 34.

[44] Principle 35.

[45] CESCR, GC 12 (n 28) para 17; CEDAW Concluding Observations Belarus' UN Doc. A/55/38 of 2000, para 374; CRC, 'Concluding Observations Uzbekistan' UN Doc. CRC/C/111 of 2001 para 576-7; CESCR, 'Concluding Observations Uzbekistan' UN Doc. E/2006/22 of 2006, para 503; CRC, 'Concluding Observations Honduras' UN Doc. CRC/C/87 of 1999, para 112; HRC, 'Concluding Observations DPRK' UN Doc. CCPR/CO/72/PRK of 27 August 2001, para 12, cited by Marlies M.E. Hesselman, 'Establishing a Full 'Cycle of Protection' for Disaster Victims: Preparedness, Response and Recovery according to Regional and International Human Rights Supervisory Bodies' (2013) 18 Tilburg Law Review 106, 125-6.

or search international help for affected States when overwhelmed, both in General Comments and State reporting, or to requirements to not arbitrarily refuse and accept offers made by international actors'.[46] What is confirmed, therefore, is the existence of the obligation to move to the second step of the legal framework on accepting assistance, but for moving on to the next step of accepting only the rule that consent may not be withheld arbitrarily is explicitly recognized. The Maastricht Principles speak explicitly of a duty to seek international assistance and cooperation, but they are, although regularly accepted as an authoritative and well-researched interpretation of the status quo of ESC-rights and of the extraterritorial obligations of states in relation to these rights, not legally binding.

In conclusion, although it is established that states have an obligation to *seek* international humanitarian assistance (in rather unspecified cases) it is very difficult to define the obligation to *accept* international assistance and cooperation as a general obligation. In this case the 'devil lies not in the detail' but more detail is needed to determine the exact nature of the duty to accept assistance as a part of the obligation to international assistance and cooperation. The CESCR has followed the same line when staying on the surface in General Comments, but defining duties in more detail in Concluding Observations in the light and context of individual cases. It must be stressed, though, that '(d)ue to Article 2(1) international co-operation, as an obligatory ingredient to full realization, is implicit in all provisions of the ICESCR part III provisions'.[47] The general obligation also follows from the distinction the CESCR made between unwilling and unable states. An unable state can prove that it has done everything in its power to obtain international assistance. If it did not succeed, it at least did not violate any obligation. Unwilling states cannot justify non-compliance as they have not tried to obtain international assistance.

### 3.4 Using the maximum of available resources and other appropriate means

Not having sufficient resources for the realization of the ESC-rights was not meant by the drafters of the ICESCR as an excuse for not fulfilling obligations. It implies, in fact, an obligation to seek resources internationally. This creates a link between using the maximum of available resources and international assistance and cooperation as an obligation. The CESCR does, however, give some room for not having sufficient resources as a justification for non-compliance: if a state has done everything it can to obtain resources but has not succeeded, it has fulfilled its

[46] Valencia-Ospina, 'Fourth Report' (n 34) paras 51-77; CESCR, General Comment 3 on 'The Nature of States Parties Obligations' of 14 December 1990, para 13; CESCR, 'Statement by the Committee: An Evaluation of the Obligation to Take Steps to the "Maximum of Available Resources" under an Optional Protocol to the Covenant' (UN Doc. E/C.12/2007/1 of 21 September 2007) para 10; CESCR, GC 12 (n 28) para 19.
[47] Künnemann (n 30) 205.

obligation. Only some elements must be realised at all times, like core obligations. Using the maximum of available resources is therefore an obligation of conduct.

In this context the obligation of conduct – or the obligation to make an effort – is defined by the CESCR as to 'strive to ensure the widest possible enjoyment of the relevant rights under the prevailing circumstances'.[48] Even in situations of severe resource constraints, states must try to achieve as much as possible, and 'at least vulnerable groups must be reached by low-cost targeted programmes'.[49] Again, there is a difference between unwilling and unable states, where the latter category can show it has done everything in its power to obtain resources and violations due to a lack of resources may be excused. Unwilling states have not attempted to attain additional resources and are in violation of their obligations. In monitoring state compliance, it is advisable to first assess to what extent a state has fulfilled its obligations. If a state did not comply, it can be assessed whether failure is due to not having sufficient resources, and if that is the case, a state's effort to obtain more resources can be evaluated. The state party must at that point show that it has done everything in its power to obtain additional resources. If it cannot do this, it would not necessarily be a violation of substantive rights (although the inquiry starts at finding such a violation), but at least a violation of the duty to use the maximum available resources and the duty seek international cooperation and assistance.

It must be noted that resources do not merely relate to financial resources, but also to more material items like tents, vehicles, field hospitals, food, water, et cetera, and to human resources, like rescue workers, medical personnel and construction experts. In disaster context, using 'all appropriate means' must also be understood to include different types of resources which can satisfy the obligation 'to take steps' and may also include creating legislation for example following the IDRL Guidelines. The state can decide what it deems appropriate, but if it comes to establishing violations of ESC-rights the CESCR has the final saying in this. The means used must be reasonable and effective and must produce results compatible with Covenant obligations. Using appropriate means is therefore an obligation of conduct.

Quite often it is not the availability of resources which poses a problem, but the way in which these resources are spent. In the case of Hurricane Katrina, for example, with all the offers of assistance made, the US had no problem to come by

[48] CESCR, GC 3 (n 46) para 11.

[49] Ibid, para 11-2. Also in General Comment 5 it is stated that 'the duty of States parties to protect the vulnerable members of their societies assumes greater rather than less importance in times of severe resource constraints; CESCR, General Comment 5 on 'Persons with disabilities' of 9 December 1994, para 10; see also CESCR, General Comment 6 on 'The Economic, Social and Cultural Rights of Older Persons' of 8 December 1995, para 17, CESCR, General Comment 15 on 'The Right to Water' (UN Doc. E/C.12/2002/11 of 20 January 2003) para 13; CESCR, GC 17 on 'The Right of Everyone to Benefit From the Protection of the Moral and Material Interests Resulting From Any Scientific, Literary or Artistic Production of Which He is the Author' (UN Doc. E/C.12/GC/17 of 12 January 2006) para 20; CESCR, General Comment 21 on 'The right of everyone to take part in cultural life' (UN Doc. E/C.12/GC/21 of 21 December 2009) para 23.

sufficient resources, but the problems in New Orleans were mainly related to the way of using these resources.[50] Getting assistance to the people living in the affected area 'took several days'.[51] The same problems were experienced in another relatively wealthy state: Japan. Despite the thorough preparation by Japan, there were problems in responding to the earthquake and tsunami of 2011. There are reports claiming that in the region affected by the floods there was a shortage of food, power and gasoline and for some time people were not assisted by the government.[52] The Japanese military was mobilized at large scale to assist in the disaster response: around 100,000 troops were sent to go on a search-and-rescue operation, while relatively few people were injured and trapped underneath rubble.[53] It therefore took longer to bring relief goods to surviving victims. Also the response relating to the nuclear leak was flawed. Reports claimed that access to the contaminated area took so long that many initial disaster survivors were much later found dead because of starvation.[54] The presumed failure of Japan's response was reflected in the opinion of the Japanese population: 70 percent was of the opinion that the government failed in its response, arguing that Prime Minister Naoto Kan should resign.[55] In such cases a state arguably complied with its duty to use the maximum of its available resources, but failed in complying with obligations relating to substantive rights, as will be illustrated in section 4 below where four rights will be discussed.

### 3.5 Progressive realization and retrogressive measures

Progressive realization has been interpreted as moving as expeditiously and effectively as possible towards realizing the rights of the ICESCR. It is therefore an obligation of conduct aimed at achieving the obligation of result and is both an immediate obligation (to start immediately by taking steps) and a long-term obligation (to come to full realization). The formulation has been used as a means to

---

[50] The international community offered over 1 billion US dollars in cash and supplies; Tyra R. Saechao, 'Natural Disasters and the Responsibility to Protect: From Chaos to Clarity' (2006-7) 32 Brookings Journal of International Law 663, 692. It must be stressed that the US is not a party to the ICESCR and this case serves merely as an illustration.

[51] Ibid.

[52] Andrew Higgins, 'Japan's Slow Tsunami Response Stirs Anger' *The Washington Post* 16 March 2011.

[53] Daniel Kaufmann & Veronika Penciakova, 'Preventing Nuclear Meltdown: Assessing Regulatory Failure in Japan and the United States' *Brookings* 1 April 2011 <http://www.brookings.edu/research/opinions/2011/04/01-nuclear-meltdown-kaufmann> accessed 23 April 2015.

[54] Hiroko Tabuchi, 'An Anniversary of 'Heartbreaking Grief' in Japan' *The New York Times* 12 March 2012.

[55] ——, 'Japanners willen dat Premier Opstapt na Slechte Hulp Ramp' *De Volkskrant* 30 May 2011.

stay flexible as every state party has to start working from different circumstances. This flexibility is also very useful in post-disaster situations.

To monitor progressive realization, plans prepared and adopted by state parties are evaluated through the state reporting mechanism, which was also seen with the duty 'undertakes to take steps'. State parties are expected to comply with the requirement of 'continuous improvement', meaning that states can violate a right by not acting when deterioration of rights take place. In the words of the CESCR: states 'should modify the domestic legal order as necessary in order to give effect to their treaty obligations'.[56] The benchmarks which states must set according to the CESCR so that progress can be measured are an example.[57]

Making progression is one of the key duties of article 2(1) and retrogressive measures are – in principle – not allowed.[58] Examples of retrogressive measures discussed in state reports are: adoption of legislation with a direct or collateral negative effect on the enjoyment of the rights; abrogation of legislation consistent with rights; unjustly making a reduction in public expenditures devoted to these rights and the adoption of regional human rights measures while not integrating ESC-rights.[59] Apart from these examples, retrogressive measures have not been extensively discussed in the Concluding Observations and where it has been discussed, the CESCR has not been very strict.[60] One explanation for this is that it is difficult for the CESCR to determine whether any retrogressive measures have been taken.[61] The amount of attention paid to retrogressive measures increased after the adoption of the Maastricht Guidelines. In Guideline 14 it is provided that the adoption of any deliberately retrogressive measure that reduces the level of human rights enjoyment, or the reduction or diversion of specific public expenditure

[56] CESCR, General Comment 9 on 'The Domestic Application of the Covenant' (UN Doc. E/C.12/1998/24 of 3 December 1998) para 3.
[57] CESCR General Comment 10 on 'The Role of National Human Rights Institutions in the Protection of Economic, Social and Cultural Rights', UN Doc. E/C.12/1998/25 of 10 December 1998, para 3(d).
[58] Retrogressive measures – or also called regressive measures – are discussed in the CESCR's General Comments 13 on 'The Right to Education' para 45; CESCR, GC 14 (n 29) para 32 and 48; CESCR, GC 15 (n 49) para 19 and 42; CESCR, General Comment 16 on 'The Equal Right of Men and Women to the Enjoyment of All Economic, Social, and Cultural Rights' (UN Doc. E/C.12/2005/4 of 11 August 2005) para 42; CESCR, GC 17 (n 49) para 27 and 42; CESCR, General Comment 18 on 'The Right to Work' (UN Doc. E/C.12/GC/18 of 6 February 2006) para 21; CESCR, GC 19 (n 25) para 42 and 64; and CESCR, GC 21 (n 49) para 46 and 65.
[59] Sepúlveda extracts these examples from various concluding observations. However, she also notes that the Committee has taken a rather flexible approach to retrogressive measures: 'For many years, with a few exceptions, the Committee did not strictly monitor the adoption of deliberately retrogressive measures'. Sepúlveda, *The Nature of the Obligations* (n 16) 323-4.
[60] Ibid, 325.
[61] According to Sepúlveda, ibid.

resulting in the lowering of the level of rights enjoyment constitutes a violation of ESC-rights.[62]

When a state is recovering from armed conflict or natural disaster, the CESCR has adopted a more flexible approach on retrogressive measures.[63] Still, in order to justify a retrogressive measure, a state must adhere to a number of conditions, including that of proving that it has unsuccessfully sought international assistance.[64] It can be argued therefore that not using sufficient resources and not seeking international assistance and cooperation may clash with the duty to 'continuous improvement' when it hampers progression, and may even lead to retrogression. Not accepting humanitarian assistance could possibly be seen as taking a retrogressive measure.

When considering the practice of disaster response, many examples can be found where the affected state's response is discussed in terms of progression made, although not extensively by the CESCR or other treaty bodies. Usually, reports of progression made are published around the first or second anniversary of a disaster. Around 11 March 2012, for example, the first anniversary of Japan's earthquake and tsunami was evident through the many items in newspapers. Although many people were unable to return to their homes due to nuclear danger, it is acknowledged that 'Japan's reconstruction has accomplished much in the past year'.[65] According to one reporter, '(v)irtually all of the tsunami zone's roads have been fixed, and many landscapes once strewn with debris are now lined with tidy plots and a growing number of restored buildings'.[66] In relation to Hurricane Katrina's fifth anniversary, US President Obama acknowledged the difficulties still existing in New Orleans, yet added that there has been 'steady progress' and that there is still 'a long way to go'.[67] Although information like this is available, it does not constitute an objective, thorough and structured assessment into the ESC-achievements made by a state, leading to rather subjective and not necessarily reliable information. On Italy's response to the earthquake in L'Aquila in 2009, for example, a variety of opinions can be found.[68] Apart from the praise for the government's response, there were reports stating that people were still living in

---

[62] Maastricht Guidelines, guideline no 14 under (e) resp. (g), cited by Sepúlveda, *The Nature of the Obligations* (n 16) 326.

[63] For example in the Concluding Observations on the report by Honduras, as the country was recovering from hurricane Mitch (UN Doc. E/C.12/1/Add.57 para 11); Sepúlveda, *The Nature of the Obligations* (n 16) 329.

[64] As is in line with the Maastricht Guidelines, Guideline no 13, cited by Sepúlveda, *The Nature of the Obligations* (n 16) 331.

[65] Tabuchi (n 54).

[66] Ibid.

[67] Helene Cooper, 'Progress Will Continue, Obama Tells New Orleans' *The New York Times* 30 August 2010.

[68] See Chapter III, section 2 above.

emergency housing and hotels in April 2010[69] and the IFRC reported that it was still running nine tent camps by mid October 2009.[70] That the recovery work certainly did not end 'before the winter', becomes clear from the DREF Final Report which provides that the plan of action of the Italian Red Cross was intended to be concluded at the end of October 2010 and that 'social health assistance activities will be carried out in the field until full recovery and return to normality are insured'.[71] The Red Cross as such calculated that it would need to work on recovery at least for 18 months after the disaster.

When insufficient progress creates new problems, an argument of rights violations may be more easily accepted, as illustrated by Haiti's earthquake. The problem in Haiti was that 'tremendous generosity at the giving end has not, in almost two years, been translated into even adequate progress on the ground for Haiti's earthquake victims, infrastructure, and economy'.[72] In a report made more than a year after the disaster, the situation was described as follows:

> Thousands of blue and grey tents continue to sit sandwiched between developments and rubble along Port-au-Prince's roads and hundreds of thousands of internally displaced persons (...) survive in camps that fail to meet even minimum international standards, severely lacking in access to clean water, latrines, and security.[73]

In June 2011 Haiti was struck by heavy rains, creating floods and landslides. As a result, 23 persons lost their lives, amongst which people who were still living in tents a year and a half after the earthquake.[74] Tents as temporary housing are highly inadequate for a country like Haiti which knows a rainy season and even a hurricane season; a lesson learned already in the context of the Indian Ocean tsunami where it was requested to 'provide transitional shelter – not just tents'.[75] Another illustration is the outbreak of cholera on Haiti. By August 2011, an estimated 6000 persons lost their lives because of the cholera epidemic. In one year, around 420.000 people were infected, of which the largest part lived in the refugee camps where the circumstances are described as 'abysmal'.[76] When discussing the

---

[69] See John Hooper, 'L'Aquila Earthquake Survivors Seek Answers from Government' *Guardian.co.uk* 5 April 2010.
[70] IFRC, 'DREF Operation Final Report: Italy: Earthquake' (DREF operation no MDRIT001, report of 9 December 2009) <http://reliefweb.int/sites/reliefweb.int/files/resources/086EEA94F04A9DBCC1257688003CED65-Full_Report.pdf> accessed 10 July 2012.
[71] Ibid.
[72] Brian Concannon Jr. & Beatrice Lindstrom, 'Cheaper, Better, Longer-Lasting: A Rights Based Approach to Disaster Response in Haiti' (2011) 25 Emory International Law Review 1145.
[73] Centre for Human Rights & Global Justice, NYU School of Law et al., 'Right to Food, Water and Sanitation' Universal Periodic Review, Republic of Haiti: Submissions to the UN Human Rights Council 71, 78-79 cited by Concannon & Lindstrom (n 72) 1145-6.
[74] ——, 'Tientallen Doden door Noodweer Haïti' *De Volkskrant* 8 June 2012.
[75] ——, 'Analysis: Are Humanitarians Learning the Lessons from Haiti?' *IRIN* 28 October 2010.
[76] The Dutch word used in the original text is 'erbarmelijk'; ——, 'Elke Dag 600 Nieuwe Cholerabesmettingen op Haïti' *De Volkskrant* 15 August 2012.

provision of, amongst others, water, health care and shelter, John Holmes, head of OCHA, stated that 'with the rainy season looming, these unmet needs are taking on additional urgency, not least from the health and protections points of view and given the potential consequences in terms of both politics and security of large demonstrations in some sensitive places'.[77]

In the Concluding Observations to state reports, the CESCR can develop certain standards on the progression it expects after a disaster, although so far not many state reports have coincided with the occurrence of a disaster, nor has the CESCR referred to disaster-specific achievements. For now, it can be concluded that there is at least an obligation to move forward and continuously improve, although as seen in the examples of disaster situations as given above the context of a specific state can co-determine what progress may be expected from states.

The obligations following article 2(1) seen in the light of disaster response reflect the steps of the legal framework on accepting international humanitarian assistance after a disaster and the standards that were found on moving from one step to the next are also mirrored. However, at this point the obligations of article 2(1) are not concrete enough to make the standards clearer. In the next section, four substantive rights will be analysed so that the general obligations can be applied to these rights resulting in more concrete standards on accepting international assistance.

## 4 Disaster-specific obligations stemming from substantive rights

### 4.1 Introduction

The content of ESC-rights has been subject to extensive debate over the years. While it has been established that ESC-rights contain concrete obligations, defining the exact content of the obligations for each right remains challenging. In the General Comments, the CESCR has tried to describe the content of each right. In doing so, the CESCR started to make use of defining the 'core content' or 'minimum obligations' to give concrete obligations for each right. This core of each right must be realized at all times: '(t)he CESCR considers that all States Parties to the ICESCR are to ensure, as its *raison d'etre*, particular minimum essential levels of all rights, such as basic food, shelter, health or education, if necessary with the help of internationally available resources'.[78] This description of core contents seems to fit seamlessly into the structure of general obligations laid down above: it provides the step that a state must at the very least take, with the use of international assistance when necessary. Yet, what comes after this very first step remains unclear and a number of questions remain that must be answered in this section. In

[77] John Holmes in a critical e-mail <http://turtlebay.foreignpolicy.com/posts/2010/02/17/top_un_aid_official_critiques_haiti_aid_efforts_in_confidential_email> accessed 18 June 2012 cited by Linda A. Malone, 'The Responsibility to Protect Haiti' (2010) 14 ASIL Insights [7].

[78] Hesselman (n 45) 121. See also CESCR, GC 3 (n 46) para 10.

the first place, it can be wondered what the effect would be of the level of development of a state: should there be higher expectations from a developed state than from a developing state? And how can it be determined what the expectations are in correlation to the level of development? What is the influence of the pre-disaster level of rights enjoyment within a state? Can non-compliance prior to a disaster be an excuse for lower performance? Before going into the obligations that exist under the rights to housing, food, water and health, it is first necessary to look into these questions. In a way, all these questions revolve around a single theme: setting benchmarks that determine what states must achieve considering their specific circumstances in terms of availability of resources and severity or type of disaster. In the next section it will be explained how benchmarks will be used and how they can be determined. Core contents will fulfil a key role in setting post-disaster benchmarks, so in the further sections, the rights to housing, food, water and health will be described in terms of their core obligations. Departing from this core, further benchmarks and standards will be looked for to establish the obligations for state parties in post-disaster settings.

## 4.2 On benchmarks and core contents

Defining the exact content and scope of ESC-rights and corresponding obligations has been a challenge ever since the adoption of the ICESCR. Due to the 'progressive realization'-formulation of ESC-rights, the understanding is or was that there are no absolute rights or obligations. The formulation was indeed meant to be used as a flexible tool taking into account the level of development of each state party. At this point, however, it has already become clear that the CESCR has done much to give more general content to obligations, but it also considers the performance of states based on individual circumstances. States must make plans and the CESCR can measure to what extent these plans have been executed. These plans made by states can be used as benchmarks, taking into account the specific circumstances of a state:

> In brief, benchmarks can be defined as goals or targets that are specific to the individual circumstances of each country. As opposed to human rights indicators, which measure human rights observation or enjoyment in absolute terms, human rights benchmarks measure performance relative to individually defined standards.[79]

Especially when looking at disaster-situations, it is necessary to remain flexible. Not every disaster is equally severe nor leads to the same amount of damage.

[79] Mary Robinson, 'Introduction by the High Commissioner for Human Rights' in High Commissioner of Human Rights, 'Benchmarks for the Realization of Economic, Social and Cultural Rights, A Roundtable Discussion Organized by the High Commissioner of Human Rights' (Geneva 1998) cited by Maria Green, 'What We Talk about When We Talk about Indicators: Current Approaches to Human Rights Measurement' (2001) 23 Human Rights Quarterly 1062, 1080.

Moreover, one state is better equipped to cope with the consequences than the next. A framework for benchmarks on post-disaster obligations must therefore:

- Take account [of] resource availability;
- Take into account the level of deprivation in the country;
- Take account of the policy options available;
- Identify clearly those [parts of – SJW] rights that are not subject to progressive realization or to resource availability;
- Use at least some universal indicators to reflect universal rights.[80]

These requirements for an effective benchmark were developed for general application, yet the way it is formulated makes it especially useful for the purposes of this research. Only in the fourth requirement an adjustment is suggested to give more flexibility in terms of defining obligations. Based on this framework, benchmarks can be set to determine what state parties to the ICESCR must achieve immediately after a disaster. By allowing room to take the context into account, it is not possible here to set *the* benchmark for each right discussed below. The first three elements constitute factors that are subjective to the circumstances in the state, thereby answering some of the questions posed above. Resource availability determines the steps a state can make, so also how much progression a state can make. However, it has become clear that at certain points a state has an obligation to seek additional resources. Due to this obligation, a choice is made on what is going to be measured by the benchmark: the post-disaster enjoyment of rights or (the violation of) obligations by state parties.[81] While it is sometimes argued that these are two sides of the same coin,[82] this stance is rejected here. If a state can prove that it has done everything in its power to obtain additional resources and that it has made use of international assistance so far it was offered but still cannot live up to certain standards, the state is not in violation of its obligations, while there could be a breach of the enjoyment of a right. Especially immediately after a disaster, a state can comply with its obligations, while disaster victims find that certain rights are violated.[83]

Next, the level of deprivation – i.e. damage caused by the disaster – is also taken into account. This could either mean departing from objective standards by determining what basic needs people are lacking, or departing from subjective

[80] Sakiko Fukuda-Parr, 'Human Development Indicators and Analytic Tools as Benchmarks in Economic, Social and Cultural Rights' in High Commissioner of Human Rights, 'Benchmarks for the Realization of Economic, Social and Cultural Rights, A Roundtable Discussion Organized by the High Commissioner of Human Rights' (Geneva 1998) cited by Green (n 79) 1081.

[81] It can be argued that a human rights indicator measures by definition 'the extent to which a government is complying with its obligations under human rights law'. The extent to 'which individuals are enjoying access to basic needs' would rather be a development indicator. Green (n 79) 1091.

[82] See for example Green (n 79), 1085-8.

[83] This can be also considered the more practical solution when it comes to measurement. Ibid, 1088.

standards by looking at what people lost. In the latter case, deprivation could be more severe merely because there was more to lose to begin with. Objective standards make more sense here as it makes it possible to identify the needs for survival and therefore what is needed in terms of assistance. Moreover, these standards fit the line taken on core contents as will be explained below. The third element, the policy options available, allows room to negotiate around complicating factors within a state or the particular set-up of a state.

Because these first three elements are strongly depending on the particulars of the case, it is difficult to determine in detail what can be expected at each moment after a disaster occurred in terms of achievements on the rights to housing, food, water and healthcare. There are, however, standards available on humanitarian assistance in response to disasters that in varying detail explain what humanitarian aid must achieve. Most notably, the Sphere Standards give detailed information on the standards immediately after a disaster and at later stages. Although not being a human rights instrument, the Sphere Standards are used to give content – together with human rights sources – to the human right benchmarks.

The fourth element of the framework for benchmarks sets objective standards by referring to those parts of rights that cannot be derogated from (not through progressive realization, nor through having insufficient resources). Earlier, it was seen that core contents meet this description. Without core obligation, a right would be largely deprived of its *raison d'être* and in case of violation of the core content, the state must demonstrate that it has done everything in its power to obtain more resources as the only way of justification.[84] The core contents will therefore fulfil a prominent role in the benchmarks. In addition, the fifth element speaks of universal indicators to reflect universal rights. This element will be understood as those parts of the rights that are not culturally or context-sensitive, but which are of universal importance to all humans. There is a clear reason for taking this interpretation: in determining what the core contents are, it is possible to depart from a needs-based approach, or from a value-based approach.

Much debate has surrounded the question what the content of a minimum core obligation should be exactly. In the initial formulation of core contents by the CESCR, there is a certain emphasis on needs: 'this type of inquiry immediately orients the "core" of the right to the essential and minimally tolerable levels of food, health, housing and education. (...) [Basic needs are therefore] amounting to survival and life'.[85] It makes sense to depart from this minimum for human existence, or the minimum for human survival. Without certain preconditions, there is no life. Moreover,

> The focus on life, survival, and basic needs has the additional advantage of pointing to the requirements for rights protection that are apparently self-evident, rather than

[84] CESCR, GC 3 (n 46) para 10.

[85] Katharine G. Young, 'The Minimum Core of Economic and Social Rights: A Concept in Search of Content' (2008) 33 The Yale Journal of International Law 113, 128.

> requiring a more controversial examination of what is needed for the satisfaction of more elaborate aims, and a "thicker" understanding of the good life.[86]

In other words, looking at basic needs sets standards which are to a certain extent objective and concrete. The subjectivity of expecting certain standards of living with various gradations of luxury is avoided and looking further can lead to standards which are 'too encompassing and too unlimited'.[87] Nonetheless, objections to this approach can be made: merely looking at basic needs leaves no room (or ample room) for considerations of human dignity and 'human flourishing' intrinsic to many interpretations to the right to life.[88] An alternative approach would be a value-based approach: '(a) value-based core goes further than the "basic-needs" inquiry by emphasizing not what is strictly required for life, but rather what it means to be human.'[89] Human dignity plays a major role in determining the core content when following the value-based approach, but then the question is immediately raised what can be understood with human dignity. On the one hand, a person can feel that his or her feelings of self-worth and self-respect are affected, but it is also possible to look at human dignity as experienced by a social group or society, where there is a societal feeling of indignation.[90] It is doubtful that this way of considering the core obligations is more useful than looking at the needs-based core. After a disaster most survivors will find themselves in situations of increased dependency, resulting in feelings of indignation and dented self-respect.

When looking at post-disaster obligations, survival is the first priority, making the needs-based approach more sensible. Further development and higher standards move into the realm of rebuilding and even – where applicable – the development phase. Understanding core obligations in terms of basic needs is also placing developing and developed states on equal footing: the basic needs are the same for both, the progression made afterwards reflects the capacity of the state and the expectations of the standards. Human dignity is given due consideration in handbooks, guidelines and standards on delivering humanitarian assistance and is in that way not neglected in a needs-based approach to the core contents. The needs-based approach are therefore more fitting for the disaster-context under scrutiny here. Still, the difficulty to set standards based on needs is not underestimated:

> People have been known to survive with incredibly little nutrition, and there seems to be a cumulative improvement of life expectation as the dietary limits are raised. (...) There is difficulty in drawing a line somewhere, and the so-called 'minimum

[86] Ibid, 130. Footnote omitted.
[87] Ibid.
[88] Ibid.
[89] Ibid, 133.
[90] John Rawls, *A Theory of Justice* (1971) 225, 386-9 cited by Young (n 85) 135.

> nutritional requirements' have an inherent arbitrariness that goes well beyond variations between groups and regions.[91]

Again, the particulars of each individual case are of crucial importance to setting the benchmarks.

In the following, the rights to housing, food, water and health will be discussed. For each of these rights it will be explained, after an introduction of the general features of each right, what the core obligations are. These core obligations are based on the interpretation by the most authoritative body on the ICESCR, the Committee on Economic, Social and Cultural Rights. The core obligations will form the basis of the formulation of specific disaster obligations for each right. Here, it will be considered what has been found in the general legal framework on accepting international humanitarian assistance and what has been found in terms of general obligations under article 2(1). In addition, General Comments will be taken into account along with practical handbooks like the Sphere Standards to identify standards that determine when a state must move from its individual response to initiating or triggering the process of international humanitarian assistance in order not to violate its obligations under the ICESCR and when a state must move on to accepting international humanitarian assistance.

## 4.3 The Right to Housing

### *4.3.1 Introduction*

Article 11 ICESCR, which contains the rights to housing, food, and implicitly water, provides:

> (1) The States Parties to the present Covenant recognize the right of everyone to an adequate standard of living for himself and his family, including adequate food, clothing and housing, and to the continuous improvement of living conditions. The States Parties will take appropriate steps to ensure the realization of this right, recognizing to this effect the essential importance of international co-operation based on free consent.
>
> (2) The States Parties to the present Covenant, recognizing the fundamental right of everyone to be free from hunger, shall take, individually and through international co-operation, the measures, including specific programmes, which are needed:
>
> (a) To improve methods of production, conservation and distribution of food by making full use of technical and scientific knowledge, by disseminating knowledge of the principles of nutrition and by developing or reforming agrarian systems in such a way as to achieve the most efficient development and utilization of natural resources;

[91] Amartya Sen, 'Poverty and Famines: An Essay on Entitlement and Deprivation' (1982) 12 cited by Young (n 85) 131.

(b) Taking into account the problems of both food-importing and food-exporting countries, to ensure an equitable distribution of world food supplies in relation to need.[92]

In general, being granted the right to housing means more than 'merely having a roof over one's head'.[93] Rather, it must be understood as 'the right to live somewhere in security, peace and dignity'.[94] The main features of the right to housing are: 'the protection against forced evictions and arbitrary destruction and demolition of one's home; the right to be free from arbitrary interference with one's home, privacy and family; and the right to choose one's residence, to determine where to live and to freedom of movement'.[95] In terms of entitlements, the right to adequate housing includes 'security of tenure; housing, land and property restitution; equal and non-discriminatory access to adequate housing; participation in housing-related decision-making at the national and community levels'.[96] The term 'adequate' has been described as constituting 'adequate privacy, adequate space, adequate security, adequate lighting and ventilation, adequate basic infrastructure and adequate location with regard to work and basic facilities – all at a reasonable cost'.[97] Adequacy is determined in part by social, economic, cultural, climatic, ecological and other factors.[98] An adequate house must further have facilities essential for health, security, comfort and nutrition[99] and must be 'habitable' in the sense that it must protect inhabitants from 'cold, damp, heat, rain, wind or other threats to health, structural hazards, and disease vectors'.[100]

In terms of the tripartite typology, the duty to respect the right to housing 'requires States to refrain from interfering directly or indirectly with the enjoyment

[92] It must be noted that the right to housing is not only laid down in this provision, but in other instruments as well. Amongst these are: article 25(1) UDHR; article 21 of the 1951 Refugee Convention; article 5(e)(iii) CERD; article 17 ICCPR; articles 14(2) and 15(2) CEDAW; articles 16(1) and 27(3) CRC. The meaning of a right in one instrument is always influenced by the understanding of the right in other instruments.

[93] CESCR, GC 4 (n 37) para 7.

[94] Ibid.

[95] UN Office of the High Commissioner for Human Rights and UN HABITAT, 'The Right to Adequate Housing' Fact Sheet no 21 (rev. 1) 2009 (henceforth 'UNCHR/UN-Habitat fact sheet no 21'), 3. See also Maria Green, who identified these three key elements: '1) the right to access to adequate housing; 2) the right to security of tenure and freedom from forced evictions; and 3) the right to privacy in the home'. Green (n 79) 1074.

[96] OHCHR/UN-Habitat Fact Sheet no 21 (n 95) 3.

[97] Commission on Human Settlement and the Global Strategy for Shelter to the Year 2000 cited by the CESCR, GC 4 (n 37) para 7.

[98] Ibid, para 8. In addition, 'adequacy' is also determined by the factors that are mentioned earlier, like '(legal) security of tenure; availability of services, materials, facilities, and infrastructure; affordability; habitability; accessibility; location; and cultural adequacy', since housing cannot be considered adequate without these; para 8 under a through g; OHCHR/UN-Habitat Fact Sheet no 21 (n 95) 4.

[99] CESCR, GC 4 (n 37) para 8(b).

[100] Ibid, para 8 under (d).

of the right to adequate housing'.[101] As for the duty to protect, states are required to prevent third parties from interfering with the right to housing, for example private actors like landlords and landowners.[102] The duty to fulfil requires states to 'adopt appropriate legislative, administrative, budgetary, judicial, promotional and other measures to fully realize the right to adequate housing'.[103] Moreover, 'in essence, the obligation is to demonstrate that, in aggregate, the measures being taken are sufficient to realize the right for every individual in the shortest possible time in accordance with the maximum of available resources'.[104]

*4.3.2 Core contents*

The CESCR did not formulate explicit core obligations for each right from its beginning, and therefore there are no core obligations on the right to housing. Even so, the CESCR determined that states have immediate obligations with regard to the right to housing no matter the level of development since 'many of the measures required to promote the right to housing would only require the abstention by the Government from certain practices and a commitment to facilitating "self-help" by affected groups'.[105] For these parts, it is determined that insofar 'that any such steps are considered to be beyond the maximum resources available to a State party, it is appropriate that a request be made as soon as possible for international cooperation in accordance with articles 11(1), 22 and 23 of the Covenant, and that the Committee be informed thereof.'[106] There is no explanation in the same paragraph of what these immediate steps are exactly. The next paragraph, however, continues by explaining that due priority must be given 'to those social groups living in unfavourable conditions by giving them particular consideration'. In the same paragraph it is acknowledged that external factors can affect the right, but that 'despite externally caused problems, the obligations under the Covenant continue to apply'.[107]

A further obligation of immediate effect recognized in the General Comment is that of effective monitoring 'to ascertain the full extent of homelessness and inadequate housing within its jurisdiction'.[108] State reports must therefore contain information '"(...) about those groups within ... society that are vulnerable and

---

[101] OHCHR/UN-Habitat Fact Sheet no 21 (n 95) 33. This includes: refrain from carrying out forced evictions and demolishing homes; denying security of tenure to particular groups; imposing discriminatory practices that limit women's access to and control over housing, land and property; infringing on the right to privacy and protection of the home; denying housing, land and property restitution to particular groups; or polluting water resources'.

[102] Ibid.

[103] Ibid.

[104] CESCR, GC 4 (n 37) para 14.

[105] Ibid, para 10.

[106] Ibid, para 10.

[107] Ibid, para 11.

[108] Ibid, para 13.

disadvantaged with regard to housing".'[109] These include amongst others homeless persons and those inadequately housed.

In general, non-discrimination is recognized as an immediate obligation and can therefore be mentioned as part of the core content. A number of these elements require mostly abstention from the state, or require only little effort from states perfectly possible in disaster situations.

*4.3.3 Obligations relating to disasters*

The goal of identifying disaster-specific obligations for each right is to define standards based on which it can be determined if an affected state must move from one step to the next in the legal framework on accepting international humanitarian assistance. To this end, benchmarks must be created for the four rights. However, as explained in section 4.2, benchmarks are context-sensitive (depending on the context of the case, so the destructiveness of the disaster, the amount of resources available within the state, the amount of offers of assistance made to the affected state and the quality of these offers (i.e. whether they meet the humanitarian principles)), making it difficult to set general standards. One element is nonetheless fixed: the core obligations of each right must be realized at all times, also immediately after a disaster. Moving beyond the core obligations, states must make sufficient progression, which is largely depending on the particulars of the case. Therefore, in describing the disaster-specific obligations for the four rights selected here two layers are distinguished. First, the core obligations that must be realized at all times provide concrete standards. Next, the standards on progressive realization can be less concretely defined, but indications will be provided that help to determine in each case whether a state makes sufficient progression. It must be called to mind that very detailed frameworks on humanitarian achievements exist that are of use here like the Sphere Standards or the UN Inter-Agency Standing Committee's Operational Guidelines on Human Rights and Natural Disasters, but repeating all standards here is unnecessary.[110]

The standards set by the core obligations must be included in the needs-assessment so that the affected state can quickly determine whether it will be able to realize this or not. If a state cannot (or fears that it cannot) realize the core obligations it must seek international assistance and even accept international assistance if suitable offers are found. For the right to housing, no concrete core obligations were formulated by the CESCR. It cannot therefore be said with full certainty what the obligations are that must be realized at all times, although above

[109] Ibid.

[110] UN Inter-Agency Standing Committee, 'Protecting Persons Affected by Natural Disasters: IASC Operational Guidelines on Human Rights and Natural Disasters' (2006). These guidelines are supported by the Special Rapporteur on the Right to Housing who encourages further work on the right to housing in disaster situations. UN Human Rights Council, 'Promotion and Protection of All Human Rights, Civil, Political, Economic, Social, and Cultural Rights, Including the Right to Development' UN Doc. A/HRC/7/16 of 13 February 2008 paras 81-84.

some obligations were identified as constituting the core contents. Of these, a number is especially relevant in post-disaster settings. First, the affected state must have an idea of the number of persons that are left homeless. In addition, it must establish which people live in emergency shelter and determine how long that emergency shelter is tangible given the circumstances of the case (for example considering the weather forecast, accessibility of relief workers and goods, and influx of more disaster survivors). The Sphere Handbook gives concrete standards on the tangibility of emergency housing.[111]

When looking at the core obligations, the affected state must especially consider the needs of vulnerable and disadvantaged groups. 'Victims of natural disasters' and 'people living in disaster-prone areas' can be considered a 'disadvantaged group' and therefore need some degree of priority consideration and discrimination is not allowed.[112] Implementing these obligations in a plan of action in which the state determines which steps will be taken from this basis helps to make founded decisions on whether the state must start to seek international assistance and cooperation and whether the state must accept this. At this point, the standards consist of the obligation to realize the core contents of the right to housing. If the affected state lacks the resources to fulfil its core obligations, it is in violation of its obligations stemming from the ICESCR.

After the core obligations, the affected state has an obligation to move forward, or to make progression through taking steps. At this time, the immediate disaster response will gradually turn into reconstruction phase. It is difficult to pinpoint where one phase ends and another begins. Nonetheless, a couple of indicators can be mentioned making it possible to formulate disaster-specific obligations with regard to the right to housing. To determine the progression a state must make, the CESCR's formulation of 'adequacy' can be used. It is established what can be understood with 'adequate' housing in terms of privacy, having enough space, lighting, ventilation and access to basic infrastructure. Based on the needs-assessment, the affected state can describe in its plans which steps it will take to move from emergency shelter to housing that increasingly meet the standards of adequacy. The Sphere Handbook contains concrete standards on the amount of covered living space, including consideration for privacy and household uses which can be used as benchmarks.[113]

The IASC Guidelines provide that basic services must be available, accessible, acceptable and adaptable, which must be considered next to the CESCR's

[111] See for example the housing and shelter options and response scenarios on p. 245 and the minimum standards starting on p. 249. Sphere Project, 'Humanitarian Charter and Minimum Standards in Disaster Response' (Oxfam Publishing, Oxford 2011).

[112] CESCR, GC 4 (n 37) para 8(e); Charles W. Gould, 'The Right to Housing Recovery after Natural Disasters' (2009) 22 Harvard Human Rights Journal 169, 175.

[113] Shelter and Settlement Standard 3, Sphere Handbook (n 111) 258.

requirement of adequacy.[114] As a consequence, there must be sufficient emergency housing, this must be made available and must be of sufficient quality. In addition, the housing must be made available without discrimination. Non-discrimination is an obligation that is relevant for all rights in disaster contexts and is an issue returning often. For example, the Committee on the Elimination of Discrimination against Women (CEDAW Committee) 'noted that female tsunami victims in Indonesia did not have their needs for (reproductive) health, clothing, housing and safety met. The CEDAW Committee was also concerned that households in which women were the head of the household suffered from 'discriminatory treatment in trying to get access to housing or food aid provided to male heads of the households'. The Committee explicitly urged Indonesia to 'eliminate all forms of discrimination against women with respect to access to housing and food aid in emergency and natural disaster situations.'[115]

Further, the housing provided must be culturally appropriate and must be sensitive to gender and age, for example by granting privacy. The adaptability finally requires that the emergency shelter can be easily transformed into more permanent housing, this way making room for progression from the start. The transition from emergency shelter to permanent housing must be 'speedy'.[116]Keeping survivors in tents during a hurricane season, for example, is insufficient progression. Permanent housing must meet the requirement of 'adequacy', which is by the IASC described as 'accessibility, affordability, habitability, security of tenure, cultural adequacy, suitability of location and access to essential services such as health and education'.[117]

The shelter or housing as achieved may not be downgraded as that would constitute a retrogressive measure. To this end, the security of tenure (including prevention of forced evictions) also applies to emergency housing.[118]

In conclusion, immediately after a disaster the affected state must seek and accept assistance if it is unable to identify those persons left homeless and those living in emergency shelter and to make plans for progression for this point. Progression that must be made immediately after the occurrence of a disaster is granting sufficient privacy, living space (determined by standards of the Sphere Handbook), lighting, ventilation and access to basic infrastructure. Throughout the progress made, the shelter or housing must be affordable, culturally adequate, and there must be security of tenure. The speed with which this progression is made depends on the context, but where an affected state is not making progression, there is an obligation to accept assistance.

---

[114] Gould (n 112) 180. See also the Sphere Handbook on the standards (n 111). IASC Guidelines (n 110) B.2.1.

[115] CEDAW, 'Concluding Observations Indonesia' UN Doc. CEDAW/C/IDN/CO/5 of 10 August 2007, para 38-9, cited by Hesselman (n 45) 123.

[116] IASC Guidelines (n 110) C.3.1 and C.3.3.

[117] Ibid, C.3.2.

[118] CESCR, GC 4 (n 37) para 8(a).

## 4.4 The Right to Food

### *4.4.1 Introduction*

The right to adequate food is also laid down in article 11 ICESCR, the text of which was provided in the previous section.[119] The CESCR has been quite clear on the obligation of result of the right to food: '(t)he right to adequate food is realized when every man, woman and child, alone or in community with others, has physical and economic access at all times to adequate food or means for its procurement'.[120] Consequently, for the right to food to be realized, food must be 'available, accessible and adequate'.[121] Availability indicates that food must be available through means of production (agriculture, animal husbandry), gathering (including fishing, hunting) or that it must be purchasable in stores and markets.[122] Accessibility means that it must be affordable without 'compromising on any other basic needs'[123] and that it must be accessible also for physically vulnerable persons, like the elderly and disabled.[124] Finally, adequacy refers to the quality and type of food, so that it contains the nutrients needed for each group of individuals (i.e. children, adults, pregnant women, elderly etc.), also meaning that it must be safe and culturally acceptable.[125]

In terms of the tripartite typology, states must respect the access to food that is already established and the means of obtaining food already established in any way.[126] The obligation to protect indicates that states must prevent third parties from destroying sources of food and states must make sure that food available at national markets is safe and also that food is nutritious and healthy.[127] The first aspect of the obligation to fulfil - to facilitate - tells states to be 'proactive in strengthening people's access to and use of resources and means of ensuring their

---

[119] And in *inter alia* article 12 CEDAW, article 24 (on food) and 27 (on an adequate standard of living) CRC, Convention on the Rights of Persons with Disabilities, and a number of regional instruments.

[120] CESCR, GC 12 (n 28) para 6.

[121] Ibid, para 7; UN Office of the High Commissioner for Human Rights, 'The Right to Adequate Food: Fact Sheet no 34' (UN, Geneva 2010) 2. The key elements as identified by Maria Green are in line: '1) the right to sustainable access to adequate food; 2) the right to safe food, including the right to information about food and nutrition; and 3) international aspects of the right to food'. Green (n 79) 1074.

[122] CESCR, GC 12 (n 28) para 12.

[123] OHCHR, Fact Sheet no 34 (n 121) 2.

[124] CESCR, GC 12 (n 28) para 13.

[125] Acceptability is therefore also mentioned as a separate category; Federica Donati & Margret Vidar, 'International Legal Dimensions of the Right to Food' in George Kent (ed), *Global Obligations for the Right to Food* (Rowman & Littlefield Publishers Inc., Lanham 2008) 51. CESCR, GC 12 (n 28) para 11.

[126] OHCHR, Fact Sheet no 34 (n 121) 18. This includes recognizing (customary) land rights, the rights of persons to seek an income to come by food through free choice of work, and abstention from projects which potentially harm the production of food. Eide (n 16) 150.

[127] OHCHR, Fact Sheet no 34 (n 121) 18.

livelihoods, including food security'.[128] The aspect 'to provide' dictates states to provide food assistance or to ensure social safety nets for those who are unable, for reasons beyond their control, to enjoy the right to food by the means at their disposal,[129] so to 'give poor people food, or giving them money by which to buy the food'.[130]

In an extraterritorial context, there is at the very least an obligation to respect the right to food in other countries.[131] Also, states should 'take steps (...) to protect that right, to facilitate access to food and to provide the necessary aid when required' in other countries.[132] In this respect it is noted that recognizing 'international assistance and cooperation' as relating to 'more than development assistance and a duty to 'provide', is essential'.[133] Moreover, 'states have an obligation to support the fulfilment of the right to food in other countries'.[134] For the accepting-side it is acknowledged that not seeking assistance and prevention of access of food aid is a violation of the right to food: '(a) State claiming that it is unable to carry out its obligations for reasons beyond its control therefore has the burden of proving that this is the case and that it has unsuccessfully sought to obtain international support to ensure the availability and accessibility of the necessary food'.[135]

### *4.4.2 Core contents*

The right to food does not constitute an entitlement to receive food from the state. The state must create the environment in which people can obtain food themselves. Only where people are unable to provide for themselves for reasons beyond their control, the state must provide food.[136] The minimum core obligation of the right to food therefore is 'to ensure the satisfaction of, at the very least, the minimum essential level required to be free from hunger'.[137] As the right to food may be realized progressively, states must at least create a roadmap towards full realization

---

[128] OHCHR, Fact Sheet no 34 (n 121) 18.

[129] Ibid, 19.

[130] Eide (n 16) 152.

[131] CESCR, GC 12 (n 28) para 36; Donati & Vidar (n 125) 60, 68; Sigrun I. Skogly, 'Right to Adequate Food: National Implementation and Extraterritorial Obligations' (2007) 11 Max Planck Yearbook of United Nations Law 339, 352.

[132] CESCR, GC 12 (n 28) para 36.

[133] Skogly, 'Right to Adequate Food' (n 131) 351.

[134] Rolf Künnemann & Sandra Ratjen, 'Extraterritorial Obligations: A Response to Globalization' in George Kent (ed), *Global Obligations for the Right to Food* (Rowman & Littlefield Publishers Inc., Lanham 2008) 42.

[135] CESCR, GC 12 (n 28) para 17. Künnemann recognizes that a 'state could need to co-operate internationally to meet its territorial obligations, for example in a state of emergency for securing domestic access to food through international assistance'. Künnemann (n 30) 204.

[136] Donati & Vidar (n 125) 52.

[137] CESCR, GC 12 (n 28) para 17. This minimum level is described as 'food that will maintain an adult and ensure normal growth of children'; Donati & Vidar (n 125) 53.

of the right to food.[138] Moreover, 'States have a core obligation to take the necessary action to mitigate and alleviate hunger as provided for in paragraph 2 of article 11, even in times of natural or other disasters.'[139] Other core obligations are: making sure that there is such availability of food that dietary needs are satisfied; that food is culturally appropriate and that it is accessible in such a way that it is sustainable and that there is no interference with the enjoyment of other human rights.[140] Finally, in situations of 'severe resource constraints, whether caused by a process of economic adjustment, economic recession, climatic conditions or other factors, measures should be undertaken to ensure that the right to adequate food is especially fulfilled for vulnerable population groups and individuals.'[141] If a state claims it does not have the resources to realize this, 'the state has to demonstrate that every effort has been made to use all the resources at its disposal in an effort to satisfy, as a matter of priority, those minimum obligations'.[142]

*4.4.3 Obligations relating to disasters*

The core obligations on the right to food give the most concrete standards on when an affected state must seek and/or accept assistance. Immediately after a disaster, the affected state must make sure that disaster survivors are free from hunger (under the obligation to mitigate and alleviate hunger). As a consequence, the affected state must actively provide food assistance to those without access to food.[143] At this point, adding the need for food items in the needs-assessment is not enough. Immediately after a disaster an obligation to accept food assistance exists if the state cannot alleviate hunger and the state cannot await the needs-assessment.[144] The needs-assessment can be used to plan the next steps and to specify what further food aid is required. At this stage (as core obligations), the food assistance must satisfy dietary needs, and the food must be culturally appropriate and must be accessible in a sustainable way so that there is no interference with other human rights.[145] These criteria give grounds for judging the offers of assistance and give

[138] Making such a plan is an immediate obligation, as is the prevention of discrimination, taking steps towards full realization, the prohibition of retrogressive measures, and the realization of the minimum core content. UN-OHCHR, Fact Sheet no 34 (n 121) 20-22.
[139] CESCR, GC 12 (n 28) para 6.
[140] Ibid, para 8.
[141] Ibid, para 28.
[142] Ibid.
[143] Donati and Vidar claim in this respect that a state violates its obligations 'if it let people starve when they were in desperate need and had no way of helping themselves'. Donati & Vidar (n 125) 58.
[144] UN Development Programme, 'Disaster Assessment' (2$^{nd}$ edition 1994) 24 cited by David Fisher, 'Fast Food: Regulating Emergency Food Aid in Sudden-Impact Disasters' (2007) 40 Vanderbilt Journal of Transnational Law 1127, 1131.
[145] CESCR, GC 12 (n 28) para 39. Sustainability and long term-planning is generally recommended in delivering food assistance: 'the response is based on people's immediate food needs but will also consider the protection and promotion of livelihoods strategies'. Sphere Handbook (n 111) 151, 153. See for example Barry Armstrong, British Red Cross disaster

room for states to refuse an offer. The Sphere Handbook gives indicators on requirements of nutrition based on which a state can determine which food assistance can satisfy dietary needs.[146] Apart from immediately providing food assistance, the affected state must – as a core obligation – create a roadmap towards full realization (the CESCR formulated a clear definition of the full realization of the right to food). In this roadmap there is room for particular consideration of the situation at hand.

After the core obligations, the progression that a state must make is determined by the factors 'availability' and 'accessibility', both being a part of 'adequacy'.[147] Here, the affected state must continue the core obligation of providing food, yet now the standard is providing the *access* to food for those who cannot obtain it (either cannot purchase it for lack of means or lack of offer). The CESCR formulated this as follows: 'an individual or group is unable, for reasons beyond their control, to enjoy the right to adequate food by the means at their disposal, States have the obligation to *fulfil (provide)* that right directly. This obligation also applies for persons who are victims of natural or other disasters'.[148] Throughout the disaster response, states must therefore accept assistance if they cannot provide food to disaster survivors: '(e)ven where a State faces severe resource constraints, whether caused by a process of economic adjustment, economic recession, climatic conditions or other factors, measures should be undertaken to ensure that the right to adequate food is especially fulfilled for vulnerable population groups and individuals'.[149]

The requirement of 'availability' indicates that food must either be obtained from productive land or other resources (which is usually hampered after a disaster) or through well-functioning distribution or market systems (the first steps in disaster response).[150] The affected state must therefore set up such a system or request assistance to this end. 'Accessibility' requires that food is economically accessible, so in the beginning usually free of costs with a gradual increase of costs, and that food is physically accessible, also to those groups more vulnerable (elderly, children, disabled). The affected state must therefore actively provide food to those

---

response manager in ——, 'Emergency Food Aid' *Disaster Emergency Committee* 25 August 2011 <http://www.dec.org.uk/appeals/east-africa-crisis-appeal/emergency-food-aid> accessed 15 August 2012 stating: '(e)mergency food aid is the option of last resort. It is desperately needed now to save lives, but it does not solve any of the underlying causes. One thing which has made a long term difference in areas of Kenya is helping people strengthen their livelihoods, which can help them withstand future crises'

[146] See the scheme on p. 142 and Food Security and Nutrition Assessment Standard 2: Nutrition in the Sphere Handbook (n 111) 154.

[147] These factors were explained in the introduction to the right to food above.

[148] CESCR, GC 12 (n 28) para 15.

[149] Ibid, para 28; Donati & Vidar (n 125) 58. In the same paragraph, Donati and Vidar also note that 'States that, through neglect or misplaced national pride, make no such appeals or deliberately delay such appeals are violating their obligation'.

[150] CESCR, GC 12 (n 28) para 12.

who cannot obtain it or provide the means to obtain food. Ensuring access to food not only entails providing the actual food, but also materials to prepare and possibilities to store food, and means of distribution.[151] According to the CESCR and to the Sphere Handbook, states may not hamper the access to food, so if a third party is providing food aid, the state may not block access to the assistance.[152]

Consequently, the affected state must accept international humanitarian assistance if it cannot provide basic food aid immediately after a disaster. If the affected state is not able to provide basic food, it violates its obligations under the CESCR and must therefore give its consent to suitable offers. The obligation to provide exists throughout the disaster response phase, where the affected state must meet increasing standards of nutrition. These standards can be used to determine the amount of progression the affected state must make.

## 4.5 The Right to Water

### *4.5.1 Introduction*

The right to water is not laid down explicitly in the ICESCR, but is derived from articles 11 and 12 ICESCR. Without clean and safe water it is impossible to enjoy the right to food and health and certain aspects of the right to housing cannot be achieved (like access to infrastructure). It is possible to consider the right to water as 'subordinate and necessary' to realize other human rights, yet by now it can be argued that the right to water is an independent human right as well.[153] This suggestion is reinforced by the adoption of the right in various treaties[154] and by the General Comment made by the CESCR on the right to water, recognizing it as a part of articles 11 and 12 ICESCR and also of the right to life and human dignity.[155]

According to the CESCR, '(t)he human right to water entitles everyone to sufficient, safe, acceptable, physically accessible and affordable water for personal and domestic uses'.[156] On the one hand this means that people have the 'right to maintain access to existing water supplies' and the 'right to be free from interference', on the other hand that the state foresees in a 'system of water supply and management that provides equality of opportunity for people to enjoy the right to water'.[157] The CESCR determines further that water must be adequate for human dignity, life and health and gives a number of indicators to determine adequacy: availability (sufficient for daily household use); quality (safe and of acceptable

[151] Fisher, 'Fast Food' (n 144) 1141.

[152] CESCR, GC 12 (n 28) para 19. In the Sphere Handbook: states 'should also facilitate safe and unimpeded access for international assistance'. The Sphere Handbook (n 111) 144.

[153] Erik B. Bluemel, 'The Implications of Formulating a Human Right to Water' (2004) 31 Ecology Law Quarterly 957, 967-8.

[154] For example article 14(2) CEDAW and article 24(2) under (c) CRC.

[155] CESCR, GC 15 (n 49) para 3.

[156] Ibid, para 2.

[157] Ibid, para 10.

colour, odour and taste); and accessible (physical, economical and without discrimination).[158] If persons do not have sufficient means they should be provided with the necessary water and water facilities and discrimination must be prevented.[159] Especially certain groups must be protected, amongst which are mentioned IDPs and refugees.[160]

States have immediate obligations to realize the right to water (non-discrimination and the obligation to take steps). States 'have a constant and continuing duty (...) to move as expeditiously and effectively as possible towards the full realization of the right to water'[161] and no retrogressive measures may be taken.[162] Further, states are under duties to respect, protect and fulfil, where they must fulfil 'the right when individuals or a group are unable, for reasons beyond their control, to realize that right themselves by the means at their disposal'.[163]

If a state is unwilling to use the maximum of its available resources to realize the right to water, it is in violation of its obligations. Where a state is in violation of its obligations due to resource constraints, it has to justify that every effort has been made to use all resources at its disposal to realize the right to water.[164]

### *4.5.2 Core contents*

The CESCR has identified a number of core obligations. These core obligations constitute the duty to ensure access to the minimum essential amount of water; to ensure the right of access to water and water facilities without discrimination and especially for disadvantaged or marginalized groups; to ensure physical access to water without long waiting times and at reasonable distance; safe physical access; equitable distribution; to adopt a plan of action; to monitor; to adopt relatively low-cost targeted programmes to protect vulnerable and marginalized groups[165] and to take measures to prevent treat and control water-based and water-borne diseases.[166] These obligations are explicitly recognized to be non-derogable and a state cannot justify non-compliance with these core obligations.[167]

### *4.5.3 Obligations relating to disasters*

It is noticeable that the system of core contents had evolved by the time the General Comment on the right to water was created: the contents mentioned are both relatively extensive and elaborate. In disaster contexts, water is of essential

[158] Ibid, para 12 under (a) to (c).
[159] Ibid, para 15.
[160] Ibid, para 16 and 16(f).
[161] Ibid, para 18.
[162] Ibid, para 19.
[163] Ibid, para 25.
[164] Ibid, para 41.
[165] Apart from being mentioned under paragraph 37, this core obligation is also recognized as a general obligation in paragraph 13 of CESCR, GC 15 (n 49).
[166] Ibid, para 37 under (a) to (i).
[167] Ibid, para 40.

importance and is immediately linked to the fulfilment of other rights. Water is for example needed to make use of food aid, which often consists of dried food stuffs like dried noodles and rice.[168] Another example is provided as a core obligation: the right to health can be violated through water-based and water-borne diseases, which must be prevented, treated and controlled under the right to water.

Immediately after the occurrence of a disaster, the affected state party has a number of obligations to fulfil. In the first and foremost place, the state must provide access to safe water, where a number of specifications are given. First, the affected state must provide the minimum essential amount, for which the Sphere Handbook contains standards.[169] Next, water must be provided without discrimination. Third, physical access must be guaranteed, where the affected state must make sure that there are no long waiting times,[170] that the distance to the water source is reasonable,[171] and that the access to the water sources is safe, for example by having sufficient lighting at night and having separate facilities for men and women.[172] Within the progression the state must made, these standards give indications on what must be achieved (less waiting time, closer distances, more safety to users). The Sphere Handbook gives for example standards on the number of facilities for certain amounts of people, and the progression from latrines to actual toilets.[173] Where groups are 'facing difficulties with physical access to water, such as (...) victims of natural disasters, (...) are provided with safe and sufficient water'.[174] To achieve this, the state must be well-equipped. As with the right to food, the danger is that waiting for the needs-assessment takes too long and that fast decisions are required in order not to violate the core obligations.

The basis for the progression is also laid down in the core obligations by referring to the plan of action, to monitoring and to adopting relatively low-cost targeted programmes to protect vulnerable and marginalized groups (under which disaster victims can be ranged). Further progression is again determined by the elements that constitute 'adequacy' (availability, quality, accessibility). Using these factors as guidelines and taking the context of the state and disaster into account, the affected state party must make sure that it takes steps towards the full realization. In the IASC Guidelines, the formulation used is that of the 'right to sufficient, safe, acceptable, physically accessible and affordable water for personal and domestic use without discrimination'.[175]

---

168 Fisher, 'Fast Food' (n 144) 1137.

169 The Sphere Handbook divides the needs for water in various purposes, like hygiene, excreta disposal and drainage. For each purpose there are different minimum amounts. Sphere Handbook (n 111) 82.

170 See for example the maximum queueing time of 30 minutes provided by the Sphere Handbook, ibid, 97.

171 The Sphere Handbook prescribes a maximum distance of 500 metres, ibid.

172 IASC Guidelines (n 110) B.2.2.

173 See Appendix 3 to the Sphere Handbook (n 111) 130 and the table at 109.

174 CESCR, GC 15 (n 49) para 16(h).

175 IASC Guidelines (n 110) B.2.2.

Ultimately, if a group is or individuals are unable to obtain water, the state party must fulfil the right. In the context of the right to water it is explicitly recognized that progression includes the preparation for the occurrence of a new disaster: states must plan for response mechanisms for emergency situations[176] and the failure to adopt such mechanisms constitutes a violation of the right to water.[177]

Apart from identifying obligations with regard to the right to water stemming from the ICESCR, '(t)he Committee notes that during armed conflicts, emergency situations and natural disasters, the right to water embraces those obligations by which States parties are bound under international humanitarian law'.[178] Here, the CESCR argues that in cases of natural disaster, international humanitarian law applies, which is a striking comment as there is no ground to assume that in a peacetime disaster humanitarian law can be applied.[179] Large parts of IHL can be considered as customary international law and can generally be applied, and the comment of the CESCR may be understood as referring to general principles depicted by IHL.[180] These are the very basic needs with regard to access to clean water, as laid down in the core contents of the right to water.

Affected states must seek assistance when disaster survivors do not have access to sufficient amounts of safe water and the state cannot facilitate this access immediately after a disaster. This obligation remains in place during the progression the state must make afterwards, where indicators like adequacy, availability, quality and accessibility determine what can be expected from a state. Although the steps remain dependent on the specifics of the case, the Sphere Handbook give concrete standards that the affected state can use in its plan.

## 4.6 The Right to Health

### *4.6.1 Introduction*

Article 12 ICESCR, containing the right to the highest attainable standard of health (and implicitly also the right to water), provides:

> (1) The States Parties to the present Covenant recognize the right of everyone to the enjoyment of the highest attainable standard of physical and mental health.
> (2) The steps to be taken by the States Parties to the present Covenant to achieve the full realization of this right shall include those necessary for:

---

[176] CESCR, GC 15 (n 49) para 28(h).

[177] Ibid, para 44(v).

[178] Ibid, para 22.

[179] The CESCR comments in a footnote that the ICJ Nuclear Weapons-case (1996) can be consulted for the interrelationship of human rights law and humanitarian law.

[180] Although the option must be considered that the CESCR referred to IHL only in relation to armed conflicts, possibly in combination with the occurrence of a disaster. See for an overview of the relation between IHL and disaster response Michael H. Hoffman, 'What is the Scope of International Disaster Response Law?' in IFRC, *International Disaster Response Laws, Principles and Practice: Reflections, Prospects and Challenges* (IFRC, Geneva 2003) 13-20.

(a) The provision for the reduction of the stillbirth-rate and of infant mortality and for the healthy development of the child;
(b) The improvement of all aspects of environmental and industrial hygiene;
(c) The prevention, treatment and control of epidemic, endemic, occupational and other diseases;
(d) The creation of conditions which would assure to all medical service and medical attention in the event of sickness.[181]

Reading this article makes clear that the right to the highest attainable standard of health is quite elaborate and complex. It consists of physical and mental health and the elements vary from reproductive health to workplace environments, control of epidemics and working on the services providing health care.[182] The key elements can be narrowly defined as: '1) rights involving freedom and control over one's health, including for instance reproductive freedom and freedom from torture; 2) the right to health care; 3) the right to underlying determinants of health, including for instance clean water, sanitation, healthy and natural workplace environment and information about health'.[183] The CESCR provides a more layered analysis of the content of the right to health in one of its General Comments. It emphasizes that the right to health is not to be understood as a right to be healthy, but through freedoms and entitlements people should be able to pursue the highest attainable standard of health.[184] Freedoms relate to the abstention of governments in choices made regarding one's health and body and elements like freedom from torture. Entitlements 'include the right to a system of health protection which provides equality of opportunity for people to enjoy the highest attainable standard of health.[185]

Because the right to health is so broad and all-encompassing, a useful way to define the content of the right to health is making use of the aspects of 'availability', 'accessibility', 'acceptability', and 'quality', as the CESCR has also done in the context of other rights. Availability relates to the presence of health-care facilities and goods, but also to availability of underlying determinants, like clean water.[186] Accessibility must be understood in terms of non-discrimination, physical accessibility, economic accessibility (affordability) and accessibility of

[181] The right to health is also provided in, *inter alia,* article 25(1) UDHR and article 24 CRC.
[182] The CESCR gives this list of topics in the General Comment and explains there that the list is not exhaustive. It is explained what each of the issues under article 12(2) ICESCR entails and it is further emphasized that certain groups may need specific attention, like women, children, the elderly, the disabled and indigenous people. CESCR, GC 14 (n 29) paras 18-29.
[183] Green (n 79) 1074.
[184] CESCR, GC 14 (n 29) para 8. It is obvious that states cannot prevent people from becoming ill entirely, but they must protect against illnesses wherever they can. Even so, certain lifestyle choices are also of influence, but are not necessarily related to the right to health in disaster-contexts.
[185] Ibid.
[186] Ibid, para 12(a).

information.[187] Next, health facilities, goods and services must by culturally appropriate, so acceptable in the society.[188] Finally, the quality must be such that staff and goods are safe and that equipment and facilities are clean and furnished.[189] The CESCR further states – again – that states must take targeted steps towards full realization with an obligation to move forward and that retrogressive measures are not allowed.

As with the other rights, the duties to respect and protect relate to not blocking access to health care or medicines in any way, or allow other to block this access. Under the obligation to fulfil, states are encouraged to at least adopt recognition of the right in national political and legal systems and to set up programmes and campaigns related to health. Moreover, states must 'ensure provision of health care' and 'ensure access for all underlying determinants of health', like safe food, water and adequate housing.[190] States must further provide for a specific right of the ICESC when persons 'are unable, for reasons beyond their control, to realize the right themselves by the means at their disposal.'[191]

### *4.6.2 Core contents*

As core obligations, the CESCR identifies a number of duties: ensuring the right of access to health facilities, goods and services on a non-discriminatory basis, especially for vulnerable or marginalized groups; to provide essential drugs; to ensure equitable distribution of all health facilities, goods and services; to adopt and implement a strategy and plan of action, including benchmarks with particular attention to all vulnerable or marginalized groups.[192] Under the core contents of the right to health other rights are mentioned as well: to ensure access to the minimum essential food; to ensure access to basic shelter, housing and sanitation and an adequate supply of safe and potable water.[193]

The CESCR continues by providing a list of obligations which are 'of comparable priority'. It may be assumed that these obligations are of the same level as the core obligations, but why the CESCR did not choose to just make one longer list is not clear. This second list provides: to ensure reproductive, maternal and child health care; to provide immunization against the major infectious diseases occurring in the community; to take measures to prevent, treat and control epidemic and endemic diseases; to provide education and access to information concerning the main health problems in the community, including methods of preventing and controlling them; to provide appropriate training for health personnel, including

[187] Ibid, para 12(b).
[188] Ibid, para 12(c).
[189] Ibid, para 12(d).
[190] Ibid, para 36.
[191] Ibid, para 37.
[192] Ibid, para 43 under (a), (d) to (f).
[193] Ibid, para 43 under (b) and (c).

education on health and human rights.[194] Again, the CESCR stresses that 'a State party cannot, under any circumstances whatsoever, justify its non-compliance with the core obligations (...), which are non-derogable.'[195]

### *4.6.3 Obligations relating to disasters*

Since it is very broad and consisting of many factors, realizing the right to health is already challenging in ordinary times and in times of emergency it has proved 'exceedingly complex'.[196] States must provide for access to health care, meaning access to facilities, staff, goods, medicines, etc. The IASC Guidelines formulate the right to health in emergency contexts as the right 'to timely and appropriate, accessible, culturally acceptable and gender sensitive health care without discrimination'.[197] Access to health care also includes access to underlying determinants, like clean water, safe and nutritious food and adequate shelter.[198] Especially for marginalized and vulnerable groups, and for those who are unable to obtain health care for reasons beyond their control, like disaster victims, the state must provide access. After a disaster, states must therefore provide for the whole package, and cannot afford to only focus on one of the aforementioned rights.

Granting access means making health care affordable, which post-disaster means in most cases free of charge. This goes especially for obtaining essential drugs, which is one of the core obligations of the right to health. Health care must also be in the vicinity of disaster survivors so that it is physically accessible. This entails an equitable distribution of emergency facilities throughout the disaster area and in the areas where IDPs or refugees are staying. An example of a violation of the obligation to respect include the 'denial of access to health facilities, goods, and services', so where states refuse to accept assistance that must contribute to realizing the right to health, it may be understood as denial of access.[199] An overview of what essential health services encompass is provided in the Sphere Handbook.[200]

Providers of humanitarian assistance relating to health care must make sure that the assistance is culturally appropriate. States also have a role in ensuring that the assistance is meeting this requirement and also that it meets certain standards of quality. An example is provided by the sensitivity to gender, to which end the state must make sure that female health care is accessible for women and girls.[201]

---

194 Ibid, para 44 under (a) to (e).
195 Ibid, para 47.
196 Obijiofor Aginam, 'The Right to Health in Emergencies: Natural or Man-Made Disasters' in Andrew Clapham & Mary Robinson (eds), *Realizing the Right to Health* (Zurich, Ruffer & Rub 2009) 175.
197 IASC Guidelines (n 110) B.2.5.
198 Ibid.
199 CESCR, GC 14 (n 29) para 50.
200 Essential Health Services Standard 1: Prioritizing Health Services, Sphere Handbook (n 111) 309.
201 See for example the IASC Guidelines (n 110) 36.

Because of its many aspects, the right to health therefore 'can be used to monitor the humanitarian response by local, regional, national and international actors'.[202] While immediately after a disaster the health care may be of emergency-level, states have an obligation to make progression and to make steps towards full realization of the right to health, so emergency health care is only acceptable right after a disaster. Making plans and setting benchmarks are steps that states can take immediately and will help to determine how to move on from the post-disaster phase to the recovery phase, and will allow a state to make targeted requests for assistance.

Finally, the right to health must also aim at preventing the outbreak of epidemics and endemic diseases, which includes 'the creation of a system of urgent medical care in cases of accidents, epidemics and similar health hazards, and the provision of disaster relief and humanitarian assistance in emergency situations'.[203] Especially after water-related disasters, special measures must be taken to prevent the outbreak of diseases, like disposing of bodies and cleaning sources of drinking water. To this end, the Sphere Handbook contains clear standards on the control of communicable diseases, where general prevention measures refer to the rights mentioned before: shelter, water and food security.[204]

The CESCR has summarized these disaster-specific obligations in the General Comment on the right to health, stating that states and international organisations should:

> Cooperate in providing disaster relief and humanitarian assistance in times of emergency, including assistance to refugees and internally displaced persons. (...) Priority in the provision of international medical aid, distribution and management of resources, such as safe and potable water, food and medical supplies, and financial aid should be given to the most vulnerable or marginalized groups of the population.[205]

This is repeated in relation to the role of international organisations in realizing the right to health. The role of these organisations is of special importance

> In relation to disaster relief and humanitarian assistance in times of emergencies, including assistance to refugees and internally displaced persons. Priority in the provision of international medical aid, distribution and management of resources, such as safe and potable water, food and medical supplies, and financial aid should be given to the most vulnerable or marginalized groups of the population.[206]

The set of obligations for affected states under the right to health is quite complex as it includes standards from the aforementioned rights. In any case, the

---

[202] Aginam (n 196) 176.
[203] CESCR, GC 14 (n 29) para 16.
[204] Sphere Handbook (n 111) 312-3.
[205] CESCR, GC 14 (n 29) para 40.
[206] Ibid, para 65.

affected state must be able to provide access to basic health care, immediately after a disaster free of charge, with access to essential medicines. Standards following the core obligations are again determined by formulations of adequacy, accessibility, quality and availability and must be measured by including standards of the other rights.

## 4.7 Disaster-specific obligations under the substantive rights

When considering the four rights discussed here together a number of issues become clear. Throughout the General Comments, the CESCR has used the same words to define obligations, yet often this has also led to general obligations and not to specific obligations relating to each right. The advantage of this is that certain conclusions can be drawn on what is at least expected from states in disaster situations. However, certain gaps remain with regard to each right on the details and specifics of the obligations.

The core contents contain obligations that must be realized at all times and for which, according to General Comments 14 and 15, no justification for non-compliance is possible. An evolution in the usage of core contents can easily be discerned in the work of the CESCR. Where the formulation of core obligations was missing in the General Comment on the right to housing, the mechanism was already used for the right to food and with respect to the rights to health and water the formulation of non-derogable obligations was used. Core contents provide the minimum of obligations that states must realize at all times, also immediately after a disaster. If a state does not have the resources to do this, it must seek additional resources and therefore accept international assistance when necessary. Consequently, the core obligations provide a clear standard on when an affected state is obliged to accept international humanitarian assistance.[207] Core contents have been formulated quite elaborately and not all (parts of) the core obligations are of particular relevance in disaster settings. Those parts that are relevant in the aftermath of a disaster and for which an obligation exists to accept international humanitarian assistance if the affected state cannot realise it by itself are to:

- Give particular consideration with respect to housing to social groups living in unfavourable conditions;
- Monitor to ascertain the full extent of homelessness and inadequate housing;

[207] If an affected state party to the ICESCR does not realise the core contents it violates an obligation under international law. As explained in section 5.4 of Chapter II, this could result in state responsibility for committing an internationally wrongful act. Invocation of the state responsibility by third states could occur based on draft articles 48 and 54 of the draft articles on State Responsibility for Internationally Wrongful Acts (UNGA Resolution 56/83). See also Annie Bird, 'Third State Responsibility for Human Rights Violations (2011) 21 European Journal of International Law 883. The core contents therefore at least give standards to the 164 state parties (April 2015), and under the customary core theory also to the remaining non-party states.

- Ensure the satisfaction of, at the very least, the minimum essential amount of water and minimum level required to be free from hunger;
- Take the necessary action to mitigate and alleviate hunger;
- Make sure that food is culturally appropriate, accessible and sustainable;
- Ensure that the right to food is especially fulfilled for vulnerable population groups and individuals;
- Ensure the right of access to water and water facilities (including safe and quick access);
- Adopt relatively low-cost targeted programmes to protect vulnerable and marginalized groups;
- Take measures to prevent, treat and control water-based and water-borne diseases and provide immunization against major infectious diseases;
- Treat and control epidemic and endemic diseases;
- Provide access to information concerning health issues, including preventing and controlling diseases;
- Ensure access to health facilities, goods, and services, especially for vulnerable and marginalized groups;
- Provide essential drugs.

Moving beyond core obligations, the question immediately arises what states must achieve further in terms of progression. In the context of each right, the CESCR has given its interpretation of 'adequacy'. The elements constituting 'adequacy' can be used to determine the progress a state party must make, like availability, accessibility, acceptability and quality.[208] However, the progress is depending on availability of resources, the size of the disaster, and the specifics of the affected state. One obligation that was identified for all rights is the positive obligation to provide for those persons who cannot obtain or fulfil a right for reasons beyond their control. If persons do not have access to housing, food, water or health care after a disaster, a state must provide this access. This obligation is mentioned under the duty to fulfil where the CESCR discusses the tripartite typology and does not fall under the core contents. Consequently, a state must make sure that it seeks additional resources (and as such has an obligation to accept assistance) when it does not have sufficient resources to provide, but where a state has made sufficient efforts to obtain additional resources and can still not provide, it does not violate its obligations. Nonetheless, where states are unable to provide for access to one of the aforementioned rights, there is an obligation to accept international assistance. The other duties of the tripartite typology are treated in the same way. The duties to respect and to protect lead to the same results for each right: states must abstain from interfering in the enjoyment of a right and must make sure that third parties do not interfere either.

[208] This was not this explicit in relation to the right to housing, but also there 'adequacy' was determined in equal terms (security of tenure; availability; affordability; habitability; accessibility; location; and cultural adequacy). With regard to the right to health, the elements were used to define the content of the right to health, as 'adequacy' is not a part of the right to health.

## 5 Conclusion

It has become clear that during and immediately after a disaster state parties to the ICESCR have obligations that cannot be set aside merely by the occurrence of a disaster. Most notably, the core contents that the CESCR has defined for most rights are non-derogable and justification for violating these core contents is not possible. As a consequence, if an affected state party to the ICESCR is unable to realize the core contents of a right after the occurrence of a disaster, that state has an obligation to seek and accept international humanitarian assistance for the realization of the core contents. Departing from this initial obligation, affected states must also comply with the general obligation to take steps towards full realization of the rights of the ICESCR. What the further steps beyond the core obligations should look like is less easy to define, nor is it possible to clearly demarcate where disaster response in terms of human rights standards ends and the rebuilding-phase begins, at which point more progression can already be expected. It is acceptable that states make less progression in the realization of the ESC-rights than they would otherwise do, although this lenience is subject to a number of ifs and buts. As soon as a state finds that its performance is limited by resource constraints, it must seek additional resources and make use of international assistance and cooperation. This indicates a clear transition from the first to the second step of the legal framework on accepting international humanitarian assistance. The standard dictating the point of transition is in line with what was found in the first part of the research: if the national capacity is overwhelmed, a state must seek assistance (by triggering the process). Within the reach of available resources (including those available internationally), a state must take steps towards full realization. Even though these steps are – as said – limited in scope due to resource constraints, a state must nonetheless move forward. Where a state made an effort to obtain additional resources, it is not violating its obligations.

The obligation to use (and therefore accept) international assistance and cooperation – i.e. humanitarian assistance in the context of disasters – is not recognized as a general obligation, yet exists in the context of what has just been said: if resource constraints cause lack of progression (or standstill or regression) as no steps can be taken and as such obligations under the ICESCR are violated, the state has an obligation to accept. Again, the ICESCR provides a standard for moving to the next step of the legal framework on accepting international humanitarian assistance in line with the standards of Part I of this research: the needs-assessment must determine whether the affected state has sufficient capacity to respond to a disaster. Human rights standards can be used in this needs-assessment. If the capacity is overwhelmed, so if at least the core contents cannot be realized, there is an obligation to accept. At this point lies a check for the CESCR: a willing state is able to demonstrate what it has done to obtain assistance. An unwilling state that does not make sufficient progression through even the smallest steps cannot demonstrate what it has done to obtain international assistance and is in that case in violation of its obligation to accept humanitarian assistance. The way in which article 2(1) is formulated therefore functions to a certain extent as a derogation clause. In situations of severe resource constraints, less progression can be expected from states than in ordinary situations, yet what exactly the standards are must be determined for each right.

With regard to the rights to housing, food, water and health the minimum obligations can be found in the core contents. These must be realized at all times and where a state lacks the resources to do this, it must seek and accept additional resources. Further, as a next step there is for each right a clear positive obligation to provide access to that right for disaster victims. The standard of this duty is not clearly defined for each right. Rather, it is part of the general obligation to fulfil. Yet, when looking at the standards that determine adequacy, more becomes clear on what progressive realization must lead to. However, here the transition is made from the disaster-proper-phase to the recovery-phase, which is excluded from the present research. Nonetheless, making plans for progressive realization is part of the core contents and therefore the needs-assessment must already take into account how the affected state will progress.

In conclusion, refusing offers of international assistance after a disaster when a) core contents are not realized or b) access of disaster victims to certain rights is not provided leads to a violation of obligations under the ICESCR. Also, not accepting international humanitarian assistance when it is needed to make progress in the realization of human rights after a disaster could also be seen as taking a retrogressive measure, which is only allowed when meeting certain conditions.

# CHAPTER VI
# FINAL CONCLUSIONS

## 1 INTRODUCTION

Disasters have devastating effects on the lives of people. The occurrence of a disaster can kill thousands in an instance, injure many others, damage homes and destroy livelihoods. Reconstruction takes a long time and the traumas last even longer. Natural disasters will not cease to exist and their impact appears to be ever growing. It is therefore of great importance that the response to a disaster is as effective and adequate as possible. If the disaster is too large for the affected state to cope with, other states, international organisations and NGOs are usually willing to assist. Although there is no guarantee that the situation of disaster survivors will greatly improve by external assistance, such help could be the difference between suffering due to a lack of supplies and being able to obtain at least the most basic resources. Nonetheless, some states affected by a disaster refuse international humanitarian assistance. They do this for a variety of reasons, a decision which can aggravate the effects of the disaster. Public international law offers hardly any instruments explicitly directing states' behaviour regarding humanitarian assistance in response to a disaster. This research has therefore aimed to answer the following question:

*To what extent does public international law contain standards for affected states determining whether they must accept international humanitarian assistance after the occurrence of a disaster?*

As a first part of the research, a number of (legal) instruments and documents has been selected which potentially can be used to find clues for answering the main research question. Together with an analysis of the past attempts to organize the response to disasters on the international level, the consideration of fields of international law, resolutions, guidelines and other instruments has resulted in an overview of legal rules and principles depicting where the law on accepting humanitarian assistance in response to a disaster currently stands. Based on this a framework is designed departing from the primary role of the affected state and giving three steps for initiating and accepting international humanitarian assistance, together with three limitations of the affected state's freedom to withhold consent. Next to that, these findings have been placed in the light of and have been confronted with practice to determine what nuances, details and difficulties exist in the application of the rules 'in real life'. Here it was found that although the rules give certain direction for states on accepting assistance, more concrete standards are required before it is possible to speak of an obligation for states to accept international humanitarian assistance in response to disasters. From the analysis of legal sources it followed that the most promising field for concretizing standards is human rights law. In particular the International Covenant on Economic, Social and Cultural Rights (ICESCR) turned out to be useful since a number of its rights is of particular importance for disaster contexts, like the right to housing, food, water and health. In addition, the general obligations of the ICESCR speak of using 'international assistance and cooperation'.

In the following, the results will be discussed. First, it will be considered what the current legal framework (apart from the ICESCR) entails and where the limitations and challenges lie. After this, it will be explained how especially the ICESCR contributes to the legal framework, before ending with an overview of obligations directing states on accepting international humanitarian assistance in response to a disaster.

## 2 The current standing of public international law on accepting international humanitarian assistance in response to a disaster

### 2.1 International approaches to disaster response versus state sovereignty: the origin of the conflicting notions

Public international law does not contain a clearly demarcated field of law created for the sole purpose of disaster response. The sources that form the basis of a common set of rules and principles identified in this research are mostly of soft-law character and created for specific practical purposes, like improving the quality of humanitarian operations. This scattered legal framework is the result of conflicting views on disaster response, reflected in past attempts to organize this response on the international level.

The only attempt to set up an international organization with the main task of actively responding to a disaster, the International Relief Union (IRU), created in 1927 under auspices of the League of Nations, rested on the assumption that affected states must be helped by an international collective, but was handicapped by the preservation of state sovereignty and territorial integrity in its mandate. It was generally accepted that a disaster can be beyond an affected states' capacity to respond and that international support is therefore necessary, but at the same time states were reluctant to set the door open widely for others to enter. These conflicting views have resulted in an unsuccessful organisation. The IRU's mandate was limited to responding only to exceptionally devastating disasters and it needed permission of the affected state to operate. Only in two disasters did the IRU come to action, but only managed to channel resources through the Red Cross. After merely focusing on its scientific tasks for some decades after its imbedding in the

UN system, the IRU's end became final with the transfer of its remaining scientific tasks to UNESCO in 1967.

The two conflicting views on international disaster response – i.e. preserving state sovereignty whilst acknowledging the importance of a coordinated international response in some cases – determine the working methods of today's main international organisations dealing with humanitarian assistance in response to disasters. Within the UN context, there is a specific body that is created for the coordination of humanitarian responses to disasters. This Office for the Coordination of Humanitarian Affairs (OCHA) is headed by the Emergency Relief Coordinator and is the result of the development of the UN's branch of disaster response since the establishment of the UN Disaster Relief Organisation in 1971. OCHA works with affected states that are willing to cooperate with the organisation and in this way respects the sovereignty of states. With permission of the affected state, OCHA can coordinate the international response to a disaster or assist in the coordination.

The other main organisation working on humanitarian assistance in response to disasters is the International Federation of the Red Cross and Red Crescent (IFRC). The IFRC is a private initiative that was first set up in 1919 as the League of Red Cross and Red Crescent Societies, being the umbrella organisation of National Red Cross and Red Crescent Societies which aim at delivering humanitarian assistance in peacetime disasters. The IFRC leans strongly on principles like impartiality, neutrality and independence making affected states more comfortable to accept assistance from the IFRC. In addition, the IFRC often has access to disaster situations through national Red Cross and Red Crescent Societies already on the ground. Accordingly, from the first attempt to organise the response to a disaster internationally, state sovereignty has limited the possibilities of the organisations set up for this purpose. These conflicting notions have also found their way into the legal framework on humanitarian assistance.

## 2.2 The common rules and principles on humanitarian assistance in disaster response

When looking at the sources from which common rules and principles are derived on accepting international humanitarian assistance in response to a disaster, it can be clearly seen that on the one hand it is acknowledged that an affected state sometimes needs external assistance, yet that at the same time the sovereignty and territorial integrity of states must remain intact. The document currently forming the basis for most peacetime humanitarian relief operations, UN General Assembly Resolution 46/182, adopted in 1991, reflects this conflicting idea and encompasses the main common rules and principles also found in other instruments. Here, the main common rules and principles will be mentioned where it will suffice to refer to Resolution 46/182 as the basis instead of including again all documents and instruments that confirm the rules and principles.

The Resolution explicitly recognizes the importance of sovereignty, territorial integrity and national unity. Departing from these principles, the affected state has the primary responsibility to take care of the victims of disasters. If additional assistance is required because the magnitude and duration of a disaster is beyond the response capacity of the affected state, Resolution 46/182 articulates that assistance should only be provided with the consent of and on the basis of an appeal by the affected state. Without the leading role of the affected state (and the requirement of consent), the response to a disaster could potentially be very chaotic because too much goods and personnel enter at the same time, clogging distribution chains with items that are perhaps not even needed. Offers of international humanitarian assistance must meet the humanitarian principles of humanity, neutrality, impartiality and independence, making it easier for the affected state to decide on the acceptance of the offer, and Resolution 46/182 determines that the provision of assistance must also be in line with these principles (although the Resolution does not mention the principle 'independence', which is mentioned by others like OCHA).

According to Resolution 46/182 it is the primary task of the affected state to respond to a disaster by bringing relief to the affected population. International assistance and cooperation is 'of great importance' when the affected state comes to the conclusion that its own response is inadequate or will be inadequate in the near future. Other states, international organisations and NGOs must await the request of the affected state and subsequently the consent by the affected state before they can provide humanitarian assistance. These rules are to a large extent recognizable in the entire set of (legal) sources on humanitarian assistance, although it is now accepted (in practice) that external actors do not have to await a request by the affected state but that they can also make an unsolicited offer.

Comparing this set of rules to that found in the field of international humanitarian law – often believed to be more advanced in this respect than the field of peacetime disasters – leads to the conclusion that the same rules dictate the delivery of humanitarian assistance within IHL, albeit in different phrasings. The point at which a state must seek external assistance is, for example, based on the undue hardship suffered by a civilian population. Consent is also explicitly required. The main difference between the rules for armed conflict situations and for peacetime disasters is that for the first category the rules are laid down in the Geneva Conventions and their Additional Protocols. This means that the rules can be found in widely ratified conventions which for a large part even constitute customary international law. Another difference between humanitarian access in armed conflict situations and in peace-time disasters is that in the case of Syria the Security Council has taken the step to grant access for humanitarian organisation in the state's stead. This decision has been preceded by earlier resolutions asking the state to grant access (to which the state did not comply) and has been based upon considerations of the severity of the humanitarian crisis and the many refugees and IDPs in the case. It is questionable whether the Security Council would ever come to such a decision in response to a peace-time disaster. Considering what has been found in the field of IHL, it can be concluded that even in this field many questions and difficulties remain regarding humanitarian access and giving consent thereto.

Taking the findings from the sources relating to disaster response and humanitarian assistance together results in the following legal framework. The process of international humanitarian assistance consists of three steps where certain rules or standards determine whether an affected state must move on to the next step. The affected state has the primary role to respond to a disaster. First, the affected state must make a needs-assessment to determine whether it has the capacity to respond to the disaster (1). If the affected state is of the opinion that it needs additional assistance because its capacity is overwhelmed or because it will violate a norm of international (human rights) law without external assistance, it moves on to the next step, which is (2) the triggering or initiation of international humanitarian assistance. In this stage, states make requests for assistance based on the needs-assessment and they consider offers of assistance made by other actors to determine whether the offer is needed, whether what is being offered is suitable and whether the offer meets the humanitarian principles. However, there are three rules, summarized in the work of the International Law Commission in its work on the 'Protection of Persons in the Event of Disasters' and derived from a variety of sources like UNGA Resolution 46/182, general obligations under human rights law and refugee law, the Guiding Principles on Internal Displacement, the IFRC's International Disaster Response Laws Guidelines and many other instruments of a soft-law character, dictating the transition to the point at which the affected state *must* give its consent (3). This point is reached when the capacity of the affected state is overwhelmed, if a norm of international law will be violated by withholding consent (which could result in an internationally wrongful act) and/or when the affected state only has arbitrary reasons for withholding consent. At this stage, the affected state can only withhold consent when there is a valid reason, for example if the offer does not meet the humanitarian principles. Depicted schematically, the legal framework looks as follows:

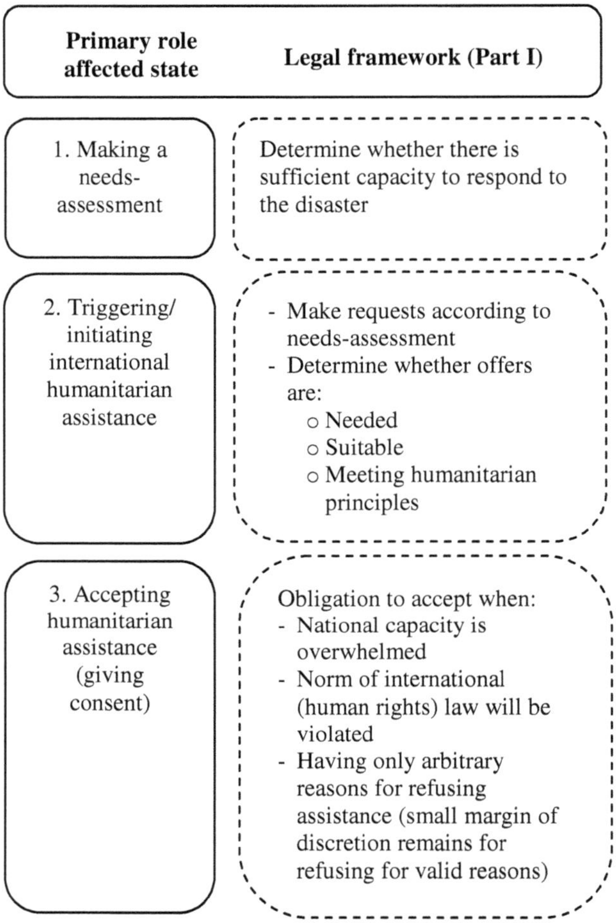


**Figure 1: Legal framework on accepting assistance**

This legal framework on international humanitarian assistance follows the line highlighted so far: it is recognized that there should be room for international assistance, but sovereignty and territorial integrity give plenty of room for the affected state to withhold consent. When looking at the practical applicability and actual application of the framework, it has become clear that the standards are not concrete enough to really determine at what point an affected state must accept aid. Currently, three developments are ongoing that each in their own way (perhaps implicitly) seek to find a solution to the dilemma.

### 2.3 Ongoing developments trying to combine international humanitarian assistance and state sovereignty

#### *2.3.1 Preparing national legal frameworks for accepting international assistance*

Quite often, accepting humanitarian assistance is delayed because the affected state is not equipped to make a needs-assessment, to coordinate targeted requests for assistance and to create the room for speedy transfer of goods and personnel. The International Disaster Response Law-project (IDRL) of the IFRC, started in 2001, aims at preparing national legal systems for the future possibility that the state comes into the position that it needs international humanitarian assistance. Departing from the same common principles as found throughout the legal framework (consent is required, initiation of assistance through a request), the IFRC helps states to make the necessary adjustments to the national legal systems during the time that no disaster is taking place. Within this project there is no hurry or pressure from an occurring disaster leaving more room to gently convince states to critically assess their national systems.

Because the IDRL-project works with states that are willing to participate, there is no breach of sovereignty or territorial integrity. Yet the voluntary basis and the explicit recognition of the requirement of consent make that the IDRL-project cannot solve the problem of a state that refuses to accept assistance when that assistance is necessary. It does, however, help to reduce underhandedly refusing assistance through delaying the entry of goods and personnel.

#### *2.3.2 Development of a new legal basis: the ILC's draft articles on the Protection of Persons in the Event of Disasters*

The International Law Commission (ILC) is working on the issue from a different angle. In the project 'Protection of Persons in the Event of Disasters', included in 2007 in the ILC's programme of work, the ILC is establishing rules on state action in response to a disaster, going into a full range of issues like disaster preparedness and mitigation, the primary role of the affected state, the duty to international cooperation, the role of consent, delivery of external assistance and underlying considerations like human dignity and respect for human rights. The draft articles adopted so far by the ILC depart from acknowledging state sovereignty and territorial integrity, but link these principles to the existence of certain duties. It is recognized that the primary role lies with the affected state, but that affected state must make use of international cooperation and must seek external assistance when its national capacity is overwhelmed. States are granted the right to give consent, but it is at the same time determined that consent may not be withheld for arbitrary reasons. According to the ILC, a refusal is not arbitrary when the affected state has sufficient resources to respond to a disaster, when assistance is accepted from other actors, or when the offer does not meet the humanitarian principles. In addition, the ILC argues that it is possible that a limitation of a state's freedom to withhold consent grounded in international law may be justified. When looking at certain fields of public international law, this argument can be supported. If states have certain obligations under, for example, human rights law or refugee law and cannot fulfil these obligations due to a lack of resources or capacity, there is an argument that the state has no room for withholding consent.

The strength of the draft articles lies in the all-encompassing basis it provides for humanitarian assistance in disaster settings. Since Resolution 46/182 (dating from 1991), it is the first instrument establishing clear legal rules on the acceptance and delivery of humanitarian assistance. The draft articles further give a full overview of the entire process by providing underlying principles and including disaster preparedness, by discussing the initiation and provision of assistance, the termination of operations and by looking at questions of protection of relief staff. Nonetheless, due to those parts of the draft articles that dent state sovereignty and territorial integrity, many states do not appear inclined to ratify the draft articles in case these would turn into a treaty. The question is whether opening the treaty for ratification would indeed be a sensible future step. The possibility exists that only a handful of states will ratify the treaty. Rather, given the support the draft articles have received from humanitarian relief workers and organisations, the draft articles can be used as guiding principles replacing the former operational basis provided by Resolution 46/182. Possibly, when picked up by those working in practice, states, and in time perhaps even by courts, some of the provisions will become rules of customary international law.

The draft articles clearly acknowledge the existence of sovereignty and territorial integrity and grant states the primary role of responding and the right to give or withhold consent accordingly. However, at the same time the draft articles link these privileges with the existence of certain obligations. In this way a framework is created in which the rights of affected states are qualified by duties, laying the foundation for a legal framework on accepting international humanitarian assistance. Only the legal status of the draft articles makes it difficult to value the impact of the rules.

*2.3.3 Bypassing sovereignty through humanitarian action: usefulness of RtoP*

That sovereignty comes with responsibilities towards the population is certainly not only acknowledged in the ILC's draft articles on the Protection of Persons in the Event of Disasters, but is in the meantime broadly accepted in international law. Running parallel with emerging concepts like 'human security', the Security Council started to authorize action for humanitarian purposes against the will of states primarily insofar the humanitarian situation at hand poses a threat to international peace and security. In addition, over the last few decades sometimes the concept of (non-authorised) humanitarian interventions has been used in situations where (a group of) states felt that action was necessary to protect the needs of a civilian population but where no Security Council authorization could be obtained. However, this has never been done in relation to natural disasters. Contrary to that, within the relatively new concept of the Responsibility to Protect (RtoP) the response to disaster has been originally foreseen. The idea behind RtoP is to embed responses to gross human rights violations resulting in international crimes in a conceptual framework. Under this framework, various options exist for preventing gross violations of human rights, for responding to such violations and for rebuilding after the response. Underlying RtoP is the idea of responsible sovereignty, meaning that sovereignty entails certain responsibilities towards the population.

Within the framework of RtoP, sovereignty is understood as having responsibilities to protect the population against gross human rights violations and other security concerns (hence 'responsible sovereignty'). If a state fails this responsibility, the responsibility transfers to the wider community of states. Within the responsibility to react the peaceful means are strongly emphasized, but if necessary and when meeting certain precautionary criteria more invasive action is in principle – with Security Council authorization – possible.

The original report laying the foundations for RtoP explicitly foresaw in applicability of the framework in response to a disaster. However, in the document depicting the general consensus of states on the concept RtoP, the UN World Summit Outcome Document of 2005, no reference to disasters can be found. When Myanmar refused practically all humanitarian assistance offered to it in response to devastating cyclone Nargis, an international debate arose on whether or not RtoP should be invoked to force humanitarian assistance into the country.

Opponents of invoking RtoP argued that the World Summit Outcome of 2005 only speaks of applicability in case of genocide, ethnic cleansing, war crimes and crimes against humanity. Those supporting the use of RtoP in the case of Myanmar saw the refusal to accept assistance and the apparent lacking national response to the cyclone in the context of earlier acts against the population and argued that the refusal to accept resulted in a crime against humanity. Although it is difficult to determine if there was truly a crime against humanity in the case of Myanmar, it cannot be denied that *in principle* poor disaster response in a context of severe crimes already committed against a population can in extreme cases result in a crime against humanity. In such extreme cases, it does not matter whether the crime against humanity is the result of armed conflict or of a disaster. Thus, while the occurrence of a disaster in itself is not enough to invoke RtoP, application of RtoP in disaster-contexts cannot be excluded on forehand.

Even when accepting that RtoP can be used in some disaster settings, the question remains what the implications would be. If a civilian population is suffering from the lack of basic resources, it is possible to take increasing intervening steps (from negotiations to sanctions to more forceful action) to deliver relief to that population. As the case of Myanmar has illustrated (where the regional organisation ASEAN played an important role in Myanmar's ultimate consent to relief), negotiations can take place outside the scope of RtoP. Intervening measures require Security Council authorization (which also poses a potential barrier, possibly leaving the non-authorised humanitarian intervention as an alternative under very special conditions) and it can be wondered whether the population benefits from pressure put on their state. Especially if there is any kind of force used, disaster survivors are worse off if they find themselves in the midst of a conflict. Only when RtoP is used to put slight pressure on a state to accept humanitarian assistance, without using armed force, it may be beneficial for the civilian population but it can be wondered if the concept RtoP is crucial for such pressure. It appears therefore that RtoP can be used in extreme situations of inadequate disaster response, but it is difficult to pinpoint where the added value lies.

### 2.4 The persisting problems in applying the legal framework

The most important developments within the field of international assistance in response to disasters do not provide an immediate answer to situations in which states refuse to accept assistance after a disaster while they clearly need it for the survival of the disaster victims. The IDRL-project does not give any standards on giving consent. Within the work of the ILC such standards are given, but for now it is unclear what the legal status will be. The discussion surrounding humanitarian intervention and RtoP goes beyond the question when a state must give its consent and focuses mainly on the subsequent phase. As a consequence, the problems surrounding the practical application of the legal framework on accepting humanitarian assistance remain because the standards directing states from one step to the next are not concrete enough to constitute clear obligations. The IDRL Guidelines and RtoP do not give new legal indicators based on which it can be determined when the capacity of the affected state is overwhelmed, what norm of international law is violated by refusing aid or what arbitrary reasons for withholding consent are. The Draft Articles on the Protection of Persons in the Event of Disasters do to a certain extent, but it is not clear what their legal status will be in the future. What remains, therefore, is the legal framework with its accompanying difficulties in practical application.

While studying the possibly applicable standards it soon became clear that the ICESCR in the end is the most promising instrument for concretizing the legal framework due to the basic needs which disaster survivors are often deprived of (shelter, food, water and access to basic health care) which are laid down as rights in the ICESCR and also due to the Covenant's general obligation to make use of international assistance and cooperation. In the following, it will be explained how the ICESCR complements the legal framework.

## 3 Using the ICESCR to complement the legal framework

### 3.1 Using the ICESCR for making a needs-assessment and for triggering international assistance

Through the phrase 'individually and through international assistance and cooperation' in the general obligations of article 2(1) ICESCR it has been made clear that state parties are not expected to merely work alone on the progressive realization of the rights of the ICESCR, but that international assistance and cooperation is a necessary supplement. State parties must make use of that supplement when the resources available within the state prove insufficient for meeting the obligations under the Covenant, according article 2(1). What these obligations are follows from the substantive rights (to which end the well-known tripartite typology can be used) but is co-determined through the formulation of progressive realization. The Committee on Economic, Social and Cultural Rights (CESCR) has defined what is expected from state parties. It has done so especially in its General Comments, while also standards have been set through the state reporting mechanism, although these standards are less general in character. With the phrase 'maximum of its available resources' the ICESCR obliges its state parties to seek additional resources internationally if insufficient progress can be made, as such indicating when an affected state must move from its individual response to seeking assistance.

For each of the rights included in the research (i.e. the rights to housing, food, water and health) it is at least clear that state parties must realize the core obligations, even immediately after a disaster. Based on the needs-assessment which an affected state must make after the occurrence of a disaster, the affected state determines if it can fulfil its core obligations. If insufficient resources are available for this goal, international assistance must be sought. Moving beyond the core obligations, the criterion is that sufficient progression must be made. This aspect arguably falls under the recovery-phase of disaster response and to that extent lies outside the scope of the research. Still, making plans for the full realization of rights falls under the core obligations and therefore these plans must be part of the needs-assessment. While certain standards can be discerned for each right, it depends on the context of the state and the size of the disaster how much progression may be expected. A method that appears useful for disaster settings is the adequacy-formulation used by the CESCR in the General Comments. Temporary housing in the form of tents is for example no longer adequate during a hurricane season. By considering what is adequate in specific contexts, states can use these standards in their needs-assessments and in their requests for assistance. This way, it becomes possible to make more targeted requests because the human rights standards help determine what is needed in terms of shelter, food, water and health care.

Although the strained resources are taken into account in determining how much progression can be expected from a state party, the fact that a disaster occurs cannot be used as an argument for derogation. Truly, by limiting the expectations on progression, standards are lowered, but the general obligations to move forward (continuous improvement) and to seek international assistance to this end remain intact. Only if no progression is made due to insufficient resources and the state party can demonstrate it has done everything in its power to obtain additional resources the lack of progression can be justified. Article 2(1) therefore serves only to a limited extent as a derogation-clause during a state of emergency.

### 3.2 The role of the ICESCR in limiting the freedom to withhold consent

The core contents of each right of the ICESCR are non-derogable and must therefore be realized at all times, even immediately after a disaster. If a state party (fears that it) does not have the capacity to achieve this, it must seek additional resources internationally and is under an obligation to accept international assistance. This means for example with regard to the right to food that state parties have an obligation to alleviate hunger, so after a disaster they must provide food aid. Taking too long to conduct a needs-assessment could in this case already result in a violation of obligations.

States have an obligation to make plans on how they will progress from the core obligations towards full realization (making such plans is often even mentioned as a core obligation). Within these plans, there is room to take the disaster into account, yet states have an obligation to move forward. With regard to the right to housing, the transition from shelter to permanent housing must be 'speedy'. The elements determining progression are privacy, having enough space, lighting, ventilation and access to basic infrastructure. In relation to the rights to water, food and access to basic health care it is explicitly determined that the state party must provide food and water when people are unable for reasons beyond their control to obtain it. In addition, disaster victims can be considered as a marginalized and vulnerable group, for whom special attention is required in terms of obligations of state parties. This means, for example, that affected states must give due priority to groups living in unfavourable conditions and must ascertain how many people are homeless or live in inadequate housing.

For the rights to water and health also disaster-specific obligations have been identified. With regard to the right to water, it is explicitly recognized that progression includes the preparation for the occurrence of a new disaster. Realization of the right to health must also aim at preventing the outbreak of epidemics and endemic diseases by creating a system of urgent medical care and the provision of disaster relief and humanitarian assistance.

Based on the obligations stemming from the ICESCR as described above, it can be concluded that refusing offers of international assistance after a disaster when a) core contents are not realized or b) access of disaster victims to certain rights is not provided results in a violation of obligations under the ICESCR. Through this, standards are set for measuring whether the capacity of an affected state is overwhelmed or when an affected state violates a rule of international law by refusing assistance. Consequently, offers of assistance can be refused when an affected state party is able to realize the core contents immediately after a disaster (so when it does not need assistance). In addition, affected state parties have a margin of discretion for refusing assistance when that assistance is not meeting certain standards like the humanitarian principles, for example by being conditional. Nonetheless, this discretionary room for refusing offers of assistance decreases as the affected state struggles to comply with its obligations under the ICESCR. Especially where the state cannot meet the core obligations, the state must have very weighty and valid reasons for refusing. Whether or not a refusal to give consent is arbitrary is depending on context and content of the offer and on the needs within the affected state, but not giving consent to international humanitarian assistance when core obligations are not realized would in most cases be a violation of international human rights law and a breach of an obligation to accept.

With the findings from the ICESCR, the legal framework as provided in figure 1 above can be given more concrete standards, making it possible to determine more concretely when a state must move from one step to another and when a state must accept assistance.

| **Primary role affected state** | **Legal framework (Part I)** | **Standards ICESCR (Part II)** |
| --- | --- | --- |
| 1. Making a needs-assessment | Determine whether there is sufficient capacity to respond to the disaster | The affected state must be able to:<br>- Realize the core contents<br>- Provide basic needs |
| 2. Triggering/ initiating international humanitarian assistance | - Make requests according to needs-assessment<br>- Determine whether offers are:<br>o Needed<br>o Suitable<br>o Meeting humanitarian principles | - Use maximum of available resources (through international assistance)<br>- Use core contents to make targeted requests<br>- Use core contents and plans for progression to determine which offers are needed |
| 3. Accepting humanitarian assistance (giving consent) | Obligation to accept when:<br>- National capacity is overwhelmed<br>- Norm of international (human rights) law will be violated<br>- Having only arbitrary reasons for refusing assistance (small margin of discretion remains for refusing for valid reasons) | Consent must be given when:<br>- Core obligations are violated<br>- The state is unable to provide access to basic needs<br>- Any other ICESCR-obligations will be violated |

**Figure 2: Legal framework on accepting assistance with inclusion of the ICESCR**

# SUMMARY

## 1 INTRODUCTION

Whenever a disaster occurs, the affected state responds by coordinating and delivering assistance. In situations where the affected state's capacity is overwhelmed, international actors are usually willing to assist. Problems arise when the affected state is unable (or unwilling) to adequately respond to a disaster and refuses to accept international humanitarian assistance. There is no explicit legal framework on humanitarian assistance in disaster response explaining to what extent states should accept international humanitarian assistance. A variety of sources of international law can nonetheless be identified which contain rights, rules and principles on state action after a disaster took place. Within this legal framework, principles of state sovereignty, non-intervention, non-interference and territorial integrity grant the freedom to an affected state to determine which aid is needed after a disaster and to decide which international actors are allowed to cross the borders of its territory to provide assistance.

Considering that the affected population is suffering even more in the aftermath of a disaster when the affected state refuses to accept international humanitarian assistance and does not adequately respond itself and taking into account that the largely scattered legal framework is not helpful here, this research answers the following question:

*To what extent does public international law contain standards for affected states determining whether the affected state must accept international humanitarian assistance after the occurrence of a disaster?*

To answer this question, the (legal) instruments containing pieces of the puzzle have been analysed resulting in a framework of rules on accepting international humanitarian assistance. These findings have been placed in the light of the practice of disaster response to determine to what extent they constitute clear standards for states. Here it was found that the rules are not concrete enough for this purpose and the International Covenant on Economic, Social and Cultural Rights (ICESCR) has been identified as the most promising solution to this problem. Therefore, it is analysed what standards can be derived from the ICESCR.

Throughout the study, examples of disaster situations have been used to illustrate points made. These cases do not together form a case study. Rather, they explain how the legal framework on disaster response described here can be and is applied in practice. In selecting the cases and being the point of departure for this research, a definition of 'disaster' is used inspired by definitions made by a variety of organisations for different purposes. In this research a 'disaster' is: *an event occurring in peace-time with natural causes, man-made causes or a combination of both, which causes harm to the affected population to an extent that it is beyond the affected state's capacity to address. This includes situations in which the affected state is not willing to address the consequences and refuses to accept international assistance.*

## 2 Disaster Response and International Humanitarian Assistance: Background and Legal Framework

The current legal framework on disaster response and international humanitarian assistance has been influenced by developments taking place in the nineteenth and twentieth Centuries. Especially the creation of the Red Cross system and developments taking place within the context of the UN left their marks on the contemporary rules and principles on accepting humanitarian assistance. The Red Cross (and mainly the International Federation of the Red Cross and Red Crescent Societies, IFRC) and the UN are part of a system in which the need for international humanitarian assistance in addition to the national response to a disaster is colliding with state sovereignty and where reconciliation of these two elements of disaster response is ever under consideration. The failure of the only international organisation ever set up for the sole purpose of disaster response, the International Relief Union, illustrates the consequences of not being able to reconcile international disaster response and state sovereignty. Still, in the (legal) instruments relevant for answering the main research question, the incompatibility becomes immediately visible.

Although situations of armed conflicts are excluded from the definition of 'disaster' in this research, international humanitarian law is nonetheless included to understand the difference between the rules applicable in peace-time disasters and disasters taking place in armed conflict. From international humanitarian law it becomes clear that states – whether occupying powers or parties to an armed conflict – are under an obligation to accept relief when the civilian population is in need of humanitarian assistance. However, before humanitarian relief can be delivered, consent must be obtained from the state and this consent may not be withheld arbitrarily. Also, if (offers of) humanitarian assistance meets the humanitarian principles (these are the principles of neutrality, impartiality and humanity) it cannot be understood as unfriendly or as interference in domestic affairs, which is in line with the ruling of the International Court of Justice (ICJ) in the Nicaragua-case.

In peace-time, human rights law is highly relevant in disaster settings. Through a rights-based approach to assistance survivors of a disaster can be considered as right holders and affected states as duty-bearers. The question is whether these duties of states could result in an obligation to accept humanitarian assistance where the rights of survivors cannot be fulfilled. Due to the relevance of certain rights of the ICESCR in post-disaster settings (i.e. the rights to housing, food, water and health) and because of the formulation of the general obligations for state parties, the ICESCR appears to be a useful instrument for considering whether an obligation to accept assistance exists.

Other fields and instruments included in the legal framework are refugee law and the rules on IDPs, instruments taking away practical barriers of delivering humanitarian assistance (like customs regulations or the Tampere Convention on Telecommunication), General Assembly resolutions (of which Resolution 46/182 of 1991 is still the basis for most relief operations today), regional mechanisms (for example that of ASEAN which proved useful in the context of Myanmar) and instruments containing principles on humanitarian operations and delivering disaster relief (the Sphere Handbook, IFRC Guidelines). In addition, two standard-setting developments are ongoing relevant for the field of international humanitarian assistance. The IFRC started its International Disaster Response Laws, Rules and Principles (IDRL) programme in 2001 to explore the role of law in the response to disasters, particularly in international disaster relief. Also, in 2006, the UN's International Law Commission (ILC) included the 'Protection of Persons in the Event of Disasters' in its long-term programme of work which has to date resulted in almost twenty draft articles on disaster response.

Still, currently sovereignty still plays a dominant role in the field of humanitarian assistance in response to disasters. Commonly, sovereignty can be used to prevent international humanitarian assistance from entering, which is an expression of a rather traditional reading of the concept. Such a reading of sovereignty appears to be caught up by developments within international law and politics. While originally meant to maintain or restore international peace and security exclusively, it has been gradually accepted that the Security Council also uses its powers to react on gross and systematic human rights violations since also non-military causes of instability can form a threat against peace and security. The new (non-legal) concept of 'Human Security' captured this and placed the protection of civilians and respect for human rights as priorities on the international agenda, arguing that gross human rights violations could also constitute a threat to international peace and security, and thus qualify for Security Council intervention. With this focus on the protection of civilians a method of action in case of gross human rights violations was created.

Returning to situations of disaster, it is possible that a civilian population is suffering undue hardship after a disaster as a consequence of their state's decision to not come to their aid and where the state is at the same time not accepting international humanitarian assistance. In extreme situations, this may prompt the international community to discuss the option of undertaking action to come to the assistance of the civilian population. Being such an extreme situation, in the case of cyclone Nargis in Myanmar it was debated whether a humanitarian intervention (if the other option under discussion, an intervention with Security Council authorization, would not be realized) should take place. Also, with regard to the same disaster, it was being discussed whether the concept of RtoP (endorsed at the World Summit outcome of 2005) would be applicable (this discussion is summarized under section 3). As no clear answer was found in these discussions, presently the story of sovereignty finds its temporary end in the developments underway (like the work of the ILC), yet while acknowledging that both assisting and victim states retain virtually unfettered sovereignty in the context of natural disaster policy.

Based on the (legal) sources described here and keeping the current role of sovereignty in mind, the following framework on accepting international humanitarian assistance is identified. The primary role to respond to a disaster lies with the affected state. The affected state must make a needs-assessment to determine whether it is in need of assistance. If the state is in need of assistance, it can initiate the process of delivery of such assistance. After considering the offers of assistance made to the affected state, that state is granted the right to give or withhold consent to international humanitarian assistance. Indicators are identified explaining when the affected state must give its consent to offers. These three indicators entail that the affected state must accept assistance when its domestic response capacity is overwhelmed, when not accepting assistance would result in the violation of a legal norm (in which case the refusal could arguably constitute an internationally wrongful act) or when the affected state only has arbitrary reasons to refuse. To determine what arbitrary reasons are, the humanitarian principles (humanity, neutrality, impartiality and independence) play a role: states have less ground to refuse offers meeting these principles than offers which are violating them in any way.

Two observations must be made with regard to this framework before continuing with the practical application of the framework. In the first place it is noted that although the rules identified here return in various instruments and documents, it cannot be said that these are rule of customary international law. In the second place, comparing the rules for accepting assistance in peace-time disasters to those applicable in armed conflict shows that the rules following from international humanitarian law are not that much more elaborate than those applicable in non-armed-conflict situations.

## 3 Practical Application of the Rules on International Humanitarian Assistance in Response to Disasters

The first step in the framework on international humanitarian assistance is to make a needs-assessment to establish the capacity of the affected state. The affected state should decide in a 'timely' manner whether or not to request relief and to 'communicate its decision promptly'. However, there is no set of standards that explains how to make a needs-assessment. Although the first step in the affected state's response to a disaster appears quite straightforward (determining through a needs-assessment what it can do by itself and whether international assistance is required), it is difficult to pinpoint if and when the affected state should start seeking international humanitarian assistance. It is left to the discretion of the affected state to determine whether it needs such external assistance.

If the affected state decides that it needs international humanitarian assistance, it can initiate the process by requesting what is needed (basing the requests on the needs-assessment) or by reacting to offers made. Offers can be a response to the request made by the affected state or can be unsolicited. Offers must meet the humanitarian principles of humanity, impartiality, neutrality, and independence. Especially when this is the case, offers cannot be considered as unlawful intervention in the receiving state's internal affairs and must be accepted sooner than offers which do not meet these principles. The rule that consent may not be withheld for arbitrary reasons therefore contains two components: the context in which the offer is made (for example by a political enemy or being conditional upon certain counter performances) and the content of the offer (is the content of the offer suitable for the circumstances of the case?).

After the process of international humanitarian assistance is triggered, the affected state must decide which offers of assistance are being accepted and which refused. Through giving consent, the state accepts assistance and allows activities on its territory which would otherwise be violations of non-intervention and territorial integrity. Because it has this function, consent is discretionary and can be subjected to conditions. Usually, it lays down the terms for the relief operation in question. Due to this implication, it is problematic to understand a request or the expression of the 'willingness to accept' as giving (blanket) consent. Therefore the problem remains that the providers of relief must await consent, something which can be abused by the affected state. In addition, it is accepted that a state can withhold its consent for valid reasons, making it even more difficult to value the lack of response or the refusal to give consent by the affected state.

It remains unclear what can be done if the affected state refuses to give its consent to international humanitarian relief. After the military regime in Myanmar refused to accept international humanitarian assistance in the aftermath of cyclone Nargis in 2008, the options were extensively debated but the discussion mainly evolved around possible application of RtoP. According to the World Summit Outcome Document of 2005, RtoP can be invoked when gross human rights violations amount to one of four predetermined crimes: genocide, ethnic cleansing, war crimes or crimes against humanity. Some argue that refusing to accept assistance when the affected population is in need and by not providing sufficient relief itself, this refusal could amount to a crime against humanity. Looking at the definition of a crime against humanity, it is arguable that not granting access to humanitarian assistance when it is needed for the survival of the population within a wider context of acts committed against that population, the refusal to give consent could indeed constitute a crime against humanity. That it is taking place in a context of disaster should not matter for the status.

Although only in rare and extreme cases RtoP would possibly be applicable, it is questionable whether invoking it would do any good for the population, especially when it is combined with intrusive or forceful measures. Currently, there appears to be no better response from the international community other than trying to negotiate access.

At this point, a preliminary conclusion is made to answer the main research question. From the first part it becomes clear that rules on accepting international humanitarian assistance indeed exist (although based on a scattered legal framework), but that these rules are not specific enough to create concrete standards on when to accept international humanitarian assistance. Especially when considering the three limitations to the freedom to withhold consent, the lack of concrete standards becomes visible. Affected states must accept assistance if their own capacity is overwhelmed, yet it is the affected state that decides whether this is the case (based on a needs-assessment). No objective standards exist. Second, if the affected state is violating a norm of international (human rights) law by not accepting international humanitarian assistance, it must give its consent but it is not entirely clear what norm would exactly be violated by not giving consent. Third, consent may not be withheld for arbitrary reasons. If what is being offered is needed according to the needs-assessment, is suitable for the situation at hand and meets the humanitarian principles, there is less ground – if any – for the affected state to refuse the offer.

To come to a more satisfying answer to the main research question, something is needed that gives the rules found so far more detail, so that they can constitute concrete standards. The ICESCR has proved the most promising option for concretizing the framework on accepting international humanitarian assistance. The ICESCR contains the rights to housing, food, water and health, rights that are of special importance in disaster settings. In addition, the ICESCR contains a provision on general obligations stating that apart from working on human rights realization individually, international assistance and cooperation must be used as well. To find out to what extent the ICESCR can be used to make the framework concrete enough to constitute standards, the content of the ICESCR must be assessed closely.

## 4 The content and meaning of article 2(1) ICESCR

Part II of the research is dedicated to establishing the post-disaster obligations for state parties under the ICESCR. First, the provision on general obligations for states is closely scrutinized to establish what the content and meaning is of these general obligations. In the fifth Chapter, these findings will be applied on the substantive rights of the ICESCR which are most relevant in disaster settings. To establish the content and meaning of article 2(1), the rules on treaty interpretation of the Vienna Convention on the Law of Treaties are used in a slightly adapted version.

As a first step, it is determined whether article 2(1) ICESCR is generally formulated as a provision containing concrete, justiciable obligations. Although for quite some time the ICESCR was understood to be merely consisting of policy guidelines of which article 2(1) ICESCR explains how to imply them, it is now clear, considering the place of article 2(1) within the Covenant and also due to the adoption of the Optional Protocol establishing an individual complaint mechanism, that article 2(1) contains concrete obligations. The nature of the obligations follows from the object and purpose of the ICESCR, where the purpose is understood as the goal that the Covenant aims to achieve and the object as the whole set of obligations directed at achieving the purpose. The long-term obligation of result is the full realization of rights; the obligations of conduct (immediate as well as long-term) follow from the phrases of article 2(1). Although the obligations formulated by the CESCR are directed at the state parties to the ICESCR, certain obligations to respect (and other obligations acquiring abstention from states to meet that obligation) must be adhered to by non-state parties under the 'do no harm'-principle. In addition, arguably a certain core of the rights of the ICESCR have obtained the status of customary law.

Although the full realization of the rights of the ICESCR is the obligation of result – and therefore a goal that state parties must aim to achieve – the phrases 'undertakes to take steps' and 'with a view to achieving progressively' indicate that the full realization does not have to be achieved at the moment of becoming a party. This does not mean that state parties are free in setting a pace. States must take steps from the moment of becoming a party and these steps must be deliberate, concrete and targeted towards the full realization of rights. Progressive realization indicates that there is no room for doing nothing and that retrogressive measures are in principle not allowed. Despite these clear obligations, the size of the steps or the progression made is determined by the context of a state and the capacity the state has for working on the economic, social and cultural rights. Lack of capacity cannot, however, be used as an excuse for non-compliance in all situations.

The phrase 'to the maximum of its available resources' indicates that states must not only rely on their national resources, but must seek additional resources internationally when national resources are not yielding sufficient result. Here, the states have an obligation to make use of international assistance and cooperation. If a state is in any way violating its obligations and argues that this is due to resource constraints, it must prove that it has done everything in its power to obtain additional resources. Also, certain elements of the ICESCR are non-derogable, meaning that for these elements the lack of resources can never be justified. Examples of the non-derogable elements are the principle of non-discrimination and the core contents of the substantive rights.

To determine in more detail what the obligations of state parties are in post-disaster settings, the findings of Chapter IV must be considered in a disaster-context and be applied to substantive rights, in this case the rights to housing, food, water and health.

## 5 Applying the ICESCR on Disaster Situations: Specific Obligations

Before discussing specific disaster-obligations, it is necessary to determine the extent to which states are allowed to derogate from their obligations during an emergency situation, as compared to the state of emergency derogation-clause of the ICCPR. There is no derogation-clause present within the ICESCR, but the formulation of the general obligations makes clear that due to the special circumstances and resource constraints, some flexibility is given with regard to the performance of affected states, yet there is an obligation to seek and use international assistance and cooperation when the resources of the state are insufficient for making the required progress. Derogation during an emergency is therefore only to a certain extent possible and only when the affected state can demonstrate that it has tried to obtain additional resources.

Considering the general obligations in the light of disasters and analysing the substantive rights in terms of their disaster-specific obligations lay bare a number of issues. Within the General Comments formulated by the Committee on Economic, Social and Cultural Rights (CESCR) the same terminology for determining obligations returns, making clear what is generally expected from state parties but lacking the detail to be precise in the formulation in post-disaster obligations.

One clear obligation is that the core contents of each right must be realized at all times and there is no justification for non-compliance. If a state does not have the resources for fulfilling the core contents, it must seek additional resources and therefore accept international assistance. Consequently, the core obligations provide a clear standard on when an affected state is obliged to accept international humanitarian assistance. Recognized generally as core content is to make plans for progressive realization (explaining the steps the state will take towards full realization) and to provide access to rights for those groups who are particularly vulnerable or marginalized (like disaster survivors).

At this point lies a check for the CESCR: a willing state is able to demonstrate what it has done to obtain assistance for the fulfilment of its obligations. An unwilling state that does not make sufficient progression through even the smallest of steps cannot demonstrate what it has done to obtain international assistance and is therefore in violation of its obligation to accept humanitarian assistance. The way in which article 2(1) is formulated therefore functions to a certain extent as a derogation clause. In situations of severe resource constraints, less progression can be expected from states than in ordinary situations, yet what exactly the standards are must be determined for each right.

In the plans for the realization of each right which form a part of the core obligations, states must consider the steps they will take, including the recovery after a disaster. While not falling under the scope of the present research, it must be noted that through this obligation affected states must take progression into account in their needs-assessment. The formulation by the CESCR of what 'adequate' is – consisting of elements like availability, accessibility, acceptability and quality – can help in making these plans for progression.

The obligation to use (and therefore accept) international assistance and cooperation – i.e. humanitarian assistance in the context of disasters – is not recognized as a general obligation, yet exists in the context of what has just been said: if resource constraints cause lack of progression (or standstill or regression) as no steps can be taken and as such obligations under the ICESCR are violated, the state has an obligation to accept.

## 6 Final Conclusions

The first part of the research has shown that a framework for accepting international humanitarian assistance exists, but that the steps in this framework are not concrete enough to constitute standards for affected states. The findings of the ICESCR can be used to make the framework more concrete. When the affected state makes a needs-assessment, being the first step, the obligations of the ICESCR can be used to determine whether the capacity of the affected state is sufficient. If the affected state is not able to realize the core contents, the capacity is overwhelmed and the affected state has an obligation to seek international assistance and cooperation. This is in line with the general obligations of article 2(1) ICESCR telling state parties to make use of international assistance and cooperation when insufficient resources are available. If the affected state cannot realize the core contents after a disaster occurred, it violates its obligations under international law, giving the affected state an obligation to accept assistance.

Based on the needs-assessment – specified through the use of human rights standards – the affected state can make targeted requests for assistance. It must then value any offers made to determine whether these offers are acceptable (do the offers meet the humanitarian principles and are they suitable for the context at hand?). If the state's capacity is overwhelmed (not being able to meet the core contents), if the state is violating its obligations under international human rights law (not meeting the core contents, not being able to fulfil or provide access to the rights for those unable for reasons beyond their control to access the rights by themselves), and the state has no valid reasons for refusing assistance, the state must accept assistance.

# BIBLIOGRAPHY

## BOOKS & ARTICLES


Abramowitz, Morton & Thomas Pickering, 'Making Intervention Work. Improving the UN's Ability to Act' (2008) 87 Foreign Affairs 100.

Abrisketa, Joana, 'The Right to Humanitarian Aid: Basis and Limitations' in Humanitarian Studies Unit (ed.), *Reflections on Humanitarian Action: Principles, Ethics and Contradictions* (Pluto Press, London/Sterling 2001) 60.

Aginam, Obijiofor, 'The Right to Health in Emergencies: Natural or Man-Made Disasters' in Andrew Clapham & Mary Robinson (eds), *Realizing the Right to Health* (Zurich, Ruffer & Rub 2009).

Alston, Philip & Gerard Quinn, 'The Nature and Scope of State Parties' Obligations under the International Covenant on Economic, Social and Cultural Rights', (1987) 9 Human Rights Quarterly 156.

Annan, Kofi, (with Nader Mousavizadeh), *Interventions: A Life in War and Peace* (Allen Lane, London 2012).

Arendshorst, John, 'The Dillemma of Non-Interference: Myanmar, Human Rights, and the ASEAN Charter' (2009) 8 Northwestern University Journal of International Human Rights 102.

Axworthy, Lloyd, 'RtoP and the Evolution of State Sovereignty' in Jared Genser & Irwin Cotler (eds), *The Responsibility to Protect: The Promise of Stopping Mass Atrocities in Our Time* (Oxford University Press, Oxford 2012).

Bannon, Victoria L. 'Strengthening International Disaster Response Laws, Rules, and Principles' in C. Raj Kumar & D.K. Srivastava (eds.), *Tsunami and Disaster Management: Law and Governance* (Thomson Sweet & Maxwell Asia, Hong Kong 2006).

Bannon, Victoria L., 'International Disaster Response Law and the Commonwealth: Answering the Call to Action' (2008) 34 Commonwealth Law Bulletin 843.

Bannon, Victoria L. & David Fisher, 'Legal Lessons in Disaster Relief from the Tsunami, the Pakistan Earthquake and Hurricane Katrina' (2006) 10 ASIL Insight [6].

Bannon, Victoria L. *et al.*, 'Legal Issues from the International Response to the Tsunami in Indonesia' (IFRC, Geneva 2007).

Barber, Rebecca J., 'The Responsibility to Protect the Survivors of Natural Disaster: Cyclone Nargis, A Case Study' (2009) 14 Journal of Conflict and Security Law 3.

Barber, Rebecca J., 'Protecting the Right to Housing in the Aftermath of Natural Disaster: Standards in International Human Rights Law' (2008) 20 International Journal of Refugee Law 432.

Beaulac, Stéphane, 'Emer de Vattel and the Externalization of Sovereignty' (2003) 5 Journal of the History of International Law 237.

Bellamy, Alex J., 'Disasters and 'Responsibility to Protect': Should Nations Force Aid on Others? A Cyclone is Not Enough' (2010) 34 Natural Hazards Observer [3] 1.

Bird, Annie, 'Third State Responsibility for Human Rights Violations (2011) 21 European Journal of International Law 883.

Bluemel, Erik B., 'The Implications of Formulating a Human Right to Water' (2004) 31 Ecology Law Quarterly 957.

Bothe, M., 'Relief Actions: The Position of Recipient State' in Frits Kalshoven, *Assisting the Victims of Armed Conflict and Other Disasters: Papers Delivered at the International Conference on Humanitarian Assistance in Armed Conflict, The Hague, 22-24 June 1988* (Martinus Nijhoff Publishers, Dordrecht/Boston/London 1989).

Bueno de Mesquita, Judith, Paul Hunt & Rajat Khosla, 'The Human Rights Responsibility of International Assistance and Cooperation in Health' in Mark Gibney & Sigrun I. Skogly (eds), *Universal Human Rights and Extraterritorial Obligations* (University of Pennsylvania Press, Philadelphia 2010).

Buffard, Isabelle & Karl Zemanek, 'The Object and Purpose of a Treaty: An Enigma?' (1998) 3 Austrian Review of International & European Law 311.

Burke-White, William W., 'Adoption of the Responsibility to Protect' in Jared Genser & Irwin Cotler (eds), *The Responsibility to Protect: The Promise of Stopping Mass Atrocities in Our Time* (Oxford University Press, Oxford 2012) 19.

Caballero-Anthony, Mely & Belinda Chng, 'Cyclones and Humanitarian Crises: Pushing the Limits of R2P in Southeast Asia' (2009) 1 Global Responsibility to Protect 135.

Cohen, Roberta & Francis M. Deng, *Masses in Flight: The Global Crisis of Internal Displacement* (The Brookings Institution, Washington D.C. 1998).

Concannon, Brian, Jr., & Beatrice Lindstrom. 'Cheaper, Better, Longer-Lasting: A Rights-Based Approach to Disaster Response in Haiti' (25) 2011 Emory International Law Review 1145.

Coomans, Fons, 'Some Remarks' in in Fons Coomans & Menno T. Kamminga (eds), *Extraterritorial Application of Human Rights Treaties* (Intersentia, Antwerp 2004).

Council of the International Institute of Humanitarian Law, 'Guiding Principles on the Right to Humanitarian Assistance' (1993) 33 International Review of the Red Cross [297].

Craven, Matthew C.R., *The International Covenant on Economic, Social and Cultural Rights: A Perspective on its Development* (Oxford Monographs in International Law, Clarendon Press, 1995).

Cryer, Robert *et al*, *An Introduction to International Criminal Law and Procedure* (Cambridge University Press, Cambridge 2009).

Cubie, Dug & Marlies M.E. Hesselman, 'Accountability for the Human Rights Implications of Natural Disasters: A Proposal for Systemic International Oversight' (2015) 33 Netherlands Quarterly of Human Rights 9.

Dennis, Michael J., 'Application of Human Rights Treaties Extraterritorially in Times of Armed Conflict and Military Occupation' (2005) 99 American Journal of International Law 119.

Dinstein, Yoram, 'The Right to Humanitarian Assistance' (2000) 53 Naval War College Review 77.

Dinstein, Yoram, 'The ICRC Customary International Humanitarian Law Study (2006) 36 Israel Yearbook on Human Rights 1-15.

Dunant, Henry, *Memory of Solferino* (International Committee of the Red Cross, 1986, first published 1862).

Donati, Federica & Margret Vidar, 'International Legal Dimensions of the Right to Food' in George Kent (ed), *Global Obligations for the Right to Food* (Rowman & Littlefield Publishers Inc., Lanham 2008).

Dungel, Joakim, 'A Right to Humanitarian Assistance in Internal Armed Conflicts Respecting Sovereignty, Neutrality and Legitimacy: Practical Proposals to Practical Problems' (2004) Journal of Humanitarian Assistance.

Eide, Asbjorn, 'The Right to Adequate Food as a Human Right' UN Doc. E/CN.4/Sub.2/1987/23 of 7 July 1987.

Eide, Asbjorn, 'Realization of Social and Economic Rights and the Minimum Threshold Approach' (1989) 10 Human Rights Law Journal 35.

Eide, Asbjorn, 'State Obligations Revisited' in Wenche Barth Eide & Uwe Kracht (eds), *Food and Human Rights In Development: Volume II – Evolving Issues and Emerging Applications* (Intersentia, Antwerp 2007) 147.

Fidler, David P., 'Disaster Relief and Governance after the Indian Ocean Tsunami: What Role for International Law?' (2005) 6 Melbourne Journal of International Law 458, 459.

Fischer, Horst, 'International Disaster Response Law Treaties: Trends, Patterns and Lacunae' in IFRC, *International Disaster Response Laws, Principles and Practice: Reflections, Prospects and Challenges* (IFRC, Geneva 2003).

Fisher, David, 'Fast Food: Regulating Emergency Food Aid in Sudden-Impact Disasters' (2007) 40 Vanderbilt Journal of Transnational Law 1127.

Fisher, David, 'Domestic Regulation of International Humanitarian Relief in Disasters and Armed Conflict: A Comparative Analysis' (2007) 89 International Review of the Red Cross 350.

Fisher, David, 'Law and Legal Issues in International Disaster Response: A Desk Study' (IFRC, Geneva 2007).

Fisher, David, 'The Law of International Disaster Response: Overview and Ramifications for Military Actors' in M.D. Carsten (ed) *Command of the Commons, Strategic Communications and Natural Disasters* (International Law Studies, Naval War College, Newport, Rhode Island 2007) 293-320.

Fitzmaurice, Sir Gerald, 'The Law and Procedure of the International Court of Justice: Treaty Interpretation and Certain Other Treaty Points' (1951) 28 B. Yearbook of International Law 1.

Fitzmaurice, Sir Gerald, '*Vae Victis* or Woe to the Negotiators! Your Treaty or our "Interpretation" of it?' (1971) 65 American Journal of International Law 358.

Fox, Grace 'The Origins of UNRRA' (1950) 65 Political Science Quarterly 561, 570.

Freudenheim, Ellen, 'Politics in International Disasters: Fact, Not Fiction' in Lynn H. Stephens & Stephen J. Green (eds) *Disaster Assistance: Appraisal, Reform and New Approaches* (1979) 228.

Gardiner, Richard K., *Treaty Interpretation* (Oxford International Law Library, Oxford University Press 2008).

Genugten, Willem J.M. van, Fred Grünfeld & Dick Leurdijk, 'Internationale Rechtshandhaving' in Nathalie Horbach, René Lefeber & Olivier Ribbelink (eds), *Handboek Internationaal Recht* (T.M.C. Asser Press, The Hague 2007).

Genugten, Willem J.M. van & Nico Schrijver, 'Kroniek Internationaal Publiekrecht' (2015) 90 Nederlands Juristenblad (De Staat van het Recht 15) 982.

Gould, Charles W., 'The Right to Housing Recovery after Natural Disasters' (2009) 22 Harvard Human Rights Journal 169.

Green, Maria, 'What We Talk about When We Talk about Indicators: Current Approaches to Human Rights Measurement' (2001) 23 Human Rights Quarterly 1062.

Grow Sun, Lisa, 'Disaster Mythology and the Law' (2011) 96 Cornell Law Review 1131.

Grow Sun, Lisa & RonNell Andersen Jones, 'Disaggretating Disasters' (2013) 60 UCLA Law Review 884, 931.

Hardcastle, Rohan & Adrian Chua, 'Victims of Natural Disasters: The Right to Receive Humanitarian Assistance' (1997) 4 The International Journal of Human Rights 35.

Heath, J. Benton, 'Disasters, Relief, and Neglect: The Duty to Accept Humanitarian Assistance and the Work of the International Law Commission' (2010) 43 Journal of International Law & Politics 419.

Heintze, Hans-Joachim, 'Humanitarian Assistance and Failed States: Still an Issue of Sovereignty? The Case Study of Haiti' in A. Zwitter *et al* (eds), *Humanitarian Action: Global, Regional and Domestic Legal Responses* (Cambridge University Press, Cambridge 2014).

Henckaerts, Jean-Marie & Louise Doswald-Beck (eds), *Customary International Humanitarian Law: Volume I: Rules* (Cambridge University Press, Cambridge 2005).

Henkin, Louis, 'Kosovo and the Law of "Humanitarian Intervention"' (1999) 93 American Journal of International Law 824.

Hesselman, Marlies M.E. 'Establishing a Full 'Cycle of Protection' for Disaster Victims: Preparedness, Response and Recovery according to Regional and

International Human Rights Supervisory Bodies' (2013) 18 Tilburg Law Review 106.

Hilhorst, Dorothea 'Dead Letter or Living Document? Ten Years of the Code of Conduct for Disaster Relief' (2005) 29 Disasters 351.

Hilhorst, Dorothea & Bram J. Jansen, 'Humanitarian Space as an Arena: A Perspective on the Everyday Politics of Aid' (2010) 41 Development and Change 1117.

Hoffman, Michael H., 'What is the Scope of International Disaster Response Law?' in IFRC, *International Disaster Response Laws, Principles and Practice: Reflections, Prospects and Challenges* (IFRC, Geneva 2003).

Hoof, F. van, 'Problems and Prospects with Respect to the Right to Food' in P. van Dijk *et al.* (eds.) *Restructuring the International Economic Order: The Role of Law and Lawyers* (1987).

Horbach, Nathalie & René Lefeber, 'Staatsaansprakelijkheid' in Nathalie Horbach, René Lefeber & Olivier Ribbelink (eds), *Handboek Internationaal Recht* (T.M.C. Asser Press, The Hague 2007).

Hoyer, Brian, 'Lessons from the Sichuan Earthquake' (2009) Humanitarian Exchange [43] 14.

Hutchinson, John F., 'Disasters and the International Order – II: The International Relief Union' (2001) 23 International History Review 253.

Jacobs, Francis G., 'Varieties of Approach to Treaty Interpretation: With Special Reference to the Draft Convention on the Law of Treaties Before the Vienna Diplomatic Conference' (1969) 18 International and Comparative Law Quarterly 318.

Katoch, Arjun, 'International Natural Disaster Response and the United Nations' in IFRC, *International Disaster Response Laws, Principles and Practice: Reflections, Prospects and Challenges* (IFRC, Geneva 2003).

Kent, George, 'Disasters and 'Responsibility to Protect': Should Nations Force Aid on Others? Rights and Obligations' (2010) 34 Natural Hazards Observer [3], 18.

Kuijt, Emilie E., *Humanitarian Assistance and State Sovereignty in International Law: Towards a Comprehensive Framework* (forthcoming).

Künnemann, Rolf, 'Extraterritorial Application of the International Covenant on Economic, Social and Cultural Rights' in Fons Coomans & Menno T. Kamminga (eds), *Extraterritorial Application of Human Rights Treaties* (Intersentia, Antwerp 2004).

Künnemann, Rolf & Sandra Ratjen, 'Extraterritorial Obligations: A Response to Globalization' in George Kent (ed), *Global Obligations for the Right to Food* (Rowman & Littlefield Publishers Inc., Lanham 2008).

Langford, Malcolm, Fons Coomans & Felipe Gómez Isa, 'Extraterritorial Duties in International Law' in Malcolm Langford, Wouter Vandenhole, Martin Scheinin & Willem J.M. van Genugten (eds), *Global Justice, State Duties: The Extraterritorial Scope of Economic, Social and Cultural Rights in International Law* (Cambridge, Cambridge University Press 2013).

Loof, Jan-Peter, *Mensenrechten en staatsveiligheid: verenigbare grootheden? Opschorting en beperking van mensenrechtenbescherming tijdens noodtoestanden en andere situaties die de staatsveiligheid bedreigen* (Wolf Legal Publishers, Nijmegen 2005).

Macalister-Smith, Peter, *International Humanitarian Assistance: Disaster Relief Actions in International Law and Organization* (Martinus Nijhoff Publishers, Dordrecht 1985).

Macalister-Smith, Peter, 'The International Relief Union: Reflections on the Convention Establishing an International Relief Union of July 12, 1927 (1986) 54 Legal History Review 363.

Malone, Linda A., 'The Responsibility to Protect Haiti' (2010) 14 ASIL Insights [7].

March Tappan, Eva (ed), *The World's Story: A History of the World in Story, Song and Art,* 14 Vols. (eyewitness report, Boston: Houghton Mifflin, 1914), Vol. V: *Italy, France, Spain, and Portugal.*

Nelson, Travis 'Rejecting the Gift Horse: International Politics of Disaster Aid Refusal' (2010) 10 Conflict, Security and Development 379.

Mowbray, Alastair, 'The Creativity of the European Court of Human Rights' (2005) 5 Human Rights Law Review 57.

Oraá, Jaime, *Human Rights in States of Emergency in International Law* (Clarendon Press, Oxford 1992).

Oraá, Jaime, 'The Protection of Human Rights in Emergency Situations under Customary International Law' in Guy S. Goodwin-Gill & Stefan Talmon, *The Reality of International Law: Essays in Honour of Ian Brownlie* (Clarendon Press, Oxford 1999).

Orakhelashvili, Alexander, 'Restrictive Interpretation of the Human Rights Treaties in the Recent Jurisprudence of the European Court of Human Rights' (2003) 14 European Journal of International Law 529.

Orakhelashvili, Alexander, *The Interpretation of Acts and Rules in Public International Law* (Oxford University Press, Oxford 2008).

Patnaik, Dabiru S., 'Issues of State Consent and International Humanitarian Assistance in Disasters: The Work of the International Law Commission' in A. Zwitter *et al* (eds), *Humanitarian Action: Global, Regional and Domestic Legal Responses* (Cambridge University Press, Cambridge 2014).

Pinheiro, Paulo Sérgio & Meghan Barron, 'Burma (Myanmar)' in Jared Genser & Irwin Cotler, *The Responsibility to Protect: The Promise of Stopping Mass Atrocities in Our Time* (Oxford University Press, Oxford 2012).

Postema, Gerald J., 'Custom in International Law: A Normative Practice Account' in Amanda Perreau-Saussine & James B. Murphy, *The Nature of Customary Law: Legal Historical and Philosophical Perspectives* (Cambridge University Press, Cambridge 2007).

Prebensen, Soren C., 'Evolutive Interpretation of the European Convention on Human Rights' in Paul Mahoney *et al* (eds), *Protection des droit de l'homme: la perspective europeenne* (Carl Heymanns Verlag, 2000).

Saechao, Tyra R., 'Natural Disasters and the Responsibility to Protect: From Chaos to Clarity' (2006-7) 32 Brookings Journal of International Law 663.

Sarooshi, Danesh, 'Humanitarian Intervention and International Humanitarian Assistance: Law and Practice' Conference Report Based on Wilton Park Special Conference: 2-4 July 1993 (HMSO, London 1994).

Sawyer, Wilbur A., 'Achievements of UNRRA as an International Health Organization' (1947) 37 American Journal of Public Health 41.

Sepúlveda, Magdalena, *The Nature of the Obligations under the International Covenant on Economic, Social and Cultural Rights* (Intersentia, Antwerp 2003).

Sepúlveda, Magdalena, 'Obligations of 'International Assistance and Cooperation' in an Optional Protocol to the International Covenant on Economic, Social, and Cultural Rights' (2006) 24 Netherlands Quarterly of Human Rights 271.

Shaw, Malcolm N., *International Law* (Cambridge University Press, New York 6th edition, 2008).

Shue, Henry, *Basic Rights: Subsistence, Affluence, and U.S. Foreign Policy* (Princeton University Press 1980).

Skogly, Sigrun I., *Beyond National Borders: States' Human Rights Obligations in International Cooperation* (Intersentia, Antwerp 2006).

Skogly, Sigrun I., 'Right to Adequate Food: National Implementation and Extraterritorial Obligations' (2007) 11 Max Planck Yearbook of United Nations Law 339.

Spieker, Heike, 'The Right to Give and Receive Humanitarian Assistance' in Hans-Joachim Heintze & Andrej Zwitter (eds.), *International Law and Humanitarian Assistance: A Crosscut Through Legal Issues Pertaining to Humanitarianism* (Springer, Heidelberg/Dordrecht/London/New York 2011).

Stoffels, Ruth A., 'Legal Regulation of Humanitarian Assistance in Armed Conflict: Achievements and Gaps' (2004) 86 International Review of the Red Cross 515.

Tomuschat, Christian, *Human Rights: Between Idealism and Realism* (Oxford University Press, Oxford 2003).

Tsui, Ed & Thant Myint-U, 'The Institutional Response: Creating a Framework in Response to New Challenges' in OCHA, *The Humanitarian Decade: Challenges for Humanitarian Assistance in the Last Decade and into the Future* (Volume II: General Assembly Resolution 46/182: The Development of Practice, Principles and the Humanitarian Framework) United Nations, Geneva/ New York 2004.

Vattel, Emerich de, *Les Droits des Gens; Ou Principes de la Loi Naturelle Appliques à la Conduite & Aux Affairs des Nations &des Souverains* (London 1758).

Verwey, W., *The Establishment of a New International Economic Order and the Realization of the Right to Development and Welfare* (1980).

Whipple, Dan, 'Wrestling with Generals: Pinning Down the 'Responsibility to Protect' (2010) 34 Natural Hazards Observer [3] 17.

Young, Katharine G., 'The Minimum Core of Economic and Social Rights: A Concept in Search of Content' (2008) 33 The Yale Journal of International Law 113.

Zwitter, Andrej, 'United Nations' Legal Framework of Humanitarian Assistance' in Hans Joachim Heintze & Andrej Zwitter (eds), *International Law and Humanitarian Assistance: A Crosscut Through Legal Issues Pertaining to Humanitarianism* (Springer, Heidelberg/Dordrecht/London/ New York 2011).

Zwitter, Andrej & Christopher K. Lamont, 'Enforcing Aid in Myanmar: State Responsibility & Aid' in A. Zwitter *et al* (eds), *Humanitarian Action: Global, Regional and Domestic Legal Responses* (Cambridge University Press, Cambridge 2014).

## Cases and Concluding Observations

### Cases

ECtHR *Golder v. United Kingdom* (App no 4451/70) (1975) Series A no 18, 1 EHRR 524.

ECtHR *Tyrer v. United Kingdom* (App no 5856/72) (1978) Series A no 26; (1979-80) 2 EHRR.

PCIJ *Lotus* (Turkey v. France), Series A, No. 10, 1927.

ICJ *North Sea Continental Shelf,* (Judgment) ICJ Reports 1969, p. 3.

ICJ *Military and Paramilitary Activities in and Against Nicaragua* (Nicaragua v United States of America) (Merits) [1986] ICJ Rep 14.

ICJ *Libya/Malta*, ICJ Reports 1995, pp. 13, 29; 81 ILR, p. 239.

ICJ *Legality of the Threat or Use of Nuclear Weapons*, Advisory Opinion, ICJ Reports 1996, p. 226.

ICJ *Legal Consequences of the Construction of a Wall in the Occupied Palestinian Territory,* Advisory Opinion, ICJ Reports 2004, p. 136.

ICTR *Prosecutor v. Akayesu* (Trial Chamber) Case No ICTR 96-4-T (2 September 1998) (Judgement).

ICTY *Karadzic and Mladic* (T. Ch. I 11.7.1996).

ICTY *Mrksic* (IT-95-13/1-T) 'Vukovar Hospital' (27 September 2007).

Jerusalem District Court case *A-G of Israel v. Eichmann* (1968).

### Concluding Observations Human Rights Treaty Bodies

CEDAW, Concluding Observations Belarus (UN Doc. A/55/38 of 2000).

CEDAW, Concluding Observations Indonesia (UN Doc. CEDAW/C/IDN/CO/5 of 10 August 2007).

CESCR, Concluding Observations Colombia (UN Doc. E/1996/22).

CESCR, Concluding Observations Honduras (UN Doc. E/C.12/1/Add.5 of 28 May 1996).

CESCR, Concluding Observations Ukraine (UN Doc. E/1996/22).

CESCR, Concluding Observations El Salvador (UN Doc. E/1997/22).
CESCR, Concluding Observations Guatemala (UN Doc. E/1997/22).
CESCR, Concluding Observations Russian Federation (UN Doc. E/1998/22).
CESCR, Concluding Observations Nigeria (UN Doc. E/1999/22).
CESCR, Concluding Observations Sri Lanka (UN Doc. E/1999/22).
CESCR, Concluding Observations Mexico (UN Doc. E/2000/22).
CESCR, Concluding Observations Solomon Islands (UN Doc. E/2000/22).
CESCR, Concluding Observations France (UN Doc. E/C.12/1/Add.72 of 30 November 2001).
CESCR, Concluding Observations Sweden (UN Doc. E/C.12/1/Add.70 of 30 November 2001).
CESCR, Concluding Observations Slovakia (UN Doc. E/C.12/1/Add. 81 of 19 December 2002).
CESCR, Concluding Observations Luxembourg (UN Doc. E/2004/22).
CESCR, Concluding Observations Uzbekistan (UN Doc. E/2006/22).
CRC, Concluding Observations Australia (UN Doc. CRC/C/15/Add.79 of 10 October 1997).
CRC, Concluding Observations Honduras (UN Doc. CRC/C/87 of 30 July 1999).
CRC, Concluding Observations Uzbekistan (UN Doc. CRC/C/111 of 28 November 2001).
CRC, Concluding Observations Madagascar (UN Doc. CRC/C/MDG/CO/3-4 of 8 March 2012).
HRC, Concluding Observations DPRK (UN Doc. CCPR/CO/72/PRK of 27 August 2001).
HRC, Concluding Observations Thailand (UN Doc. CCPR/CO/84/THA of 8 July 2005).

## United Nations

### General Assembly Documents

UNGA Third Committee, Meetings 1181 to 1185 (UN Doc. A/C.3/SR.1181 of 13 November 1962).
UNGA Resolution on 'Assistance in the Case of Natural Disaster' (UN Doc. A/Res/2034 [XX] [195] of 7 December 1965).
UNGA Resolution on 'Strengthening the capacity of the United Nations system to respond to natural disasters and other disaster situations' (UN Doc. A/Res/36/225 of 17 December 1981).
UNGA and ECOSOC, 'Draft Convention on Expediting the Delivery of Emergency Assistance' (UN Doc. A/39/267/Add.2, E/1984/96/Add.2 of 18 June 1984).
UNGA Resolution on 'Principles Relating to Remote Sensing of the Earth from Outer Space' (UN Doc. A/41/65 of 3 December 1986).
UNGA Resolution on 'Humanitarian assistance to victims of natural disasters and similar emergency situations' (UN Doc. A/Res/43/131 of 8 December 1988).

UNGA Resolution on 'Strengthening of the coordination of humanitarian emergency assistance of the United Nations' (UN Doc. A/Res/46/182 of 19 December 1991).

UNGA Resolution on 'Strengthening the effectiveness and coordination of international urban search and rescue assistance' (UN Doc. A/Res/57/150 of 27 February 2003).

UNGA, '2005 World Summit Outcome' (UN Doc. A/Res/60/1 of 16 September 2005).

UNGA, 'Implementing the Responsibility to Protect: Report of the Secretary-General' (UN Doc A/63/677 of 12 January 2009).

UNGA, 'Declaration of Principles of International Law Concerning Friendly Relations and Cooperation between States' (GA Res. 2625 (XXV) of 24 October 1970)

UNGA, 'Implementing the Responsibility to Protect: Report of the Secretary-General' (2009) UN Doc A/63/677

**Security Council Resolutions**

UNSC Resolution 1244 (UN Doc. S/Res/1244 of 10 June 1999).

UNSC Resolution on 'Protection of Civilians in Armed Conflicts' (UN Doc. S/Res/1674 of 28 April 2006).

UNSC Resolution 2165 (UN Doc. S/Res/2165 of 14 July 2014).

UNSC Resolution 2191 (UN Doc. S/Res/2191 of 17 December 2014).

**International Law Commission**

ILC, 'Draft Articles on the Law of Treaties with Commentaries' (Yearbook of the International Law Commission 1966 Vol. II).

ILC 'Preliminary Report on the Protection of Persons in the Event of Disasters by Mr. Eduardo Valencia-Ospina, Special Rapporteur' (UN Doc. A/CN.4/598 of 5 May 2008).

ILC 'Second Report on the Protection of Persons in the Event of Disasters by Eduardo Valencia-Ospina, Special Rapporteur' (UN Doc A/CN.4/615 of 7 May 2009).

ILC 'Fourth Report on the Protection of Persons in the Event of Disasters by Eduardo Valencia-Ospina, Special Rapporteur' (UN Doc. A/CN.4/643 of 11 May 2011).

ILC 'Fifth Report on the Protection of Persons in the Event of Disasters by Eduardo Valencia-Ospina, Special Rapporteur' (UN Doc. A/CN.4/652 of 9 April 2012).

ILC Drafting Committee, 'Protection of persons in the event of disasters: Texts of draft articles 1, 2, 3, 4 and 5 as provisionally adopted by the Drafting Committee' (UN Doc. A/CN.4/L.758 of 24 July 2009).

ILC Drafting Committee 'Protection of Persons in the Event of Disasters: Text and titles of draft articles 6, 7, 8, and 9 provisionally adopted by the Drafting Committee' (UN Doc. A/CN.4/L.776 of 14 July 2010).
ILC Drafting Committee 'Protection of Persons in the Event of Disasters: Text and titles of draft articles 10 and 11 provisionally adopted by the Drafting Committee on 19 July 2011' (UN Doc. A/CN.4/L.794 of 20 July 2011).
ILC Drafting Committee 'Protection of Persons in the Event of Disasters: Text and titles of draft articles 5 *bis*, 12, 13, 14 and 15, provisionally adopted by the Drafting Committee from 5 to 11 July 2012' (UN Doc. A/CN.4/L.812 of 12 July 2012).
ILC Drafting Committee, 'Texts and titles of the draft articles adopted by the Drafting Committee on first reading' (UN Doc. A/CN.4/L.831 of 15 May 2014).
ILC, Report of the International Law Commission, fifty-eight session (1 May-9 June and 3 July-11 August 2006) (UN Doc. A/61/10 of 2006).
ILC, Report of the International Law Commission, fifty ninth session (7 May-5 June and 9 July-10 August 2007) (UN Doc. A/62/10 of 2007).
ILC, Report of the International Law Commission, sixty-second session (3 May-4 June and 5 July-6 August 2010) (UN Doc. A/65/10 of 2010).
ILC, Protection of Persons in the Event of Disasters: Memorandum by the Secretariat (UN Doc. A/CN.4/590 of 11 December 2007).

**Committee on Economic, Social and Cultural Rights**

CESCR, General Comment 1 on 'Reporting by State Parties' of 24 February 1989.
CESCR, General Comment 2 on 'International Technical Assistance Measures' of 2 February 1990.
CESCR, General Comment 3 on 'The Nature of States Parties Obligations' of 14 December 1990.
CESCR, General Comment 4 on 'The Right to Adequate Housing' of 13 December 1991.
CESCR, General Comment 5 on 'Persons with disabilities' of 9 December 1994.
CESCR, General Comment 6 on 'The Economic, Social and Cultural Rights of Older Persons' of 8 December 1995.
CESCR, General Comment 8 on 'The Relationship between Economic Sanctions and Respect for Economic, Social and Cultural Rights' (UN Doc. E/C.12/1997/8 of 12 December 1997).
CESCR, General Comment 9 on 'The Domestic Application of the Covenant' (UN Doc. E/C.12/1998/24 of 3 December 1998).
CESCR, General Comment 10 on 'The Role of National Human Rights Institutions in the Protection of Economic, Social and Cultural Rights' (UN Doc. E/C.12/1998/25 of 10 December 1998).
CESCR, General Comment 11 on 'Plans of Action for Primary Education' (UN Doc. E/C.12/1999/4 of 10 May 1999).

CESCR, General Comment 12 on 'The Right to Adequate Food' (UN Doc. E/C.12/1999/5 of 12 May 1999).
CESCR, General Comment 13 on 'The Right to Education' (UN Doc. E/C.12/1999/10 of 8 December 1999).
CESCR, General Comment 14 on 'The Highest Attainable Standard of Health' (UN Doc. E/C.12/2000/4 of 11 August 2000).
CESCR, General Comment 15 on 'The Right to Water' (UN Doc. E/C.12/2002/11 of 20 January 2003).
CESCR, General Comment 16 on 'The Equal Right of Men and Women to the Enjoyment of All Economic, Social, and Cultural Rights' (UN Doc. E/C.12/2005/4 of 11 August 2005).
CESCR, General Comment 17 on 'The Right of Everyone to Benefit From the Protection of the Moral and Material Interests Resulting From Any Scientific, Literary or Artistic Production of Which He is the Author' (UN Doc. E/C.12/GC/17 of 12 January 2006).
CESCR, General Comment 18 on 'The Right to Work' (UN Doc. E/C.12/GC/18 of 6 February 2006).
CESCR, General Comment 19 on 'The Right to Social Security' (UN Doc. E/C.12/GC/19 of 4 February 2008).
CESCR, General Comment 21 on 'The right of everyone to take part in cultural life' (UN Doc. E/C.12/GC/21 of 21 December 2009).
CESCR, 'Statement by the Committee: An Evaluation of the Obligation to Take Steps to the "Maximum of Available Resources" under an Optional Protocol to the Covenant' (UN Doc. E/C.12/2007/1 of 21 September 2007).

## Other

Annan, Kofi (The Millennium Assembly of the United Nations), 'We the Peoples: The Role of the United Nations in the 21st Century: Millennium Report of the Secretary General' (UN Doc. A/54/2000 of 27 March 2000).
Commission on Human Rights, 'Economic, Social and Cultural Rights: Report of the Open-Ended Working Group to Consider Options Regarding the Elaboration of an Optional Protocol to the International Covenant on Economic, Social and Cultural Rights on its First Session' (UN Doc. E/CN.4/2004/44 of 15 March 2004).
Commission on Human Rights, 'Elements of an Optional Protocol to the International Covenant on Economic, Social and Cultural Rights - Analytical Paper by the Chairperson-Rapporteur Catarina de Albuquerque' (UN Doc. E/CN.4/2006/WG.23/2 of 30 November 2005).
CPRD, 'Report of the Committee on the Rights of Persons with Disabilities to the General Assembly' (UN Doc. A/66/55 of 2011).
CRPD, 'Statement of the CteeRPD on the Rights of Persons with Disabilities on the Situation in Haiti' of 8 February 2010.

CRPD, 'Statement of the CtRPD in Connection with the Earthquake in Qinghai China' of 23 April 2010.
ECOSOC Resolution on 'Review of the composition, organization and administrative arrangements of the Sessional Working Group of Governmental Experts on the Implementation of the International Covenant on Economic, Social and Cultural Rights' (ECOSOC Res. 1985/17 of 28 May 1985).
ECOSOC, Commission on Human Rights, 'Guiding Principles on Internal Displacement' (Annex) (UN Doc. E/CN.4/1998/Add.2 of 11 February 1998).
ECOSOC, 'The Limburg Principles on the Implementation of the International Covenant on Economic, Social and Cultural Rights' (UN Doc. E/C.12/2000/13 of 2 October 2000).
Kälin, Walter, 'Report of the Representative of the Secretary-General on the Human Rights of Internally Displaced Persons: Addendum on Protection of Internally Displaced Persons in Situations of Natural Disasters' (UN Doc. A/HRC/10/13/Add.1 of 5 March 2009).
OCHA Haiti Earthquake Situation Report #34 of 16 April 2010, 1.
Office of the High Commissioner for Human Rights, 'Frequently Asked Questions on a Human Rights-Based Approach to Development Cooperation' (United Nations, New York/Geneva 2006).
Office of the High Commissioner for Human Rights and UN HABITAT, 'The Right to Adequate Housing: Fact Sheet no 21' (rev. 1, UN, Geneva 2009).
Office of the High Commissioner for Human Rights, 'The Right to Adequate Food: Fact Sheet no 34' (UN, Geneva 2010)
UNDHA, 'Internationally Agreed Glossary of Basic Terms Related to Disaster Management' (UN Doc. DHA/93/36 of December 1992).
UN Inter-Agency Standing Committee, 'Protecting Persons Affected by Natural Disasters: IASC Operational Guidelines on Human Rights and Natural Disasters' (2006).
UN International Strategy for Disaster Reduction, 'Hyogo Framework for Action 2005-2015: Building the Resilience of Nations and Communities to Disasters' (Geneva 2007).
UN Human Rights Council, 'Promotion and Protection of All Human Rights, Civil, Political, Economic, Social, and Cultural Rights, Including the Right to Development' (UN Doc. A/HRC/7/16 of 13 February 2008).

## Reports (other)

### International Committee of the Red Cross and Red Crescent

ICRC, *Draft Additional Protocols to the Geneva Conventions of August 12, 1949* (1973).
ICRC, *Commentary on the Additional Protocols of 8 June 1977 to the Geneva Conventions of 12 August 1949* (Geneva-Dordrecht 1987).

## International Federation of the Red Cross and Red Crescent

IFRC, 'World Disaster Report 2000' (IFRC, Geneva 2000).

IFRC, 'International Disaster Response Laws, Principles and Practice: Reflections, Prospects, and Challenges' (IFRC, Geneva 2003).

IFRC, 'Introduction to the Guidelines for the Domestic Facilitation and Regulation of International Disaster Relief and Initial Recovery Assistance' (IFRC, Geneva 2008).

IFRC, 'Introduction to the Guidelines for the Domestic Facilitation and Regulation of International Disaster Relief and Initial Recovery Assistance' (IFRC, Geneva 2008).

IFRC, 'DREF Operation Final Report' (DREF operation no MDRIT001, report of 9 December 2009).

IFRC, 'DREF Operation Final Report: Italy: Earthquake' (IFRC 2009).

IFRC, 'IDRL Programme: Plan 2010-2011' (IFRC, Geneva 2010).

IFRC, 'World Disaster Report 2014: Focus on Culture and Risk' (IFRC, Geneva 2014).

## Other

Commission on Human Security, 'Human Security Now!' (New York, 2003).

ETO Consortium, 'Maastricht Principles on Extraterritorial Obligations of States in the Area of Economic, Social and Cultural Rights' (FIAN International, Heidelberg 2013).

Global Risk Miyamoto, 'L'Aquila Italy Earthquake Field Investigation Report' (2009).

IASC, 'Protecting Persons Affected by Natural Disasters: IASC Operational Guidelines on Human Rights and Natural Disasters' (Brookings-Bern Project on Internal Displacement, Washington DC 2006).

ICISS, 'The Responsibility to Protect: Report of the International Commission on Intervention and State Sovereignty (International Development Research Centre, Ottowa 2001).

ILA, 'Resolution on International Medical and Humanitarian Law' adopted at the 54th ILA Convention (The Hague, 1970) Part I.

ILA, 'Resolution on International Medical and Humanitarian Law' (1976).

Institute of International Law, 'Duty of Affected States not arbitrarily to Reject a Bona Fide Offer of Humanitarian Assistance' (2003).

International Criminal Court, 'Elements of Crimes' (ICC, The Hague 2011).

Johns Hopkins Bloomberg School of Public Health Center for Public Health and Human Rights, 'After the Storm: Voices from the Delta' (2nd ed., 2009).

Mohonk Criteria for Humanitarian Assistance in Complex Emergencies (1995).

Oxfam & Save the Children, 'A Dangerous Delay: The Cost of Late Response to Early Warnings in the 2011 Drought in the Horn of Africa' (18 January 2012).

Robinson, Mary, 'Introduction by the High Commissioner for Human Rights' in High Commissioner of Human Rights, 'Benchmarks for the Realization of Economic, Social and Cultural Rights, A Roundtable Discussion Organized by the High Commissioner of Human Rights' (Geneva 1998).
Sphere Project, 'Humanitarian Charter and Minimum Standards in Disaster Response' (Oxfam Publishing, Oxford 2011).
US Department of State, Office of the Historian, 'Milestones: 1914-1920 – The League of Nations, 1920'.
The White House, 'The Federal Response to Hurricane Katrina: Lessons Learned' (February 2006) 1.

## NEWS ARTICLES

### 2005

——, 'Food Aid Held for Taxes to be Released Says Government Official' *IRIN* (16 August 2005).
——, 'Urging Greater Generosity: Annan Arrives in Pakistan for Quake Donor Conference', *UN News Centre* (17 November 2005).

### 2008

Borger, Julian & Ian MacKinnon, 'Bypass Junta's Permission for Aid, US and France Urge' *The Guardian* (9 May 2008).
Buncombe, A. 'Burma under pressure to let outside world help after cyclone kills hundreds' *The Independent* (5 May 2008).
Lillis, M. 'Debate Storms over Burma Aid' *Washington Independent* (20 May 2008).
O'Neill, Andrew, 'Kosovo Aid: The Model for Burma' *The Australian* (14 May 2008).
Pisik, B. 'Cyclone toll feared above 100,000; Burma blocks aid; workers await visas' *The Washington Times* (8 May 2008).
Sengupta, S. 'International Pressure on Myanmar Junta is Building' *The New York Times* (18 May 2008).

### 2009

——, 'Death Toll Rises in Italy Quake' *BBC News* (7 April 2009).
——, 'Sichuan Earthquake' *New York Times* update (6 May 2009).
——, 'China Jails Earthquake Activist' *The Guardian* (23 November 2009).
Eimer, David, 'Sichuan Earthquake Anniversary: Parents of Victims Told Not to Hold Memorials' *The Telegraph* (8 May 2009).

## 2010

——, 'L'Aquila Earthquake Survivors Plan Protest March' *Guardian* (5 April 2010).
——, 'Analysis: Are Humanitarians Learning the Lessons from Haiti?' *IRIN* (28 October 2010).
Benedetti, Laura, 'After a Quake, Reclaiming their City' *The Washington Post* (11 April 2010).
Cooper, Helene, 'Progress Will Continue, Obama Tells New Orleans' *The New York Times* (30 August 2010).
Hooper, John, 'L'Aquila Earthquake Survivors Seek Answers from Government' *The Guardian* (5 April 2010).
Winward, Fiona, 'Italy Snubs Cannes after Row Over Berlusconi Documentary' *The Guardian* (10 May 2010).

## 2011

——, 'Japanners willen dat Premier Opstapt na Slechte Hulp Ramp' *De Volkskrant* (30 May 2011).
——, 'VN: Tienduizenden Doden Zuid-Somalië' *NOS* (20 July 2011).
——, 'Somalia: Aid Agencies Gain Access to Al-Shabab Areas' *IRIN* (26 July 2011).
——, 'VN Komt met Luchtbrug naar Noodlijdend Somalië' *De Volkskrant* (26 July 2011).
——, 'Al-Shabaab Houdt Somali's Op Weg Naar Voedsel Vast' *De Volkskrant* (2 August 2011).
——, 'Somalia: Al-Shabab Pullout – The Beginning of the End?' *IRIN* (9 August 2011).
——, 'Somalia: Coordinate Aid and Build for Long Term, Agenices Urged' *IRIN* (16 August 2011).
——, 'Pakistan: Forgotten 2005 Quake Victims Still Need Help' *IRIN* (18 August 2011).
——, 'Emergency Food Aid' *Disaster Emergency Committee* (25 August 2011).
——, 'Al-Shabaab Dreigt Kenia Met Invasie' *De Volkskrant* (17 October 2011).
——, 'Somalia: Al-Shabab Ban on Agencies Threatens Aid' *IRIN* (28 November 2011).
Higgins, Andrew, 'Japan's Slow Tsunami Response Stirs Anger' *The Washington Post* (16 March 2011).
Kaufmann, Daniel & Veronika Penciakova, 'Preventing Nuclear Meltdown: Assessing Regulatory Failure in Japan and the United States' *Brookings* (1 April 2011).
McCurry, Justin, 'Naoto Kan resigns as Japan's Prime Minister' *The Guardian* (26 August 2011).

**2012**

——, 'Somalia: ICRC Suspends Aid Deliveries' *IRIN* (12 January 2012).
——, 'Oxfam: Voorbode Hongersnood Steevast Genegeerd' *De Volkskrant* (18 January 2012).
——, 'Fukushima One Year On: Poor Planning Hampered Fukushima Response' *SAGE Publications* (2 March 2012).
——, 'Disasters: Learning from Japan's Tsunami' *IRIN* (9 March 2012).
——, 'Briefing: Myanmar's Ethnic Problems' *IRIN* (29 March 2012).
——, 'Tientallen Doden door Noodweer Haïti' *De Volkskrant* (8 June 2012).
——, 'Elke Dag 600 Nieuwe Cholerabesmettingen op Haïti' *De Volkskrant* (15 August 2012).
——, 'IDPs: African IDP Convention Comes into Force' *IRIN* (6 December 2012).
Tabuchi, Hiroko, 'An Anniversary of 'Heartbreaking Grief' in Japan' *The New York Times* (12 March 2012).

**2013**

——, 'Builders Found Guilty in L'Aquila Quake Deaths' *The Australian* (17 February 2013).
——, 'Why Does the US Need Our Money?' *BBC News Magazine* (6 September 2013).
Koch, Martin, 'After the Floods: Relief Work and Cleanup' *DW* (21 June 2013).

# INDEX

# CURRICULUM VITAE

Stefanie Jansen-Wilhelm (Sliedrecht, 1983) completed her Bachelor International and European Law and Master in International Public Law with an accent on human rights law (*cum laude*) at Tilburg University. Following her interest in international (human rights) law, she did the Research Master in Law (*cum laude*) and was appointed a PhD position by Tilburg Law School based on her research proposal on accepting assistance in the aftermath of disasters. While working on her PhD, Stefanie Jansen-Wilhelm was closely involved in educational activities of the Department of International and European Law at Tilburg Law School, teaching courses on international and European law on both bachelor's and master's level and supervising students writing a thesis, and she obtained her University Teaching Qualification. Outside the Department, she assisted Special Rapporteur Eduardo Valencia-Ospina on his Fourth Report on the Protection of Persons in the Event of Disasters for the ILC, co-organized the conference on International Humanitarian Assistance and International Law with fellow PhD-researcher (at Leiden University) Emilie Kuijt, held in Leiden in January 2013 and gave presentations at a number of international conferences. Not related to the field of international humanitarian assistance, Stefanie worked on research assignments for the Statelessness Programme (now the Institute on Statelessness and Inclusion) and for her own consultancy (set up together with friend and colleague Eefje de Volder).

# School of Human Rights Research Series

The School of Human Rights Research is a joint effort by human rights researchers in the Netherlands. Its central research theme is the nature and meaning of international standards in the field of human rights, their application and promotion in the national legal order, their interplay with national standards, and the international supervision of such application. The School of Human Rights Research Series only includes English titles that contribute to a better understanding of the different aspects of human rights.



For previous volumes in the series, please visit http://shr.intersentia.com.

Published titles within the Series:

62. Ramona Biholar, *Transforming Discriminatory Sex Roles and Gender Stereotyping: The implementation of Article 5(a) CEDAW for the realisation of women's right to be free from gender-based violence in Jamaica* ISBN 978-1-78068-167-2
63. Jasper Krommendijk, *The Domestic Impact and Effectiveness of the Process of State Reporting under UN Human Rights Treaties in the Netherlands, New Zealand and Finland. Paper-pushing or policy prompting?* ISBN 978-1-78068-244-0
64. Jennifer Anna Sellin, *Access to Medicines. The Interface between Patents and Human Rights. Does one size fit all?* ISBN 978-1-78068-247-1
65. Gustavo Arosemena Solorzano, *Rights, Scarcity, and Justice. An Analytical Inquiry into the Adjudication of the Welfare Aspects of Human Rights* ISBN 978-1-78068-275-4
66. Etienne Ruvebana, *Prevention of Genocide under International Law. An analysis of the obligations of states and the United Nations to prevent genocide at the primary, secondary and tertiary levels* ISBN 978-1-78068-273-0

67. Evgeni Moyakine, *The Privatized Art of War. Private Military and Security Companies and State Responsibility for Their Unlawful Conduct in Conflict Areas* ISBN 978-1-78068-281-5
68. Esther Janssen, *Faith in Public Debate. On Freedom of Expression, Hate Speech and Religion in France & the Netherlands* ISBN 978-1-78068-309-6

www.ingramcontent.com/pod-product-compliance
Ingram Content Group UK Ltd.
Pitfield, Milton Keynes, MK11 3LW, UK
UKHW051922100926
8556IPUK00021B/1314

9 781780 68329